Learning from Disas

University of Pennsylvania Press
Law in Social Context Series

A complete list of the books in this series
appears at the back of this volume.

Learning from Disaster

Risk Management After Bhopal

Edited by Sheila Jasanoff

University of Pennsylvania Press

Philadelphia

Library of Congress Cataloging-in-Publication Data

Learning from disaster : risk management after Bhopal / edited by Sheila Jasanoff.
   p.   cm.—(Law in social context series)
  Includes bibliographical references and index.
  ISBN 0-8122-3250-X (cloth).—ISBN 0-8122-1532-X (pbk.)
1. Technology—Risk assessment.   2. Technology and state.
3. Technology—Social aspects.   4. Bhopal Union Carbide Plant
Disaster, Bhopal, India, 1984.   I. Jasanoff, Sheila.   II. Series.
T174.5.L415   1994
363.17′91′0954—dc20   93-48100
                                                         CIP

For Alan

Contents

Preface

The lethal gas leak that occurred at a Union Carbide pesticide plant in Bhopal, India on the night of December 3, 1984 may well be the most extensively studied industrial disaster in history. In the intervening years, dozens of books and articles, as well as countless conference and workshop proceedings, have grappled with the questions of what happened in Bhopal that night and why. What, then, is the reason for adding still another contribution to this voluminous literature? What new illumination does this book hope to provide?

We believe that this book stands in a fundamentally different relationship to the events in Bhopal from most previous reports and analyses. While other commentators focused largely on the causes of the tragedy, our object is to look most critically at its consequences. Surveying the changes in law and public policy that followed Bhopal, the contributors to this volume ask what we and our institutions have learned of lasting value from the mistakes of commission and omission that led to the disaster. Are modern societies any better prepared today than they were in 1984 to manage the risks of hazardous technologies, especially those that are transferred across national boundaries? Could an accident like the one at Bhopal happen again—in India, in the United States, in Europe? And if the same toxic cloud were to strike Bhopal once more, would the consequences be as dire, the agony for the victims as protracted and inconclusive?

The chapters in this volume address these questions by examining the impact of Bhopal on both national and international policymaking. In a series of essays written from different disciplinary perspectives—including law, political science, sociology, policy studies and public administration—the authors explore the capacity of varied social actors to learn from an event whose causes were as complex and multiply layered as its consequences. Their essays ask how learning takes place among individuals and in institutions, in legal systems and in administrative agencies, in the "low politics" of unorganized and often isolated victims' groups and in the "high politics" of the state. Throughout the volume, there is an attempt to understand whether events of such destructive ferocity as Bhopal simply overwhelm the human ability to learn or whether they stimulate efforts to impose meaning upon tragic events, thereby setting in motion a constructive process of change. The book, then, is directed not only to followers of the Bhopal story but also to academic, industrial, and governmental audiences that share a commitment to understanding and preventing technological disasters.

Appropriately enough, the book itself is the endpoint of an extended period of learning. It grew out of informal conversations among a scattered group of writers and scholars who were united primarily by the sense that Bhopal demanded a different kind of commemoration from ordinary happenings in law and politics. At the time of the accident, many of us were already working on issues that were sharpened and given new immediacy by Bhopal: the transnational traffic in hazardous industries, the risks of industrialization in developing countries, environmental policy-making in India and the United States, the uses of information in risk management, and the normative and procedural inadequacies of the law for compensating victims of mass disasters. As private individuals, we were moved, as were so many others, by the enormity of the suffering in Bhopal; as professionals, we felt compelled to glean from it some lessons that could reduce the potential for such harm in the future.

The idea for a collaborative volume first germinated in the winter of 1985, when several of the contributors to the present volume met in Colombo, Sri Lanka at a conference on transnational industrial hazards sponsored by the Ford Foundation in India. Subsequently, another subset of the authors, mainly lawyers, met at the Centre for Socio-Legal Studies at Oxford University and discussed societal responses to what we described at the time as "big, bad events," a term that embraced a range of socially transforming accidents, both natural and human-made. Further discussions at a meeting of the Law and Society Association in 1987 led to the establishment of an informal network of "Bhopal watchers" who agreed to share information and exchange written work on the still unfolding medical, legal, administrative, and political dimensions of the tragedy. Bhopal, we agreed, was a big enough event to merit attention on its own as a richly textured case study in social learning. Our interactions led in turn to a weekend workshop on "Bhopal: Policy Implications and Research Priorities" at Cornell University in May 1988.

About half the authors who eventually contributed to this book attended the Cornell workshop; several others were invited but could not come because of prior commitments. All agreed that the topic of learning from Bhopal was worth pursuing in a more formal way than we had previously planned. We decided as well that an interdisciplinary approach was best suited to probing the depths of a story that seemed equally momentous to lawyers and political scientists, to sociologists and policy analysts, to journalists and management experts. An edited volume seemed the most reasonable vehicle for bringing together the heterogeneous but usefully intersecting perspectives represented in the now expanded circle of Bhopal watchers.

The years between the Cornell workshop and the completion of this collection have also been years of learning, though in a more closely structured environment. Once we had decided to go forward with an interdisciplinary volume of essays, we needed time to divide up a topic that seemed at times unmanageably complex into analytically coherent pieces. Time was also needed to learn about, adapt to, and occasionally disagree with the views or approaches of the other contributors. The authors of all but one of the chapters attended a meeting in Cambridge, Massachusetts in February 1991, where divergences in coverage, argument, style, and method were creatively explored and common themes were identified and brought into sharper focus.

The book that emerged from all these preparatory exercises does not—and should not—presume to be the definitive account of the aftermath of Bhopal. There are topics and actors that it addresses poorly or not at all. For example, there is no single chapter that does justice to the chemical industry's massive efforts to improve its monitoring, reporting, and public communication practices at hazardous facilities around the world. Some disciplinary perspectives, too, are under-represented here, among them organizational sociology and technology studies. This book, however, is the first serious attempt by a group of scholars and analysts to break out of the retrospective habits of thought that accidents and mishaps so often engender: to stop asking what caused the tragedy or who is to blame, and to consider instead how human beings and their fault-prone institutions can learn to do better.

To look forward in this way one must, of course, have looked backward first; past events have to be invested with meaning and fitted out with causal structures before one can draw from them persuasive lessons about the future. Accordingly, each contributor to this volume begins implicitly or explicitly with some explanation for what happened in Bhopal on that night in December 1984 and immediately after. The purpose of these accounts, however, is not to affix responsibility for the conjunction of failures that uniquely defined Bhopal.

The book's intent is both less particularistic and less judgmental. Bhopal becomes a symbol for an entire complex of flawed relationships among technology, power, and social organization. The book addresses technology and its social control in a world that is at once more interdependent and more economically and socially unequal than at any other period in modern history.

A book like this represents a relatively unusual undertaking in discipline-dominated academic circles, and we owe special thanks to the institutions and individuals who facilitated its development. The Centre for Socio-Legal Studies in Oxford, where the project in a sense began, provided a hospitable environment for broaching wide-ranging questions about law and society long before they were ready for distillation into researchable units; much of the credit for maintaining this open intellectual climate belongs with Don Harris and Keith Hawkins. At the Ford Foundation India, R. Sudarshan recognized the human rights implications of a major industrial tragedy and provided both funds and intellectual support for continuing exchanges between Indian and U.S. academics working on Bhopal. Particularly important was a grant from the Ford Foundation that enabled two experienced and talented Indian lawyers, Rajiv Dhavan and M. C. Mehta, to attend the Bhopal workshop at Cornell in 1988. That workshop was also funded in part by a grant from the Hewlett Foundation to Cornell's Center for Environmental Research; additional Hewlett funds for furthering interdisciplinary, problem-oriented work on the environment made possible the final authors' meeting in Cambridge in 1991, which was hosted by the Harvard University Center for Population and Development Studies.

Several of my Cornell colleagues recognized the importance of the Bhopal-watchers' network and provided generous support for our activities even before this book loomed as a serious possibility. I would like to acknowledge a special debt to Simon Levin, Gil Levine, and Neil Orloff, all past directors of the Center for Environmental Research, and to Walter Lynn and Judith Reppy, past directors of the Program on Science, Technology and Society. Deborah Van Galder, my administrative assistant, showed her usual patience and resourcefulness in communicating with some sixteen authors on three continents. Amy Mansfield and Lori Hamilton provided invaluable help in marshalling texts composed in varied styles and word processor formats into a coherent, readable manuscript. I am grateful as well to William C. Clark, Lee Clarke, Trevor Pinch, Michael Reich, and Judith Reppy for their illuminating comments on some or all of the manuscript; their critical readings provided an essential and much appreciated check on editorial near-sightedness.

I must, finally, add a personal note of thanks to each of the chapter authors, whose encouragement and faith in the project were indispensable in transforming an appealing but amorphous idea into a fruitful collaborative volume. All of the contributors responded to my criticisms and suggestions with a degree of patience and good humor that greatly simplified my task as editor. The willingness of authors from so many different fields and countries to work together was admirable. The resulting book establishes what I hope will be a productive pattern for future interdisciplinary studies in law and society.

Chapter 1
Introduction: Learning from Disaster

Sheila Jasanoff

The accident at the Union Carbide pesticide factory in Bhopal, India on December 3, 1984 was by any reckoning a cataclysmic event. For a few weeks, accounts of sudden death raining from the air, of sundered families and grieving relatives, of a panic-stricken city and a pathetically disorganized relief effort seized banner headlines and were flashed around the world in wrenching images that tugged at humanity's collective conscience. Long after these accounts receded from public view, the disaster's complex aftershocks continued to send tremors through a company, an industry, a nation's political and bureaucratic leadership, and the legal and policy instruments by which two countries—India and the United States—had previously sought to compensate the victims of unexpected harm. Eight years later, this once earth-shaking event had dimmed into memory for all but a few thousand victims who still awaited redress in Bhopal, and a few hundred activists, policy-makers, lawyers, journalists, and academics whose lives and work were permanently imprinted by the tragedy. But these dwindling numbers gave at best a pale reflection of Bhopal's impact on the modern chemical industry's relationship with society. What happened in 1984 at one plant in one Indian city prompted a worldwide reexamination of industrial policy and practice. This book explores the results of that inquiry and their influence on various frameworks of national and international decision making.

Accounts of disasters are written most often in a retrospective mode. The tragic event becomes the occasion for looking backward to a prior, more fortunate time, when foresight, prudence, good behavior, or divine grace might have unscrolled history toward a happier conclusion. Disasters involving technology, in paticular, have tended through time to take the form of morality plays about human over-

reaching. From the fall of Icarus to the sinking of the Titanic, technological failures have often been represented as the result of hubris.
The fatal flaw in the machine becomes in this kind of narrative an
icon for deeper flaws in the human intellect or imagination, a refusal
to acknowledge and abide by limits set by nature.

Recent academic writing about technological disasters, however,
has begun to take a different tack, one that stresses the social and
political as well as the moral dimensions of such events. There is a
new emphasis on the organizational context in which the failed technology was embedded and, with this, a recognition that corrective
policies have to address not only the design of artifacts but also
(indeed, perhaps even more so) the human practices and presuppositions that determine their management and use. Seen from this
perspective, a serious technological mishap ceases to be merely accidental, for it opens windows onto previously unsuspected weaknesses
in the social matrix surrounding the technology. Efforts to explain
what went wrong and, most especially, to find measures for future
prevention lead to a wider social critique; in seeking to understand
the defects of our technological creations, we simultaneously deepen
our understanding of the societies we inhabit.

As the essays in this book demonstrate, the tragedy in Bhopal revealed a set of complex interdependencies between technology and
society, radiating out from the disaster's epicenter at the Union Carbide pesticide plant and encompassing the political economy of the
international chemical industry. The failures that first produced a
lethal accident and then magnified its consequences to tragic proportions cannot be dismissed as a mere catalogue of mechanical fail-
ings. Although "hard" engineering played its part in precipitating the
events, the plant's defective components—the leaking valve, the bro-
ken refrigeration system, the malfunctioning warning signal, and the
inadequate storage tank—were themselves the symptoms of more
deep-seated social problems. These included the dearth of medical
and scientific knowledge about an extremely hazardous technology,
the imperfections of information transfer across national boundaries,
the lack of regulatory resources in a still developing country, the absence of workable relief and rehabilitation plans, and the profound
imbalance of economic power and legal and managerial expertise between nations of the North and the South. Many of these deficiencies
became apparent only in the aftermath of Bhopal, as institutions in
India and abroad tried to construct a program of compensation for
the victims and a framework of law and public policy to ensure that a
disaster of this magnitude would never happen again.

The chapters that follow examine in depth many aspects of industrial risk management that changed directly or indirectly in response to Bhopal. In tracing out these consequences, the book as a whole creates a more complex accounting of the accident itself, since each policy initiative the authors describe represents the endpoint of a different story told about Bhopal, a particular way in which an otherwise senseless event was infused with meaning. But it would be a mistake to read this collection of essays simply as an extended case study of Bhopal's impact on policy; rather, what happened in Bhopal provides the occasion for addressing wider questions about the transfer and control of hazardous technologies and the capacity of human societies to learn from failure. Writing from different disciplinary and theoretical perspectives, each contributor addresses the problem of learning, calling attention to the economic, political, and institutional constraints on our ability to draw productive lessons from disaster.

My objective in this opening chapter is to introduce and contextualize two major themes that connect the subsequent chapters: the importance of the social world in producing technological disasters and, conversely, the possibility of preventing disasters by changing social rules and practices. In the first part of a three-part exercise, I therefore review several lines of scholarship that have begun to shed light on the social causes of technological failure and that can, to some degree, help make sense of events in Bhopal. In the next section, I discuss the particular ways in which studies of a disaster's consequences extend the literature on technology and society and point the way toward better risk management policies. I conclude the chapter with an overview of the individual essays and their contributions to the theme of social learning.

Why Technologies Fail

Accidents by definition are untoward events: they happen without forewarning and by unpredictable pathways. Technological accidents strike us as particularly unnerving because they represent a sudden breakdown in a smoothly functioning, inanimate world, which seemed beforehand to stand apart from human agency and the possibility of human error. The collapse of a bridge, the bursting of a dam, the failure of a tested medical device, the escape of deadly radiation from a nuclear power plant or a chemical factory—all such accidents seem at first glance to be random, freakish, and irrational, contrary to the usual orderliness of things. Yet a second look often reveals an entirely different picture, in which not only things but people and institutions played an essential and destructive role. We recognize the warning signals that intelligent observers should not have missed and the steps

that they might have taken to prevent the occurrence or, at the very
least, to mitigate its harmful effects. In a legal system, such after-the-
fact discoveries may lead to the attribution of blame and the award of
substantial damages. What appeared at first to be a chance event may
be reclassified through the law's retrospective analysis as an accident
that was "waiting to happen." The disaster in Bhopal, along with
many lesser industrial tragedies of our time, has undergone precisely
such a transformation.

Should accidents like the one that befell Union Carbide in India,
then, really be thought of as unexpected? One of the more provoca-
tive insights emerging from recent work on technology is that most
so-called accidents belong in reality to the class of "normal" events. If
they seem to strike without notice, it is because we have drawn an
artificial boundary between the technological and the social, imputing
to the former a false infallibility, and have accepted a temporarily
stable working relationship among machines, people, and their environment as the only imaginable state of affairs. Seeing technologies
as heterogeneous systems, combining technical and social elements in
a fragile equilibrium, provides the antidote to these comfortable assumptions. By putting technological artifacts back into their social
contexts, we uncover pathological patterns that hold the clues to both
past and future disasters.

Some of the destructive connections between technology and society were noted in the attacks on technological determinism mounted
in the latter part of the twentieth century by an influential array of
social theorists who argued that developments in society are never
passively conditioned by the innate and uncontrollable imperatives
of technology. Spanning theoretical perspectives from Marxism to
ecology, this body of scholarship impressively converged on the view
that technologies look the way they do because of their historical
and cultural moorings and their connections with macro-features of
economic and social organization. Phenomena such as the dispro-
portionate growth of military technology, the development of environmentally harmful products, and the rise of the large industrial
corporation provided ample proof, for modern critics of technology,
that the demonic impulses in the machinery we create reflect structural deficiencies in our society rather than merely accidental defects
of design or conception.[1]

While little of this literature dealt explicitly with disasters, it can
nevertheless be mined for insights into technological choices that have
turned sour. Powerful indictments of large-scale technologies and
their resistance to democratic control can be found, for instance, in
the work of such writers as Lewis Mumford and E. F. Schumacher.[2]

Enlarging on the problem of control, Langdon Winner called attention to the political embeddedness of all technological artifacts. Technical devices or systems, in Winner's view, can acquire politics either because they represent a solution to a particular political problem or because they are "inherently political" in the sense of being compatible only with particular (often antidemocratic) forms of politics.[3] Such technologies can be prone to failure if safety considerations are inadvertently overlooked or, worse, if the designers consciously choose to adopt unsafe options that would be rejected by a democratically accountable decision maker.

More recently, scholars working on the causes of environmental problems have begun to explore the ways in which characteristic economic and social commitments of Western societies are built into inappropriate choices for technological development in other parts of the world. Studies of the Green Revolution, for example, show that high-yield hybrid grain varieties resulted from an explicit decision by pioneering Western scientists to define the problem that they were attacking—world hunger—in scientifically reductionist terms. The resulting technology succeeded brilliantly in achieving the specific goals its designers selected, but it entailed social and environmental impacts that many now regard as deeply unfortunate for the recipient societies.[4] Policy choices for managing technology may also produce unintended negative consequences. It has been argued, for instance, that stringent environmental regulation in developed countries has driven "dirty" technologies to developing countries, where they operate under disaster-prone conditions; others have drawn connections between Western agricultural policies and unsustainable land use patterns in the Third World.[5] Analyses such as these suggest that disasters are particularly likely to happen when there is a sharp disjunction between the social order that gives birth to a technology and the one in which it is eventually deployed.

A more focused but no less compelling analysis of disasters has emerged from the work of organizational sociologists, who were among the first to recognize explicitly that technological breakdowns of any magnitude demand a social explanation. In his influential book on "normal accidents," Charles Perrow pointed out that such failures are almost unavoidable in systems with a mix of technical and social properties that make them essentially unforgiving of error.[6] High-risk technologies are characterized, in Perrow's view, by "tight coupling" and complex interactions among components; instead of recovering from mistakes, such systems slide irresistibly into catastrophe. Some risky systems can be made safer by appropriately "loosening" their coupled and interactive elements, while others, like nuclear power, may require radical and as yet unattainable changes in design and management. Perrow's systemic view of technology fully implicated human as well as non-human factors in the production of disasters. Foreshadowing what happened at Bhopal, in particular, Perrow observed that, even in the technically sophisticated petrochemical industry, such engineering defects as leaky valves might react synergistically with such human elements as poorly trained operators, faulty communication, inadequate expert support, and inefficient evacuation plans to produce runaway accidents.

Among the human causes of disasters, the role of organizations has attracted justified attention, since organizations tend to fix patterns of unsafe behavior in much the same way that technological artifacts fix risky combinations of engineering design. Barry Turner, an early analyst of "man-made disasters," concluded, for example, that organizational factors often impede the flow and utilization of knowledge that could have been used preventively.[7] Only in a minority of cases is the necessary knowledge simply not available. More frequently, as indeed was the case in Bhopal, organizational barriers stand in the way of communicating knowledge, in usable form, to people who have the will and the power to take preventive action.[8] Features of an organization's external context, such as its competitive and regulatory environment, may increase its tendency to make disastrous choices, just as features of its internal culture may prevent the critical self-scrutiny needed to promote safety.[9] Further, the ways in which organizations communicate with each other may aggravate an accident's impacts, as Lee Clarke demonstrated in his illuminating study of emergency responses to an office building fire in Binghamton, New York.[10]

Organizational theory helps to identify the social-technical settings where failures are most likely to occur or to spin out of control. But to understand and even predict how technologies may fail, organizational analysis can usefully be supplemented by more micro-level accounts of the processes by which new technologies come into being. Adapting approaches that were fruitful in studying the production of scientific knowledge, social scientists have begun to explore just this problem, asking what happens before technological innovations are "black boxed" into the "hard," and presumably successful, artifacts that enter commerce. In technology as in science, innovation begins with an area of "interpretive flexibility"—a range of possible meanings, and accompanying technical choices, that correspond to the needs of divergent user groups. A final product is selected from a number of variants by narrowing its interpretive possibilities, merging some possible uses and excluding others. For instance, the artifact we know today as a bicycle acquired something like its present form through a nineteen-year period of development that resolved the competing claims of Sunday church-goers, sports enthusiasts, long-skirted women, and even anticyclists.[11] In the process, alternative designs were permanently abandoned (such as the classic "penny-farthing" with its two disparately sized wheels).

In common with political and organizational theory, the social constructivist view stresses the interpenetration of the social and artifactual domains in the production of technology. Neither mute nor immobile, the technological object, facility, or process emerges from recent historical and sociological accounts as profoundly and dynamically social.[12] A technological system of any complexity is a network of linked and disparate elements, ranging from the simplest widget to the most sophisticated social structures: banks, corporations, political parties, and governmental agencies. It takes force and ingenuity to hold together these resistant and sometimes recalcitrant components in a functioning whole. In historian Thomas P. Hughes's happy phrase, such systems are appropriately conceptualized as "networks of power."

From this perspective, the safety of a technological design or solution is never simply a given, determined solely by the laws of nature and the constraints of the physical environment. If form successfully follows function, it is because form and function have been *interpreted* as being in harmony with one another; a change in society's expectations with respect to either form or function could destabilize or destroy a seemingly functional technology. Thus chemical pesticides (Union Carbide's product in Bhopal), which once were seen as symbols of progress and prosperity, came to be identified in the 1970s with corporate greed and disregard for nature as environmental critics chronicled their harmful effects on human health and ecosystems.[13] This degradation in the status of pesticide technology contributed in turn to the stridently negative assessments of Union Carbide's actions after the accident, including the charge that the company had engaged in "industrial genocide."

Looking through the lens of social constructivism, we recognize that the design of technology involves the simultaneous construction of an inanimate artifact and a model of society that is compatible with the chosen design.[14] The shape of a technology is determined as much by assumptions about the way society will function in relation to the thing that is being produced as by conceptions of the thing itself. Automobiles, for example, are designed in the expectation that the vast majority of drivers will be literate and obey traffic rules (cars are seldom "idiot proof"[15]), that pedestrians will stay out of roadways, that signals (themselves a technological system of some complexity) will function smoothly, that roads will be kept in a state of tolerable repair, and so on. We do not stop to question these background assumptions most of the time because they are generally close enough to being right and do not cause *systemic* disruptions even when they are wrong.

Once a technology comes into being, the apparent hardness of its design reinforces the boundary we tend to draw between the social and the material worlds and creates strong disincentives to reexamining the social presuppositions that went into its making. Yet, as technology studies have disclosed, even a hardened technological artifact retains dimensions of fluidity that may not be transparent to the naive onlooker. To make the object "work," for instance, a body of informal uses and practices may grow up around it that were not in the minds of the designers and that may even change the character of the object itself. Thus a drug approved by the Food and Drug Administration for one indication may be routinely prescribed by physicians for other, unapproved indications. A pesticide made in an industrialized country may be used at higher than recommended doses by Third World farmers unschooled in the principles of toxicity. In cases like these, a technology is invisibly adapted to meet the needs of a new user group, without any explicit reformulation of its physical design or associated formal routines and codes of practice.

Technological disasters reveal with laser precision the dangers latent in this process of invisible adaptation. Thus an apparently harmless decision to deviate from prescribed cleaning practices becomes, in Brian Wynne's telling, the prime cause of a fatal explosion in an underground water main in Abbeystead, Lancashire:

[A] large void had been allowed to form in the tunnel, partly because operators had evolved an informal work practice which left washout valves a crack open all the time. This extra drainage, against official procedures, was evolved as an alternative to the official procedure which involved fully flushing the (normally closed) valve about once every several weeks, to wash out accumulating silt.[16]

The practice of continuous drainage had been adopted in this case because local anglers (an unexpected "consumer" group for the flushing system) had complained about the river being muddied for days after an officially sanctioned desilting. As it happened, the unofficial practice that met their needs created a space for the build-up of potentially explosive levels of methane, an eventuality that was not foreseen by the tunnel's engineers, the operators, or the demanding if unwise fishing community.

When technologies are transported out of their original context, as in cases of cross-national technology transfer, the chances of such risk-enhancing reinterpretations of the original system are enormously multiplied. The artifact is joined in the receiving nation with a community of users who never participated in the negotiations leading to the technology's original construction and who thus had no opportunity to ensure that their cultural needs and preferences would be translated into appropriate technical specifications or rules of operation. The result is a disjunction between the technology that these users need and the one that they received.[17] This "user gap," in turn, increases the probability that new practices will develop around the technology that may temporarily satisfy local requirements but that may in the long run subvert its built-in safety systems. At the limit, a technology that was relatively linear and "loosely coupled" in Perrow's terms may develop complexities and tight couplings that invite disaster. All of these possibilities were realized in Bhopal, as we shall see throughout this volume, with fateful consequences for more than a hundred thousand people.

The victims of disasters represent, in a sense, the ultimate excluded community from the standpoint of negotiating the design of technology. In contrast with other "missing" social groups, such as users in an importing country, victims of technological disaster do not constitute a clearly demarcated social group until they are struck by tragedy. They possess no common identity, and hence no political voice or force that would allow them to declare in advance which hazards they are prepared to accept. Even after the fact, as Kai Erikson showed in his masterly study of the 1972 dam disaster at Buffalo Creek, the tragic event demolishes not just the physical but the psychological foundations of preexisting communities, making recovery arduous.[18] Reconstructing communities under such circumstances involves a very special and chancy kind of politics: the gradual accretion of power around a community of the dispossessed, whose only significant resource is the symbolic status engendered by their extraordinary suffering. Yet only when victims effectively regroup themselves can they hope to impress on others their particular causal interpretations of the tragedy, along with the moral and political consequences that this interpretation entails.

The search for legal redress has proved to be a most effective vehicle in industrial societies for uniting the victims of disaster into a coherent community. As individuals, disaster victims do not command sufficient influence to mobilize the established levers of power, and their progress toward relief tends to be excruciatingly slow.[19] Legal proceedings allow the plaintiffs' individual voices to be aggregated into a politically recognizable force. The U.S. legal system in particular provides a wealth of procedures and resources that facilitate the search for collective remedies. An entrepreneurial legal culture, creative and resourceful practitioners, and low entry barriers to litigation have enabled plaintiffs to achieve through the legal process a level of redress that they could not normally have hoped to gain through other channels.[20] In Bhopal, the victims were initially confronted by a less developed tort system and a far less receptive remedial tradition. The Indian judiciary's halting responses to the tragedy and its gradual enunciation of new compensatory principles—spurred by an uncomfortably close encounter with American tort law—provide one of the most poignant examples of social learning triggered by the events in Bhopal.

Disasters and Public Policy

Although disasters frequently lead to changes in public policy, policy analysts have not as a rule interacted productively with scholars in the domain of technology studies. Just as social theorists seldom look inside the black box of technology to explore its hidden interpretive flexibility, so students of technology rarely concern themselves with the inner workings of black-boxed social institutions such as regulatory agencies and courts. Yet political and policy studies, as represented in this book, have much to contribute to our understanding of modern technological systems, for they can add a dynamic, structural, and cross-cultural dimension that is frequently missing in social studies of technology. The question one confronts through such analysis is not why things came apart in one specific instance but what in general constrains the capacity of human societies to control their harmful technological impulses. By examining the ways in which social rules and institutions changed (or failed to change) after a traumatic event, one begins to apprehend what is fixed and what is relatively negotiable in the way a given society or culture constructs its relationship with technology. This exercise, in turn, may unveil previously unsuspected "couplings" between the technical components of complex technologies and the social structures in which they are embedded.

Comparative studies are especially useful in clarifying the societal presuppositions against which technological disasters play themselves out, and few episodes in history could have served better to highlight these cross-cultural similarities and differences than did the accident in Bhopal. Just as the leaking methyl isocyanate gas destroyed the lives of thousands in one Indian city, so the example of what had happened to Union Carbide demolished overnight a whole edifice of public confidence in the norms governing the multinational chemical industry. Governments, companies, trade associations, victims' groups, and the legal community in several countries scrambled to rebuild a regulatory structure that would take account of the multiple layers of technical and social unpreparedness revealed by Bhopal. The disaster thus set off a massive experiment in learning, but one that was deeply conditioned at each location and for each major actor by varying social and cultural factors. Lawyers, bureaucrats, politicians, and activists in India drew different conclusions from each other, and they in turn differed from their counterparts in Europe or the United States. In probing these divergences, and the reasons for them, the contributors to this volume add to our growing awareness of the culturally situated character of risk management policies.

The essays that follow begin to bridge an unfortunate theoretical divide that has long existed between policy analysis and the study of technological systems, mirroring the stubborn, though untenable, separation that marks off engineering design from the design of law, policy, risk management, and international technology transfer. Such an advance is long overdue. If we accept that technical artifacts are at once also political and social constructs, then the analysis of how technology both conditions and is conditioned by its social context has to be at the heart of any attempt to control its hazards. For instance, a hazard that is for the most part physically determined (methyl isocyanate at sufficient doses will kill people anywhere) will call for different treatment from one that derives instead from a pathological conjunction of human and non-human factors (a production process that "worked" in America may fail in India, where even risky technologies are differently contextualized into people's lives). Accordingly, a central objective of many of the following chapters is to examine in detail the lasting human and social deep structures over which the gas leak temporarily spread its tragic pall. For the makers and controllers of technology, the challenge is to reintegrate these insights concerning human institutions and behavior into the construction of safer technological systems.

Policy analyses such as those undertaken in this volume also offer an important vehicle for exploring how politics shapes the formation of closure around particular constructions of technology, making some hazards more probable than others. The process by which different consumer or user groups iron out their differences with respect to the choices that technology presents is deeply and necessarily political. Simply put, in any technological culture some interpretations of machines or of mechanical processes of production are more politically viable, and hence have a better chance of succeeding, than others; in Western societies, for example, high-energy and high-chemical input agriculture has won out over "alternative" farming,

and interventionist techniques like surgery and intensive chemo-
therapy have consistently drawn more public funding and support
than "alternative" medicine. To date, the power relationships that influence such patterned outcomes have been studied, as I suggested
above, largely at the macro-level of political economy. By contrast,
questions of politics and power have generally fallen outside the purview of empirical work focused on the micro-construction of particular technologies. This loss of contact with the political realm is a
criticism frequently leveled against the work of social constructivists.[21]

Probing into the policy aftermath of technological failures offers a
means of restoring politics to the center of social constructivist inquiry
without losing the benefits of empiricism. A disaster, in effect, is the
unplanned and total disintegration of the negotiated consensus that
stably held together the actors, institutions, rules, behaviors, and artifacts that constitute a heterogeneous technological system. Debates
about how to interpret such an event, how to apportion blame and
responsibility, and what restorative policies to craft in its wake provide a powerful textual basis for reading how technology and political
power interact both formally and informally in modern societies.
Whose voices are heard and whose interpretations are excluded, perhaps systematically, as the state moves to remedy the disaster? Which
legal and policy approaches find favor and whose interests do they
serve? Which institutions are challenged and which are reinforced by
the breakdown in the mechanical world? Why do solutions that seem
self-evident in one nation's policy environment find little or no reso-
nance in another? These are some of the enduring questions that are
brought to the fore in an analysis of the aftermath of Bhopal. Together, they repoliticize the social terrain within which Union Carbide
built, operated, and ultimately lost hold of its ill-fated Indian pesticide
plant. They also bring out the universal themes that connect such
seemingly "one of a kind" disasters as Chernobyl and Bhopal.

Essays in Learning

In the summer of 1991, I spent about five weeks in India researching
recent developments in risk management and environmental policy.
One question that I put to many of the people whom I interviewed,
both in government and in the private sector, was whether, in the
seven years since Bhopal, anything had fundamentally changed in
India's approach to controlling hazardous technologies. I asked Indian lawyers and civil servants what they regarded as the most significant legal and policy reforms arising out of the disaster and whether
the preconditions for other Bhopals still existed in many parts of the

country. The answers ranged widely. Not only had things failed to change for the better, said the pessimists, they had actually become worse as a result of rising pollution and poverty, as well as the government's recent decisions to liberalize the economy, a move that some saw as tantamount to widespread deregulation of hazardous industries. Others, more sanguine, felt that positive changes had indeed occurred, but in intangible forms: heightened environmental awareness in industry, closer networking among citizen groups, greater legal and political sophistication among activists, and so forth. Interestingly, and perhaps sadly, hardly anyone spoke of the many formal legislative and regulatory measures adopted by the Indian government as evidence of progressive social learning.

The following accounts of legal and policy change after Bhopal go far toward explaining the reasons for these ambivalent assessments. We see Indian institutions, with little historical investment in technology management or victim relief, struggling to create a framework of rules that will work in a culture to which hazardous technologies have only recently been imported from vastly different sociopolitical settings. But the learning processes in the United States, in Europe, and in the international community were also marked, as we shall see, by ambiguity and ambivalence. Thus, even the highly developed system of legal remedies for toxic substance victims in the United States offers a striking example of imperfect social learning, and it is not surprising that this system proved impossible to adapt to the challenges of Bhopal. The stories told throughout this volume make it clear that no state or international institution can yet claim to have mastered the problems of safety and social justice that arise from the passionate engagement of modern societies with hazardous technologies.

The remainder of the book explores the problem of learning in a framework of expanding institutional and political circles. We begin, appropriately enough, with a chapter focusing on Union Carbide, generally seen as the perpetrator, but in some ways also the least visible victim of the tragedy. Wil Lepkowski documents the impact of the accident on the company's structure, finances, self-image, and indeed its soul, in the years following the gas leak. At one level, this is a cautionary tale about what can happen to any corporate enterprise that is hit by catastrophe. The accident and its legal consequences were interwoven with a hostile takeover bid and a forced restructuring that completely altered the character of Union Carbide, undermining its ability to compete with more innovative firms in world markets. But Lepkowski's analysis shows a Carbide that was less the passive victim of circumstances than the active agent of its own dissolution. The company's decision to adopt an unyielding legal posture, showing little sensitivity to the enormity or the special cultural resonances of Bhopal, inexorably shaped its destiny. In drawing up the balance sheet on Carbide's performance, Lepkowski suggests that a more context-sensitive interpretation of its rights and responsibilities might have led to a different, and brighter, future.

The plight of the Bhopal victims and the efforts of the Indian government to provide relief form the focal points of a chapter by Armin Rosencranz, Shyam Divan, and Antony Scott on the legal and policy repercussions of Bhopal. While the authors record India's formal achievements in both the judicial and political forums, they also illuminate the tortured and exhausting pathways that led to these endpoints. Progress was especially hard to discern in the political domain, where shifting objectives and alliances hindered the pursuit of a consistent relief program. The courts, by contrast, played a more constructive and coherent role at both state and national levels, since their efforts were focused from beginning to end on the relatively narrow issue of compensation. Yet the task of manufacturing a remedial structure that was adequate to the complexity of Bhopal proved to be an elusive and intensely political undertaking. The Indian judiciary's attempts to steer between a procedurally correct adherence to existing norms and a more flexible conception of justice, tailored to the extraordinary demands of the case before them, make a remarkable study in legal innovation.

Many of the regulatory structures that could have prevented the accident were formally in place in India before 1984, but the event revealed surprising deficiencies in both the coverage of the rules and their implementation. B. Bowonder, Jeanne Kasperson, and Roger Kasperson review the legislative and regulatory initiatives through which the Indian government sought to fill these gaps in the years after Bhopal. Although the formal gains have been impressive, the authors urge caution in evaluating their cumulative impact. The government's overarching goal, they note, has been to strengthen a system of command and control regulation whose basic premises are widely questioned by informed Indian opinion. This relatively unimaginative response to a momentous event raises doubts about the state's ability to reflect creatively on its own institutional shortcomings. The broad issue to which the chapter points is the need for flexible, self-executing regulatory approaches in developing countries, where state authority is severely constrained by deficits in resources, expertise, critical awareness, and political legitimacy.

Beyond the circles of those immediately affected—the company and the victims—the Bhopal disaster was widely interpreted as a mandate to improve communication about technological risks. Destruction on such a scale could not have taken place, people argued, if the community at risk had been informed beforehand of the threat to its life and health. Pressure to enact a mandatory disclosure law gained ground in the United States, while in the European Community the monitory lessons of Bhopal were absorbed into an incremental process of learning, underway since the 1976 accident in Seveso, Italy, to make more information about chemical risks available to the public. Nationally and internationally, therefore, there was a high degree of policy convergence after Bhopal around the concept of a community's right to know about chemical hazards.

But there were interesting divergences as well in the way that state agencies and the public construed their rights and responsibilities with respect to increased knowledge. In their chapters on the U.S. and European cases respectively, Susan Hadden and Josée van Eijndhoven point to the different assumptions about state-society relationships embedded in right-to-know policies on the two sides of the Atlantic; in particular, while the U.S. legislature acted to make information broadly available (a characteristically rights-based approach), European policy focused on tailoring the information to meet expected demands (a needs-based approach). Although information was seen as an important resource in each setting, U.S. policy makers were content to let citizens decide for themselves what was important and how it could be put to use. Europeans, however, felt that the state had a duty to step in and package information in a way that would readily serve the instrumental needs of its citizens. These contrasting preferences illustrate the far-reaching impact of politics and culture on a society's ability to translate a catastrophic event into meaningful preventive action.

If Bhopal helped to crystallize a single issue for policy makers, that issue was the drastic inadequacy of compensation for the victims of mass disasters in Third World countries. The much publicized, and much maligned, descent of American plaintiffs' lawyers on Bhopal immediately after the accident underscored a glaring cross-cultural gap in legal remedies, even if it served no other socially beneficial purpose. The subsequent flow of litigation between courts in the United States and India further highlighted the disparities in legal resources that exist between industrial and developing countries. What are the long-term implications of differential access to lawyering and legal institutions in a world of growing economic interdependence, where productive technologies travel far from their places of origin? Is it reasonable to expect that the "soft technology" of lawyering should be transferred across national boundaries together with the harder engineering and process technologies developed in industrial countries? And when legal worlds collide, as they did in Bhopal, what can the clashing systems usefully learn from their enforced contact? Marc Galanter, a former consultant to the Indian government on the Bhopal litigation, speculates on these questions in his chapter on the transnational traffic in legal remedies.

Tom Durkin and William Felstiner raise additional questions about the relevance of American compensatory systems for other countries in their study of litigation generated by abestos-related diseases. Tracing the evolution of law and practice in one of the world's most highly developed tort systems, they ask whether such a sophisticated framework is well adapted to handling the needs of mass tort victims in other parts of the world. The asbestos tragedy, they conclude, was a disaster on such a massive scale that it overwhelmed the adaptive capacity of the U.S. legal process, much as war strains civil institutions to the breaking point. Bhopal in the Indian context was a similarly overwhelming event. Durkin and Felstiner argue that it may be fruitless in such cases to look to the courts for the levels and speed of relief expected by ordinary accident victims. The rough and ready equity of an administrative compensation scheme—a solution toward which both asbestos and Bhopal victims were slowly and painfully directed—may be the only realistic alternative.

And what of learning outside the established institutions of government or industry? Michael Reich explores this question in a chapter on pollution victims and the politics of redress. Learning, as noted earlier, is particularly difficult for victims, who must cope not only with the problems of dissociation and resource limitations but also, frequently, with the entrenched opposition of better-institutionalized interests. Yet, as Reich demonstrates, victim groups from Bhopal and other toxic disasters have been able to surmount these obstacles through a stepwise learning process, eventually transforming their private trouble into political issues that the state cannot ignore. While victims in developing countries are likely to meet especially strong resistance from the state, their cause may gain strength from alliances with international regulatory bodies and the environmental movement.

The next two chapters adopt an explicitly transnational perspective as they ask what impact Bhopal-like episodes can have on learning and norm building in international institutions. Frank Laird discusses Bhopal's impact on efforts by international agencies to build worldwide information networks about chemical hazards. Following Bhopal, Laird argues, policy makers, and for the most part the public, tended to think about the objectives of right-to-know laws in simple instrumental terms: more information should be made available because its availability will necessarily empower the receiver. Missing from public debate was much awareness of the problematic character of "information," which like technology is at once a strategic resource and a social construct. Thus, information can be filtered, manipulated, selectively disclosed, and presented in relatively usable or unusable forms consistently with the needs of different social and political actors. An important function of policy making, then, is to limit the range of meanings that competing actors seek to attach to "information" and to forge consensus around a subset of interpretations that serve valid collective interests. Laird suggests that international regimes have begun to serve these functions, thereby providing opportunities for information users to overcome the structural constraints built into their own national systems of information provision.

Peter Haas's survey of environmental initiatives in the United Nations system is also moderately reassuring, in that it shows the capacity of such bodies to learn adaptively from prior mistakes and shortcomings. In large part, however, this pattern of learning conforms to the "single loop" model, in which new knowledge is used to develop better means and instruments for application to preexisting ends. Few international organizations are structured to achieve more complex forms of learning, in which knowledge helps refine both the means and the ends of policy making. Yet, in a somber closing chapter, Paul Shrivastava suggests that disasters like Bhopal will continue to occur unless national as well as international institutions master just this kind of rigorously critical self-examination. Looking to the political economy of international trade in chemicals, Shrivastava argues that technological disasters originate in a series of basic economic, political, and cultural contradictions that cannot be papered over with simple technological or policy fixes. But he finds little evidence as yet that policy makers are probing for underlying causal connections between economic organization and environmental ills or are seeking to integrate such transnational considerations into national risk management decisions.

Conclusion

Looking at the policy impacts of the Bhopal disaster, we can hardly doubt that it was in journalistic terms a "big story," which Lepkowski defines as one with the capability to transform the future. The event not only left an indelible mark on a hundred thousand Indian citizens and on the company that injured them, but also fundamentally reshaped the way people perceive the risks and benefits of the chemical industry in the developing world. Measured by numbers alone, Bhopal also had a massive impact on policy, for the accident gave rise to innumerable changes in the rules by which private firms, governments, and international organizations manage the risks of hazardous technologies.

The picture of policy change that emerges from the following pages, however, is incremental rather than cataclysmic. Learning was manifested in small advances over and refinements in existing ways of doing business, rather than in wholesale reformulations of earlier practice. Many institutions reacted to Bhopal, but they did so in predictable fashion, implementing policies that were already on the horizon and for which the disaster generated persuasive political support. Particularly noteworthy was the failure of any policy-making body to take seriously the fully elaborated political and social critiques of technology that have been developed in the academic literature.

Bhopal in this sense precipitated more what Charles Lindblom has characterized as "muddling through" than the kind of "paradigm shift" in social learning that some view as essential if we are to survive the environmental crises of the coming century.[22] The critical reader will find much in this volume to support the view that the latter kind of learning is simply beyond the capacity of existing policy institutions at the national or international levels. Learning came easiest and most fruitfully to some of the actors who "knew" least to begin with: the victims, the Indian courts, and some international institutions. For more experienced actors, even a catastrophic event like Bhopal could only be understood and accommodated within established frames of practice, a fact that effectively militated against radical policy innovation.

How should we react to this message, apart from seeking to incorporate it into theories of social learning? It suggests, first, that we should be cautious about the idea, forcefully championed by political scientist Aaron Wildavsky, that resilience is a generally wiser alternative to anticipation in societal efforts to manage risk.[23] Wildavsky warned that preventive measures adopted on the basis of imperfect knowledge may siphon away resources that could be better used to build more robust and responsive societies. But if, as Bhopal suggests, innovative learning is beyond the capacity of our most powerful social institutions—if indeed learning tends to replicate socialized forms of error—then after-the-fact alleviation may prove to be as ineffectual a strategy for coping with risk as blind reliance on prevention. Where knowledge is limited, we should therefore at least learn to anticipate the worst possible outcomes. Many of the chapters in this book demonstrate that retroactive learning from disasters can prove to be a frustrating and costly experience.

Lindblom, ever the apostle of incrementalism, suggests that it would be unwise for human societies as impaired as ours are by inequality and imperfect knowledge to seek out radical forms of change, particularly at the level of institutional reforms. Indeed, he argues that the very absence of consensus on such reforms shows how unprepared we are to undertake them:

> If anyone could here and now present an array of feasible institutional reforms that would significantly reduce impairment, that is to say, reforms defensible by informed and sustained argument and feasible at least in commanding some endorsement from large groups not dismissed as eccentric, that would in itself be evidence that societies are less impaired than alleged in this study.[24]

One hopes, however, that human understanding is capable of ranging a few steps ahead of humanity's ability to convert insight into action. This after all is the expectation that underlies modern environmentalism's call to "think globally but act locally." True, most of the institutions that responded to Bhopal were too limited in administrative, political, and moral imagination to bring about the fundamental social reorderings that the event demanded. In focusing so completely on legal and regulatory reform, for instance, they collectively passed up the opportunity for a thoroughgoing global reassessment of the relationship between technological risk and political power in an unequal world. A volume such as this can help us ponder the causes of their failures and sow the seeds for a future of more revolutionary change.

Notes

1. Noteworthy contributions to this literature include Lewis Mumford, *The Myth of the Machine* (New York: Harcourt, Brace, Jovanovich, 1967, 1970); Jacques Ellul, *The Technological Society* (New York: Alfred A. Knopf, 1964); Herbert Marcuse, *One-Dimensional Man* (Boston: Beacon Press, 1964); Jürgen Habermas, *Toward a Rational Society* (Boston: Beacon Press, 1970); David Noble, *America by Design* (New York: Oxford University Press, 1977).

2. Lewis Mumford, "Authoritarian and Democratic Technics," *Technology and Culture* 5 (1964): 1–8; E. F. Schumacher, *Small Is Beautiful* (London: Blond and Briggs, 1973).

3. Langdon Winner, "Do Artifacts Have Politics?"in *The Whale and the Reactor* (Chicago: University of Chicago Press, 1986), pp. 19–39.

4. Bernhard Glaeser, ed., *The Green Revolution Revisited* (London: Allen and Unwin, 1987); William Ascher and Robert Healy, *Natural Resource Policymaking in Developing Countries* (Durham, NC: Duke University Press, 1990), pp. 33–48.

5. See particularly Michael Redclift, *Sustainable Development: Exploring the Contradictions* (London: Methuen, 1987).

6. Charles Perrow, *Normal Accidents* (New York: Basic Books, 1984).

7. Barry A. Turner, *Man-Made Disasters* (London: Wykeham, 1978).

8. Sheila Jasanoff, "The Bhopal Disaster and the Right to Know," *Social Science and Medicine* 27 (1988): 1113–1123. See also Frank Laird, "Information and Disaster Prevention" (this volume, Chapter 10).

9. The explosion of the space shuttle Challenger in January 1986 directed considerable attention to the organizational culture of NASA, leading to better elaborated accounts of the connections between organizations and technological failure. For a representative sample of the literature addressing these issues, see Presidential Commission on the Space Shuttle Challenger Accident, *Report of the Presidential Commission on the Space Shuttle Challenger Accident* (Washington, DC: U.S. Government Printing Office, 1986); Diane Vaughan, "Policy Implications of Organizational-Technical System Failure: The Challenger Accident," paper presented at Law and Society Annual Meeting, Madison, WI, June 1989; Garry D. Brewer, "Perfect Places: NASA as an Idealized Institution," in Radford Byerly, Jr., ed., *Space Policy Reconsidered* (Boulder, CO: Westview Press, 1989), pp. 158–173.

10. Lee Clarke, *Acceptable Risk? Making Decisions in a Toxic Environment* (Berkeley: University of California Press, 1989).

11. Wiebe Bijker, Thomas P. Hughes, and Trevor Pinch, *The Social Construction of Technological Systems* (Cambridge, MA: MIT Press, 1987); for a theoretical overview, as well as details of the bicycle story, see Trevor J. Pinch and Wiebe E. Bijker, "The Social Construction of Facts and Artifacts: Or How the Sociology of Science and the Sociology of Technology Might Benefit Each Other," pp. 17–46.

12. Bruno Latour, *The Pasteurization of France* (Cambridge, MA: Harvard University Press, 1988); Thomas P. Hughes, *Networks of Power: Electrification in Western Society, 1880–1930* (Baltimore: Johns Hopkins University Press, 1983); Bijker, Hughes, and Pinch, *Social Construction of Technological Systems.*

13. The book that is universally credited with raising modern environmentalism's consciousness about the risks of chemical pesticides is Rachel Carson, *Silent Spring* (New York: Houghton Mifflin, 1962). For an argument that attributes the extraordinary success of Carson's missionary writing to features in the social organization of the environmental movement, see Mary Douglas and Aaron Wildavsky, *Risk and Culture* (Berkeley: University of California Press, 1982).

14. Brian Wynne, "Unruly Technology," *Social Studies of Science* 18 (1988): 147–167.

15. After a car accident occurs, however, the victims may well claim that the offending vehicle was designed without adequate safeguards against operator carelessness. For an argument that this is exactly what happened in accidents involving the Audi, see Peter Huber, *Galileo's Revenge: Junk Science in the Courtroom* (New York: Basic Books, 1991), pp. 57–74.

16. Wynne, "Unruly Technology," p. 155.

17. The notion of "appropriate technology" current in the field of international development acknowledges that technologies need to be adapted to suit local circumstances. But the term as ordinarily used fails to capture the full implications of the critique emerging from social studies of technology, which suggests that true "appropriateness" cannot be achieved without a real element of power-sharing between the creators and the users of technology.

18. Kai Erikson, *Everything in Its Path: Destruction of Community in the Buffalo Creek Flood* (New York: Simon and Schuster, 1976).

19. For an excellent cross-national study of the difficulties faced by victims of chemical disasters, see Michael Reich, *Toxic Politics: Responding to Chemical Disasters* (Ithaca, NY: Cornell University Press, 1991); see also Adeline Levine, *Love Canal: Science, Politics, and People* (Lexington, MA: Lexington Books, 1982).

20. A telling case is that of veterans allegedly injured by Agent Orange during the Vietnam war. After failing to persuade Congress to compensate them, the veterans brought a class action suit against the manufacturers of the herbicide. Although the case did not proceed to trial, the plaintiffs won a record-setting settlement. For a highly readable and human account of the protracted legal proceedings, see Peter Schuck, *Agent Orange on Trial: Mass Toxic Disasters in the Courts,* enlarged edition (Cambridge, MA: Harvard University Press, 1987).

21. See, for example, Langdon Winner, "Upon Opening the Black Box and Finding It Empty: Social Constructivism and the Philosophy of Technology," in Joseph C. Pitt and Elena Lugo, eds., *The Technology of Discovery and the Discovery of Technology*, Proceedings of the 6th International Conference of the Society for Philosophy and Technology (Blacksburg, VA: Society for Philosophy and Technology, Virginia Polytechnic Institute, 1991), pp. 503–519; Brian Wynne, "Representing Policy Constructions and Interests in SSK," *Social Studies of Science* 20 (1990): 195–207; Edward Woodhouse and Susan Cozzens, "Science and Politics," in Sheila Jasanoff, Gerald E. Markle, James Petersen, Trevor Pinch, eds., *Handbook of Science and Technology Studies* (Newbury Park, CA: Sage Publications, forthcoming).

22. On "muddling through," see Charles E. Lindblom, "The Science of 'Muddling Through'," *Public Administration Review* 19 (1959): 79–88. For a discussion of constraints that lead to paradigmatic learning (that is, learning within existing paradigms), see Dean E. Mann, "Environmental Learning in a Decentralized World," *Journal of International Affairs* 44 (1991): 301–337.

23. Aaron Wildavsky, *Searching for Safety* (New Brunswick, NJ: Transaction Press, 1988), pp. 77–85.

24. Charles E. Lindblom, *Inquiry and Change* (New Haven, CT: Yale University Press, 1990), p. 286.

Chapter 2
The Restructuring of Union Carbide
Wil Lepkowski

The impact of the worst industrial disaster in history—Bhopal—is usually described from one of five different perspectives: legal, social, political, technological, and medical. The first three account for most of the chapters in this book. The other two can be found in various engineering and medical studies describing the technical facets of the methyl isocyanate (MIC) leak (how water entered the methyl isocyanate storage tank and why the eruption was not contained)[1] and the still-unresolved toxicological effects of MIC.[2]

There is another view, however, that might be called the "corporate perspective": the attempt to chart and interpret the changes that Bhopal wrought on the structure, values, and behavior of Union Carbide Corporation (UCC). Only one book, *A Killing Wind* by Dan Kurzman, attempted with an empathetic eye to go "inside" Carbide in the days and months following the disaster.[3] Covering events through late 1986, Kurzman provided valuable portrayals of how some Carbide executives reacted in an atmosphere of unrelenting crisis. But because his account ended in 1986, he had no opportunity to describe any deeper changes within Carbide in Bhopal's more extended aftermath.[4]

Kurzman's book did close with an excursion into the mind and feelings of Warren Anderson, Carbide's chairman during the tragedy, who by the book's end was living in reflective retirement on Long Island. On reaching age 65, Anderson left the company to a younger team of executives not associated with the Bhopal debacle. But, as Kurzman puts it, Anderson could not really exorcise the "ghosts" of the Bhopal experience, knowing that the name Union Carbide would forever be associated with a disaster that occurred under his stewardship. He would attend Carbide's annual stockholders' meetings in succeeding years, but did not, as is often customary when a chief executive retires, retain a seat on Carbide's board of directors.

Anderson's name was again associated with the disaster in 1992 when the Indian government signaled its intent to extradite him to India to stand criminal trial.[5] He himself refrained from any public comment, but Carbide lawyers essentially said they regarded the actions as without legal basis and would not comply. What Anderson left behind was a company he had once helped nurture into a giant, only to see it undergo continued shrinkage and predictions of disappearance. This, partly, is the story of that diminution and of Carbide's simultaneous efforts to remake its reputation as it systematically diminished in size and diversity.

Almost ten years after the Bhopal tragedy, Carbide continues to be depicted in two ways. The first version is its own: a compassionate company, victimized by employee sabotage at a plant it did not control 10,000 miles away; a company that did everything possible to bring succor and just compensation to the victims of Bhopal only to be hampered at every point by Indian politics and activist assaults; a company that finally agreed to a $470 million settlement, far in excess of the actual needs of the victims.[6] Of these, Carbide believes that no more than 10,000 can be numbered as permanently disabled. Others, including the Indian government's Council for Medical Research, believe upward of 150,000 is a more realistic figure.[7]

The opposing version, equally crystallized and more passionately argued, sees Carbide's behavior throughout as a crass, cynical manipulation of public opinion, consciously blind to the actual human damage caused by the methyl isocyanate leak. Carbide, in this account, trumped up a fabricated sabotage story without following it up in court, and escaped true justice with the aid of an Indian Supreme Court that colluded with the government to produce a shockingly inadequate settlement. There is no dearth of literature arguing this viewpoint.[8] Both sides make strong cases. My point in this chapter is not to settle these critical differences or advocate one against the other. The aim, instead, is to evaluate a shamed but staunch company, enormously changed since Bhopal, that will for all time be at the center of the history of industrial disaster.

The Culture of Union Carbide

Assembling a fully descriptive portrait of Union Carbide through its transformation since 1984 is an elusive undertaking (see my postscript). That is because, as with all corporations, at least four worlds intersect within its closed institutional system, each painting its own canvas. First is the financial realm, demarcated by the company's performance on Wall Street; second, the complex managerial world of covert strategies, veiled motives, and risky decisions; third, the human world of the Carbide work force; and, fourth, the symbolic world— the sturdy and reliable image that the corporation seeks to present to its customers, its shareholders, and the public.

Sharply different, too, are the confident, masculine, all-is-well, all-will-be-well mentalities of Carbide at the headquarters level in Danbury, Connecticut, and the grittier, truer-to-life existence of smells, sounds, laughter, and emergencies at Carbide's operating plants in West Virginia, Louisiana, Texas, and elsewhere. Carbide's saga is replete with drama—much known, a great deal hidden—because of the legal, financial, and media pressures that bore down on it from late 1984 through 1989, when the case reached the Indian Supreme Court. It survived, and bears its combat medals proudly—though as regards Bhopal rather stiffly, often evasively.

So the post-Bhopal Carbide brought into rough focus in this chapter is no anatomically correct rendering of a complex organization but instead a shifting cubist melange. The parts are recognizable but they frequently seem oddly disconnected. The legal Carbide hardly fits an outside observer's expectation of the ethical Carbide, though Carbide officials would clearly dispute that assessment. The scientific Carbide—especially as regards toxicological research on methyl isocyanate—would hardly live up to science's exacting demand for all the toxicological facts about a controversial molecule. And the journalist's ideal of a Carbide candid about itself, willing to take a reporter aside and describe the agonies of decision, conflicts rather predictably with the reality of a corporation bent on preserving shareholder value by protecting its image.

Historically, Union Carbide's corporate structure likewise displays a cubism of its own behind the company's hexagonal logo. Separate, unrelated fiefdoms of industrial gases, metals and alloys, carbon electrodes, agricultural products, chemicals and plastics, and specialty products each jealously adhered to their own corporate personas, presenting an image of a company perpetually searching for focus. New ventures would emerge according to fashions of the managerial moment, only to flounder in indecision and isolation, and ultimately disappear. To Wall Street, the pre-Bhopal Carbide seemed a benign, inbred, poorly managed, under-performing, company that never could quite "get its act together," an image that dogged the company from the mid-1960s until its systematic dismemberment into the monolithic ethylene-based petrochemical company it returned to by 1993.[9]

What all Carbiders have always held in common, though, was pride in technology and the feeling of being treated fairly and humanly by the company. Carbide's top managers, in my judgment, displayed the once stereotypical mentalities of the engineer: regimented, narrowly focused, business-first, hostile to the social and political values of the environmental community, but paragons of dedicated citizenship.[10]

Until the late 1980s, when continuous restructuring and layoffs led to serious declines in the morale of its workers and depressed confidence in management,[11] Union Carbide commanded extreme employee loyalty and security. Though less than a sixth the size it was before Bhopal, Carbide still ranks as a large chemical company, employing around 14,000 people in plants along the Houston Ship Channel, the petrochemical alley running down from Baton Rouge to New Orleans in Louisiana, the Kanawha Valley of West Virginia, and dozens of other places.

In the Kanawha Valley, many Carbide families reach back to the company's beginnings in 1917. Bonds are powerful among Carbiders, as well as between Carbiders and the various social and commercial institutions in the Valley. To be a Carbider—at least to be one still remaining with the company—is to wear a badge of reliability, responsibility, and stability. When reminded of the Bhopal disaster, a Carbider always replies that the cause was sabotage at a plant operated by Third World foreigners. The American company could not possibly have been responsible.[12]

Before Bhopal, "the whole chemical industry operated on the basic assumption that what we did within our fences was none of anyone's business," commented one Carbide community relations official in Charleston interviewed in 1991. "And the people outside the fences didn't think it was any business of theirs, either. Bhopal changed all that, and for the better." Yet, ironically, what really brought new consciousness to Carbide, he added, was not so much Bhopal as the serious leak of a mixture of aldicarb oxime that took place nine months later at its plant in Institute, West Virginia. "That one really shook us," he said. "We said it couldn't happen to us here and it did. That's what really kicked in these new attitudes."[12]

But Bhopal remains central to Carbide's damaged identity. The noble mythology of the chemical calling (high service to society) made the enormity of the disaster especially jarring to Carbiders. It was their children who had to face classmates in the disaster's aftermath. Carbiders felt not only the shame of identification with the affected company but also the insecurity of wondering about the survivability of their jobs. And those fears were well placed. As a result of the corporate dismemberment during the 1980s and early 1990s, tens of thousands of former Carbiders were either let go or with some degree of relief became part of such companies as Ralston Purina, Rhone-Poulenc, First Brands, UCAR Carbon (the name of a new company formed by the sale of half of Carbide's carbon products division to Mitsubishi), and Praxair. This dissection almost certainly could have been avoided had Carbide made an early $600 million settlement on damages with the Indian government.

Up to the editing of this chapter in mid-1993, Carbide was well embarked on a campaign to demonstrate to all its publics its determination to be "second to none" in environmental and safety matters. But the effort of winning over the public has been a difficult one for Carbide, owing at least partially to its past. Of no help was the 1985 aldicarb oxime leak, or the March 1991 explosion of an ethylene oxide unit at its petrochemical plant in Seadrift, Texas, which killed one person and injured thirty-two. For that accident, the Occupation Safety and Health Administration fined Carbide $2.8 million, reprimanded Carbide for ignoring several internal safety audits that urged preventive measures in the explosion area, and withdrew a safety award the agency had given Carbide months before. The report conjectured that had the accident occurred during the work day, rather than at 1:00 A.M., more than four hundred might have been killed.[14]

As a result of the Seadrift explosion, a group of community activists formed an organization they called "Citizens Concerned About Carbide" in response to what they felt was Carbide's less-than-forthcoming behavior within the surrounding community following the Seadrift explosion. By the end of the year, they were petitioning the Chemical Manufacturers Association (CMA) for violating the principles of its Responsible Care accident prevention program. The effort failed, but their actions resulted in the launching of a continuing dialogue between the two sides over the sharing of relevant safety information between the plant and the community.

I have dwelt at length on this background in order to say simply that attitudes at Carbide as a company are representative, even stereotypical, of traditional chemical industry attitudes in America before and since Bhopal. Before Bhopal, it distrusted environmentalists with lightly veiled contempt. Now, though inbred defensive attitudes persist, it recognizes the tides and even characterizes itself as a "green" company.[15] Carbide's attempt to locate two small chemical plants in Kingman, Arizona against strong public opposition offers one illustration of its new attitudes.[16] Because two chemically unrelated plants were involved, entailing different aspects of Arizona's environmental legislation, the action aroused a swirl of corporate and citizen misperceptions. But in the end Carbide learned important lessons of community relations that were not lost on corporate headquarters.[17] Carbide succeeded in building the plants through considerable compromises with the community, through almost unprecedented negotiation between plant managers and citizen groups, and at a price that barred any further chemical development in Kingman. At Seadrift it was learning, with much more difficulty, to deepen its exposure to the local public. For what community activists were pressing for was in essence internal co-management of the plant's accident-prevention system by establishing an inspection corps made up of outside experts.

As Carbide's then-president, William Lichtenberger, told shareholders during the company's annual meeting in April 1991, the high costs of environmental control and safety engineering are "absolutely necessary to meet our responsibilities to our people, our neighbors, and to the planet." It was only when the 1990s began, six years after Bhopal, that high-level Carbiders began so explicitly to express the company's responsibility to the earth's ecology and to employ such verbal icons as "planet" in their rhetoric.

The Chemical Company, 1982–1993[18]

In the pre-Bhopal year of 1982, Carbide described itself as a "global powerhouse." It led the world in polyolefins production, dry-cell batteries, and graphite electrodes for steelmaking. It was the largest producer of industrial gases in the United States. Its portfolio included an agricultural products business, the world's largest-selling brand of antifreeze (Prestone), and such specialty businesses as electronic products, food-processing and packaging materials, silicones, molecular sieves, coatings services, specialty chemicals, and specialty polymers and composites.

Yet, in the face of such size and diversity, the company's mood was somber. Carbide's income had dropped 52 percent from the previous year, to $310 million. The country was struggling through a recession, and Carbide predicted in its annual report that a decade of slow growth and austerity lay ahead. "The recession exacted a high price," Carbide's report said, "placing us in the same boat as many of our customers, suppliers and competitors."

A year later, with the recession persisting and the company's performance no better, Carbide nevertheless boasted of how well it had adapted. "We have reduced inventories and tightened the lid on costs and expenses," Carbide said in its 1983 report. "We have cut back on capital spending and refocused it into our most promising operations. Despite the weakened business conditions, we have increased our research and development spending and reduced our debt. And we wrote off a large chunk of uncompetitive facilities in the fourth quarter of 1983."

As 1984 began, Carbide began to shape a new image of itself—that of a chemical company ready to serve and take its place in the high-growth, high-tech world, making plans, even, to move away from dependence on the minimally-profitable ethylene line of chemicals. On the very day it met with editors of *Chemical and Engineering News* to elaborate its new profile—December 3, 1984—it had to open the session with the crushing news of the Bhopal leak.

Grim Carbide officers met their shareholders in the spring of 1985. The company was staggering under the impact of an event in an Indian city only a handful of Carbiders had ever heard of. The 1984 report acknowledged the Bhopal accident and the resultant drop in its per-share stock value from $60 to $30. But the accent was on the company's "basic strengths." Carbide by that time had already established its legal strategy by rejecting any responsibility other than "moral" for the accident, implicitly attributing any technical and managerial problems at the Bhopal plant to its Indian affiliate. It was banking on an early, rather inexpensive settlement of around $80 million, while maneuvering to have the trial moved from the United States to India. Its legal team consisted of its two top corporate lawyers, Joseph Geoghan and Robert Butler, along with its outside counsels at the Manhattan firm, Kelley, Drye, and Warren, led by Bud G. Holman. A special unit, headed by Ronald B. Wishart, then head of Carbide's Washington office, was assigned the full-time job of overseeing Carbide's corporate and public relations strategies.

Reeling from Bhopal, a takeover crisis, and a still sluggish economy, the year 1985 was Carbide's worst ever. "After a year that began with Bhopal and ended with our successful defense against a hostile takeover attempt by GAF Corporation," its report for 1985 said, "Union Carbide is regrouping and gathering strength." Carbide indeed had become a substantially weakened company as it fought off GAF, a considerably smaller but highly aggressive chemical producer. In a complicated series of financial dealings done well into 1986 and involving junk bonds and other financial instruments, Carbide borrowed almost $3 billion to buy back 55 percent of its stock for an inflated $85 a share, gave its shareholders a $33 bonus dividend plus $30 per share from sale of its battery business, brought share value down to $30 by a three-to-one split, and gave the top officers a total of $28 million in so-called "golden parachutes" as insurance against future takeover attempts.

To retire the bonds and pay off part of the loans, Carbide planned to divest some of its most profitable businesses, including its crown jewel, Consumer Products, which Anderson had earlier told employees he would never sell. "When the divestitures announced during the past year and the impending sale of our consumer businesses are completed," Carbide said, "the company will remain among the leading U.S. industrials. It is also becoming a more focused company—simpler in structure, more efficient and cost-effective, and a more aggressive and determined competitor." On Bhopal the report noted that a settlement continued to evade the company, that the Indian government was to blame, and that without a settlement the victims were the losers.

The following year, 1986, was an epic one in Union Carbide's history, the year when the corporation put together by the 1917 merger of five separate entities broke into pieces. One after another the sell-off announcements came forth: films-packaging business—sold to Envirodyne Industries for $215 million; worldwide metals business—sold to an employee group for $83 million; worldwide battery operations (except for Union Carbide India, Ltd.)—sold to Ralston Purina for $1.415 billion; specialty polymers and composites—sold to Amoco Chemical for $184 million; home and automotive consumer products—sold for $800 million to First Boston Corporation in a complex deal that gave rise to a new company, First Brands; agricultural products—sold to Rhone Poulenc for $575 million.

Union Carbide was now a company in pieces. As Tara Jones noted in his book on Bhopal, "The cost of compensating the victims of Bhopal pales compared with the debts incurred in fighting the takeover, the legal and banking fees and golden parachutes."[19] Interest payments alone totaled almost $500 million during that year. A settlement for $600 million, which Indian officials indicated they would accept, might have avoided the entire nightmare. For its part, however, Carbide said the settlement process was so politicized and decentralized in India that the company was never certain what sum would be acceptable.

Carbide has boasted of the creative financial maneuverings that went into its self-preservation strategy. It needed a great deal of money ($3 to $4 billion in the end) to outmaneuver GAF, and the process is fully comprehensible only to those who specialize in the financial maze of mergers, acquisitions, and bond marketeering that characterized the 1980s. (Even the infamous Wall Street arbitrageur, Ivan Boesky, inserted himself into Wall Street's manipulation of Carbide's stock by purchasing several thousand shares.) Arthur Sharplin, professor of management at McNeese State University, has studied this aspect of Carbide's history. "Clearly, by any objective measure,"

Sharplin observed, "UCC and its managers benefitted from the Bhopal incident, as did UCIL. They were politically able to close a burdensome plant, take aggressive actions to restructure both companies, and enhance management benefits. . . . It is ironic that a disaster such as Bhopal [would] leave its victims devastated and other corporate stakeholders better off." And Carbide's more activist critics saw another motive to its divestments and debt acquisition. Commented Ward Morehouse, director of the Council of International and Public Affairs, "It is naive to think that Carbide's . . . stock buy-back and divestment maneuvers were motivated solely by its defense against the takeover. Just by coincidence, these steps also placed a significant proportion of Carbide's assets beyond the reach of the victims of that disaster, and effectively immunized the company against a consumer boycott."[21] However, the Madhya Prodesh court did order Carbide to maintain, unencumbered, $3 billion in assets—a sum equal to the size of the Indian government's damage claim against Carbide.

Carbide Stabilizes

By 1988 Carbide had slimmed down to a trinity of "sharply focused" businesses—chemicals and plastics, industrial gases, and carbon products. It also began emphasizing the new health, safety, and environmental programs it began putting in place just after Bhopal. It claimed 50 percent reductions of toxic emissions from 1985 to 1987 in its plants around the world, but it made no clear verbal connection between its revamped safety commitments and the Bhopal disaster. By this time, Robert Kennedy had become chairman of Carbide and had begun promoting safety and environmental awareness through his activities in, and eventually chairmanship of, the Chemical Manufacturers Association.

Carbide's 1989 meeting was held in Houston, Texas, in April, two months after the Indian Supreme Court had ordered a $470 million settlement absolving Carbide of any further civil or criminal liability (see Chapter 3). The annual report contained no hint that the settlement was contested and was being reviewed by the court. Kennedy reported that the year 1988 was "the best in the 71-year history of Union Carbide." The company boasted a record $4.88 in earnings per share, which included the "year-end charge of 43 cents per share related to the resolution of the Bhopal litigation." Production records were set in almost all product areas, and the company improved its market share in most businesses. It also "won a record fistful of American industry's major technology peer awards, and took large strides in nailing down quality in the pursuit of our five fundamental values: safety and environmental excellence, customer focus, technology leadership, people excellence, simplicity and focus." Again, Carbide continued its policy of raising its image as a safe and environmentally responsible company.

Carbide's meeting was made tumultuous by the presence of several Bhopal victims, who were brought to Houston by American activists. The purpose was to express their objections to the settlement, to dramatize conditions in Bhopal, and to distribute information to Carbide shareholders on the plight of the victims. Three demonstrators were arrested for attempting to hand out their literature, and, although they were quickly released, relations between Carbide and pro-victim activists became further embittered.

The restructuring continued throughout 1989 as rumors grew on Wall Street that Carbide was seeking a suitor for at least parts of its businesses. It reorganized itself into three independent "core" businesses: Chemicals and Plastics, Industrial Gases, and UCAR Carbon. By 1990, the United States was beginning to undergo another recession. Carbide's sales of $7.6 billion were unchanged from the previous year, but its net income dropped to $308 million from the $573 million of a year before.

Meanwhile, the company continued to divest down to its "core" petrochemical technology. It announced late in 1990 the sale of 50 percent of its UCAR Carbon Products to Mitsubishi Corporation. During the same year it sold 50 percent of its interests in KEMET Electronics Corporation and Lincare, Inc., plus both its polysilicon and primary alcohol ethoxylates businesses. But curiously, it began diversifying into unrelated areas as well, with the purchase of Vitaphore Corporation, a maker of medical devices, and the establishment of a joint venture in dermatological products with Baker-Cummins Dermatologicals. It also announced a plant genetics venture with Agri-Diagnostics Associates. It was also exploring alliances with European chemical makers, such as Italy's Enichem Corporation.

Carbide's overall image and strategy remained unclear on Wall Street. It could not escape the stodgy appearance of a company whose life depended on unexciting ethylene, industrial gases, and only modest aspirations in value-added chemicals. In commodity chemical technology, Carbide remained a solid leader and earned the plaudits of the engineering community. But, as one industrialist told *Business Week* in October 1990, "They're uniquely unsuccessful."[22]

Carbide in 1990 bought 20.3 million shares of its common stock for $393 million in order to establish an Employee Stock Ownership Trust. "The effect of this share purchase plan," said Kennedy, "will delay a raid on the company should there be one, long enough to help ensure that the full value of Carbide shares is achieved. And it prevents an acquirer from slowly accumulating enough stock to gain control of the corporation without paying shareholders the premium that they deserve." Some on Wall Street felt that Carbide had nothing further dramatic to do for its shareholders except to sell its industrial gases or to submit to a friendly takeover.

It was not until the final days of 1991 that Carbide could be said to have completed its restructuring. It announced plans to sell to shareholders and spin off into a separate company (Praxair) its industrial gases division, appointing Lichtenberger as president and chairman. The Union Carbide that remained was essentially Union Carbide Chemicals and Plastics. Carbide stockholders gained equal shares of Praxair as a result of the deal. Kennedy described Carbide as "unfocused and overweight" before the actions and stated his intent to "get rid of the baggage." Some Wall Street analysts predicted, by contrast, that Carbide would totally disappear in a few years through purchase by a large company desiring a strong position in commodity chemicals.[23]

The one piece of baggage that remained, however, was the criminal trial in Bhopal. No press releases emerged from Carbide offering updates on the proceedings. By January 1992, the Indian government was preparing extradition proceedings against Warren Anderson so that he could in person stand trial with executives from the Indian affiliate for their alleged roles in the disaster. In the spring Carbide announced that it was putting its 50.9 percent share of the Indian affiliate up for sale, the proceeds (about $17 million) going toward the construction of a Bhopal hospital. The Indian government refused to allow the sale, and the Bhopal court announced seizure of Carbide's Indian assets. But by early 1993 the attempts to extradite Anderson had been shelved and the question remained as to whether Carbide would at any future date be drawn back into the Indian courts.

The View from Outside

To Wall Street, Carbide had always been a solid but unexciting investment. Subsequent developments have done little to change this assessment. In 1978 Carbide's stock price stood at around $15 a share. In 1983, it approached $25, rising to the low $50s just before Bhopal, then plunging to the low $30s. It was driven up to almost $90 during the takeover attempt, before its directors approved a three-for-one split, bringing it back down to $30. From 1990 to early 1992 Carbide's stock hovered persistently around $20, dropping as low as $15 as the U.S. recession deepened and the Persian Gulf crisis raised the chemical industry's feedstock prices. In early 1993, the stock of Praxair and Union Carbide Chemicals and Plastics stood at around $16 each, approximately doubling their combined value before the two companies went their separate ways.

Throughout the early 1990s Carbide was seen as an undervalued stock identified with certain stereotypes combining mediocre management, unexciting product line, lack of imagination, and bad luck. One measure of a company's imaginative thrust is the amount it spends in today's competitive world in research and development. Union Carbide in 1989 spent 3.1 percent of its sales on R&D. Monsanto, by contrast, spent 7.3 percent, and Dow spent 6.4 percent. Chemical analyst Len Bogner of Salomon Brothers said in 1991 that "Bhopal was for sure a disaster for the company. It clearly left scars on the company. And what did Carbide do to remain independent during the GAF takeover attempt? It sold its future. And by doing that it left itself a weakened company."[24] Articles in the business press[25] stressed the difficulties ahead for a Carbide so susceptible to swings in the economy. *Forbes* also devoted space to the company's continuing difficulties in India.[26]

The view of Carbide by Indians victimized by the tragedy is, of course, self-evident in Bhopal itself. The term "Killer Carbide" is painted on the walls surrounding the plant and carried on placards in parades during every anniversary. A body of artistic literature and visual art depicting the tragedy has itself become one of the more poignant legacies of the disaster. And the pain, sorrow, and resignation reflected on the faces of Indians at the mention of Bhopal is testament enough to the image Carbide will for a long time—perhaps for all time—carry in India.

As for the activists in America, the source to turn to for their view of Carbide is *Abuse of Power*, published by the Council of International and Public Affairs and carrying accounts of Carbide's corporate behavior in the years before and since Bhopal. As one summary paragraph states, "In many ways, the tragic story of Bhopal simply replicates, on a far vaster scale, Union Carbide's performance record over the past decades. That record, it appears, is one of evasion of corporate social responsibility for actions harmful to others while seeking to enhance returns to the Carbide senior management and the company's stockholders."[27]

The Symbolic World of Union Carbide

By the early 1990s Carbide was working very hard to upgrade its image among its own employees, its shareholders, and certain ill-defined segments of the public. I say "ill-defined" because Carbide's public relations operations have never tried, as other companies have done, to promote its environmental activities to the national public. "It seems that after Bhopal Danbury went into a shell and hasn't yet completely come out of it" is how one of Carbide's local plant employees expressed it to me. Carbide's main strength, however, has always been as an industrial supplier, which renders the company invisible in a way Dow and Monsanto seek not to be.

Psychically damaged, Carbide's post-Bhopal public relations strategy has been highly ambivalent. When asked at the 1991 annual meeting why the company had not launched broader efforts to publicize its efforts in safety, environmental quality, and education, Kennedy replied that the company first wanted to compile a record it could display. His winning of the chemical industry's coveted Palladium Award (a plaudit sought but never won by the deeply wounded Warren Anderson) was to industrial observers one symbol that Carbide—at least to its industrial peers—was successfully making the long climb back. Absent from Carbide's string of prizes, however, were honors from any of the many traditional environmental groups around the country.

Carbide in fact spent hundreds of millions of dollars after 1984 to upgrade safety and environmental technology—$169 million in 1990 alone—and its annual report projected further spending on emission controls at $200 million annually throughout 1995. Various types of emissions have been significantly reduced at Carbide's U.S. facilities since Bhopal. The company claims it led the rest of the chemical industry in supporting the community right-to-know act, mainly through Kennedy's outspoken support for it while he was president of the Chemical Manufacturers Association[28] (see Hadden, this volume, chapter 5). It has tried, as in Seadrift, to strengthen outreach programs with the communities where its plants are located.

Yet positive national attention continues to escape the company. The public at large still does not see Union Carbide as a top performer in environmental matters. That honor belongs more to such firms as Dow, DuPont, and 3-M. How one measures "public opinion" has always been a crude art at best. But among government chemical safety officials and emergency response experts in industry, Carbide is seldom mentioned among industry leaders. As Falguni Sen and William Egelhoff[29] stated in their evaluation of Carbide's public relations performance, "In the short run and based largely on financial measures, Carbide seems to have managed the crisis effectively. . . . But the long run costs are difficult to measure, and may prove expensive. Carbide's handling of the crisis left many people disappointed and angry. . . . Carbide is feeling the pressure of bad publicity, greater environmental review, and loss of strategic flexibility."

Carbide and the Bhopal Legacy

So up to October 1991, when the Indian Supreme Court upheld the Bhopal settlement, Carbide headquarters seemed to have relegated Bhopal to history. My own inquiries between 1989 and 1991 about the review process that was taking place in the Indian Supreme Court were discouraged by continuous streams of "no comment" and usually sluggish responses to questions directly related to Bhopal. As far as the company was concerned, the settlement was complete and final. Carbide spokespersons reiterated that the company had done all it could to make moral recompense to the victims of the disaster but that almost every attempt had been turned away by the vagaries of Indian politics.

With the Indian Supreme Court ruling, Carbide on the one hand was relieved that the $470 million settlement sum was upheld. But it seemed ambivalent about the court's decision to reopen criminal charges against itself, its Indian affiliate, and their officers in the Madhya Pradesh state district court in Bhopal. Attorneys were divided as to further Carbide liability but were unanimous in their belief that Indian attempts to extradite Warren Anderson for trial would be unsuccessful. In its brief official response to the decision, Carbide did indicate it would welcome the opportunity to prove that the cause of the accident was employee sabotage.

Throughout the post-Bhopal years, the company, fearing further legal complexities in India, refused to make moves that would lead to the identification and prosecution of the alleged "disgruntled employee" saboteur. The suspect, however, has often publicly argued against the allegations, and much of the world's safety engineering community doubts the veracity of Carbide's sabotage evidence.[30] Moreover, consistent with the company's hands-off policy on Bhopal, Carbide toxicologists made no continuous attempts to investigate the long-term effects of methyl isocyanate exposure, despite accumulating scientific evidence that such effects are more than just a possibility. Indeed, continuing research by chemical toxicologists has led to the likelihood that methyl isocyanate, upon reaching the lungs, can be carried throughout the body by glutathione, a molecule abundant in that organ.[31]

And what of UCC's affiliate, Union Carbide India, Ltd.? In early 1993, several former UCIL executives and plant managers were standing criminal trial in Bhopal. UCIL, almost exclusively a battery company with about seven plants throughout the country, is valued at around $30 million. It is still 50.9 percent owned by Union Carbide Corporation and is termed by its parent as "an unconsolidated affiliate." Two Carbide executives remain on UCIL's board of directors. They still take part in their annual shareholders meetings, and presumably still play some hand in UCIL's financial decisions. UCC's share of its affiliate's profits are not returned to Danbury, but are placed in a special reserve fund in India. UCIL for its part remains strongly profitable in the Everready battery business and by 1992 was making plans to expand its product line in South Asia.[32] Carbide's thwarted attempt to sell its 50.9 percent share is seen as a reasonable strategy in any case. A sale itself would further Carbide's desired exit from India. Short of that, seizure within India and sale of assets for the benefit of the gas victims would essentially serve the same purpose.

The Mind of Union Carbide

Is there any final summation, any accurate generalization, of the "mind" of Union Carbide as reflected in its behavior during the eight years since Bhopal? Answers must be cautious because they are personal and are mostly derived from inference.

Carbide can justly claim to have been misrepresented and unfairly abused in its attempts to bring assistance to the Bhopal victims. Self-righteousness certainly pervaded all sides—Carbide, the Indian government, and activist groups—during the entire drama. Industrialists may have a heart as individuals, but their professional devotion and sense of survival cling tenaciously to the financial bottom line. To have admitted any mistakes in managing the relationship with its Indian affiliate would, to Carbide officials, have spelled destruction to their company. Yet corporate officials do agonize, do stumble, and do get muddled in the process of establishing policy. When in 1984 I asked one Carbide officer how he would have managed UCIL, he answered simply and probably accurately: "I would have kicked ass."

Carbide worked hard to portray itself as a passive victim of foreign-investment laws and rules in India. Other companies ridiculed this stance, but, then, none of them suffered a Bhopal. According to its own account, Carbide also became a victim of India's radical politics and technological backwardness and finally of an alleged saboteur. Beginning as the party "morally responsible" for the disaster, Carbide painted itself finally with continuous brush strokes as the moral victor. And Carbide did not fail to receive its share of support from the financial and popular press.[33] Especially supportive was a 1988 broadcast of the CBS program "60 Minutes" that sympathetically described Carbide's frequently thwarted attempts to bring humanitarian aid to the victims.

Still Carbide's image during the Bhopal episode was that of a company that had decided to play legal hardball with the disaster. While it claimed moral responsibility, it seemed to shun any deeper spirit of reparation or of understanding Indian culture. How can one explain that? There is a form of dishonesty, or perhaps more properly structural self-deception, built into the process of corporate reparation in an industrial disaster. Such a posture (based on the implicit proposition that "we do everything well, carefully, caringly, and safely") may be unavoidable, because liability is always just around the corner in any chemical operation. But it exists nonetheless, supported by two kinds of institutional pressure. The first is the need to put only the best face forward to shareholders, present and future. The second is the unavoidably litigation-resisting character of the modern U.S. corporation, which translates into the position "we can make no mistakes that can be admitted to."

In the Bhopal case, the first imperative led to Carbide's attitudinal "atonement" through its establishment of new safety and environmental practices within the company. Bhopal drove Carbide to do good for its own workers, as it also led to the still deficient community right-to-know law in whose promotion Carbide played a leading role. At the same time, the second imperative pushed Carbide to distance itself from the disaster victims in Bhopal. While it "atoned," it also detached.

Union Carbide, in my view, had every reason to reach out for public understanding—to more fully atone, as it were, for an accident that occurred under its blue and white logo in a distant part of the world. Warren Anderson spoke of Carbide's "moral responsibility," and it seemed just the right tone to take in those early days. But it raised false expectations that Carbide would seek creative solutions as the legal picture became more and more tangled and contentious. Later, Carbide transmuted "moral responsibility" into self-righteousness, becoming moralistic, even close-minded, about Bhopal. To Carbide, the settlement was a closure that allowed it to walk away from India, to evade the fuller atonement that moral responsibility implies. Bhopal could have been the opportunity for Union Carbide to display legal and moral innovation: a disaster one company decided not to turn its back on. Instead, it negotiated not a commitment to continuing stewardship at Bhopal, but an uncreative, even antiquarian, way of notarizing its moral responsibility for what was (and is) a unique, ongoing tragedy.

In the summer of 1989, during a long interview at Washington's Metropolitan Club and later in his office, I asked Ronald Wishart whether Carbide bore any long-term responsibility to atone for Bhopal. The answer given by Wishart was that atonement implied guilt, which Carbide never intended to admit. But Wishart misread his Christian theology. The idea of atonement in the Christian tradition is not primarily about the atoner's guilt; it is about sacrifice as an act of reparation for the sins of others. By its silence, its self-righteousness, its lack of scientific integrity in failing to pursue the toxicology of methyl isocyanate, and its refusal to bring to justice any Bhopal plant "saboteur," Carbide shunned the ideal of corporate moral responsibility, while publicly embracing the concept.[34]

In 1989 Carbide's chairman, Robert Kennedy, was elected chairman of the Chemical Manufacturers Association (CMA). The theme of his speech before CMA's 1989 annual meeting was the chemical industry challenge of regaining the "trust and confidence of the public." He said: "We can sit back and wait for the public to come to its senses and discover us doing good, or we can stand up strong and tall and say what we're doing, what we've done already and what we're going to do. There is a growing need for predictable, consistent environmental stewardship from nation to nation and region to region around the world. The chemical industry has a great opportunity in the years ahead to make new history."

Eight days after Kennedy's speech, an internal memo was distributed among Carbide's public affairs strategy group. It concerned an environmental activist organization known as the Citizens' Clearing House for Hazardous Waste (CCHHW) formed by former Love Canal activist Lois Gibbs. The memo characterized CCHHW as "one of the most radical coalitions operating under the environmentalist banner," with "ties into labor, the communist party, and all manner of folk with private/single agenda." CCHHW's agenda, the memo said, was to "restructure U.S. society into something unrecognizable and probably unworkable. It's a tour de force of public issues to be affecting business in years to come."

Carbide officials discount the memo's significance. What it did do was expose a lingering mentality the company finds difficult to shake, even after Bhopal—that "radical" elements of society somehow conspire against the virtues embodied by American industry and, perforce, against civilization itself. But by Earth Day 1990, just as the *Washington Post* was about to publish the text of the memo, its author sent an apology to Gibbs. That gesture could also be construed as an offer of reconciliation, another step in Carbide's long voyage toward renewed respectability.

Union Carbide after Bhopal is a permanently changed company. Its officers may personally have profited by the breakup of the company after the GAF takeover attempt, but it is deeply scarred and permanently pained by the experience. Kennedy won for himself and Carbide their self-described "fistful" of awards from the chemical industry. But in the post-Bhopal era, this whole industry is in the process of transformation toward sensitivity and gentility in planetary stewardship. Belatedly, Carbide, too, seems to have learned the right vocabulary and has, by all indications, finally "got it."

At the 1991 annual meeting, Carbide's legal counsel and director, Joseph Geoghan, would tell me: "Bhopal is going to be the kind of overhang that will always drive Union Carbide and the industry toward improved results. Everything we do will be put in the context of Bhopal." Yet by 1992 Carbide seemed to be refocusing itself into oblivion. Entities bought only a few months before were being offered for sale. All that was left of the Union Carbide that before Bhopal had employed almost 100,000 people was its Chemicals and Plastics core, with a smattering of unwanted specialty operations and a work force of only 14,000. Kennedy was described as revivified at the prospect of running a company now so tightly focused. Yet in 1993 UCC continued to struggle for profitability. The world market in ethylene-based chemical commodities remained in a deep recession. Added foreign capacity intensified the competitive pressures on Carbide. Prospects were grim.

As a boy during the 1940s, I remember attending frequent movie matinees that would often run cartoons featuring the characters Bugs Bunny and Porky Pig. Each feature would close with Porky focused at the center of a large circle. Before "The End" appeared, and while the band played its merry tune, the circle would diminish in size to a narrower and narrower focus before disappearing entirely, taking Porky with it. As the circle narrowed, Porky would intone his goodbye to the audience with his cheery, "That's All, Folks." And then, Porky gone, the theater screen would darken to silence. So it may be with Carbide, except that the story is hardly a funny cartoon, and there is no applause.

Postscript: Author's Note on Technique

Many primary and secondary sources contributed to this reading of Union Carbide, not the least of which were Carbide's annual reports between 1983 and 1992. Visits to Carbide's ancestral origins in West Virginia's Kanawha Valley, my reporting assignment in Kingman, Arizona, and talks with present and former employees were, to say the least, invaluable. And reporter-source relations with Carbide's activist nemesis, the Bhopal Action Resource Center in New York, provided me with critical information and documentation that kept me alert to the "other side" of Carbide's corporate face. That organization, more than any, has kept Carbide management conscious of its negative impacts on communities within the orbit of its plants.

In covering the Bhopal disaster since its beginnings, I established satisfactory working relationships with certain individuals in Union Carbide, mainly with Robert Berzok, director of corporate and public communications, and Ronald Wishart, vice-president for public affairs, now retired, who were the spokespersons for the corporation throughout the Bhopal years. Also included were brief encounters with previous chairman Warren Anderson, current chairman Robert Kennedy, Jackson Browning, director of health and environmental affairs during the Bhopal period, a long interview with Carbide attorney Bud G. Holman, encounters with Carbide toxicologists from its Bushy Run laboratory near Pittsburgh (during a 1986 symposium on MIC effects), and other individuals assigned to one or another aspect of the Bhopal problem. I was always treated cordially, but with the caution that is the norm between journalist and industrial source on a subject with the seriousness and sensitivity of Bhopal.

The truest gauge of a company's character, however, lies in its "laundry hamper," the internal machinery that is essentially invisible to outsiders, especially journalists—the rationale for its financial decisions, its internal memoranda, the discussions at its executive strategy meetings and within its board of directors. Such meetings are always closed, and records were treated as extra-secure in a situation where both the image and survivability of Union Carbide were at stake. Carbide does maintain in the state of New Hampshire an archive where corporate records are kept, but its existence was never brought to my attention despite dozens of discussions with Carbide officials and requests for material and despite my oft-expressed wish for an understanding of the "true" Carbide.

Carbide did declare from the beginning a policy of "openness" with the media. To a journalist, corporate "openness" implies the willingness to speak for background and perspective and to offer entry into the dynamics of decision making within the firm. Bhopal was obviously too weighty a matter to leave to anything but the most controlled and premeditated release of information by Carbide's executives. Thus not until June 1993, were Carbide sources willing to speak for background to discuss debates that might have gone on between corporate attorneys, line executives, public relations staff, and board members in the evolution of Carbide policy. Carbide's public relations staff was basically passive in volunteering information unknown to me but important nonetheless. Not once in my memory did anyone suggest my contacting present or past employees of Carbide for special insights.

However, seldom were my requests for information, once made specific, denied. One of the denials was to a 1986 request for interviews with Carbide toxicologists on MIC research. Another was a request for the text of the trust agreement Carbide established in England for disposal of Carbide's 50.9 percent share of UCIL. That request essentially was ignored. My overall impression was of reluctance at Danbury to make Carbide too well known.

Finally, Robert Berzok was sent a copy of an early draft of this chapter. The hope was that by a discussion of the issues I might gain a fuller perspective on the "mind" of Union Carbide. Berzok, however, declined. A copy was sent to Kennedy, which led to the June 1993 meeting to review the manuscript for this chapter and elaborate on the atonement issues raised in it.

Notes

1. See, for example, Paul Shrivastava, *Bhopal—Anatomy of a Crisis* (Cambridge, MA: Ballinger, 1987); Ward Morehouse and Arun Subramaniam, *The Bhopal Tragedy* (New York: Council on International and Public Affairs, 1986); Union Carbide Corporation, *Bhopal Methylisocyanate Incident: Investigation Team Report* (Danbury, CT: Union Carbide Corporation, 1985); *Report on Scientific Studies on the Release Factors Related to Bhopal Toxic Gas Leakage* (New Delhi: Indian Council of Scientific and Industrial Research, December 1985).

2. Reports on MIC's systemic effects are not replete in the toxicological literature. But for an initial news account see "Scientists Find Systemic Effects of MIC," *Chemical & Engineering News* (June 13, 1988): 6. For more technical accounts see Jeffrey S. Ferguson and Yves Alarie, "Long Term Pulmonary Impairment Following Single Exposure to MIC," *Toxicology and Applied Pharmacology* 107, 2 (February 1991): 253; and *Journal of the American Medical Association* 264, 21 (December 5, 1990): 2781; Bhopal Gas Disaster Research Center, *1990 Annual Report* (Bhopal: Gandhi Medical College, June 1991); Anil Sadgopal and Sujit K. Das, *Report on Medical Relief and Rehabilitation of Bhopal Gas Victims* (done for the Indian Supreme Court, August 1988).

3. Dan Kurzman, *A Killing Wind* (New York: McGraw-Hill, 1987).

4. One article, published a year after the disaster, did attempt to describe the reactions of several Carbide employees in Institute and South Charleston, WV. See *Chemical Engineering* (December 9/23, 1985): 14.

5. "Union Carbide—Bhopal Saga Continues as Criminal Proceedings Begin in India," *Chemical & Engineering News* (March 16, 1992): 7–14.

6. Carbide's positions are well documented in its annual reports since Bhopal, its press releases, its various legal briefs, a 1989 videotape describing its rendition of the disaster, and a sympathetic account of its post-Bhopal humanitarian efforts by the CBS program "60 Minutes."

7. The exact number of those injured by the MIC leak is one of the most vexing aspects of the Bhopal disaster. Carbide's study of the MIC plume argues for the 10,000 number but the company has not responded to my request to release the study. It has, however, provided a copy of Writ Petition 843 of 1988 to the Indian Supreme Court by the Bhopal Claims Office director. The petition cites 173,382 persons as temporarily injured, 18,922 permanently injured, and 1,313 permanently disabled. But the 1990 Indian Council for Medical Research report indicates the number of persons permanently injured to be roughly 150,000.

8. The bias against Carbide on India's political left can only be described as scathing. See, for example, the continuous coverage of Bhopal in the Indian journal *Economic and Political Weekly*. For parallel critiques from Western environmental reformers, see, for example, the books *Corporate Killing: Bhopals Will Happen*, by Tara Jones (London: Free Association Books, 1988) and *Abuse of Power—The Case of Union Carbide*, by Ward Morehouse, David Dembo, and Lucinda Wykle (New York: New Horizons, 1990).

9. This judgment is based on informal conversations with former Carbiders and others familiar with the chemical industry. Carbide, however, has been considerably written about in the financial press. See, for example, *Forbes* (December 10, 1990): 106; *Business Week* (October 29, 1990): 70; and *Wall Street Journal*, January 23, 1992, p. A1, for critical accounts of Carbide's corporate prospects.

10. Corporations are careful to remain "off the record" in their honest attitudes toward the environmental community. This judgment, however, is based on my own years of reporting on the environmental movement, including involvement in several off-the-cuff conversations with industrialists over the years.

11. An internal survey of Carbide employees, conducted late in 1991 and published in its company magazine, reported a widespread decline in confidence toward top management. See *Union Carbide World* (December 1991).

12. These assessments are self-evident to anyone who has spent any time living in or visiting a chemical plant community. The chemical industry culture has indeed not been studied to any extent. But in my own visits to the Kanawha Valley and through conversations there, I repeatedly was struck by the strong sense of honesty and integrity of Carbide employees, along with a thin-skinned readiness to defend the vulnerable record of the company. Carbide, after all, was also responsible for the worst industrial disaster in American history—the infamous mass silicosis tragedy during the construction of the Gawley tunnel during the 1930s by Carbide's metals division. See Martin Cherniack, *The Hawk's Nest Incident* (New Haven, CT: Yale University Press, 1986). Carbide omits that episode from its histories.

13. Interview with Thad Epps, director of community affairs, UCC, South Charleston, WV, July 1991.

14. Memorandum dated June 28, 1991, "Request for consideration of approval of an egregious case," p. 4. Confidential internal report by the Occupational Safety and Health Administration, 1992.

15. Cornelius C. Smith (UCC vice-president, community and employee health, safety, and environmental protection), "Bhopal Aftermath: Union Carbide Rethinks Safety," *Business and Society Review* 75 (Fall 1990): 50.

16. *Chemical & Engineering News* (January 1, 1991): 15.

17. *Chemical & Engineering News* (May 13, 1991): 14.

18. Most of the material in this section is derived from Carbide's annual reports.

19. See Jones, *Corporate Killing*.

20. Arthur Sharplin, "Union Carbide India, Ltd.: The Bhopal Gas Incident," paper for the Center for Business Ethics, Bentley College, 1989. Presented at Bentley College.

21. Ward Morehouse, written communication, April 1992.

22. *Business Week* (Oct. 29, 1990): 70–71.

23. *Chemical Week* (January 18, 1992): 8.

24. Len Bogner, personal conversation, July 1990.

25. Hadden, this volume, Chapter 5.

26. *Forbes* (December 10, 1990): 106.

27. Morehouse, Dembo, and Wykle, *Abuse of Power*.

28. See Union Carbide's employee's magazine, *Carbide World*, December 1991, for the company's own progress report on its environmental performance and compliance with the Community Right to Know Act. But see also critiques of Carbide from the activist group Communities Concerned About Carbide and the report *Present Danger, Hidden Liabilities: Environmental Profile of Union Carbide Corporation in the United States* prepared by Robert Ginsburg for the National Toxics Campaign Fund, April 1990.

29. See Falguni Sen and William G. Egelhoff, "Six Years and Counting: Learning from Crisis Management at Bhopal," *Public Relations Review* 17, 1 (1991): 69–83.

30. *Chemical & Engineering News*, July 4, 1988.

31. *Chemical Research in Toxicology* 4 (1991): 157.

32. *Financial Times*, Jan. 6, 1992.

33. See, for example, *Barrons*, February 1988, lead editorial.

34. According to much Western Christian tradition (using biblical sources such as Isaiah 53:4–5 and Mark 10:45), the act of atonement in the sacrifice of Christ delivers all persons out of bondage to their sins. A self-emptying, reconciling act, the atonement does not simply cancel debts up to the present, but also covers all future debts. Belief in this theory is in turn inherent in the ethical value system in the West. Union Carbide assumed the mantle of "moral responsibility" for the Bhopal disaster, thus inviting a deeper examination of what such a claim does indeed represent for corporate human beings in a disaster on the scale of Bhopal.

Chapter 3
Legal and Political Repercussions in India

Armin Rosencranz, Shyam Divan, and
Antony Scott

Just after midnight on December 3, 1984, forty tons of highly toxic
methyl isocyanate (MIC), which had been manufactured and stored
in Union Carbide's chemical plant in Bhopal, escaped into the atmosphere and killed over 3,500 people who lived in the dispersing
chemical's pathway. As many as 150,000 others were injured, many
seriously and some permanently. Indeed, the official figures of death
and injury do not convey the enormity of the human tragedy. They
do not tell the stories of the families and communities disrupted, disabled, dislocated, and impoverished.

A complicated and costly four-year legal battle ensued, in which the
Indian government undertook to represent the Bhopal victims' claims
against Union Carbide. On February 14, 1989, the Indian Supreme
Court cut the Gordian knot and persuaded the Indian government
and Carbide to accept its suggestion for an overall settlement of the
claims arising from the disaster. Carbide agreed to pay $470 million
to the Indian government on behalf of all the Bhopal victims, in full
and final settlement of all past, present, and future claims arising
from the Bhopal disaster. The entire amount had to be and was paid
by March 31, 1989. To facilitate the settlement, the Supreme Court
exercised its extraordinary jurisdiction and terminated all collateral
civil, criminal, and contempt of court proceedings that had arisen
during the Bhopal litigation and were pending in subordinate Indian
courts.

In inducing the parties to settle, the Court hoped to move on to the
urgent task of compensating the victims. A popular uproar greeted
the settlement, however, and in its wake, the short-lived minority
government of Prime Minister V. P. Singh set the Carbide money
aside, undertook to compensate the victims from public monies, and

asked the Court to rescind the settlement.[1] This extraordinary turn of events within the government—which previously, under Prime Minister Rajiv Gandhi, had attempted only minimal compensation for the victims—seemed to be the result of reordered priorities: punishing Union Carbide was subordinated to providing compensation for the victims. For years, the courts and the central government had tried to address both these concerns, but to differing degrees, at different times, and with different levels of success.

We begin this chapter with a discussion of the victims' groups and the political setting for the litigation. We then examine the interplay between the courts, on the one hand, and the Gandhi, Singh, and Shekhar governments on the other, that ultimately led to a settlement of the lawsuit. We then evaluate the settlement and its legal and political ramifications. Finally, we examine how the Bhopal disaster helped spark efforts toward more effective environmental legislation, enforcement, and grassroots activism in India.

Victims' Groups

In the wake of the disaster, almost two dozen voluntary groups formed to help cope with the damage. They addressed a broad range of relief issues, from victims' medical and basic sustenance requirements to trying to secure work for those whose livelihoods had been affected. They also tried to organize the victims into politically cohesive units to fight for their rights. Controversies immediately arose, however, and charges of fraud abounded. Groups accused one another of being "Carbide spies" and of trying to get medical information to aid Carbide in its case. Group leaders often bickered, wrangling for political control.[2] But in all of the charges and counter-charges, two potentially conflicting positions were clearly articulated.

On one side were those—usually seriously affected victims—who wanted compensation from Carbide as quickly as possible.[3] Many of the injured were unable to work and had severe and persistent medical problems. Without compensation they could not meet their medical bills, could not work, and often were unable to get enough to eat. Dependents of breadwinners who had been killed or disabled faced similar difficulties. The desire and need for speedy compensation caused all other issues to pale in comparison. The victims wanted relief and they wanted it as quickly as possible.

On the other side were those—often the leaders of the advocacy groups—for whom compensation was an issue but retribution against Union Carbide was at least as important. These advocates were opposed to any settlement not commensurate with what could be

awarded in the United States for a disaster of comparable proportions. Thus, when there were rumblings of a possible settlement in December of 1987 involving approximately $650 million, these groups
protested vociferously. They sought $3 billion and saw anything less
as a sell-out. Indeed, some felt that agreeing to any settlement at all
would be to "fall prey to the overture of the multinational company."[4]
These groups also demanded that criminal prosecutions be brought
against Union Carbide executives. Arguing that "the guilty must be
brought to trial," they clamored for retribution. As the head of the
International Coalition for Justice in Bhopal explained, "The question of accountability for those responsible for the disaster is very important. Accountability is the first step if future disasters are to be
prevented."[5]

Those who took the more strident stance were keenly sensitive to
the historical inequalities of power between India and the United
States. Conscious of India's long years as a colony, these groups did
not want India to be under foreign influence of any kind. This position was bolstered by pride in India's leadership role with respect to
other developing countries.[6] Accepting a less than American-sized
settlement was seen from this standpoint as acceding to the view
that Indian life and health were less valuable than American life and
health. Clearly, this was not permissible. Insisting on criminal prosecutions emphasized India's rejection of a passive or "victim" role, and
these groups were deeply angered when the settlement gratuitously
terminated all criminal proceedings against Carbide officials.

The issues articulated by both groups, and the pressures they
brought to bear, are central to understanding both the government's
and the courts' roles in the Bhopal settlement. The length of time
leading to the settlement, the manner in which it was brokered, its
modest size, and the Singh government's attempts to undo it, all reflected governmental and judicial perceptions of what was necessary
and possible in the face of the moral and political dimensions of the
tragedy.

Government Action: From Prosecution to Relief

Soon after the accident, the Government of India, led by Rajiv Gandhi, set about filing criminal charges against top executives of Union
Carbide. Warren Anderson, CEO of the chemical giant, was arrested
and briefly held, as were executives of Carbide's Indian subsidiary.
Legal experts in both India and America understood that the charges
were "trumped up," that is, they were filed to put pressure on Carbide
to settle to India's advantage. The charges—including culpable homi-

cide not amounting to murder—would have been difficult if not impossible to prove. In any case, the Indian courts had no personal jurisdiction over the American "defendants." It would therefore have been impossible to impose penalties even if India could have secured convictions.

The futility of pursuing criminal charges seems not to have been understood by the Indian populace at large. In any case, the issue of criminal prosecution would not go away. Advocacy groups in India demanded that the government strictly adhere to its announced position of taking a tough stand against Carbide. *Business India*, for example, ran a cover story early in the proceedings entitled "Why the Guilty Must Be Punished."[7] This hardline rhetoric later made it politically difficult to consider a settlement. Because of the perceived popularity of criminal proceedings against Carbide officials, the restoration of those proceedings was the easiest concession for the Supreme Court to make in October 1991, when it upheld the remainder of the settlement but reinstated the criminal charges.

Meanwhile, the victims' calls for assistance went largely unanswered. While the government spent $57 million on victim relief in the first four years following the accident,[8] this sum proved meager in relation to the tragedy's actual dimensions. The harsh reality was that the victims were nobody's constituency, and their lack of political power allowed governmental aid to remain low on the Gandhi administration's agenda. Some in the government worried that a larger disbursement would be perceived as an interest-free loan to Union Carbide. The Gandhi government could not maintain its hard-line stance against Carbide and at the same time aggressively move to compensate the gas victims. Caught between these competing priorities, the Gandhi government decided to give the lower rating to the victims' needs.

The confrontational stance and the political need *not* to cooperate with Carbide caused the government to reject a UCC offer of $1.5 million in assistance. The reason offered was that this was "dirty" money. But the real worry was that accepting this meager offer would look like cooperation with the hated multinational and might weaken the government's claim in any future financial settlement. Implementing a confrontational strategy, however, gave rise to new difficulties. One of the Indian parliament's first actions after the disaster was the passage, in March 1985, of the Bhopal Gas Leak Disaster Act,[9] a law consolidating all legal claims against Carbide and making the Government of India sole representative of the victims. Designed to streamline the legal effort, the Act directed the government to set up a system of processing claims in a speedy and efficient manner. Medical examinations were to be conducted to determine the extent of each individual's injury. The claims system would thus allow the total sum of damages to be calculated, as well as seeing to it that victims were compensated when awards were made.

The Act was precipitated by the rush of American personal injury lawyers into Bhopal immediately after the accident, as well as the incapacity of the victims to battle the powerful corporation on their own. Great confusion and distrust accompanied the onslaught of foreign lawyers. Thousands of victims signed over exclusive "power of attorney" to several different lawyers. Some lawyers took the victims' medical slips—their only official proof of having suffered MIC poisoning—without giving proper receipts in return.[10] Many victims, unable to read what they were signing, agreed to contracts that allowed for large lawyers' contingency fees. The Bhopal Act was passed in an effort to mitigate this confusion.

Unfortunately, government ineptitude obstructed rather than streamlined the legal effort. By December 1987, claimants had filed forms with the government three separate times because of information gaps in poorly designed previous forms.[11] Predictably, progressively fewer claimants responded to each form, though many of the non-respondents undoubtedly had legitimate claims. Moreover, medical examinations were performed on many fewer victims than required, partly in consequence of victim ignorance and apathy and partly because of a lack of medical facilities. The machinery for performing medical examinations was not finally in place until a year after the accident, and this delay, although presumably not deliberate, had the effect of weeding out those temporarily injured. As explained by Dr. N. P. Misra, dean of the local medical college, "if someone recovered sufficiently we would not be able to tell what was there [in the way of injury] at the time of the disaster."[12] Without documented, medical disability, such claimants would never collect any compensation for their injuries.

Government-sponsored medical efforts were poorly managed even after a delayed start-up. By mid-1987, less than one third of the money spent on relief had actually gone toward assisting victims. Over half of the money appropriated in 1987 for victim relief was spent on furniture and motor vehicles for health officials.[13] More than two years after the accident, hospitals were grossly overcrowded and many patients could not get a bed. Unable to get hospital treatment, an even larger number of patients exhausted their resources pursuing private medical help.

The controversy surrounding sodium thiosulfate was a further distraction. The drug is known to combat cyanide poisoning—a possible result of the accident. Treatment with the drug, however, was dis-

couraged by the Madhya Pradesh state government, which sent out
an official circular saying that sodium thiosulfate should not be used
as there was absolutely no release of cyanide at the time of the accident.[14] This was later found to be untrue. A plausible case has since
been made that cyanide can accumulate in the bloodstream as an indirect result of MIC exposure. Six months after the accident, sodium
thiosulfate treatments produced favorable results, suggesting that
cyanide was involved. Yet the government continued to deny this possibility. Indeed, in the summer of 1985, Madhya Pradesh authorities
arrested volunteer physicians who were administering the drug and
confiscated their supplies.[15] Eventually, the courts were petitioned to
force the state government to allow distribution of sodium thiosulfate
to volunteer medical groups.[16]

Government attempts to provide work for those displaced by the
accident were also poorly conceived and executed. Government-
sponsored worksheds opened in the fall of 1985 amid much fanfare,
but several have since closed or have been open less than half-time.
Even if all the planned worksheds had been constructed and run at
full capacity, they would not have met the needs of the 25,000 families
officially classified as suffering from a total loss of income or a substantial reduction in earning capacity.[17] As it is, these families have
battled starvation.[18]

The Courts

It is against this backdrop of inadequate governmental relief efforts,
and the desperate condition of the gas victims, that the actions of the
Indian courts, both state and central, can best be understood. The
courts' number one priority seems to have been to get compensation
to the victims as quickly as possible. All of the courts' actions reflect
this mission. While District, High Court, and Supreme Court judges
all made mistakes in trying to secure speedy compensation—indeed,
their actions were even counterproductive at times—they appear at
all times to have been motivated by a desire to compensate the victims
in the face of inadequate government assistance. To this end, the
courts introduced several innovations in Indian tort law.

Absolute Liability

A year after the Bhopal disaster, the Shiriam Food and Fertilizer
Company in New Delhi let escape a cloud of oleum (pyrosulfuric
acid), a moderately toxic gas. The extent of the damage was relatively
mild; only one person died, from a heart attack brought on by the

fear of gas poisoning. With the impending Bhopal litigation in mind [19] and with unprecedented speed, the Indian Supreme Court ruled on the case, applying a standard of *absolute liability* to companies engaged in hazardous activities. Chief Justice P. N. Bhagwati, speaking for the Court, held that

> where an enterprise is engaged in hazardous or inherently dangerous activities and harm results to anyone on account of an accident in the operation of such hazardous or inherently dangerous activity . . . , the enterprise is strictly and absolutely liable to compensate all those who were affected by the accident.[20]

The *Shriram* case not only set a precedent for absolute tort liability, admitting no defenses (including sabotage), but it also declared that compensation should be guided by the company's ability to pay.[21] This was a striking departure from the previous rule that compensation be measured by the earning power of the victim. The motivation for setting the new standard of compensation was a desire to deter reckless behavior, especially on the part of well-heeled foreign companies.

The *Shriram* ruling put obvious pressure on Carbide to settle. Carbide had spent much of the previous year trying to build a case of sabotage. The notion of absolute liability effectively quashed this defense. The ruling also addressed some of the concerns of the more politicized victims' rights groups. The new standard of compensation, if strictly applied, would mean that accidents in India should be just as expensive for multinational corporations as accidents in the developed countries. This would help stop the exportation of "dirty" or unsafe technologies.

Interim Payments

In November 1986, two nongovernmental organizations representing some victims applied to the District Court for "immediate relief," that is, relief pending the final resolution of the controversy.[22] Vibhuti Jha, the victims' advocate, hoped that his motion would stir the government into doing more for the victims or at least into supporting the application.[23] Little did he realize that some months away the idea first raised in his motion would radically alter the nature and direction of the lawsuit. Initially, the government ignored the motion, and District Court Judge W. M. Deo appeared unmoved. But Jha's application must have impressed Judge Deo. In April 1987 he drafted a similar proposal to grant "reconciliatory substantial interim relief," and placed it before the parties.[24] This proposal remained dormant until the fall of 1987, when Union Carbide and the Government of India were attempting, at Judge Deo's request, to come to a settlement and to prevent the case from going to a lengthy trial. Their efforts were not fruitful. When word of a possible settlement of $650 million leaked out, demonstrations were organized by victims' groups. Shops were closed, lawyers boycotted the court, and people took to the streets.[25] On November 17, Judge Deo was told that talks had broken down, in part because of the protests.

When the litigants met again on November 24, they told Deo that they would proceed toward a trial, "keeping open the option to negotiate" a settlement.[26] His efforts thwarted, Judge Deo reviewed his draft proposal that Carbide pay substantial interim compensation to the victims.[27] Three weeks later Judge Deo issued a seventeen-page ruling ordering the multinational to pay $270 million in interim compensation. The money was to go to health care and the creation of jobs for the more than 500,000 claimants.[28] Explaining his action, Judge Deo said:

Attempts at an overall settlement appear to have bogged down in the din of diverse loud voices, leaving the poor gas victims pathetically past even the third anniversary of the unprecedented disaster to fight [their] legal battle.[29]

Although Deo had explained in his ruling that the order was "interlocutory in nature . . . without prejudice to the rights and defenses of the parties to the suit,"[30] it was appealed by Carbide. The company's attorneys argued that Deo's judgment "amounts to awarding damages without trial, a practice that runs counter to the laws of India and other democracies."[31] In any case, the move to help speed aid for the victims backfired. Neither interim compensation nor a speedy settlement was achieved. Instead, the victims' wait was prolonged by an appeal on the legality of interim compensation to the Madhya Pradesh High Court.

English courts have permitted interim payments in water-tight cases where the defendant has admitted liability, or where judgment has been obtained and damages remain to be assessed, or where the eventual trial would result in the plaintiff obtaining judgment for substantial damages against the defendant.[32] Astonishingly, after a cursory examination of the merits, High Court Justice S. K. Seth found the third condition fulfilled.[33] He issued a new ruling, reducing the amount of the interim compensation to $192 million, which was within the $200 million of Carbide's insurance coverage. The *Shriram* precedent enabled Seth to render all Carbide's possible defenses irrelevant. In refusing to acknowledge liability, Carbide had raised a number of defenses that seemed entitled to be considered under Indian law before *Shriram*. The corporate veil separating Carbide from its Indian subsidiary and the theory that sabotage had caused the leak of MIC were arguments that could conceivably have absolved Carbide of liability. But none of these defenses impeded Justice Seth's upholding of interim compensation.

Judge Seth seemed more conscious of the need to ensure the enforceability of his order than did Judge Deo. Deo's order was issued without reference to the case's merits and could not be enforced as a decree. A decree was essential before the Indian government could enlist the aid of a U.S. court to reach Carbide's U.S. assets. The U.S. Court of Appeals decision in the Bhopal case[34] contains the following explicit language: "A foreign-country judgment that is *final, conclusive and enforceable where rendered must be recognized and will be enforced as 'conclusive between the parties to the extent that it grants or denies recovery of a sum of money'* except that it is not deemed to be conclusive if the judgment was rendered under a system which does not provide tribunals or procedures *compatible with the requirements of due process of law*" (emphasis added). Seth attempted to surmount this hurdle simply by stating that his pretrial judgment was on the merits, that it was final and conclusive, and that it could be executed as if it were a decree. He cited no precedent for this extraordinary pronouncement.[35]

In American legal terms, disposing of the case after such a fleeting examination of the merits and without trial would have amounted to a grant of summary judgment. No American court, however, would have tolerated such a conclusion based on the facts alleged and the defenses offered in this case. Moreover, conservative American judges, with American industrial interests and American jobs in mind, would probably have been unimpressed by Justice Seth's strained reasoning. They would almost certainly have dismissed his "decree" as a denial of due process.

Like Deo's ruling, Seth's actions proved counterproductive in securing speedy relief. Carbide's attorneys appealed. Assuming that the judgment would be unenforceable in an American court, they did not even request a stay in the ruling pending their appeal. Not to be outdone, the Indian government also appealed the ruling. Seeking to demonstrate once again that it would not in any way compromise with the multinational, the Government complained against Seth's having reduced the interim payments.

Opting for Settlement

Surveying the Bhopal litigation in December 1988, the five-judge Supreme Court bench could only have been dismayed at the lack of progress in the principal lawsuit. The ineffectiveness of the Indian government's maneuvers, combined with Carbide's apparent disregard for the victims, had dimmed all hopes for early compensation. Proceedings in the original lawsuit before the Bhopal District Judge had stalled. Pretrial matters such as the mutual discovery of documents and interviewing of potential witnesses under oath had yet to be addressed. Four years after the tragedy, the government still had to issue a final list of authentic claimants.

The Supreme Court was in a quandary. Though it desired compensation for the victims, it knew that, without the support of U.S. courts, it would be futile to uphold the High Court decision. On the other hand, reversing the Seth judgment would plunge the victims into a trial of uncertain outcome, which could last up to ten years. With people still dying almost daily from MIC-related injuries, and countless others starving as a result of unemployment and the expenses of the accident,[36] a lengthy trial was not acceptable on humanitarian or political grounds. Extricating itself from the tangle on February 14, 1989, the Supreme Court brokered a settlement in which it ordered Carbide to pay $470 million in compensation. All other proceedings, including the criminal charges against Carbide, were terminated by the Court's order.

The drama in the Supreme Court's chamber on the day of the settlement has been well documented. The Court formally ordered that the suit be settled and the parties on both sides—without hesitation or consultation—agreed. Observers in India and abroad understood that the Supreme Court's action was in no sense a genuine "order" or "verdict," despite the government's announcement to the contrary.[37] The parties agreed to the figure of $470 million far too easily for anyone to believe that the "order" had not been prearranged.[38] Indeed, the Supreme Court explained in a subsequent order that:

Learned counsel for both parties stated that they would leave it to the court to decide what should be the figure of compensation. The range of choice for the court in regard to the figures was, therefore, between the maximum of 426 [million] US dollars offered by Shri Nariman [counsel for UCC] and the minimum of 500 million US dollars suggested by the learned attorney general [on behalf of the government].[39]

This excerpt illustrates two salient facts. First, it shows that the Government of India was prepared to accept whatever the court deemed appropriate within the $426–500 million range. Second, it seems that the government was using the Court to shield itself from political fallout; after all, the government's own previous attempt to settle for $650 million in late 1987 had met with such an outcry that the plan had had to be abandoned. It is clear in any event that without the Court's aid no agreement would have been reached. A Carbide lawyer said: "We could have talked to the government till the cows came home and still have been without a settlement if it had not been for the Supreme Court and its involvement. That made all the difference this time, both sides knew it, and it was the last chance to settle."[40]

Evaluating the Settlement

How should the Bhopal settlement be evaluated? We begin by asking whether the settlement achieved the traditional tort goals of compensation, corrective justice, and deterrence.

The goal of *compensation* under tort law is to ensure that innocent victims are adequately reimbursed for their injuries. In its Order of May 4, 1989, the Court explained its rationale for the total figure of $470 million, which was based on an aggregated estimate of the appropriate compensation for varying degrees of injury.[41] This sum was to provide $44 million for an estimated 3,000 dead, $160 million for the 30,000 permanently disabled, $60 million for the 20,000 temporarily disabled, and an additional $50 million for 2,000 victims who had suffered other serious injuries. The Court also set aside $16 million for specialized medical treatment, after-care, and rehabilitation of the victims. The remaining $140 million was allocated to meet the claims of those with less serious injuries, such as those who had lost personal belongings and livestock. The order implied that the entire $470 million would go to the victims. Neither the central government nor the Madhya Pradesh state government was entitled to draw reimbursements from that amount for the litigation and rehabilitation expenditures they had incurred.

Compensation for the deceased was thus to average $14,600. Though small by U.S. standards, this amount was three times higher than might have been awarded in motor vehicle accident claims under Indian tort law.[42] Moreover, since the 1987 average annual income in India was $311,[43] the $14,600 is forty-seven times the national average annual income, comparing in this respect reasonably well with U.S. settlements in class action suits.[44] Insofar as compensation was based on lost earning potential, the families of the deceased would be well compensated by the settlement.

A second question about compensation was whether all those who suffered would be compensated. Official figures of the numbers of Bhopal victims, released by the government for the first time in April 1990,[45] support the Supreme Court's estimate of the amounts required to recompense those who had suffered manifest injuries or had died. According to the amended figures submitted to the Supreme Court in November 1990, 3,828 persons died due to the gas leak, 40 individuals suffered permanent total disablement, and 21,602 suffered permanent injury or permanent partial disablement. The number of victims who were temporarily disabled was 8,484.[46]

However, as the Indian government argued before the Supreme Court during a review of the settlement in December 1990, the Court's estimate made no allowance for latent injuries that might be manifested in the future, for minor injuries suffered by Bhopal residents, for rehabilitation and employment schemes, and for the building and maintenance of community infrastructure that was adversely affected by the disaster. Indeed, data and analyses released by the Indian Council of Medical Research (ICMR) in 1990 challenged the Madhya Pradesh government's figures and stressed the long-term impact of MIC poisoning. According to R. Ramachandran, the study

puts serious doubts on the categorization scheme adopted by the Madhya Pradesh Government, based arbitrarily on an extrapolation of the mortality patterns of the first four days of the tragedy, for the purpose of disbursal of monetary compensation depending on the severity of the injuries. Since the classification methodology also formed the rationale for arriving at the sum for the out-of-court settlement, the amount of $470 million paid by the UCC is too meager for the enormity of the tragedy.[47]

The ICMR study lists a wide range of respiratory diseases, early onset of cataracts and other ocular impairments, psychiatric disorders, and a high rate of miscarriages (7.5 percent) among the legacies of the MIC release.[48]

There are other reasons to think that the settlement did not provide coverage for all those who suffered damages. Over 600,000 claims were initially filed by supposed victims of the Bhopal gas leak. While the government eliminated 250,000 of these because claimants failed to respond to all three calls for medical exams,[49] it is unlikely that all these claims were bogus. The claims of 105,000 children who either were exposed to MIC or were born to gas-exposed mothers were not considered by the government on the grounds that such claims would complicate the process of classifying victims.[50] The government, moreover, had an interest in eliminating as many claims as possible, so its numerical estimates are inherently suspect. Reducing the number of officially injured persons improved the appearance of the settlement, since there was more to go around. Indeed, victims' groups charged the Government with artificially reducing the number of "officially" gas-injured for just this reason.

Retributive or corrective justice requires that the tortfeasor not benefit from his or her action or negligence, but instead be forced to pay for the misconduct. Although the Supreme Court's orders did not ascribe liability to Carbide, the settlement implicitly recognized the company's culpability. Carbide probably paid enough to counteract the perception that it had achieved a net benefit by operating with insufficient safety; and Carbide's standing was damaged in more subtle ways that are documented in Chapter 2. The settlement also arguably furthered the aims of international corrective justice. This was the first time in a mass tort case that a multinational paid for the actions of its local subsidiary, strengthening the emerging norm of international law that parent corporations are strictly liable for accidents resulting from their hazardous activities around the globe. Insofar as the aims of corrective justice depend on the *amount* of compensation, however, $470 million was not adequate punishment. Many victims' rights groups protested the settlement on exactly these grounds,[51] perceiving correctly that Carbide had settled for far less than it would have done in the United States.

With respect to *deterrence*, the $470 million paid by Carbide was more than double the corporation's $200 million insurance coverage. This would seem large enough, at first glance, to deter foreign and domestic entrepreneurs from recklessly investing in hazardous technologies in India. As noted above, the settlement order also substantially weakened the theory that a corporate shell shields a parent corporation from its subsidiary. Thus the Bhopal settlement demonstrated that hazardous industries must assume some of the social costs arising from activities outside their countries of origin.

At the same time, by consenting to a readily affordable settlement, India signaled its continued desire for foreign investment in hazardous industries. The meaning of this "signal" for industrial safety is difficult to interpret. It is widely recognized that, by U.S. standards, Carbide "got off easy,"[52] even though its Bhopal plant was operated at insufficient levels of safety. This implies that investors in hazardous technologies face a lower financial risk when their operations are conducted in developing rather than in industrialized countries. In short, while the settlement may deter "reckless" behavior, it is not likely to erase the discrepancy between richer and poorer countries' safety standards.

Reaction to the Settlement

Popular reaction to the settlement was loud, immediate, and negative, focusing mainly on its modest size. Demonstrators representing victims' groups argued that the awards were too small, that too few victims were covered, and that long-term effects of MIC were not considered.[53] Particularly strident were the assertions that the awards did not conform to U.S. norms.[54] Victims' advocates argued that hazardous industries were insufficiently deterred from operating with reduced safety standards in India, and they objected to the overt disparities in the valuation of human life in India and the West.

The dropping of criminal charges evoked similar outrage. Some jurists demanded that the charges be pursued and claimed that Carbide had bought its way out of the criminal liability. They argued that criminal proceedings should in no way be influenced by the outcome of civil actions. Implicitly, they rejected the Supreme Court's apparent assessment that the need for compensation was compelling, that convictions were unlikely to be secured, and that any convictions would be almost impossible to enforce. Some protestors asserted that *any* settlement would disadvantage India's long-term interests,[55] because it would not establish legal liability, deter inadequate safety measures, or contribute strongly enough to an emerging norm of international liability. Virtually every victims' rights group protested along one or more of these lines, but many of the 25,000 or so seriously incapacitated victims supported the settlement.[56] While the amount was below their highest expectations, it was substantial. As one gas victim said, "at least there is some hope we will get the money."[57]

Beyond organizing public demonstrations, protestors also filed appeals with the Supreme Court to have the settlement overturned. The Court had made clear that it would hear appeals if

the benefit of some contrary or supplemental information or material, having a crucial bearing on the fundamental assumptions basic to the settlement, have been denied by the Court and that, as a result, serious miscarriage of justice, violating the constitutional and legal rights of the persons affected, has been occasioned.[58]

The first plan of attack was to have the Bhopal Act declared unconstitutional: if the Government did not have standing to represent the victims, then it could not negotiate a settlement. Not surprisingly, however, the Court upheld the Bhopal Act in December 1989.[59] Having put its reputation on the line in engineering the settlement, the Court was unlikely to undercut itself. Upholding the Bhopal Act solidified the *parens patriae* principle—the right of a State to bring suit on behalf of its injured citizens—and thereby firmly established it as an instrument for future mass tort cases in India.

The next line of attack was to challenge the settlement on the grounds that criminal charges cannot be dropped through a civil settlement, especially since the Supreme Court was quashing the criminal charges of a district court. The attackers reasoned that, if an important component of the settlement were disallowed, the settlement as a whole would have to be renegotiated. Carbide, predictably, defended the clause, but also pleaded that criminal immunity was not a central part of the settlement and could be invalidated without imperiling the rest of the argument. Pushed to the wall, Carbide seemed willing to give up its criminal immunity to limit its financial liability.

In December 1989 the Government of Rajiv Gandhi fell and V. P. Singh became the new Prime Minister. As a result, the groups filing these appeals were joined by a surprising ally—the Government of India itself. On January 12, 1990, the Prime Minister repudiated the settlement, declaring, "No one has the right to bargain with the corpses of people."[60] His actions were greeted with an outpouring of popular support.[61] Singh's government wanted not only to set aside the settlement but to keep Carbide's money in India. The Attorney General of India asserted that Carbide had brought the $470 million into India "voluntarily." If the settlement were set aside, Carbide was not entitled in law or equity to the return of the money. There was more than a hint in the government's argument that this money could be attached in fulfillment of the High Court's interim award, which had never been stayed.

The Singh government's hostility to the settlement arose more from its politics than from juristic principle. Having condemned Carbide's escape when they constituted the parliamentary opposition, members of the new administration felt obliged to reverse the pro-settlement policy of their predecessors. Although this could have been done by supplementing Carbide's money with government aid, the new government took a more radical position.

Of the individuals who now held the reins of litigation on behalf of the government and the victims, Attorney General Soli Sorabji had, as a private lawyer, argued the victims' case in the 1989 challenge to the Bhopal Act. Other leading victims' counsel, notably Shanti Bhushan and Upendra Baxi, were also close to the Singh administration. The efforts of these lawyers and their access to power helped the victims' groups—which until then had been battling the central government, Carbide, and a reluctant Supreme Court—to capture and convert one of their principal adversaries.

Meanwhile, the legal challenges were impeding disbursement of the settlement money. Prime Minister Singh was thus prompted to do what his predecessors would not, namely, compensate the victims with Government of India funds. The payment scheme, begun in late June 1990, allowed for the distribution of $220 million. Under the plan, all 484,000 residents of the 36 severely gas-affected wards were to receive Rs 200 ($12) each month. The purpose was to provide the victims with basic sustenance, so that they could survive while the Supreme Court reconsidered the validity and adequacy of the settlement.

While the plan met with general approval, it was not without critics. In the first place, providing for all residents of the thirty-six severely gas-affected wards meant that 78,000 people who had not even claimed damages would receive funds. While the government understood this, it argued that all the people of Bhopal had suffered. In reality, the move tacitly recognized the fact that any requirement to have claims sorted out and evaluated more accurately would result in hopeless delay. Further, the decision was a concession to victims' groups that had maintained that the medical tests previously administered were overly stringent in determining who was affected.

While some undeserving claimants would receive funds, there were also deserving claimants who would not. The medical documentation on file indicated that at least 6 percent of the victims—about 12,000 people—lived permanently outside the 36 wards scheduled to receive aid and would therefore receive nothing under the plan.[62] Finally, the plan was criticized on the grounds that compensating the undeserving, as well as compensating everyone equally, deprived those who had suffered severely of their "proportionate" share.

The infusion of $6 million per month into the Bhopal economy under the government relief plan also had adverse economic and social impacts. The sudden availability of money triggered a price spiral; the consumption of liquor increased; and some residents, content to live off the government dole, gave up their jobs. Other effects were positive or at least neutral. Many families left the squalor of shanties for better homes; there was a boom in the television and transistor markets; and household help became scarce.[63]

In summary, the relief action of the Singh government raised a compelling question. Why was the new Prime Minister able to accomplish, with general favor, what the Gandhi government believed it could not? Five years after the accident, the neglected condition of the gas victims was widely recognized. Political considerations surrounding a "loan" to the hated multinational had paled in importance. Because the Singh government had not already taken a stand on *not* providing such a "loan," it was able to offer compensation without any reversal of policy. More importantly, the opportunity to assist the victims came within the context of popular discontent surrounding the settlement. Some victims' rights groups had charged that Rajiv Gandhi's Congress government had colluded with Union Carbide to "break the victims' backs," making them more amenable to a small settlement.[64] By repudiating the settlement, the Singh government demonstrated that it was "against" both Carbide and official collusion with the multinational. Gandhi's tragic assassination while campaigning for reelection in May 1991 probably means that the truth or falsity of these charges will never be sorted out.

Settlement Affirmed

On October 3, 1991, the Supreme Court upheld the $470 million settlement but reinstated criminal proceedings against Carbide officials. The Court acknowledged that the criminal proceedings were separate from the victims' civil lawsuits, and had been improperly dismissed in 1989. Criminal charges were quickly filed against former Union Carbide Corporation chairman Warren Anderson and officials of Carbide's Indian subsidiary. It seemed virtually certain that Warren Anderson would not place himself under the jurisdiction of the Indian courts. Senior officials of Carbide's Indian subsidiary were likely to be prosecuted for manslaughter, if not for murder.

Shortly before the settlement's affirmation, the Indian government devalued the rupee against the American dollar. Coupled with the interest that had accrued since the Supreme Court directed the money to be deposited with the Reserve Bank of India in the spring of 1989, the devaluation brought the total settlement to Rs 15 billion—more than double the rupee amount in February 1989.[65] From an Indian perspective, the settlement now appeared more substantial, though the government delayed announcing whether the increased value would go to the victims. But the Supreme Court's affirmation of the settlement did not seem to accelerate the process of getting money to the victims.

On October 16, 1992, the Supreme Court asked the central government to pay Rs 14.82 billion to the gas relief commissioner, K. Shankaranarayan, for distribution among the victims. Forty claims courts (one in each of the 36 gas-affected wards and four appellate courts) were set up to verify claims and award compensation in individual cases. In December 1992, eight months after they began work, only 800 cases had been decided. At this rate, it could take up to twenty years to settle all claims. To speed up disbursal of funds, some victims' groups have urged for a simplified uniform compensation scheme.[66]

Judicial Learning in Response to the Disaster

While the Bhopal accident pointed up many weaknesses in the Indian judicial system, it also gave the courts an opportunity to learn from and correct these deficiencies. In keeping with our overall theme of social learning, we now assess the judicial responses to these opportunities. The legislative and administrative repercussions of Bhopal are discussed at length by Bowonder, Kasperson and Kasperson in Chapter 4.

The disaster presented opportunities to the Indian judiciary to expedite its process, implement legal aid programs, develop its case law on civil liability, and expand its class action rules. The legal aid landscape, however, remains as bleak as when the tragedy occurred. While a few public interest lawyers appeared free of cost for the victims' groups, their efforts were fragmentary and not part of an organized effort to help the needy secure justice. And there has been no reform at all in the area of expediting trial procedure. Arcane and lengthy civil court procedures in India continue to emphasize process over justice.

But there was noteworthy progress in reforming India's liability and class action framework. The *Shriram Gas Leak* decision, a by-product of Bhopal, not only set a new standard of "absolute liability" for ultra-hazardous enterprises [67] but also decreed that damages paid by hazardous enterprises should be commensurate with the corporation's assets and not tied to the actual damages suffered by the victim. The reaction to *Shriram*'s principle for quantifying damages was ambivalent. Supreme Court Justice Ranganathan cautioned, "It is premature to say whether this yardstick has been, or will be, accepted in this country, not to speak of its international acceptance."[68] Nevertheless, it is likely that the allocations suggested by the Supreme Court for the Bhopal victims will nudge upward the meager damages that Indian courts have been accustomed to award in tort actions.

Another significant innovation by the Indian judiciary was the notion of interim damages. In a country where delays of *Bleak House* proportion are endemic, interim awards in strict liability cases seem to make good sense. It is unclear whether pre-judgment awards are sustainable in the absence of express statutory support. In any case, Justice Seth's interim award judgment has not been overturned. Although it proved unenforceable in the Bhopal litigation itself, Seth's judgment, unless overruled, will remain a precedent for interim relief in mass tort cases.

The major development in the field of class action procedures was the use of the *parens patriae* principle, as embodied in the Bhopal Act. With no history of mass tort cases, India possessed virtually no institutional mechanism for dealing with the mass of legal claims that Bhopal generated. Had it not been for the government's consolidated action on behalf of the victims, Carbide most probably would have settled more cheaply in separate deals with a multitude of poor, uneducated, and increasingly desperate individual claimants. The creative use of the *parens patriae* doctrine brought parity between the adversaries in what developed into a complex and bitterly fought contest. Indeed, given the initial desire to pursue damages in the U.S. courts, the Bhopal Act provided the victims' only realistic hope for securing damages in a distant and alien forum.

In India, judge-made laws such as the absolute liability regime announced by Chief Justice Bhagwati in the 1986 *Shriram* case[69] and Justice Seth's interim compensation ruling may prove even more potent than an act of Parliament. Statutes are subject to searching judicial review, whereas judge-made laws cannot be challenged on constitutional grounds. Had the legislature enacted a new liability standard or introduced interim compensation, Union Carbide would probably have challenged the laws as unconstitutional in separate proceedings. This tactic was prevented, however, since Chief Justice Bhagwati and Justice Seth articulated standards that they asserted were implicit in the law. In this manner, the judges were able to fashion entitlements that were less susceptible to challenge.

Partial and imperfect as India's response to Bhopal has been, it gave rise to a number of new legal precedents and mechanisms—absolute liability, interim relief, and *parens patriae*—that may serve as lessons for other countries. The judges of the Supreme Court fashioned a settlement. Carbide was made to pay in a mass tort case for the deficient safety measures of its subsidiary. And as we shall see in later chapters, the battle against Carbide strengthened the institutional framework for legal compensation and industrial hazard management in India. Tragic industrial accidents will occur, but the new policies adopted by India's judiciary may reduce the harm. While it is too early to judge their efficacy, these policies demonstrate praiseworthy sensitivity to public welfare, social justice, and environmental improvement.

Notes

1. The government under Prime Minister Chandra Shekhar, which succeeded the Singh administration in November 1990, continued the Bhopal policies of its predecessor.
2. N. K. Singh, "Knocked Out," *India Today*, October 15, 1986, p. 54.
3. Tamleen Singh, "Ending an Inquiry," *India Today*, March 15, 1989, p. 44.
4. N. K. Singh and David Devades, "The Settlement Drama," *India Today*, December 15, 1987, pp. 42–46.
5. Ibid.
6. P. N. Bhagwati, "Travesty of Justice," *India Today*, March 15, 1989, p. 45.
7. *Business India*, December 2–15, 1985.

8. Government of India press statement reprinted in *Hindustan Times*, March 8, 1989.

9. "Bhopal Gas Leak Disaster (Processing of Claims) Act," *Gazette of India*, March 29, 1985.

10. Ramindar Singh, "The Legal Damage," *India Today*, January 15, 1985, pp. 100–104.

11. Singh and Devades, "Settlement Drama."

12. N. K. Singh, "The New Nightmare," *India Today*, September 15, 1986, pp. 128–132.

13. N. K. Singh, "The Bhopal Bonanza," *India Today*, September 30, 1987, pp. 94–96.

14. Sreekant Khandekar, "An Area of Darkness," *India Today*, June 30, 1985, pp. 134–136.

15. Wil Lepkowski, "Bhopal: Indian City Begins to Heal But Conflicts Remain," *Chemical & Engineering News* (December 2, 1985): 18–32.

16. N. K. Singh, "False Hopes," *India Today*, July 15, 1987, pp. 64–69.

17. Singh, "New Nightmare."

18. Lepkowski, "Bhopal."

19. Apparently Chief Justice Bhagwati expected his *Shriram* absolute liability ruling to govern the Bhopal case when and if it came before the Supreme Court, even though the Bhopal case originated before the *Shriram* ruling. In other common law jurisdictions, such an application would be a denial of due process.

20. *M. C. Mehta v. Union of India* (A.I.R. 1987 S.C. 1086).

21. It was not clear how the company's ability to pay would be measured—whether as a percentage of earnings or of total net worth.

22. The NGOs were the Zahreeli Gas Kand Sangharsha Morcha and the Jana Swasthaya Kendra. Their application is reprinted in Upendra Baxi and Amita Dhanda, eds., *Valiant Victims and Lethal Litigation: The Bhopal Case* (New Delhi: Indian Law Institute, 1990), p. 235.

23. Cameron Barr, "Carbide's Escape," *American Lawyer*, May 1989, pp. 99–100.

24. *Union of India v. Union Carbide Corp.*, Gas Claim Case No. 1113 of 1986, District Court, Bhopal, Order passed by Judge Deo dated December 17, 1987, reprinted in Baxi and Dhanda, *Valiant Victims*, p. 240.

25. Singh and Devades, "Settlement Drama."

26. Ibid.

27. UPI Wire Service, December 7, 1987.

28. *Union of India v. Union Carbide Corporation*, Gas Claim No. 1113 of 1986, District Court, Bhopal Order passed by Judge Deo dated December 17, 1987, reprinted in Baxi and Dhanda, *Valiant Victims*, p. 283.

29. Ibid.

30. Ibid.

31. AP Wire Service, December 18, 1987.

32. R.S.C. (Amendment No. 2) 1980 (S.I. 1980 No. 1010), "Order for interim payment in respect of damages" (Order 29, rule 11).

33. *Union Carbide Corp. v. Union of India*, Civil Revision No. 26 of 1988, Madhya Pradesh High Court, Order passed by Justice Seth dated April 4, 1988, reprinted in Baxi and Dhanda, *Valiant Victims*, p. 338.

34. *In re* Union Carbide Disaster at Bhopal, India in December 1984, 809 F.2d 195 (2d Cir., 1987) (emphasis added).

35. *Union Carbide Corp. v. Union of India*, Civil Revision No. 26 of 1988, Madhya Pradesh High Court, order passed by Justice Seth dated April 4, 1988, reprinted in Baxi and Dhanda, *Valiant Victims*, p. 338.

36. N. K. Singh, "The Horror Continues," *India Today*, March 15, 1989, pp. 42–43.

37. Ramindar Singh and Amrit Kakaria, "Unsettling Verdict," *India Today*, March 15, 1989, pp. 42–46. Also see Government of India press statement, *Hindustan Times*, March 8, 1989.

38. *Union Carbide Corp. v. Union of India* (A.I.R. 1990 S.C. 273), Supreme Court's orders dated February 14, 1989 and February 15, 1989.

39. Clause 117, Constitutionality of Act Judgement, see Baxi and Dhanda, *Valiant Victims*, p. 610.

40. Stephen Labaton, "Bhopal Outcome: Trial Is Avoided," *New York Times*, February 15, 1989, p. D3.

41. Typical of the government's inefficiency, even four years after the disaster it was unable to assist the Court with reliable figures on the number of victims. It was a year later, in April 1990, that the Madhya Pradesh state government released official figures for the first time, and elected to forgo the hearing of review petitions in the Supreme Court.

42. Order of the Supreme Court, May 4, 1989 (A.I.R. 1990 S.C. 281).

43. World Resources Institute, *World Resources, 1990–91: A Guide to the Global Environment* (New York: Oxford University Press, 1990).

44. G. M. Stern, *The Buffalo Creek Disaster: The Story of the Survivors' Unprecedented Lawsuit* (New York: Random House, 1976). The average award to injured miners in this U.S. class action suit was $21,000.

45. Mark Williams, "Challenges to the Bhopal Settlement: An Update," *The Lawyers*, May 1990, p. 30.

46. Affidavit dated November 10, 1989 filed by the Madhya Pradesh government in the Supreme Court in review petitions challenging the settlement.

47. R. Ramachandran, "How Killer MIC Lives on in Bhopal," *Economic Times* (New Delhi), November 25, 1990.

48. Ibid.

49. Sheila Tefft, "India's Bhopal Victims Lose Out in Legal Wrangling," *Christian Science Monitor*, October 24, 1989, p. 3.

50. Nitya Jacob, "Bhopal Gas Victims: Red Tape and Corruption Delay Compensation," *Down to Earth*, December 15, 1992, pp. 5–9.

51. Satinath Sarangi, representative for the Bhopal Group for Information and Action, colloquium given at the University of California, Berkeley, April 28, 1991.

52. Compare the Bhopal settlement to the $2.5 billion paid by the Johns Manville Corporation to 60,000 claimants, or the $500 million by A. H. Robins to 9,450 claimants.

53. Singh and Kakaria, "Unsettling Verdict."

54. Bhagwati, "Travesty of Justice."

55. Upendra Baxi, "The Bhopal Award: Another Calamity for Gas Victims," *Times of India*, February 16, 1989.

56. See Singh and Kakaria, "Unsettling Verdict."

57. Ibid.

58. Supreme Court Order dated May 4, 1989, reprinted in Baxi and Dhanda, *Valiant Victims*, pp. 539–549.

59. *Charan Lal Sahu v. Union of India* (A.I.R. 1990 S.C. 1480).

60. Sanjoy Hazarika, "Bhopal Victims Still Wait for Carbide Money," *New York Times*, January 30, 1990, p. A9.

61. AP Wire Service, "India Seeks to Reopen Bhopal Case," *New York Times*, January 22, 1990, pp. D1–4.

62. Uday Mahurkar, "Partial Relief, Controversy Dogs Scheme," *India Today*, April 15, 1990, pp. 52–53.

63. Taroon Bhaduri, "Relief Doles Ruining Bhopal Economy," *Independent*, March 12, 1990.

64. N. D. Jayaprakash, "Perilous Litigation: The Leak Disaster Case," *Economic and Political Weekly* 25, 51 (December 22, 1990): 2761–2766.

65. "Devaluation Rises UCC Compensation," *Hindustan Times*, July 31, 1991.

66. Jacob, "Bhopal Gas Victims."

67. *M. C, Mehta v. Union of India* (A.I.R. 1987, S.C. 1086). Absolute liability met with little resistance from lawyers in India because tort actions are rare. In jurisdictions where tort litigation is well developed (U.S., Australia, New Zealand), introduction of a strict liability regime would reduce the work and income of trial lawyers and would undoubtedly be resisted by them.

68. *Charan Lal Sahu v. Union of India* (A.I.R. 1990 S.C. 1480).

69. *Mehta v. Union of India.*

Chapter 4
Industrial Risk Management in India Since Bhopal

B. Bowonder, Jeanne X. Kasperson,
and Roger E. Kasperson

The Bhopal accident marked a watershed in twentieth-century industrial safety. It injured, displaced, or killed record numbers of people, and caused untold delays in treating and compensating victims (Bowonder, Kasperson, and Kasperson 1985; Shrivastava 1987a, 1987c; 1992; Morehouse and Subramaniam 1986). The accident also had far-reaching effects on the chemical industry's management of hazards in both developed and developing countries. Many studies have addressed the responses in Europe and North America (van Ejindhoven, this volume, Chapter 6; Hadden, this volume, Chapter 5; Kletz 1988; Shrivastava 1987a, 1992; Stover 1985). But India, of course, was the country most directly and profoundly affected by the accident. Accordingly, we inquire in this chapter into social learning and institutional responses to industrial risk in India after Bhopal, particularly in the area of legal and regulatory developments and the implementation of hazard assessment and management systems.

"Social learning" is the process by which a society or nation perceives, assesses, and acts upon harmful experiences or past mistakes in purposeful ways. With respect to environmental risk, the learning process may incorporate decisions to bear or spread the risk, to prevent or reduce the risk, to mitigate the consequences of a particular incident, or to adapt to or accommodate the risk. As other chapters in this volume demonstrate, the Bhopal experience offered a host of possible lessons to industrial societies. This is not to say, however, that the event led to radical change instead of mere incremental adjustment. Bhopal stimulated extensive soul-searching in India about technological threats and the Indian capacity to anticipate and manage them. Our objective is to assess the extent to which the Indian institutional responses reflected true social learning.

Social learning in its simplest form involves ongoing, incremental changes that render the institutional fabric of a society more responsive and efficient in dealing with future events and stresses. Learning from disaster, however, has the potential to be more purposive and may be more complex, radical, and broad-based. A crisis such as Bhopal may trigger signals or early warnings from which society can infer new causes for concern about the environment or discover that institutional structures are insufficient to appraise and respond to such stresses. P. W. Meyers (1990) distinguishes four types of learning: *maintenance learning* involves incremental improvements in organizational procedures and performance, all the while retaining the basic organizational fabric; *adaptive learning* aims at building the "right system" and entails changes in roles, rules, and procedures; *transitional learning* occurs when an organization shifts its major strategic emphases and often requires the "unlearning" of methods and procedures that are no longer functional; *creative learning* involves a radical redefinition of both problems and solutions, along with more conflict and openness in assessment and decision-making processes.

Social learning, it is important to emphasize, is not the same as institutional change, which may or may not accompany increased learning and, indeed, may proceed without increased knowledge. Learning must include an element of generalizability that "goes beyond simple replication to application, change, refinement" (Jelinek 1979, 161). Crises such as Bhopal obviously are apt to stimulate both learning and change.

The Bhopal accident laid bare a number of significant shortcomings in India's legal and regulatory structure for managing risk. First, the state pollution control boards, India's primary agencies for enforcing environmental regulations, had no power to close down facilities, even those that posed imminent danger. Between 1978 and 1983, for example, the Bhopal plant experienced six major accidents, three of which involved spills of toxic materials. People notified the government that the facility had become intolerably risky (Bowonder and Miyake 1988), and yet it continued to operate. Second, the Factories Act of 1948 failed to distinguish between non-hazardous and hazardous facilities, and the Factory Inspectorate lacked the power to halt a facility's operations even in the face of documented safety lapses. Third, the failure of Union Carbide Corporation to provide information on how to handle methyl isocyanate (MIC) exposures, apparent in the Bhopal accident, spotlighted the absence of any statutory requirement to disclose needed emergency-response information. Fourth, plant siting and modification procedures failed to require hazard assessments for new facilities or for proposed changes in existing ones. Fifth, citizens lacked recourse to the courts even if they had been exposed to high levels of hazards or if firms had violated safety provisions. Finally, firms typically found it more economically advantageous to avoid compliance and pay the penalties than to meet statutory requirements. Legal proceedings against violators were hampered by a host of institutional factors: huge backlogs of cases, the difficulty of proving criminal liability, tortuous laws of evidence, and the lack of technical sophistication among judges (Singh 1984).

Legislative Initiatives

In the years following Bhopal, India enacted new legislation and amended existing laws to upgrade the national system of industrial hazard assessment and control. What can be said about the efficacy and impact of these new initiatives? How much did India really learn from Bhopal?

The Environment Protection Act (EPA), 1986

In 1986, India enacted an umbrella law—the Environment Protection Act (EPA)—to provide a holistic approach to risk management and to remedy shortcomings in existing environmental pollution laws (most notably, the Water Act and Air Act). The new statute, which came into force on November 19, 1986, sought both to protect and improve the environment and to prevent major hazards. It differed from earlier environmental acts in several notable respects.

The EPA for the first time covers the control of hazardous substances and provides for inspection of facilities handling hazardous materials and for control of the storage, handling, and transportation of such materials. It requires firms to disclose to the Ministry of Environment and Forests information on hazardous materials to which humans are likely to be exposed. It also establishes environmental laboratories for analyzing water and soil samples.

Any person so authorized by the central government has the right to enter and inspect a plant at all reasonable times, may search any building for actual or potential offenses under the Act, and may seize any evidence necessary to prevent or mitigate pollution. Another significant provision, introduced for the first time, is the power to close down a facility. The central government may direct the closure, prohibition, or regulation of any industry or operation, or regulate the supply of electricity or water or any other service. During

the reporting year 1989–1990 the Government of India issued closure directives to some 51 units for not implementing the required
environmental-protection measures (Central Pollution Control Board
1991, 27–28).

A more controversial provision allows citizens to approach the
central government or the court directly to report violations by corporations or government agencies, but the complainant must first
give sixty days notice so that the authority concerned can pursue an
action in court. During 1988–1991 citizen groups used this provision
extensively to challenge corporations for alleged safety lapses arising
from emissions, discharges, and the storage of hazardous materials.
Citing harassment, industry associations and representatives counter-
petitioned the government to withdraw this provision (*Economic Times*
1992b). Multinational corporations such as DuPont have made their
coming to India (now that the government has embraced economic
liberalization) contingent on the withdrawal of the provision. Meanwhile, the sixty-day notification period continues to draw fire from
citizens' groups for essentially providing time for offenders to delay
clean-ups (Abraham and Abraham 1991, 359; Chitnis 1987, 155). Recently, a proposed amendment to EPA seeks to cut the notification
period to thirty days (*Business and Political Observer* 1991a).

In a further direct response to Bhopal, the EPA permits top corporate managers to be held personally responsible for violations of
the law. Companies previously had the freedom to designate "the occupier of the factory," who was responsible for any offense committed. The EPA, however, requires the management to involve itself
actively in preventing pollution or accidents. The law thus marks a
substantial improvement over earlier legislation, though its effectiveness will depend on the central government's ability to develop and
implement its key provisions.

The Factories (Amendment) Act, 1987

Indian factories legislation was first enacted in 1881 and has passed
through numerous subsequent modifications. Immediately after independence, the Government of India enacted the Factories Act of
1948, revising and extending a 1934 law, to include welfare, health,
cleanliness, and overtime payments. Modeled after U.K. legislation,
the 1948 Act first codified the principle that the health, safety, and
welfare of workers employed in hazardous manufacturing processes
should be legally protected. Following Bhopal, the 1987 amendment
introduced additional safeguards in the use and handling of hazard-

ous substances in factories. It imposed a statutory obligation upon management for emergency-response procedures and sought to control the siting process so as to minimize risk to host communities. It also included provisions for the participation of workers in safety management and upgraded the penalties for noncompliance.

Hazardous industries

A key section of the 1987 legislation identified a list of industries that Government officials consider to be hazardous. The list, which encompasses "all major chemical and other potentially hazardous operations and facilities," is not very significant in itself but has far-reaching implications in conjunction with other sections of the Act. Paralleling the EPA, the statute also changed the definition of "occupier" to "the person who has ultimate control over the affairs of the factory." This definition again sought to make the top management more personally committed to the safe operation of hazardous facilities and to compliance with existing safety regulations.

Duties of the occupier

The Act specifies the occupier's *duties*, all of which aim at improving risk management. Thus the occupier must undertake plant maintenance in a way that is safe and without risk to the health of workers; safeguard health and safety during the use, handling, storage, and transport of hazardous substances; provide information, instruction, training, and supervision to ensure the health and safety of all workers; and monitor the health and safety of workers. The occupier must also prepare a written statement of corporate policy with respect to the health and safety of workers and must give notice to workers regarding the hazards that they face. The onus of disclosing safety information, both to the Factory Inspectorate and to workers, is directly on management, a change from earlier regulations. The Act also institutionalizes management responsibilities for reducing risks to people in the vicinity of the plant; earlier laws did not deal with risks to nearby residents.

Siting of hazardous facilities

To keep hazardous facilities away from major population centers, the Act provides a new siting procedure. A Site Appraisal Committee, chaired by the state's Chief Inspector of Factories, will examine applications for the establishment of factories that involve hazardous products or processes. It has the power to require a broad range of information from the applicant. Careful scrutiny and review prior to siting an industrial establishment has significant potential for minimizing exposure of the public to materials released during a breakdown or accident. In practice, however, the committees in many states frequently forego stringency in favor of courting industry, as every state seeks lower hurdles to industrial development. Thus the Maharashtra Pollution Control Board recently locked horns with the central government over the proposed expansion of a petrochemical complex in a densely populated area (*Business and Political Observer* 1991b). And in Madhya Pradesh, the state that ought to have learned most from Bhopal, "ad hocism" prevails in the shadow of an inconsistent siting policy (Joshi 1991, 59). Factory owners with existing units complain of the extreme difficulty, given their ability to acquire and fence off a suitable buffer zone, of discouraging shantytown developments. Yet only the government can legally acquire the large tracts of land that would be needed for this purpose. In addition, siting or relocation in remote locations is often costly in other terms, so that owners frequently try to avoid this outcome (Hadden 1987, 716).

Disclosure of information

Disclosure obligations under the Act take several forms:

- The occupier of every factory involved in a hazardous process must disclose all information involving dangers, including health hazards and mitigation measures, to the workers employed in the factory, the Chief Inspector of Factories, the local community within whose jurisdiction the factory is situated, and the general public living in the vicinity of the facility.
- The occupier must establish a detailed policy regarding worker health and safety, communicate this policy to the Chief Inspector of Factories, and draw up a site emergency plan and detailed disaster control measures.
- The occupier must inform the Chief Inspector of Factories in detail of the nature of all hazardous processes.
- The occupier must establish measures, approved by the Chief Inspector of Factories, for the handling, usage, transportation, and storage of hazardous substances inside the factory, and the disposal of such substances outside the factory. The occupier must

also publicize these measures to the workers and the general public living in the vicinity.

Hazard information

The Act specifies several responsibilities with respect to compiling and maintaining information. For example, the occupier must maintain medical records for workers exposed to any chemical, toxic or otherwise harmful, during manufacture, handling, or transportation. Workers must have access to their medical records and to means for protection from exposure to hazardous substances. These requirements have tremendous implications for the empowerment of workers, but since levels of literacy are low, effective implementation will require determined education of workers and involvement of trade unions in areas that have few traditions and experiences on which to build.

Permissible exposure

The Act calls for permissible exposure limits for chemicals and other toxic substances in manufacturing processes and sets standards in terms of both eight-hour, time-weighted average concentrations and short-term (fifteen-minute exposure) concentrations. The standard-setting process is not at all interactive. Indeed, the Ministry usually sets exposure limits by simply copying standards from other countries. Concentration-based, as opposed to mass-emission-based, standards have produced no real reductions in pollution. Even when individual factories in a highly industrialized area (e.g., Bombay) are in compliance, the combined emissions from several plants may reach deadly levels. Aware of the problem, the Ministry of Environment and Forests has begun "to lay down mass based standards which will set specific limits to encourage the minimisation of waste, promote recycling and reuse of materials as well as conservation of natural resources particularly water" (MEF 1991, 43). Meanwhile, the cost of implementation is high; many small facilities lack the necessary infrastructure and resources to comply with regulations.

Danger warnings

The amended Factories Act gives workers the right to warn the occupier or person in charge about an imminent danger. The warning can be given directly by the worker or through the worker safety committee and *must* be brought to the notice of the Factory Inspector. Upon receiving the warning, the occupier is required to take immediate action and to send a report to the Factory Inspector.

Penalties

Violation of any of the provisions of the Factories Act is punishable with a two-year term of imprisonment, a fine of Rs 100,000, or both. If the violation continues after conviction, the fine may be extended to Rs 10,000 for each additional day.

These new amendments make the Factories Act, in principle, a powerful regulatory instrument. In fact, however, state governments lack both the resources and the regulatory infrastructure to implement the upgraded provisions. In Madhya Pradesh State, an average Factory Inspector must inspect about 280 facilities annually. Inspectors, moreover, are mostly mechanical and electrical engineers, with precious little experience in hazard assessment, industrial medicine, toxicology, emergency management, and occupational health issues. Worse yet, as one Indian journalist quips: "The ball-point pen is the only 'equipment' with a factory inspector to monitor hazard in industrial units and help check pollution in Madhya Pradesh" (Joshi 1991, 59). The inadequacy of coordination among central, state, and local government agencies exacerbates the problem of implementation. A series of industrial accidents since Bhopal—a chlorine leak in densely populated Bombay in 1985; a serious oleum leak in Delhi in 1985; a fire in a large semiconductor complex in Chandigarh in 1989; an accident in a gas cracker unit in Bombay in 1991; and a trucking accident in Mahul (near Bombay) in 1991—all illustrate persistent inadequacies in the management of risks at hazardous plants.

The Air (Amendment) Act, 1987

The 1987 amendment to the 1981 Air Act also took note of problems observed at Bhopal. As discussed above, every industry must have the consent of the State Pollution Control Board to release pollutants in accordance with applicable emission standards. Under earlier laws, such consent was irrevocable, once granted. Under the 1987 amendments, however, the State Board may cancel its consent at any time or refuse renewal if regulatory conditions have not been fulfilled. Prior to canceling or refusing a further consent, however, the authorities must grant the person concerned a reasonable opportunity to be heard. State pollution control boards may also petition a court to restrain persons from causing air pollution, mainly as a means of handling individual release events.

The Hazardous Wastes (Management and Handling) Rules, 1989

On July 28, 1989, the Government of India promulgated new rules concerning the management and handling of hazardous wastes. These rules specify what constitutes a hazardous waste and require that a person who owns or operates a facility for collection, reception, treatment, storage, or disposal of hazardous wastes take all the practical steps needed to ensure proper handling of such wastes. All generators and managers of hazardous wastes must apply to the state pollution control board for authorization to pursue any of these activities. The rules also prohibit the import of hazardous wastes from any country to India for dumping or disposal.

Though the rules have been on the books since 1989, implementation has been slow. The state pollution control boards lack adequate technical skills for handling the technologically complex problems posed by hazardous wastes. The Central Pollution Control Board, for its part, has failed to conduct the background work needed to determine the sources and quantities of hazardous wastes. As of early 1992, most of the states had not yet specified sites for the disposal of hazardous wastes. Developing the needed technical competence to implement upgraded regulatory procedures continues to be one of the weakest links in India's environmental management system.

The Public Liability Insurance Act, 1991

Bhopal highlighted the need for a procedure to provide immediate relief to the victims of industrial accidents and to address the now-legendary economic and psychological difficulties confronting the poor. Accordingly, on January 7, 1991, Parliament passed the Public Liability Insurance Bill, which requires every owner to carry insurance to cover death, injury, or property damage resulting from an accident and provides for compensation for permanent or partial disability. This act is designed mainly to protect people living in the vicinity who are not covered under any other compensation law (workers, for example, are currently covered under the Workmen's Compensation Act of 1923). The procedures for settlement of claims are very simple, with disbursement provided by the district collector.

Although this act may be seen as another striking example of social learning in the aftermath of Bhopal, full implementation again may prove elusive. For an existing industry, both the extent of liability and the basis on which it will be estimated are unclear. The law fails to distinguish between highly hazardous and less hazardous facilities, and, more important, it does not address how the dynamics of settlement growth in the vicinity of a hazardous plant will be incorporated into the liability-estimation process. Nevertheless, it is an important step in institutionalizing compensation arrangements for persons other than workers who are affected by accidents or releases from hazardous facilities.

Environment (Protection) Second Amendment Rules, 1992

A recent amendment to the Environment (Protection) Rules, 1986 requires all firms that operate under the EPA to conduct environmental audits. Beginning with the period April 1992–March 1993, any firm that discharges effluents or emissions must submit to the relevant state pollution control board a report that details (1) consumption of water and other raw materials, (2) air and water pollution, (3) quantities (by category) of solid and hazardous wastes generated, (4) waste-disposal practices, and (5) investments in environmental protection and pollution control.

The worthwhile objective of environmental audit is to encourage companies to work aggressively to reduce their pollution burden and to make optimal use of natural resources, but the regulation is fraught with weaknesses. It is difficult to verify or use the audit information submitted to the already overburdened pollution control boards. Even as the Government of India has endorsed environmental audits (MEF 1992, 7), it has failed to identify certified environmental auditors, and requisite expertise is virtually nonexistent in most firms, which, incidentally, had no say in designing and formulating audit formats. A handbook might have helped. Indeed, the Indian government might have taken a page from the U.S. Environmental Protection Agency (EPA 1986) or UN agencies (UNEP/IEO 1990) and prepared a detailed audit manual prior to launching the new regulation. Such preparatory work would have eased the task for implementing agencies and audit-performing firms alike and enhanced the prospects for achieving pollution reduction. As it is, the essentially volunteer procedure for disclosure offers no way to cross-check the information provided. Prior stringent regulations have not themselves yielded effective compliance, so it is unlikely that environmental audits will improve the environmental-pollution status of industries.

The Impacts of Legislative Initiatives

Taken together, these six laws have developed a new and potentially far-reaching management structure for reducing or mitigating industrial risks in India. But two major realities restrict their potential. First, the legislation overemphasizes the very regulatory approaches and procedures that had proved ineffective in Bhopal, while neglecting economic instruments that might have helped to internalize damage costs. Numerous studies have demonstrated the effectiveness of economic incentives in enhancing environmental quality, particularly in developing countries (Project 88 1988; Stavins 1989). In countries as disparate as Malaysia and Germany, for example, high charges for pollution provide a continuing disincentive to discharge contaminants. Malaysia's introduction of discharge fees proportional to the pollution load has effectively induced corporations to reduce emissions. Meanwhile, the Malaysian government lowered the permissible standards for various pollutants slowly over a five-year period. Economic instruments also stimulate permanent efficiency improvements, so that the costs of pollution prevention and conservation are gradually internalized into the production process.

Yet in India the continuing reality is that the cost of compliance with standards often far exceeds the cost of noncompliance, and reliance on regulation only encourages industries to find ingenious methods for avoiding or delaying compliance. The recently enacted requirement for environmental audits speaks to an overuse of regulatory mechanisms or "command-and-control" approaches to curbing pollution and reducing industrial hazards. India has still to learn that yet another regulation, devoid of built-in incentives for compliance, will not improve implementation of existing regulations. It will only weaken the working of existing institutions, since it will force them to spread meager resources very thin over a variety of regulatory procedures rather than concentrating on critical environmental problems or major polluters.

Second, regulatory reform after Bhopal has run substantially ahead of broader institutional changes. Existing institutions often lack the structure, skills, and resources to implement the new regulations. Hazard management requires diverse specialized skills not currently represented on India's pollution control boards, which are staffed mostly by civil engineers from public health departments with little expertise in hazardous substances control. Worse yet, recent years have witnessed a proliferation of political appointees, whose sometimes selective prosecution of violators has eroded public confidence (Lalvani 1985). Similarly, factory inspectors, who are mostly mechanical or electrical engineers without appropriate training, have been assigned additional responsibility for hazard assessment, hazardous substances control, and emergency management. Pollution control boards and factory inspectorates remain seriously understaffed. Recent piling on of duties attendant on enactment of environmental-audit regulations will only further compromise ongoing monitoring and implementation of existing regulations. The shortfall between new responsibilities and needed expertise is likely to undermine the implementation of the environmental protection measures included in the six recent laws.

Developments in the Courts

The Indian judiciary's role in institutionalizing risk management and risk compensation extends beyond the specifics of the Bhopal litigation (see Rosencranz et al., this volume, Chapter 3). Judicial actions have reinterpreted existing constitutional provisions to incorporate a new awareness of the deterioration of environmental quality and the potential for industrial accidents. Certainly, the Bhopal accident and the passage of the Environmental Protection Act stimulated a quick response from the courts. Several cases deserve special notice.

The Public Litigation Cases

The Constitution of India originally made no mention of environmental protection. In 1976, however, Parliament added two new articles: Article 48(A), which stipulates that the State shall endeavor to protect and improve the environment and to safeguard forests and wildlife, and Article 51(A(g)), which establishes the fundamental duty of every citizen of India to protect and improve the natural environment, including the forests, lakes, rivers, and wildlife, and to have compassion for all living creatures. In recent years the Supreme Court has agreed to hear public-interest lawsuits filed by voluntary organizations, by public-minded citizens, and by judges (Shastri 1988). Since the Bhopal accident, the Supreme Court has taken a particularly serious view of environmental offenses, as illustrated by a recent mining controversy.

In the Doon Valley in the State of Uttar Pradesh, a number of mining companies quarry limestone in hilly areas covered with forests. A voluntary agency—the Rural Litigation and Entitlement Kendra—filed a public-interest suit alleging that mining was destroying the environment. The Supreme Court issued an interim judgment on October 19, 1987, ruling that stone quarrying in the valley should generally be stopped. In its final judgment of August 30, 1988, the Court ruled that the ongoing mining lease should be terminated without provision for compensation. Observing that natural resources are permanent assets of mankind and are not intended to be exhausted in one generation, the Court found that such termination was in the broad interests of the community.

The judiciary has also interpreted the basic articles of the Indian constitution as supporting environmental protection and minimization of industrial hazards. Prompted in part by the Bhopal catastrophe and the massive suffering it induced, the judicial arm of the Government has taken a long-term view that mandates the curtailment of human activity resulting in serious or irreversible environmental damage. The judiciary's relatively forward-looking stance on environmental issues has counterbalanced to some degree the more conservative and incremental perspective of the administrative and regulatory wing of the government.

The Absolute Liability Case

As noted in earlier chapters, the oleum leak that occurred in Delhi in December 1985 at an industrial unit of the Shriram Food and Fertilizer Industries (SFFI) represented a milestone for Indian tort law. On December 7, 1985, the Supreme Court accepted for consideration a public-interest petition requesting that the SFFI unit be relocated away from Delhi and that a permit be required to restart it. A little more than two years later, the court issued a landmark judgment dealing with safety management, the liability of hazardous facilities, and compensation for workers and the public (*All India Reporter* 1988a). The judgment made it clear that corporations in India in charge of hazardous facilities have an absolute and non-delegable responsibility to prevent hazards; this liability, moreover, was not subject to any of the standard common-law defenses (see Rosencranz et al., this volume, Chapter 3). Finally, the Supreme Court held that for any damage arising from a hazardous activity the measure of compensation must be commensurate with the magnitude and capacity of the enterprise. In other words, the deepr the pocket, the larger the fine must be to achieve an adequate level of deterrence.

From the standpoint of risk management, however, the SFFI accident revealed that even one year after Bhopal, the chemical industry and the government had not really learned how to reduce the risks of serious industrial accidents or how to respond effectively to emergencies. SFFI's various units occupied a single complex in the Delhi metropolitan area and were surrounded by thickly populated settlements. Some 200,000 people resided within a radius of three kilometers. Nevertheless, at the time of the accident no emergency-response system was in place and no coordinated effort was made to communicate to people in the vicinity of the plant. Instead, confusion reigned, with various agencies providing conflicting advice to local citizens. The events at SFFI clearly indicated that hazard-assessment capability had not yet developed in major industrial facilities. On the positive side, the Delhi Municipal Corporation did take up the safety issue on receiving a complaint about SFFI, and the Supreme Court, of course, did rule on a public-interest writ petition. Neither action would have occurred but for the heightened awareness of risk created by Bhopal.

The Vicarious Liability Case

Another major case dealt with the issue of the vicarious liability of senior executives in cases of chemical damage. A distillery located at Modinagar discharged untreated effluents into a river, producing a fish kill. The Uttar Pradesh State Pollution Control Board brought suit, arguing a violation of the Water Act. The chairman, the vice chairman, the managing director, and the directors of Modi Industries filed an application with the state high court asking to have the charges set aside, since the executives were not directly responsible. The state court accepted this contention and absolved the officers of vicarious liability, but the Supreme Court set aside the decision and ruled that top executives in manufacturing firms are indeed responsible for implementing the Water Act. They are liable for offenses under the Act unless they can prove that the violation was committed without their knowledge or that they exercised due diligence to prevent its commission (*All India Reporter* 1988b).

The Tannery Pollution Case

Many small-scale industrial enterprises in India are household units or cottage industries that, for the most part, do not adhere to hazardous-waste or pollution-control regulations. This smaller and generally unorganized industrial sector remained relatively unconcerned about its risk problems until the Supreme Court of India intervened. Leather tanneries are a major example. At one time, they used non-polluting natural products from trees and barks, in a process known as East India tanning. The chrome tanning that came into India after 1950 caused water pollution and land degradation. Since most of the leather tanning units were in the cottage-industry sector and were operated with very little capital or technical expertise, it was difficult to secure their compliance with pollution control regulations. Pollution from tanneries continues to be a serious national problem, particularly since many untreated effluents make their way to the Ganges.

A public-interest lawsuit in the Supreme Court of India argued that tanneries should be prevented from discharging effluents until they had installed appropriate treatment systems. For their part, the tanneries pleaded that they were small and could not afford such remedial action. After considering all the issues, the Supreme Court ruled that the financial capacities of industrial establishments should be considered irrelevant and ordered the tanneries to undertake primary treatment of the effluents. The court also held that, just as an industry that cannot pay minimum wages to its workers cannot be permitted to continue, so the adverse environmental effects caused by the discharge of effluents justified the closure of the tanneries, despite the inconvenience caused to management and labor (*All India Reporter* 1988a).

Inspection and Enforcement

Changes in inspection procedures and regulatory enforcement constitute the third set of Indian institutional responses to Bhopal. Two changes occurring in the past five years deserve special notice.

Hazard Assessment

Following the Bhopal accident, all of the major industrial states in India appointed multidisciplinary task forces to analyze their existing hazardous facilities. These teams visited large industrial sites, reviewing emergency management plans, safety practices, and storage facilities, and, based on preliminary hazard assessments, made recommendations for improving safety management and emergency planning. In certain cases in which facilities were located in close proximity to dense human settlements, the task forces recommended shifting industries to new sites. In Karnataka state, for example, the task force studied nineteen hazardous facilities for which it identified safety problems and inadequacies that required correction. Similar exercises were also carried out in all states with major hazardous processing or storage facilities. The officials of the Factory Inspectorate also used a task-force approach for identifying and assessing hazards (Government of Karnataka 1987; Bowonder and Arvind 1989). These review exercises have helped state governments to develop local expertise in hazard assessment. They also produced widely publicized reports, through which ordinary citizens in many states became aware for the first time of the hazards of industrial facilities.

Another new development is the requirement that manufacturing facilities must prepare detailed hazard assessment reports, which must be approved by the Factory Inspectorate before they may construct and operate new facilities. Firms may be asked in this process to make specific—and burdensome—changes in equipment and procedures, as well as in the location of facilities. In Bombay, a number of units were required to move outside the city limits when they planned further expansion, even though trade unions opposed such actions because of their employment implications. The major shortcoming of these activities was that the hazard-assessment task forces could only make recommendations, since they lacked any statutory powers. The Factory Inspectorate, however, has enforced the safety-related recommendations as part of its safety inspections, which are statutory. Further, the assessment by an external committee was in most cases a one-shot affair, with little or no follow-up. Nevertheless, the exercises established the principle that private as well as public units could be inspected for safety by an external agency; many units, in fact, improved their safety procedures and made safety investments as a direct result of the committee recommendations.

Environmental Impact Assessment

Since 1985, the Government of India has required that every new project obtain environmental clearance. The operational framework for this requirement is a set of administrative procedures (Figure 4.1) that as yet lack the backing of any law. All projects are first screened at the state level to decide whether an Environmental Impact Assessment (EIA) is required. The State Department of the Environment then clears those projects that do not require an EIA and refers those that do to the Ministry of Environment and Forests.

EIA procedures require various agencies to examine the necessary safeguards at the project-initiation stage. To initiate the review, the project developer completes and submits to the State Pollution Control Board a project questionnaire provided by the Ministry of Environment and Forests. The Board reviews the environmental-management plan and either rejects the proposal or, if the plan is satisfactory, issues a "no objection certificate" and recommends the project to the State Department of Environment. No specific format has been proposed for the EIA as yet, however, and this has resulted in the exclusion of certain important impacts (for example, growth-inducing impacts) from review. The administrative apparatus for EIA at the state level is also technically very weak. If model EIAs or model environmental-management plans were prepared, and project sponsors were properly trained and sensitized, the anticipatory value of the EIA process would be greatly enhanced.

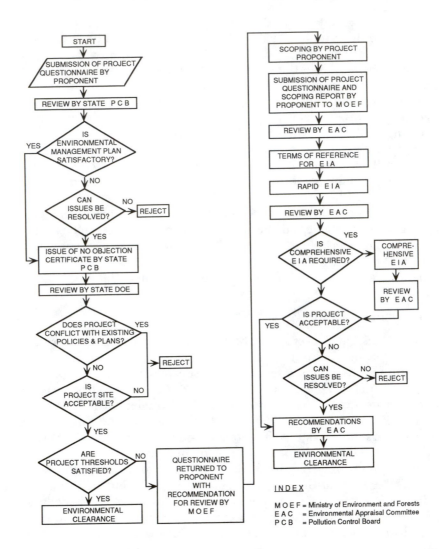

Figure 4.1. An operational framework for conducting an environmental review (Bowonder and Arvind 1989, p. 187; used by permission).

The norms and procedures for environmental clearance were vague until February 1992, when the Ministry of Environment and Forests classified all projects and industries according to two schedules (*Hindu* 1992). Projects listed in Schedule 1—which includes atomic power, thermal power, river-valley projects, refineries, chemi-

cal facilities, and so on—require clearance by the relevant state government as well as the Ministry. Schedule 2 lists projects that require
only state clearance. Yet the Ministry reserves the right to review state
clearances if it receives challenges in writing or if the project lies
within ten kilometers of ecologically sensitive areas. For projects under Schedule 1, a committee will assess the environmental impacts
prior to issuing a preliminary clearance. Although the procedures are
clearly stated, the detailed format of the EIA and the specific aspects
to be included are left to the developing agency. Moreover, since no
formal law exists to support a given site clearance, subjective elements inevitably compromise the process and may well render an EIA
ineffective.

Implementation of Pollution-Control Regulations

The implementation of pollution-control regulations was generally
ineffective in India prior to the enactment of the Environmental Protection Act of 1986. A study by Bowonder (1988; see also Bowonder
et al. 1988), based on extensive interviews and a survey covering
about two hundred industries, provides insight into the major obstacles and areas of weakness (Figure 4.2). Since 1986, however, the central government has taken a tougher stance on pollution. As noted
earlier, the 1986 Act empowers the Ministry of Environment and Forests to order plant closures without going through the state pollution
control boards. In 1991, the Ministry closed fifty-one polluting units.
In addition, it now has the authority to intervene directly in cases
where a company or government agency has failed to comply with
environmental standards.

Units that do not plan to install pollution-control equipment within
a specified time period receive closure notices, which are in turn a
prelude to the closure directive that the Ministry issues for continued
failure to comply with regulations. The Ministry may ask for a time-
table for compliance, as well as proof of the firm's commitment to
comply with the regulations.

Inspection and Classification of Industries

The Bhopal accident indicated the need to revamp completely the
inspection procedures of the factory inspectorates and state pollution
control boards. Beginning in 1988, the Government of India divided
industries into three major categories and proposed a tentative inspection schedule. All large-scale industries were placed in the "red"
category; for this class, the frequency of inspection was to range from

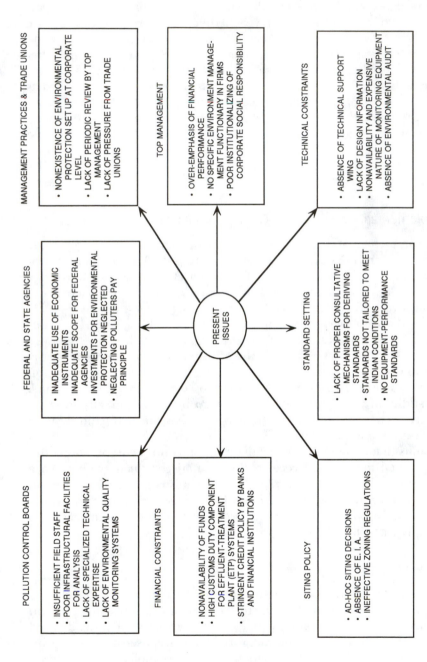

Figure 4.2. Major obstacles to environmental management in India (Bowonder 1988, p. 5; used by permission).

once a month to once every six months, depending on the size of the industry. Medium-scale industries in the "orange" category were to be inspected once every two years, whereas small industries in the orange category were to be inspected once a year. Finally, those in the "green" category were to be inspected once every two years.

This classification represents a laudable attempt to standardize and prioritize inspection procedure, but it has serious shortcomings. Since the nature of the inspection is not specified, considerable ambiguity remains about the depth and scope of review. The depth of inspection is not related to the age of the facility and its equipment, although older facilities frequently demand more in-depth inspection to uncover and correct hazardous situations. A system for comprehensive analysis of near-mishaps has yet to be developed. Procedures for the comprehensive logging and analysis of data have yet to be specified. More problematically, automatically classifying all large industries as hazardous appears to defeat the very purpose of ranking industries according to the degree of hazard. Finally, until the hazard-assessment expertise and skills of inspectors are seriously upgraded, the quality of inspection is unlikely to improve significantly.

Conclusions

It is clear that the Bhopal accident was a traumatic event that stimulated enormous attention to industrial hazards by Indian legislators and policy makers. The resulting actions were national in scope, unlike the activities of various groups whose advocacy of environmental conservation in India had concentrated on local problems and on rectifying particular harms rather than addressing more generic ones. Thus, in the Doon Valley case mentioned earlier, the concern was to preserve a specific mountain ecosystem in the north of India. The agony of the Bhopal gas victims greatly increased public awareness about the need for controlling pollution, protecting the environment, conserving natural resources, and improving safety-management practices in hazardous industrial facilities. The media devoted special attention to the consequences of Bhopal and subsequently, at repeated and regular intervals, highlighted the hazards that other Indian industrial facilities posed to humans and environment. A wide array of institutional changes since Bhopal bears witness to the depth of concern in Parliament and the central government over future accidents and threats to the environment.

A great deal of social learning, then, occurred in India as a result of the Bhopal accident, particularly in the formal regulatory arena. Bold legislative and regulatory reforms, bolstered by activist judicial decisions, put into place some much-needed institutional frameworks, but fell short of providing the infrastructure, resources, and support needed to ensure implementation. Passage of the Public Liability Insurance Act of 1991 made India one of the first countries to introduce mandatory hazard insurance for people other than workers, but the formidable problems of implementation were not assessed before the law's enactment. Regulators continued, as before, to ignore affected parties in decision making, thereby forgoing opportunities for creative learning. Indeed, most of the institutional responses to Bhopal reflected maintenance or adaptive learning; transitional or creative learning appeared to be in much shorter supply. The goal of making the environment a public good, and of ensuring that environmental values would take precedence over private economic interests, remained distant as India moved incrementally to secure better compliance with environmental regulations. Indeed, an inclination toward economic liberalization, which facilitates the start-up of new industries, threatens to compromise India's environmental gains. A prime minister's assurance that "no feasible power project will ever be held up for want of environmental clearance" heralds the accommodating "green channel" that essentially waives licensing requirements (*Economic Times* 1992a).

Nongovernmental organizations (NGOs) and trade unions played at best a peripheral role in the process of social learning. Trade unions remained largely passive and reactive in their attitude to industrial hazards. An emphasis on economic benefits to workers, an indifferent trade union leadership, and low worker awareness about safety and hazards account for this passivity. NGOs did somewhat better (see Rosencranz et al. and Reich, this volume, Chapters 3 and 9), but strong professional leadership and expertise are still very limited. The large increase in the number of NGOs and in their membership has not yet produced a commensurate increase in technical expertise and technical information support (Khator 1988). India still needs professionally competent organizations with a sound and effective base of technical expertise as well as political access.

Scant attention went into training and the development of skills: skills for carrying out hazard assessment and evaluation, for planning emergency responses, for undertaking emergency evaluation, for communicating risks to populations and workers, some of whom may be illiterate, and for improving industrial risk management generally. These shortcomings are particularly troubling in the wake of Bhopal, which starkly pointed up the need for better risk communication. As one analyst puts it: "If we give dangerous plant or material to people who have not demonstrated their competence to handle it we are responsible for the injuries they cause" (Kletz 1988, 89).

In the long run, pollution-prevention strategies and the polluter-pays principle, along with improved risk anticipation and prevention systems, may be the most effective way of controlling pollution in India. Long before Bhopal, Trevor Kletz (1978) championed *intrinsically safe plants*—namely, plant designs that use fewer and less hazardous raw materials (Kletz 1985, 1993). "Clean" new process technologies and "environmentally friendly" products will have to be pursued progressively through the ecological modernization of the economy, as proposed by Simonis (1987). Indeed, the Ministry of Environment and Forests (1991, 43) has recently initiated a system for certifying such products and encouraging consumer awareness. The growth of the economy also needs to be reoriented so as to minimize environmental impacts through the promotion of cleaner, safer, and less resource-intensive industries.

And so, even as the World Bank (1988) champions the development of national capacity, industrial risk management efforts move forward in India in a fragmented and haphazard way, involving overlapping agencies and institutions and a byzantine administrative process (Bowonder and Arvind, 1989; Hadden 1987; Hadden and Reich, this volume, Chapters 5 and 9). Industrial risk management has made important strides since Bhopal but has yet to be institutionalized in a comprehensive and systematic way. A kind of collective organizational amnesia virtually assures the recurrence of Bhopals (Kletz 1993). The end of a "decade of determined response" that we called for in 1985 (Bowonder, Kasperson, and Kasperson 1985, 36) approaches, and much more must be done to achieve a holistic framework for managing industrial risks to humans and the natural environment. One promising sign is the embracing of "sustainable development" by the Associated Chambers of Commerce and Industry of India (ASSO-CHAM), which has presented a slate of suggestions for effective cooperative management of environmental pollution (Sankar 1992). Meanwhile, the ideal of sustainable development of India's economy and technology continues to beckon.

References

Abraham, C. M., and Sushila Abraham. 1991. "The Bhopal Case and the Development of Environmental Law in India." *International and Comparative Law Quarterly* 40, 2 (April): 334–365.
A.I.R. (*All India Reporter*). 1987. *M. C. Mehta v. Union of India*. Supreme Court, 965–1010.

————. 1988a. *M. C. Mehta v. Union of India*. Supreme Court, 1037–1048.

————. 1988b. *UP Pollution Control Board v. M/s Modi Distillery*. Supreme Court, 1128–1133.

Antony, J. M. 1991. "SC Leaves Industrial Accident Laws in a Flux." *Business and Political Observer*, October 5, p. 1.

Bogard, William. 1989. *The Bhopal Tragedy: Language, Logic, and Politics in the Production of a Hazard*. Boulder, CO: Westview Press.

Bowonder, B. 1988. *Implementing Environmental Policy in India*. New Delhi: Friedrich Ebert Stiftung.

Bowonder, B. et al. 1989. *Corporate Responses to Environmental Policies*. Hyderabad: Centre for Energy, Environment and Technology, Administrative Staff College of India.

Bowonder, B. and S. S. Arvind. 1989. "Environmental Regulations and Litigation, India." *Project Appraisal* 4: 182–196.

Bowonder, B., Jeanne X. Kasperson, and Roger E. Kasperson. 1985. "Avoiding Future Bhopals." *Environment* 27, 7: 6–13, 31–37.

Bowonder, B., and T. Miyake. 1988. "Managing Hazardous Facilities: Lessons from the Bhopal Accident." *Journal of Hazardous Materials* 19: 237–269.

Business and Political Observer. 1991a. "5 Major Amendments to EPA on Anvil." November 12, p. 5.

————. 1991b. "MPCB Well Within Powers to Give NOC to NOCIL." November 22, p. 3.

Central Pollution Control Board. *Annual report, 1989–90*. Delhi: The Board.

Chitnis, V. S. 1987. "Environment Protection Act, 1986: A Critique." In Paras Diwan, ed., *Environment Protection: Problems, Policy Administration, Law*, pp. 152–156. New Delhi: Deep and Deep.

Dwivedi, O. P. 1985. "Environmental Regulations in India." *Environmental Professional* 7: 121–127.

Dwivedi, O. P. and B. Kishore. 1982. "Protecting the Environment from Pollution: A Review of India's Legal and Institutional Mechanisms." *Asian Survey* 22, 9 (September): 894–911.

Economic Times. 1992a. "PM Assures Green Channel for Delayed Power Projects." April 5, p. 1.

————. 1992b. "Prosecution of Pollution Units Strongly Resented." February 8, p. 2.

EPA (U.S. Environmental Protection Agency). 1986. "Environmental Auditing Policy Statement." *Federal Register* 51 (July 9): 25004–25009.

Goswami, Dilip. 1988. *A Handbook on Pollution Control by Industries and Government Bodies with Supreme Court Decisions*. New Delhi: Emcon Business Review.

Government of Karnataka. 1987. *Report of Task Force on Safety in Hazardous Industries in Karnataka*. Bangalore: Government of Karnataka.

Hadden, Susan. 1987. "Statutes and Standards for Pollution Control in India." *Economic and Political Weekly* 22, 16 (April 18): 709–720.

Hindu. 1992. "Govt. Norms for Environmental Clearance of Projects." February 20, p. 28.

Jasanoff, Sheila. 1986. "Managing India's Environment." *Environment* 28, 8: 12–16, 31–38.

Jelinek, Mariann. 1979. *Institutionalizing Innovation: A Study of Organizational Learning Systems*. New York: Praeger.

Joshi, V. T. 1991. "Madhya Pradesh: Not Learning from Experience." In *The*

Hindu Survey of the Environment, 1991, pp. 59, 61. Madras: Kasturi and Sons Ltd.

Karan, P. P., Wilford A. Bladen, and James R. Wilson. 1986. "Technological Hazards in the Third World." *Geographical Review* 76: 195–208.

Khanna, P. 1989. "Conceptual Framework and Role of EIA in Decision Making." Paper presented at Indo Dutch Seminar on EIA, New Delhi, 1989.

Khator, Renu. 1988. "Organizational Response to the Environmental Crisis in India." *Indian Journal of Political Science* 49, 1 (January–May): 14–39.

Kletz, Trevor A. 1978. "What You Don't Have Can't Leak." *Chemistry and Industry* 9 (May 6): 287–292.

———. 1985. *What Went Wrong? Case Histories of Process Plant Disasters*. Houston: Gulf Publishing Company.

———. 1988. *Learning from Accidents in Industry*. London: Butterworths.

———. 1993. *Lessons from Disasters: How Organizations Have No Memory and Accidents Recur*. Rugby, Warwickshire, England: Institution of Chemical Engineers.

Lalvani, G. H. 1985. "Law and Pollution Control." In J. Bandyopadhyay, N. D. Jayal, U. Schoettli, and C. Singh, eds., *India's Environment: Crisis and Responses*, pp. 284–290. Dehra Dun: Natraj Publishers.

Lepkowski, Wil. 1985. "Bhopal: Indian City Begins to Heal But Conflicts Remain." *Chemical and Engineering News* 63, 48 (December 2): 18–32.

———. 1989. Bhopal settlement: Carbide to pay India $470 Million." *Chemical and Engineering News* 67, 8 (20 February): 4–5.

Lok Sabha Secretariat. 1991. *The Public Liability Insurance Bill, 1991, Bill 103-C of 1990*. New Delhi: Lok Sabha Secretariat.

Meyers, P. W. 1990. "Nonlinear Learning in Large Technological Firms. *Research Policy* 19: 97–115.

Ministry of Environment and Forests, 1989. Hazardous Wastes (Management and Handling) Rules. *The Gazette of India Extraordinary*, Part II, Section 3(ii), July 28, 1989. New Delhi: Government of India Press.

———. 1991. *Annual Report, 1990–91*. Delhi: The Ministry.

———. 1992. *Policy Statement for Abatement of Pollution*. No. H. 11013(2)/90-CPW. New Delhi: The Ministry.

Morehouse, Ward, and Arun Subramaniam, 1986. *The Bhopal Tragedy*. New York. Council of International and Public Affairs.

Project 88. 1988. *Project 88: Harnessing Market Forces to Protect the Environment*. Washington, DC: U.S. Government Printing Office.

Ramakrishna, K. 1985. "The Emergence of Environmental Law in the Developing Countries: A Case Study of India." *Ecology Law Quarterly* 12: 907–935.

Sankar, N. 1992. "Industry Alone Not to Blame." In *The Hindu Survey of the Environment, 1992*, pp. 137, 139, 141. Madras: *The Hindu*.

Shastri, Satis. 1988. "Public Interest Litigation and Environmental Pollution." In G. S. Nathawat, Satis Shastri, and J. P. Vyas, eds., *Man, Nature and Environmental Law*, pp. 131–150. Jaipur: RBSA.

Shenoy, M. N. 1989. "Amendment to Factories Act and Its Implications for Management." Paper presented at 17th Workshop on Environmental Management, Administrative Staff College of India, Hyderabad, January 17, 1989.

Shrivastava, Paul. 1987a. *Bhopal: Anatomy of a Crisis*. Cambridge, MA: Ballinger.

———. 1987b. "A Cultural Analysis of Conflicts in Industrial Disaster." *International Journal of Mass Emergencies and Disasters* 5, 3 (November): 243–264.

———. 1987c. "Preventing Industrial Crises: The Challenges of Bhopal." *International Journal of Mass Emergencies and Disasters* 5, 3 (November): 199–221.

———. 1992. *Bhopal: Anatomy of a Crisis*. 2nd ed. London: Chapman.

Simonis, Udo E. 1987. *Ecological Modernisation: New Perspectives for Industrial Societies*. New Delhi: Friedrich Ebert Stiftung.

Singh, C. 1984. "Legal Policy for the Control of Environmental Pollution." In P. Leelakrishnan, ed., *Law and Environment*, pp. 1–27. Cochin, India: University of Cochin, Department of Law.

Stavins, Robert H. 1989. "Harnessing Market Forces to Protect the Environment." *Environment* 31, 1 (January/February): 5–7, 28–35.

Stover, W. 1985. "A Field Day for the Legislators." In *The Chemical Industry After Bhopal*. Proceedings of a two-day international symposium, November 7–8, 1985. London: Oyez IBC.

Technica, Ltd. 1988. *Techniques for Assessing Industrial Hazards-A Manual*. World Bank Technical Paper No. 55. Washington, DC: World Bank.

UNEP/IEO (United Nations Environment Programme/Industry and Environment). 1990. *Environmental Auditing: Report of a United Nations Environment Programme/Industry and Environment (UNEP/IEO) Workshop, Paris, 10–11 January 1989*. Paris: UNEP/IEO.

White, Allen L., and Srinivas Emani. 1990. *Environmental Regulation in Developing Countries: Case Studies of India, Thailand, and Venezuela and Priorities for a Capacity-Building Program*. Boston: Tellus Institute, July.

World Bank. 1988. "World Bank Guidelines for Identifying, Analysing, and Controlling Major Hazard Installations in Developing Countries." Appendix B in Technica, Ltd., *Techniques for Assessing Industrial Hazards*, pp. 126–138.

Chapter 5
Citizen Participation in Environmental Policy Making

Susan G. Hadden

The accident at Bhopal raised concerns about both participation and information because failures of information flow were central to both the accident and its aftermath. One analyst has written:

These failures occurred at various levels: inadequate worker understanding of MIC's toxicity and health threat; lack of knowledge by local government and medical officials of the plant's chemicals and their hazards; poor information during the accident to guide nearby residents; and lack of advice to local medical personnel as to recommended treatment.[1]

Environmental issues more generally provide a useful focus for thinking about the relationship between information and institutions for participation, because decisions to protect the environment must be taken and implemented collectively.

The complex interplay between public access to information and participatory institutions is illustrated in the law passed as part of the United States response to the Bhopal accident. One part of the law, which has proved relatively ineffective, established new institutions intended to bring diverse interests together to develop community emergency-response plans. A different part of the law made available startling new information about environmental risks and has led to significant participatory activity. If the new institutions under the former part could be expanded to allow consideration of the new information provided under the latter, a very effective model for citizen participation might evolve.

India's statutory response to Bhopal, as noted in earlier chapters, consisted largely of extending governmental regulatory power to cover toxics. Although new rules call for additional information from regulated facilities, they require that it be submitted to government authorities rather than to the public. Indian law constituted in this respect less of a break with the past than the U.S. statute. In large part, this response is a reflection of India's as yet less well developed environmental statutes and agencies. A statute to enable local activists is only thinkable after citizens have gained years of experience in expressing their policy preferences and developing responsive institutions. India's top-down statutory response is consistent with the point its environmental policy had reached and may be better suited to the current capacity of its political institutions.

I argue in this chapter that the lessons learned from Bhopal or any other disastrous event depend very strongly on the existing institutional and political context. Societies, like people, can only learn when they are ready. This chapter seeks to identify both the outcomes and the contexts that promote or inhibit societal learning about participation and information provision.

Right to Know

The primary U.S. response to Bhopal was a new statute, the Emergency Planning and Community Right-to-Know Act of 1986. It was passed as the third part or title of the Superfund Amendments and Reauthorization Act (SARA), and is most often called SARA Title III, or simply Title III.[2] The law calls for four different reporting formats, covering three different categories of reporting industries, and defining three different lists of chemicals subject to reporting. This complexity can be explained in large part by the legislative history of Title III.

In the months following Bhopal, more than ten bills were introduced in Congress that included various provisions either concerning emergency response to chemical accidents or giving the public access to information about chemicals in their communities. Meanwhile, Congress was also considering the reauthorization of the Comprehensive Environmental Response, Compensation, and Liability Act of 1980 (CERCLA), better known as "Superfund." Nine committees claimed jurisdiction over the Superfund reauthorization bill, called SARA. During mark-up, the Senate Environmental and Public Works Committee adopted a suggestion of Senator Frank Lautenberg of New Jersey that provisions of his Bhopal-inspired bill be incorporated into SARA. Thus two different environmental issues, hazardous waste disposal and emergency response to toxic chemicals, became closely tied.

This linkage further complicated an already complex issue. Drawing on experiences in their own states or listening to demands from constituents, members of Congress developed four policy responses to Bhopal: emergency planning and response, emergency notification, right to know, and an emissions inventory.[3] Requirements intended to address each of the four concerns were thrown into the statutory pot as the bill moved through its many committees. So massive was SARA that it took two conference committees rather than the usual one to reconcile the differences between the two houses. In conference, moreover, the issues presented by the Superfund portion of the bill were so contentious that the Bhopal-response portions were not considered at length, and overlaps among the four different approaches were not eliminated.

Under the emergency planning program, state governors were required to designate State Emergency Response Commissions (SERCs), which in turn designate local planning districts and Local Emergency Planning Committees (LEPCs). The law specifies that the LEPCs must contain representatives of diverse local groups including emergency responders, health professionals, elected officials, facility representatives, and citizens. Their primary task is to develop an emergency response plan that focuses especially, but not exclusively, on 366 "extremely hazardous chemicals," most of which are airborne toxics like MIC in Bhopal.

Second, the emergency notification provisions, which cover a broader set of chemicals, require facilities to report immediately the identity of the chemical, health effects, and precautions to be taken when more than the "reportable quantity" of one of these chemicals is released. Third, the "community right to know" provisions require most facilities to provide the LEPCs and SERCs with information about the chemicals they store or use in excess of certain threshold quantities. LEPCs may request facilities to provide a Material Safety Data Sheet (MSDS) describing physical characteristics, health effects, handling precautions, and emergency response procedures for any chemical. Any data provided to the LEPC must be made available to the public.

Finally, the "mass balance" or toxic chemical release inventory provisions require manufacturing facilities to provide the Environmental Protection Agency (EPA) with extensive information on releases and disposal of about 350 listed chemicals. Although this information is of interest to regulators in evaluating and updating emissions standards and permits, citizens, too, have access to the data through a computerized data base and can use it to assess their environmental exposures to hazardous substances. This is the most readily comprehensible part of the data made public by Title III, and it has occasioned the greatest interest in the media and among public interest groups.

Given the complexity of Title III, it should come as no surprise that its multiple purposes were fulfilled with varying degrees of success. One important impediment was the failure of Congress to appropriate any funds for its implementation. States and localities were forced to use funds from other related programs or to make special appropriations for Title III activities. EPA, too, was forced to find money within existing programs to carry out its duties under Title III.

A second impediment to achieving the goals of Title III is the structure of the law itself. Quite apart from its complexity, which created uncertainty and slowed compliance, the statute's absolute distinction between local emergency planning and the federal toxic release inventory (TRI) made it difficult for citizens to obtain all the information about a facility in one place: storage information was available at the local and state levels, while release information was available primarily at the national level. The delay in availability of the TRI also inhibited citizen access to the data: 1987 data were submitted in June 1988 and became available in electronic form only in June 1989; 1988 data became available in April 1990.

Finally, the different actors implementing the law often had very different ideas of the true purpose of the right to know. Emergency-response professionals, who tended to dominate state and local Title III activities, saw the right to know more as an aid to their planning activities than as of direct relevance to citizens. Industry, too, focused on increased safety and, in response to the TRI data, on reducing emissions, believing that the data were generally too technical for citizens. Many public interest groups, in contrast, saw in right to know an opportunity to change the power structure in the community, with data providing a hitherto unavailable basis for demonstrating how powerful industries were compromising the health and safety of ordinary citizens. These different perspectives underpinned the inconsistent orientations of the law itself, since each group had the ear of one or more Congressional staff during the long battle over SARA.

Citizen Participation in Emergency Planning and Response

As noted, Title III established State Emergency Response Commissions (SERCs), which in turn designated local planning areas to be covered by Local Emergency Planning Committees (LEPCs). In part because LEPCs are required to have citizen representation, while SERCs are not, and in part because LEPCs are easier to reach physically, citizen activities have tended to focus on LEPCs. Since there are approximately 3,500 LEPCs, generalization is difficult. Not only are citizens usually the least well-informed and smallest contingent within LEPCs, but emergency planning itself seems not to excite much interest except in communities where accidents have occurred recently. In those communities, citizens have evinced great interest in participating on the LEPC, but industry domination has often frustrated them. Nevertheless, LEPCs represent a serious effort to create institutions through which citizens can receive and act upon information, so the causes of their relative inefficacy are worth considering.

The statutory duty of LEPCs was to write an emergency-response plan by October 17, 1988, the second anniversary of Title III's passage. A successful response plan accounts for the nature and quantity of the hazardous chemicals stored and used in the community, ensuring that responders are properly equipped to control accidents involving very different types of hazards. These provisions reflect the most basic lessons from Bhopal, where lack of information about the nature and even the presence of MIC stymied early response efforts. A full-scale plan requires that a risk-benefit analysis be conducted at each site where hazardous chemicals are stored or used. Based on the results of that analysis and an assessment of the community's response capability, a locality can take a variety of actions, from working with particular sites to reduce the risk of serious accidents to increasing response capability through training or resources.

A primary impediment to successful emergency response has been the lack of coordination among varied experts and agencies. Fire departments, police, and emergency medical service personnel from one or more political jurisdictions are often called to an accident. In the past, many of these people were either untrained in methods appropriate to different hazardous chemicals or did not have access to the necessary specialized equipment. Various federal and state agencies may also have been involved in the response. Finally, large private facilities may maintain their own response equipment and personnel, hoping in part to minimize liability from inappropriate actions by untrained people.

Congress specifically designed LEPCs to overcome the lack of coordination in emergency response. LEPC members with expertise in all aspects of emergencies were brought together to formulate a coherent plan. In practice, however, LEPC activities often exacerbated jurisdictional disputes among existing agencies. In some areas, cities and surrounding counties were included in one LEPC but had separate fire, emergency medical, and planning departments; in others, cities had such capabilities but counties did not. In a surprising number of jurisdictions, fire departments and emergency medical services were unused to working together and subverted attempts to develop a unified plan. Contending agencies tended to hide their real concerns about turf behind technical arguments, making it very difficult for citizens to understand or participate in these debates.

Lacking resources and expertise, LEPCs often achieve "coordination" by allowing industry to create a coherent plan; this tendency is especially marked in the several hundred communities where chemical manufacturers had banded together to create emergency plans even before SARA's passage. Many LEPCs have also been reluctant to conduct risk analyses of individual facilities for fear of antagonizing those found to be most risky. The LEPC on which I served was prevented from publishing information about toxic releases by a county attorney with sensitivity to industry concerns. She argued that it was "illegal" for the county LEPC to publish the data submitted to state and federal, not county, agencies. Between industry domination and agency turf battles, therefore, few LEPC plans can be said to represent a true community consensus.

In order to improve citizen participation in decision making about hazardous materials, LEPCs must ensure that citizens understand and can act upon the data about storage and use. As noted, the statute did not address this concern. For example, citizen members are generally at a considerable disadvantage in a body composed of many technical experts, whether from government or industry. This common problem is especially important in groups considering risk, because experts usually limit their definitions of risk to probability and magnitude, while lay assessments of risk often take into account such qualitative factors as equity, fairness, and controllability.[4] Thus citizens might seek a plan that would take special notice of facilities near schools or nursing homes or of facilities storing carcinogens. Unless the number of citizen members is relatively large, however, such concerns could easily be ignored by the technical majority.

Citizens, however, do not constitute a majority or even a significant minority in most LEPCs. In one multistate survey, few members were found to be "citizens" (people without any industry ties) and still fewer (10 percent) represented environmental groups.[5] A survey of all members of the major LEPCs in Texas conducted in late 1988 found that many who had been appointed as "community" or "environmental" representatives did not identify themselves as such: 15 of 40 supposed environmental group appointees and 14 of 35 community-group members identified themselves as representing other interests, especially business.[6] In August 1987 I attended a Texas SERC meeting that was reviewing LEPC appointments from around the state; in several cases, members of the local Chamber of Commerce were appointed as "community group" representatives. Under such circumstances, it is not difficult to see why appointees have mixed loyalties and why the citizen perspective may be diluted. In both surveys mentioned above, LEPC membership was found to be distorted in other ways: 86 percent of members were male and more than 30 percent in each case had postgraduate degrees.[7] Whether such citizens represent the concerns of their less educated or less business-oriented neighbors is open to question.

The attitudes of LEPC chairmen (all were male) and agency personnel toward citizens also inhibit participation. An informal survey of LEPC chairmen in Texas showed that most believed citizens were not capable of understanding Title III information.[8] The multistate survey confirmed that LEPC members have a high interest in but low time commitment to citizen participation, with chairmen caring even less about participation. Most defined the task of the LEPC narrowly, focusing on the plan rather than on citizen outreach.

In short, available data give cause for concern about citizen participation on LEPCs. Neither the numbers of "citizen" members nor their perceptions of the role of the LEPCs seem to indicate a high degree of activity or effectiveness. The experience of the Durham, North Carolina, LEPC is an exception. Early on, this body adopted a guideline that the number of citizen representatives would be equal to the number of facility representatives. Elaborate subcommittees, access to the resources of nearby universities, a prior history of strong citizen participation in hazardous waste activities, and a recent accident have all helped citizen members to change the design of the plan and to determine additional outreach activities by the LEPC.[9] A vice-chairman with long experience in citizen participation in Durham and continual "hounding" of citizens to participate also account for the relative success of this LEPC.

In the large Texas survey, nearly half the respondents believed that the most important role of the LEPC is to facilitate meetings between citizens and industry.[10] But LEPCs may also participate in activities initiated by citizen groups. The Coalition Against Toxics (CAT) in New Jersey used the TRI emissions data to target five facilities and approached them seeking opportunities for plant inspections. Dynasil Corporation of America, a manufacturer of high-purity glass located in Berlin, New Jersey, responded positively and invited the LEPC and some neighbors to join in the tour along with CAT. The New Jersey group also brought along an industrial hygienist whose services were paid for by the National Toxics Coalition.[11] After the inspection tour, the group made five recommendations for reducing risk and improving worker safety. Within a month, Dynasil had implemented them all.

The successes and failures of LEPCs highlight fundamental questions about the nature of citizen participation in policy arenas with a strong technical component and, ultimately, about a society's ability to learn from disaster. On the one hand, the predominance of emergency response specialists on many committees may have resulted in increased safety for the entire community. On the other hand, few LEPCs have managed to increase the level of awareness in the broader community or to involve citizens in a meaningful way. Some of this failure has occurred not because of the LEPC professional members' willful elitism but because the storage of hazardous materials in fixed facilities is of low salience to citizens. LEPCs that have actively discouraged citizen participation are far outnumbered by those that have simply not actively sought it. But if the opportunity is offered and not taken, it may be fair to say that the goal of participation has been met at least in part. The LEPCs' limited mandate may also account in part for the somewhat disappointing level of citizen participation, in contrast to the toxic-release data, which successfully mobilized many citizen groups.

Citizen Participation in Reducing Hazardous Emissions

Section 313 of Title III requires manufacturing facilities to report their emissions of about 350 hazardous chemicals. Each seven-page report covers one chemical emitted from a particular facility, detailing how the emissions estimate was obtained as well as which streams or water-treatment plants the emissions reach. These data are entered, by law, into an electronic database, so that citizens and regulators can identify emissions problems by region, company, facility, or chemical. Publicized by the media and environmental groups, the data have stimulated considerable participation by citizens at every level of government.

The toxic-release data serve several purposes: to identify a problem (or provide hitherto unavailable hard evidence of a problem), to mobilize people to seek political remedies, and to suggest means of resolving or reducing the problem. However, in almost every case, already-organized environmental groups were needed as intermediaries to make the data useable. The services they performed included knowing what facts were available and how to acquire them; knowing how to use computerized data systems; knowing how to analyze the data and where to find relevant supplementary information; and mobilizing citizens or politicians to achieve desired results.

Without the aid of intermediary groups, even the electronic database created under Title III (called the Toxic Release Inventory, or TRI) is not entirely adequate to the task of providing access to data, because it is difficult to locate and not "user-friendly."[12] Once citizens do acquire data through the TRI, they must interpret it, determine whether risks are a cause for concern, and, if they are, persuade manufacturers to reduce their emissions. Title III does not grant citizens access to the supplementary information needed to interpret the data, although EPA and many private groups are providing such assistance. In short, access to data is but the first step in a complex process of analysis, risk assessment, and mobilizing political participation. Title III concerns only the first step—a necessary one, to be sure, and one that was previously extremely difficult. A wide variety of public interest groups were poised to assist citizens in taking one or more of the later steps.

The first activity undertaken by public interest groups (and journalists) was to print reports about chemical releases at the local or state level. EPA did not computerize the data for more than a year, so that citizens first had access to the computerized database containing reports for 1987 only in June 1989.[13] Groups lucky enough to live in states that took responsibility for computerizing their own data could publish reports much earlier; in some cases the states themselves published reports. Other groups simply entered the emissions data for their localities by hand and manipulated it using spreadsheet or database programs available for personal computers. Table 5.1 summarizes the reports issued in 1989 and early 1990.

As public interest groups continued to acquire data, transform it into comprehensible form, and publicize it, four types of policy outcomes became feasible: new laws, emissions reductions, legal actions, and improved enforcement of other environmental laws. A few illustrations of each will suggest the richness of participatory activities stimulated by access to the toxic release data.

Legislation

In response to concern generated by the TRI data, new legislation to regulate toxic emissions was introduced in several states, including Louisiana and North Carolina. Massachusetts and Oregon passed toxics-use reduction laws, with the state Public Interest Research Group (PIRG) taking a leading role in both lobbying and drafting legislation.

Table 5.1. Emmissions Reports Issued Through January 1990 from TRI Data

Issuer	Federal	State	Regional	Local	Other
			Level		
Interest group	6	15	7	5	2
State agency	7				
Congressional office	1		1		
EPA	1				
Industry-specific			2		2

Source: Compiled from Working Group on Community Right-to-Know, "Reports Using Toxic Release Inventory Data" (Washington, DC: Working Group, January 1990).

As Table 5.1 shows, many of the reports developed by public interest groups concerned emissions in a locality or region rather than the state. Two examples from California illustrate how groups used the reports to achieve increases in citizens' well-being. In one case, the San Diego Environmental Health Coalition worked with two low-income, minority neighborhood groups to develop land-use amendments that would limit industry's ability to use hazardous materials near schools and residences. Under the ordinance, new businesses cannot enter the zoned areas if they use large quantities of listed hazardous materials; existing businesses are given a conditional-use permit that requires them to reduce the quantities of materials stored and used on site.[14] In the second case, in the south Bay area, the Coalition for a Better Environment used the TRI and supplementary local data to identify pollutants being dumped into three sewers and persuaded the state water board to ban discharges of these substances into the public water system.[15]

Emissions Reduction

The most dramatic result of the TRI data is actual reductions in emissions of toxic substances. Many companies voluntarily pledged to reduce their emissions because they feared the negative publicity attendant upon announcing large quantities of emissions; perhaps the most famous was the off-the-cuff pledge made by Monsanto's president to reduce emissions by 90 percent over five years.[16]

After the data were collected, many more companies decided to announce emissions reductions; they simply had not realized how much money they were wasting through fugitive emissions. Plans for reducing emissions appeared sound from an immediate budgetary standpoint as well as from the standpoint of community relations. A number of companies also created advisory panels of residents and employees, some of which have been in existence long enough to provide specific recommendations about operating procedures that companies can adopt.[17] Finally, the Chemical Manufacturers Association developed a program called "Responsible Care," which requires all members to agree to a range of activities including community outreach, emissions reduction, and assistance to non-member facilities with fewer technical resources.

In a few cases, citizens tried to negotiate directly with industry for specific reductions. For example, Texans United (TU), a state affiliate of the National Toxics Campaign Fund, targeted an Exxon facility in Baytown, Texas. The facility contains two chemical plants and a refinery, and listed more than 80 million pounds of releases in the TRI reports for 1987. Following a large and well-publicized spill of hydrofluoric acid in nearby Texas City, the Exxon facility manager, who had long been committed to public outreach, approached Texans United about further improving community relations.[18] Texans United had helped organize a community group, Baytown Citizens Against Pollution (BayCAP) in the neighborhood of the facility, and TU suggested that Exxon work with BayCAP to develop a "good neighbor" agreement.[19] Exxon discussed its emergency response and environmental practices with BayCAP, which then submitted a list of questions concerning the four chemicals that constituted the primary emissions from the facility—benzene, toluene, hydrogen sulfide, and chlorine—as well as requesting a history of accidents. With TU's assistance, BayCAP was able to interpret Exxon's responses and to formulate demands to present to the company. Negotiations for a "good neighbor" agreement were well underway when, in the wake of the Exxon Valdez oil spill, Exxon suddenly broke them off, arguing that TU organizers had betrayed the spirit of the negotiations.[20] The dispute ended eventually with a pledge by Exxon to reduce emissions by half over five years.

The Baytown events highlight the importance of experienced citizen groups like TU in emissions reduction. First, TU organized the neighborhood group, BayCAP, using the TRI data to scare them. Citizens in low-income neighborhoods have typically been afraid to challenge industry unless mobilized in this way by outsiders. Second, TU provided much of the technical analysis needed for the negotiations. Citizens are usually at a disadvantage and must have access to technical assistance in order to participate as equals in interactions with industry. Third, TU had concerns other than achieving emissions reductions—namely, increasing its membership and visibility. TU apparently was willing to sacrifice the negotiations at a key moment for the sake of these other goals, perhaps knowing that the facility would reduce emissions anyway. We will return to these features of citizen participation in the discussion of Indian environmental activism.

Legal Actions

Title III provides that citizens may file suits against facilities that are failing to report emissions data. Courts may award legal fees to the prevailing party, and penalties for non-complying facilities may range up to $25,000 per violation. Citizens proposing to file suits must notify facilities, state agencies, and EPA, after which EPA has sixty days to preclude the suit by taking enforcement actions itself. The Atlantic States Legal Foundation filed its intent to sue seven companies on October 10, 1989. Within the sixty-day period, EPA conducted investigations, found five companies in violation, and brought action against them. This precluded ASLF from taking action against the two remaining companies. The notices achieved their goal in part, however: six of the facilities filed their emissions reports within the same sixty-day period. Subsequently, the regional EPA office and ASLF worked out a "cooperative enforcement strategy" in which both organizations will play a role in holding apparent violators accountable.[21]

Enforcement of Other Environmental Laws

Title III data can assist in enforcing other environmental laws. Section 304(l) of the Clean Water Act, for example, requires each state to identify waters polluted by certain toxic organics and heavy metals—toxic "hotspots." States must alter the permits of facilities discharging into such hotspots. In autumn 1989, citizens were given the opportunity to petition EPA to add more hotspots to the list.[22] Using the TRI database, the Natural Resources Defense Council assisted citizens in Virginia and Georgia in finding additional hotspots, which they petitioned EPA to add. The Environmental Defense Fund and the Clean Water Fund of North Carolina petitioned EPA to add fifteen new spots; another group, Clean Water Action, filed a petition to add the Houston Ship Channel and Galveston Bay to the list of Texas hotspots.[23] In each case, TRI data had to be supplemented with additional data and analysis supplied by organized environmental groups.

Title III toxic emissions data not only stimulated and revived many environmental groups, but also caused several existing groups to come together to form networks. For example, under the auspices of a private foundation, about thirty organizations came together to form a computer network, called RTKNet. The computer system, developed especially for the group, provided e-mail, conferences, and access to relevant documents and computer programs. Representatives from each participating group were trained in using the network.[24] Sharing information and resources has characterized Title III activities perhaps more than any other environmental arena. Whether this is because the data are so rich that they can only be mined collectively, or whether the spirit of right to know has begun to pervade relations among often competitive groups, it is surely a trend to be applauded.

Why did toxic emissions and the TRI become focal points for participatory activities and general excitement while the institutionally more innovative LEPCs were characterized by apathy or low effectiveness? The fact that there was an emergency-response establishment that could capture the LEPCs is surely one contributory factor. Emergency planning—forestalling possible problems—may also be a topic of lower salience than toxic emissions already affecting people's environments. The specificity of the emissions data contributed to the relative ease of publicity; so the media often became more involved with emissions than with emergency response. Finally, the very large size of many of the emissions, which by law are reported in pounds per year, gave them a dramatic impact that could not be matched by the storage data.

The different characteristics of the two sets of activities (which, in fairness, should not be overstated) suggest some important lessons about the relationship between institutions and information. Clearly, information alone does not empower people. The information must be in a form that can be understood and, frequently, community organizers or someone else must both publicize and interpret it. (In Europe, this function is served by the government; see this volume, Chapter 6.) In turn, the interpreters and publicizers gain opportunities to steer public concern in directions that do not necessarily correspond to the greatest level of risk reduction. Thus, in most communities, the risks from accidents involving stored chemicals are higher than those involving the long-term, low-level exposures associated with toxic emissions, but the more dramatic emissions data have either elicited or been used to elicit more public concern than the storage data. Participation in LEPCs has been less intense than participation in emissions issues, even though LEPCs may have had a more immediate effect on public safety and health than public interest groups wielding the TRI. In sum, LEPCs are an innovative institution still looking for a mission, while concerns about toxic emissions have been channeled through older institutional mechanisms that are better able to assist citizens both in interpreting information and in undertaking appropriate political action.

Environmental Activism in India

The most striking feature of the U.S. response to Bhopal is that it engendered much involvement among government and industry as well as community residents. Title III marked a break with the past by making citizens as well as government a recipient of reporting data, thereby enabling participation. If so much activity was generated in the United States by an incident ten thousand miles away, it seems reasonable to ask whether similar ferment was occasioned nearer to the scene of the disaster. This section briefly considers this question. One important Indian response to the Bhopal accident was a new environmental statute, just as in the United States. However, differences between the two countries in the infrastructures for environmental activism, an important determinant of the ability to learn from disaster, resulted in a response that focused more on extending governmental oversight than on enabling citizen participation.

India's new environmental law was enacted in 1986 at a time when the state of environmental concern and activism in India in many ways resembled that in the United States in the late 1960s. Although India had laws to protect air and water, for example, primary responsibility for environmental protection remained at the state level. Similarly, toxic substances were not covered by existing statutes, which focused on "conventional" pollutants. Environmental groups were largely national in scope and focused on relatively abstract and large-scale concerns such as wildlife or natural areas preservation. At the same time, the environmental movement was changing. Many local voluntary groups active in relief or development had discovered that environmental degradation directly affected their poor constituents and begun to take an interest in protecting or restoring forests, water quality, and air quality. New development projects in particular were scrutinized for their effects on the poorest sectors, and outside activists often helped mobilize citizens to oppose such projects.

The typical mode of action of pre-Bhopal environmental groups is perhaps best illustrated by the highly publicized environmental controversy in India's Silent Valley, where a large dam for hydroelectric power was to be erected by the Kerala State Electricity Board. The Valley, which purportedly gets its name from the absence of otherwise ubiquitous cicadas, contained a large stand of virgin tropical rain forest. The controversy, which emerged in late 1977, engaged complex political issues, including federal-state relations, the politics of Communist-dominated Kerala state, and the exploitation of Third World resources by First World nations, as well as traditional environmental concerns—preservation versus development, endangered species, deforestation, and loss of potentially valuable species.[25]

The activists who brought Silent Valley to the attention of the nation and the world represented the old school of Indian environmentalists—educated, relatively wealthy, and predominantly urban citizens involved in Bombay-based groups such as the World Wildlife Fund, Friends of the Trees, and Save Bombay Committee. In addition, members of the Kerala Sastra Sahitya Parishad (KSSP), founded in 1962 to translate science articles for the benefit of Malayalam-speaking Keralans, the most literate of all India's linguistic communities, played a very strong role. The KSSP, whose members are also generally well educated, organized a mass signature campaign in 1978, conducted a "techno-economic and socio-political assessment" of the project in 1979, and mobilized its membership of teachers and students to spread information about the hydroelectric dam. Yet, although concern was widespread, most analysts attribute the eventual cancellation of the project to Prime Minister Indira Gandhi's personal intervention and to a political deal that owed little to public participation.

Another feature of environmental activism prior to Bhopal was the growing awareness by thousands of non-governmental organizations involved in charitable, relief, or development work in India's countryside that environmental degradation was central to poverty. Many began to undertake projects, such as reforestation or provision of alternative fuel stoves, that contributed both to development and to restoring the environment. In addition, activist groups discovered that the unintended side-effects of many development projects affected the poorest especially adversely. The report entitled *The State of India's Environment, 1982*, published by the Centre for Science and Environment in New Delhi, contained story after story about the health effects suffered by neighbors of development projects such as dams and factories.[26]

As understanding became more widespread, activists took steps to assist local groups in protesting against proposed new facilities. For example, thousands of local residents, primarily tribals, halted for more than five years a partly completed bauxite mining project of Bharat Aluminum Company Ltd. (Balco) at Gandhamardan in Orissa state. Concerned at the signs of destruction they witnessed when the project finally got underway, residents, primarily women, blocked roads and conducted demonstrations. Forty villages participated, each one responsible for the road blockade on a particular day. A group of Orissan intellectuals in Delhi ensured that the issue was heard at the national level; at the site, another steering committee, formed with the aid of educated activists from outside the area, met regularly with local and state officials to pursue the villagers' objections.[27]

The accident at Bhopal altered the focus of environmental activism in two important ways: by causing a new law to be passed (the Environment Protection Act of 1986) and by heightened awareness of the environment in the courts. The strong potential of the new law has yet to be fulfilled for reasons closely related to Indian activists' expectations of the state. The proximate cause of delay was the failure of the Ministry of Environment and Forests to implement the portions of the Environment Protection Act (EPA) concerned with toxic chemicals until 1989, though these were clearly responsive to concerns raised by Bhopal (see Chapter 4, this volume, for more detail on this point). But the ambivalent attitude of activists toward government as the agent even of desirable change also accounts in part for the deliberate pace at which the rules were formulated.

The EPA was introduced by the Administration and passed with little debate and still less public demand; indeed, in the summer following the incident at Bhopal, few activists perceived the new law as a direct or suitable response. Perhaps the early emphasis on provisions concerning "conventional," or non-toxic, pollutants contributed to this perception. In any event, given environmental groups' longstanding perception that laws serve more as symbols than as statements of real intentions, it is not surprising that the EPA did not engender the same public enthusiasm that greeted Title III in the United States.

The problems in implementing the law have been exacerbated by a general decline in political effectiveness in India.[28] The erosion of party (especially Congress Party) infrastructure at the local level, the continued economic squeeze on the clerical class by rising costs of housing and necessities, and continued ethnic and class violence have all contributed to a state of affairs in which it is increasingly difficult to pursue such collective goals as environmental protection. While such a crisis may increase the extent of grass-roots environmental activism in the near term, it also limits groups' long-term abilities to achieve their goals, because no institutions are powerful enough to achieve closure on decisions. These factors place severe constraints on Indian society's ability to learn.

In this context, it is perhaps not surprising that the events at Bhopal were followed by an increase in environmental litigation. Although citizens could not bring environmental lawsuits directly under the

Air or Water Acts, the Supreme Court accepted such suits under Section 133 of the Criminal Procedure Code, which prohibits nuisances, and under Article 21 of the Constitution, which grants rights to life and personal liberty—rights that petitioners asserted were infringed by having to live in a polluted environment. Despite the difficulties of pursuing such suits, the courts have become an important avenue for citizen activism and protest. The Supreme Court has entertained environmental cases filed by voluntary organizations and by public-spirited individuals as well as those initiated by judges.[29]

The Environment Protection Act supports public interest litigation by allowing citizens to file suits against offending facilities, provided they give sixty days notice to appropriate governmental authorities. If the agency takes action itself during that period, the citizens are precluded from filing a suit. This section of the law followed closely similar provisions in U.S. environmental laws, including SARA Title III. The purpose of the delay is to discourage overuse of the courts and to encourage use of standard enforcement mechanisms. In short, the notice of intent to file suit offers a means for citizens to help regulatory agencies identify offenders without necessarily participating directly in enforcement procedures. Unlike Title III, however, the Act does not provide new participatory institutions, nor does it provide citizens with access to new information that would aid them in assessing environmental impacts. Instead, it imitates older Indian laws in leaving the primary responsibility for assessing and mitigating environmental risks with the government.

At the moment, then, the context for environmental decision making in India limits activism to two major forms: local protest movements and lawsuits, both of which are more effective in blocking development than in guiding it wisely. These negative participatory formats gave environmentalism a bad name in the United States for many years. As attractive as more proactive and non-adversarial mechanisms would appear to be, however, the lack of the necessary infrastructure—low cost and efficient communications, institutions through which grass-roots advocates may affect policy making, and a culture of regulatory compliance in industry—raises questions about their viability in India, at least in the short term.

Social Learning and Citizen Participation

The events in Bhopal raised concern worldwide about toxic chemicals in the community, emergency response, and worker training—subjects directly linked to the accident itself. In the United States, Bhopal motivated passage of a new law that had important implications for public participation. It ensured citizen access to formerly unavailable data and provided new opportunities for community-based planning for hazardous chemicals. U.S. environmentalists had long been frustrated by the lack of data for policy making, including data about the nature and quantity of chemicals stored at or emitted from local facilities. Bhopal prompted an examination of U.S. statutes that revealed how easy it was for local facilities to store, use, manufacture, or emit chemicals as toxic as MIC without local residents' knowledge. The right to information then became an accepted part of the policy agenda. Activists stepped in to acquire, manipulate, interpret, and disseminate information to the public as soon as SARA Title III offered a mechanism for obtaining it.

Although Indian environmentalists were also well aware of the lack of information, they faced other problems of greater immediacy. Among these were the absence of any laws clearly covering toxic substances, the domination of the planning process for new industrial facilities by non-environmental concerns, the continuing pollution of water and air by non-toxics, the inability of regulators to oversee more than a small portion of facilities, and, always, the environmental degradation attendant upon widespread poverty. Environmentalists in India also operated in a milieu in which public participation in facility siting was virtually unknown, and industry had a tradition of non-compliance with environmental standards. Finally, a widespread perception that government was often in cahoots with industry made the concept of industry-provided, government-monitored data inherently suspect.

These contrasts suggest that disasters pick up on resonances already present in social discourse. An accident such as the one at Bhopal, with a complex chain of causation, provides a wide range of possible lessons that different societies may learn. But, in a given society, crises and disasters do not create entirely new ideas or concerns so much as enhance existing ones. In India, the accident called into question existing procedures, largely closed to the public, for siting chemical or other industrial facilities. In the United States, where siting was already a matter for at least limited public participation, Bhopal clarified the need for greater access to information about facilities already in place. Because hazardous chemicals were already partly covered by U.S. laws, new initiatives could focus on extending and refining that coverage; India's laws generally did not cover toxics, and revisions focused in part on filling that gap.

With less than six years experience in implementing SARA Title III, we can already abstract some important lessons. While information remains an essential component of political power, information alone does not empower the recipients. The nexus between data and action is not obvious to most people; of those who can see the relationship, many do not find an issue sufficiently salient or the cost of acting low enough to merit participation. Various supportive mechanisms are needed, including institutions through which people can act if they wish. Institutions themselves gain strength when people need, use, and act through them, even altering them as necessary to suit their purposes. Thus LEPCs provided an unusual opportunity for a wide range of interests to work together, but their focus on emergency response limited their utility primarily to communities where a spill had recently occurred. Recently, people in some localities have begun to talk·about extending the purview of the LEPC to environmental issues other than hazardous materials, a development that would surely increase their vitality and salience.

Can these lessons about the right to know usefully be transferred to other nations, especially India? Some of the infrastructure needed to use information as an effective enabler of citizen participation is present in India: effluent standards and permits to serve as yardsticks, organized environmental activists, and a growing public and industry awareness of the costs of environmental degradation. Other elements necessary to an effective information program are lacking, however, the most important of which may be a high threshold level of economic development (see Reich and Shrivastava, this volume, Chapters 9 and 12). Countries and communities have an implicit ordering of risks and turn their attentions to those lower on the list only after higher concerns are met. Thus long-term health risks from exposure to toxics became a concern in the United States only after the more obvious risks from conventional pollutants had been mitigated. The Indian political agenda may still be focused primarily on short-term technological risks or on even more basic human needs, such as food and shelter. A final precondition, perhaps the most unlikely to be achieved soon, is a culture of collective decision making. LEPCs and similar institutions can only work when some notion of the collective good, however inchoate, motivates disagreeing interests to work together.

Although the accident in Bhopal led, in the short run, to more direct public participation in the United States than in India, the central role of information in motivating effective public control of hazards can no longer be doubted. The rules concerning toxics promulgated under the Environment Protection Act show that Indian policy makers appreciate the value of open information as much as their U.S. counterparts. The rules require, for instance, that imported hazardous chemicals be accompanied by product-safety information and that port authorities be notified of shipments of hazardous chemicals. Whether the Indian government will be as responsive when citizens ask for disclosure concerning domestic facilities remains to be seen. But the important point is that they will surely ask. In democracies everywhere, the platitude that knowledge is power has taken on new meaning as citizens seek to regain control over their environment. Perhaps that is the most important legacy of the accident in Bhopal.

Notes

1. Armin Rosencranz, "Bhopal, Transnational Corporations, and Hazardous Technologies," *Ambio* 17, 5 (1988): 341.

2. This statement was true until mid-1991, when the U.S. Environmental Protection Agency, the primary implementing entity, decided that EPCRA (for Emergency Planning and Community Right-to-Know Act) would be the official name for the law.

3. For additional details about the history, intent, and provisions of the law as well as a discussion of its early implementation, see Susan G. Hadden, *A Citizen's Right to Know: Risk Communication and Public Policy* (Boulder, CO: Westview Press, 1989).

4. Paul Slovic, "Perception of Risk," *Science* 236 (April 17, 1987): 280–285.

5. W. David Conn, William L. Owens, and Richard C. Rich, *Communicating with the Public About Hazardous Materials: An Examination of Local Practice* (Washington, DC: U.S. Environmental Protection Agency, 1990)..

6. The survey had a 33 percent response rate. Vickie V. Sutton, "Perceptions of Local Emergency Planning Committee Members Responsibility for Risk Communication and a Proposed Model Risk Communication Program for Local Emergency Planning Committees under SARA Title III," Ph.D. dissertation, University of Texas at Dallas, 1989, p. 105.

7. Ibid., p. 113.

8. Hadden, *Citizen's Right to Know*, p. 74.

9. Frances M. Lynn, "Citizen Involvement in Using Community Right-to-Know Information for Emergency Planning and Source Reduction," paper presented at the 82d annual meeting, Air and Waste Management Association, Anaheim, CA, June 1989; supplemented by telephone interview with Frances Lynn, February 20, 1990.

10. Sutton, "Perceptions of Local Emergency Planning Committee Members," p. 127.

11. Interview with Jane Nogaki, Chair, CAT, April 2, 1990. The National Toxics Coalition provides these services to many groups around the country.

12. For a discussion of the process of developing the database, see Hadden, *Citizen's Right to Know*, chapter 5.

13. Data covering 1987 were required to be submitted by July 1, 1988. In

June 1988, in preparation for the July release date, many industry groups conducted activities that are discussed below.

14. *Working Notes* (newsletter of the Working Group on Community Right-to-Know, Washington, DC), December 1989, p. 3.

15. Telephone interview with Julia May, Coalition for a Better Environment, February 20, 1990.

16. Robert Steyer, "Monsanto Volunteers to Cut Toxic Emissions at All Plants," *St. Louis Post-Dispatch*, July 1, 1988, p. 1.

17. See the case studies in Chemical Manufacturers Association, *Advisory Panels: Options for Community Outreach* (Washington, DC: The Association, 1990).

18. *Working Notes*, August 1989, p. 3.

19. Bill Dawson, "Pollution Gets Public Scrutiny," *Houston Chronicle*, February 12, 1989, p. B1. Also stories in *Working Notes* and communications from both sides to the author.

20. Bill Dawson, "Talks on Toxic Air Emissions Break Off," *Houston Chronicle* July 24, 1989, p. 9. Other informants told me that TU placed a "Shame on Exxon" banner on the plant gate and then chained Bhopal victims who were touring the United States to the gate, so that the "Shame" banner appeared to refer to emissions rather than the oil spill.

21. Interview with Charlie Tebbutt, attorney, Atlantic States Legal Foundation, May 3, 1990.

22. *Federal Register* 54:23868 ff., especially p. 23894, June 2, 1989.

23. *Working Notes*, December 1989, p. 1.

24. Although RTKNet was dissolved in its initial form after about eighteen months, the information and membership were moved to Econet, a larger electronic network covering a range of environmental issues, and the training function was significantly expanded to meet the requests of members who felt their underutilization of the telecommunications tool was partly a result of lack of experience and competence. See memo from Millie Buchanan, Chair, RTKNet, to members, on October 20, 1989 meeting. I was present at all the meetings of the full group. Like the Indian groups discussed below, it seemed that many of the groups' resources were so constrained that they could not afford the additional effort needed to participate fully in computer networking. A critical mass of information providers was not reached; so users did not continually find new information to stimulate continued interest. Finally, the network was not fun to use, especially for novices, and did not encourage exploration of additional capabilities. These difficulties should be overcome with the new emphasis on training and ties to a network with a much larger user base.

25. For a good discussion of the chronology and content of the Silent Valley controversy, see Darryl D'Monte, *Temples and Tombs* (New Delhi: Centre for Science and Environment, 1985).

26. Centre for Science and Environment, *The State of India's Environment* (New Delhi: CSE, 1983). Follow-up volumes of the same title but nearly double in length were published in 1985 and 1991.

27. *Hindustan Times*, January 15, 1989, p. 1. For a history of the events, see A. B. Mishra, "Mining a Hill and Undermining a Society: The Case of Gandhamardan," in Anil Agarwal, Darryl D'Monte, and Ujwala Samarth, *The Fight for Survival: People's Action for Environment* (New Delhi: Centre for Science and Environment, 1987), pp. 125–144.

28. Pranab Bhardan, lecture at the University of Texas at Austin, March 15, 1990.

29. Satis Shastri, "Public Interest Litigation and Environmental Pollution," in G. S. Nathawat, Satis Shastri, and J. P. Vyas, *Man, Nature, and Environmental Law* (Jaipur: RBSA, 1988), pp. 131–150.

Chapter 6
Disaster Prevention in Europe

Josée van Eijndhoven

Risk regulation has developed somewhat differently in Europe than in either the United States or India. Two important explanatory variables are differences in regulatory strategy and differences in the incidents that shaped public attention to hazards. With respect to strategy, most European countries, unlike the United States, require that a license be granted for a chemical plant to start operating. In some countries licensing requirements have been in effect for more than a hundred years. Prussia, for instance, first adopted regulations on the safety of steam engines and boilers in 1828.[1] By 1845 these had evolved into a licensing system. A licensing procedure tends to shift the burden of proof on safety to an early point in time, namely to a moment before operations have started. Debate on the acceptability of a plant's effects on its employees or its environment become part of the process of starting up the plant. A licensing system also shifts the responsibility for the safety of the plant in the sense that the authorities, in granting a license, accept that the plant can be safely operated.

The second difference between Europe and the United States is related to the accidents that have influenced policy. I argue in this chapter that the actual shape of disasters and the perception of their cause and relevance are very important in determining the reaction to them. The major accidents, most notably Bhopal, that helped shape risk management in other parts of the world were not nearly so important in Europe.[2] Accidents that were seen as locally relevant were at least as influential, before as well as after 1984. The 1976 Seveso accident stands out as most important from the standpoint of risk regulation in Europe. Specific features of this accident can be recognized in the European Directive (Council Directive 82/501/EEC) that is commonly called the Seveso Directive.

But Europe does not stand isolated in the world. Interactions between Europe and other countries ensure that trends in risk management do not differ appreciably from those in other countries, although the way things are organized may differ, mainly because of differences in accident histories and differences in legal and political culture. In what follows, I discuss the management of industrial risks in Europe as a process of mutual accommodation between a large number of actors, leading to a result that can be seen as the temporary end point of a process of institutional learning. The specific conceptualization and practices in each country, however, are influenced by local accidents and circumstances.

Disasters and National Legislation

In the 1970s several industrial disasters throughout Europe drew attention to the hazard potential of chemicals and the chemical industry. These were the accident at the Nypro plant in Flixborough in the United Kingdom (1974, 28 casualties), the ethylene explosion at the Beek site of Dutch State Mines in the Netherlands (1975, 14 casualties), and the explosion of a tank car at a camp site in Los Alfaquez in Spain (1978, 225 casualties).

Especially influential as well as earliest was the accident in Flixborough. On June 1, 1974 at 16.54 hours local time, an explosion of cyclohexane at the Nypro plant in Flixborough caused 28 fatalities and wounded 36 people. Because the explosion occurred on a Saturday, the number of deaths was much lower than could have been expected on a normal working day. Although the neighborhood was relatively thinly populated, a large number of residents were injured, and almost all the 2,000 houses in the three neighboring villages were damaged.

The inquiry after the disaster showed that a broken-down reactor had been bypassed by a pipe that was not well enough supported. As a result the pipe broke down during operation. A competent engineer would have observed that the replacement was inadequate, but according to the report prepared after the accident no process engineer had been available at the site in the weeks immediately preceding.[3] The unnoticed defect in the operation of the plant was important in shaping the British response to the accident.

In the year of the Flixborough disaster a foundation was laid for the regulatory control of major hazards in British industry by the 1974 Health and Safety at Work Act (HSW Act). The HSW Act set down the principles and structures by which health and safety in the workplace could be ensured. At the same time, it extended the duties of employers and regulators (the Health and Safety Executive) to include public safety. Flixborough demonstrated the reality of the off-site accident potential that the HSW Act sought to control.[4] As a consequence, a system of hazardous site identification and land-use planning controls was developed in the United Kingdom in the years after the accident. The Health and Safety Commission (HSC) and its operational arm the Health and Safety Executive (HSE) are the central government bodies that enforce and apply the Act. They were guided for a period by an Advisory Committee on Major Hazards. This committee wrote three reports, in 1976, 1979, and 1984, that were landmarks in major hazard control in the United Kingdom.

Other countries saw comparable developments. In France, for instance, the government established a 1976 law on "Classified Installations," which (although occasionally revised) remains the basic framework for the control of major hazards. This law is the ultimate outcome of deliberations that started after an accident in 1966 at Feyzin, on the Rhône River near Lyon in which eighteen people died and eighty-four were injured.

More generally, the 1970s were a period in which a number of European governments became sensitized to chemical hazards, partly because of disasters but partly also because of a climate that favored a certain amount of industrial regulation, especially with respect to safety at work. The starting point for regulation in many cases was the political debate after an accident in a given country, but accidents in other countries helped to keep the issue on the European agenda.

The specifics and the timing of regulation, however, varied from country to country because of differences in the accidents to which the authorities reacted, as well as in political climate and bureaucratic organization. In a number of countries hazard-control legislation went hand in hand with legislation on worker safety. Examples include, besides the Health and Safety at Work Act in the United Kingdom, the 1980 Work Conditions Act in the Netherlands and the 1980 Law on Dangerous Substances in the Federal Republic of Germany.[5] In the UK, the external effects of Flixborough were reflected in land-use control legislation that developed after the accident, but was linked to the same control body as worker safety. In the Netherlands, on the other hand, land-use planning and worker safety were (and still are) the responsibility of different authorities. The Dutch State Mines accident, like Flixborough, started a debate on land-use planning, but the existence of separate responsible authorities meant that no legislative link was established between the two areas of concern. Subsequently, environmental issues became an important vehicle for linking safety and land-use planning in the Netherlands. Unlike the Work Conditions Act in the Netherlands, however, which explicitly sought to give workers the opportunity to help enhance their safety, the French legislation that resulted from the 1966 Feyzin accident, and especially its implementation, placed a strong emphasis on the availability of technical information. As Brian Wynne remarks in his study of the implementation of the Seveso Directive,[6] France pays relatively little attention to the resulting level of safety.

On the whole, the safety legislation enacted in Europe in this period consisted mainly of provisions in the various nation states and not at the level of the European Community (EC). The impact of one accident, however, clearly was international in character. This was the accident at Seveso in 1976.

Seveso: The Accident and Its Interpretation

On July 10, 1976 the small Italian town of Seveso was startled by a nasty-smelling cloud escaping from the plant operated by Icmesa, a subsidiary of the multinational chemical and pharmaceutical company Hoffman-LaRoche. At first, the accident did not frighten residents because it was not the first time the plant had caused a nuisance. But during the weekend they slowly became concerned when they developed rashes and eye complaints and many animals began dying. After two weeks local authorities finally decided to evacuate the area.[7]

Among other chemicals, the Icmesa plant produced TCP (trichlorophenol), one of the starting products for hexachlorophene, a disinfectant used in medicinal soaps. Compounds produced from TCP include 2,4,5,-T (trichlorophenoxyacetic acid) one of the ingredients of Agent Orange, the defoliant used in Vietnam. It is well known that Agent Orange contained dioxin, a highly toxic compound that is inevitably found as a contaminant in TCP.

TCP production had a history of runaway events, in which the temperature rose to above 230° C. Dioxin is always formed as a byproduct of TCP production, but above 230° C the amounts of dioxin rise quickly and uncontrollably. Accidents similar to the one in Seveso had already happened at several places in the world. Among them were an accident at the Monsanto works in Nitro, West Virginia, in 1949 and several others in Germany in the early 1950s (at BASF in Ludwigshafen in 1953 and at Boehringer in Hamburg in 1954). It was not until 1960, however, that the nature of the compound involved and the types of effects it caused became clear. These research results led to a series of measures to reduce the possibilities of accidental human contact with the compound. But again in 1963 TCP production went out of control in Amsterdam at Philips-Duphar, and again it took some days before people realized the possible effects. Contrary to the situation in Seveso, however, in all the above cases the pollution was contained within the building where production was situated.

At Seveso, the effects of the accident were only slowly realized. In the first two weeks after the accident the local authorities did not understand what had happened. They did not know that dioxin was involved nor the extent of the accident's effects. When they finally realized the magnitude of the hazard, residents from the surrounding area were evacuated, but only after they had spent a fortnight in the contaminated region. The company, too, did not seem to realize the full effects till a week had gone by, although the negative history of TCP production was well known in the industry.

In light of this history, the company had sought a low-temperature production process, to prevent a rise of temperatures above 230° C. Production at the Seveso plant therefore took place at a relatively low temperature. A possible explanation for the initial slow response, then, is company overconfidence that a runaway reaction (leading to higher temperatures) was impossible in the production process in use. Officials apparently not only believed that such an accident could not happen, but did not even take additional precautionary measures to contain an emission should their belief be proved wrong. The tendency to minimize what might happen at the plant may well have contributed to the company's early failure to react.

The company's conduct relative to the outside world aggravated the delay following the accident. The plant at Icmesa, as noted earlier, was a subsidiary of a daughter company of Hoffman-LaRoche. Communication to the public was therefore initially left to local plant officers. If the rumor of the accident had subsided quickly, the parent company might not have been implicated and its reputation might have remained undamaged. When experts at Hoffman-LaRoche finally concluded that the situation was serious, it took much additional time for that message to reach the local population and the Italian authorities.

The single issue that emerged most forcefully after the Seveso accident was the lack of information available to the public and to the authorities responsible for taking remedial action after the event. Individuals and organizations outside the plant were not informed of what had happened or what behavior they should adopt to reduce risk. The accident did not directly claim human lives (some women underwent voluntary abortions, but there were no fatalities). In this respect it might be seen as a relatively minor event compared with the accident in Bhopal. But Seveso clearly stands out, in the context of European industrial history, as an information disaster.

Two other features of the Seveso accident were important for the way it affected the regulation of industrial hazards. First, it became an international event, because barrels containing waste from the contaminated soil were transported through a number of European countries before being disposed of.[8] Second, the fact that it was an accident in the European South, a region that is seen in the EC as less developed, had political implications. Although the characterization "less developed" is not completely appropriate for the industrialized north of Italy where Seveso is located, the regulatory atmosphere in Italy was substantially different from that in the industrialized north-western regions of Europe. By around 1980, however, the EC was slowly gaining importance, and Italy was recognized as the most important southern country in Europe. Things that happened in Italy could no longer be dismissed as something happening in a developing country for which the other European nations took no responsibility. Both features of the accident demanded centralized action by the EC, which eventually issued the regulating instrument that came to be known as the Seveso Directive.

The Seveso Directive

The Treaty of Rome gives the Commission of the European Communities the exclusive right to propose European laws, but there is an exchange of views between member-state experts and the Commission before a proposal is published formally. The Community has five legislative tools at its command: regulations, directives, decisions, recommendations, and opinions. Recommendations and opinions have no binding force. A regulation is a law that is directly applicable in Community member states; it is rarely used in the area of chemical regulation. A decision is binding in its entirety on the Community groups to which it is addressed. The most common form of legislation in the area of chemical regulation is the directive, the terms of which are binding but which leaves member states free to choose forms and methods of implementation. Community directives only become effective once they have been embodied in national laws.[9]

On June 24, 1982 the EC passed Council Directive 82/501/EEC on the major accident hazards of certain industrial activities.[10] It was the first community law requiring environmental information to be provided and exchanged across national frontiers, both among governments and between governments and the public. The Seveso Directive came into force on January 8, 1984 and had to be implemented in national laws before January 1, 1985. It covered both new and existing industrial activities.

The principal aims of the Directive were described in an EC brochure.[11] The first is "to reduce the likelihood of a major accident by requiring industry to incorporate preventive measures into the design of a plant or a manufacturing process from the beginning." The second is "to ensure that if an accident occurs, it does not escalate into a disaster." The Directive requires chemical-plant managers to install control and safety measures and prepare emergency plans. Thus described, the aims of the Directive focus on risk management.

These objectives have been operationalized by information obligations. Industrialists are required to prove to the "competent authority" (that is, to designated national control bodies) that they have identified major accident hazards, adopted appropriate safety measures, and provided the people working on the site with information, training, and equipment to ensure their safety. As noted above, in many member countries these requirements were already in place, or partly in place, through legislation on health and safety at work or via licensing procedures. More specific demands are linked to particular hazards. An annex to the Directive covers a list of about 200 substances that are (highly) toxic, carcinogenic, or explosive. For these chemicals the Directive sets out thresholds of storage and processing ranging from one kilogram to several thousands of metric tons. For amounts above the threshold, industry has to prepare a complete report on hazards, as well as safety and emergency response measures.

A major part of the Directive consists of obligations to inform the authorities about risk and safety on site. The more innovative part of the Directive, however, is the obligation to provide information to other parties, most notably the public at risk. Under Article 8, member states are required to ensure that people liable to be affected by a major accident are informed, in an appropriate manner, of the safety measures and correct behavior to adopt in the event of an accident. This obligation applies to all industrial activities covered under the Directive, but not to the potential hazards of chemical plants in general.[12] As H. Otway and A. Amendola have observed, the Directive can be seen as establishing an information network between public authorities and industry, and also between them and parties potentially at risk.[13]

As the first EC regulation requiring information to be provided to the public, the Seveso Directive occasioned great concern within industry. This is one of the reasons why Article 8 (on public information) was framed in very imprecise language.[14] This imprecision gave some countries the impression that they had already implemented this part of the Directive, because information provision was already part of their licensing procedure. Additionally, they felt[15] that information provision on hazards is conceptually inconsistent with information provision in the framework of licensing. In the usual European licensing process the public can obtain information about the hazardous properties of the plant to be licensed. Anyone who considers the activity unsafe can object to the granting of the license. The granting of a license, however, implies that the level of safety of the plant is deemed acceptable by state authorities. In some cases, authorities or industry may feel that informing the public about the probability of major accidents amounts to admitting that a risk exists, which is not normally the message one wishes to convey through the licensing process.

There is, however, another more substantial reason for fearing conflict between the two frameworks of information provision. In countries where information was not normally available to the public, the new requirements fit easily into existing legislative structures, because it was possible simply to add them to prior law. Thus, in a country like the United Kingdom, where no previous information requirements had existed, the structure of the Seveso Directive was incorporated almost intact into national legislation. By contrast, in the Netherlands, where hazard information was already regulated under licensing procedures, it took some time to realize (in the dual sense of both conceiving the idea and implementing it) that the type of information required by the Seveso Directive would be better handled under the Disaster Act than in the framework of environmental protection, where the obligation to inform the authorities was already embedded.[16]

Both the imprecision of the Directive and the difficulty of reconciling existing and new requirements shifted official attention away from the requirement to inform the public. Ironically, as well, those countries that had previously "learned" best to provide public information about risks appeared at the greatest disadvantage in learning how to implement the Seveso Directive.

The Bhopal disaster was important in keeping the information issue on European policy agenda, because it offered another case where people would have been less vulnerable if they had known more. The tragedy helped cement the awareness that informing the public how to respond to an accident was an important part of disaster prevention. Additionally, the Bhopal accident had some effects on concepts of responsibility, since it posed the question of how to view chemical production in parts of the world where safety standards were less strict or the general attitude toward safety less informed than in Europe. The feeling before Bhopal had been that some freedom should be granted to local plant managers, since they should not be patronized by their foreign counterparts. After Bhopal the more general perception—or at least the rhetoric—was that safety standards should be equal worldwide. Companies based in the United States were particularly important in disseminating this idea.

In general, however, Europeans tended to think that Bhopal was an event that could not happen in Europe. This sense was partly because of the differences between industrial siting in Europe and India. As a result of physical planning in many parts of Europe, a certain distance is required between plants and large housing districts. In the United Kingdom, for instance, the HSE gives advice about acceptable locations and concentrations for housing in the vicinity of industrial plants. In the Netherlands no new housing is allowed within a certain distance of plants that are considered hazardous, a marked contrast with the state of affairs in India. Another reason why Europe remained undisturbed by Bhopal was that regulations and general safety standards in Europe were felt to be much better enforced than in developing countries like India. And no analogue to the "Institute accident" in the United States occurred to change that feeling of security. Finally, the fact that Union Carbide was a United States-based multinational created a legal nexus between Bhopal and the United States that was in no way paralleled in Europe.

Apart from these social and psychological factors, European legislation on hazardous technologies was also reasonably well developed at the time of the Bhopal disaster. The type of risk-monitoring activity that the U.S. chemical industry engaged in after Bhopal and the enactment of SARA Title III was already formally required. In that sense, Bhopal can be seen as diminishing the lag in disaster preparedness between the United States and Europe. But the perception that Bhopal could not have happened in Europe contrasts markedly with the impact of two accidents that did happen in Europe in 1986, one at the Sandoz plant in Switzerland and the other at the nuclear power plant in Chernobyl in the USSR.

The Recognition of Disaster: Chernobyl and Sandoz

Chernobyl

The accident that started at Chernobyl on April 26, 1986 is somewhat different from other accidents discussed in this book because it was a nuclear disaster. Since it influenced European disaster management, however, it is important to acknowledge its effects in this chapter. The episode showed, first of all, that nuclear accidents may not stay contained within a certain locality. Public knowledge of the accident began when increased levels of radioactivity were measured in Sweden, some thousand miles from the original location. The spread of radiation made it very clear that disasters can produce unpredictable effects and that disaster preparedness cannot remain restricted to local activities. Chernobyl therefore underscored the importance of information provision across political borders, an issue addressed in Article 8.2 of the Seveso Directive.

In the first few weeks after Chernobyl, it proved very difficult to compare data from different parts of Europe; measurements of radioactivity were made in different ways and data were recorded in units that were not easily comparable.[17] The Chernobyl accident, therefore, showed as no previous disaster had done that not only the availability but also the form of information is extremely important to disaster preparedness and mitigation.

Sandoz

In the fall of 1986 a huge fire broke out in a chemical plant owned by Sandoz in Basel, Switzerland. It was extinguished with large amounts of water that streamed into the river Rhine, heavily polluting it with pesticides and degradation products. The town of Basel is situated relatively high up in the river basin, and as a result the water in all the downstream countries became polluted. Drinking water companies had to stop their intake of water. Massive fish kills occurred and some speculated that the Rhine ecosystem had virtually died. The ecosystem was restored relatively quickly after the chemicals disappeared, however, because of renewal from tributaries.

Nonetheless, the accident had a large impact. It again showed that disasters do not respect national borders and that nation states within a single river basin are inextricably linked by ecological interdependence, whether or not they are connected politically. Although Switzerland is not part of the EC, the accident called for measures at the European level, and the Seveso Directive was seen as the natural vehicle for regulating this type of disaster as well. The Directive was adapted to accommodate additional requirements for preventing environmental damage. Some new chemicals were added to the list of regulated compounds, because pesticides and their combustion products were now more clearly recognized as a potential threat to the environment. These adaptations were made despite the ongoing policy debate as to whether environmental regulation could best be organized in a framework that also regulated disaster management for human populations.

An important further effect was that the Seveso Directive stayed on the agenda, formally as well as informally. Changes that the European bureaucracy was already contemplating, as a result of implementation experiences in member states, became part of the agenda for adapting the Directive. The implementation process also gained renewed impetus, since it again became clear that better management was needed to reduce the disastrous potential of modern technology.

Public Information Provision

We turn now to the actual provision of public information on major accident hazards to illustrate the interactive processes that transform a final agreement into implemented policy. In 1976, the Seveso accident showed the importance of informing the public about the risks of neighboring industrial activities and about the way to protect oneself against the possible effects of an accident. In many European countries, public interest groups demanded to be so informed. This was the climate in which the requirement to provide people with risk information was incorporated into European legislation. However, European legislation is not equivalent to legislation in the member states, nor is it a guarantee of implementation in practice. At first, the implementation of the public information article lagged far behind the implementation of the other less innovative articles. Countries where some kind of information requirement was already in force were not prepared to add to their existing legislation because they felt confident that they were performing adequately.

After Bhopal, the movement to inform the public about emergency response strategies gained new impetus. EC authorities discussed possible further specifications of the information article. At the same time, Europeans became aware of the response of U.S. industries to the Bhopal accident. Information brochures and guidelines from the United States became available in Europe. Meanwhile, the implementation date for the Seveso Directive (January 1986) drew near. In some countries with no previous tradition of informing the public, both government and industry felt that something concrete had to be done. In the United Kingdom the combination of all these factors led to an almost complete implementation of Article 8 (in legislation as well as in practice), although it must be remarked that the amount of information disseminated was relatively small and was entirely restricted to those considered to be at risk. Some 200 plants covered by the Directive gave out information leaflets with or without cooperation from local governments.[18]

In 1986 the EC commissioned a study of the implementation of article 8,[19] which eventually led to revisions in the requirements for information provision. Prior to this time, EC officials had no clear idea how the Article could be implemented, although some informal guidelines had been discussed among representatives from the EC countries. The guidelines specified certain types of information that should be provided, for instance, a general description of the processes conducted at the site, the main hazardous properties of the chemicals in use, and possibilities for gaining further information. It was unclear, however, whether these guidelines were adequate.

The study showed that the guidelines were indeed practicable, as evidenced by their almost complete implementation in the United Kingdom. But it also became clear that countries diverged in their views of the adequacy of existing routes of information provision. Some adopted information policies that can only be characterized as passive. In the Federal Republic of Germany and the Netherlands, for instance, the types of information that should be available about possible impacts of industrial activity were already extensively regulated. In the course of implementing the Seveso Directive, these information requirements were further extended. However, the available information was only indirectly brought to public attention. When a license was filed, people were informed of this fact, which meant that they could inform themselves using the available material if they so chose. In the Netherlands people could in principle freely look through the files of a plant, but in practice this material was not easily accessible: it was highly technical in character and often filled many file cabinets. Some measures were adopted to facilitate public access to licenses and their contents. Dutch law, for example, requires a version of the license to be provided that can be read by lay people. Officials are supposed to assist the public to understand information about licenses under consideration, and there is also a legal requirement to hold a meeting with concerned parties. These requirements all evolved in response to citizen activism in the 1970s. Nevertheless, all the information generated during licensing is restricted to people who actively seek it. Despite the facilitating requirements, information tends to be difficult to obtain, and not all of it is available for all plants that can cause major accidents. Licensing in most countries is geared heavily toward regulating an activity as it starts and much less toward keeping hazard information up to date. Licensing information also is not adequate to inform people about the most effective precautionary or protective measures to adopt in the event of an accident.

As I noted earlier, countries that had the most extensive licensing requirements already in place were least inclined to add new information requirements in the light of the Seveso Directive. The EC implementation study brought this problem into the open and prompted the additional requirement that information provision would only be deemed adequate when people were actively informed. It also became clear that further support was needed to get the EC countries to move beyond formal implementation. Several countries were shown to have implemented the Directive in their national legislation, but they had not yet installed any executive structures. The countries that had failed to implement parts of the Directive either had trouble locating the position in their bureaucracy where the Directive best fit (for example, Italy) or felt confident that they conformed to the Directive (or even were ahead of it).

In the European context, then, the primary impact of Bhopal was a more systematic focus on implementation. On the one hand, this new attention revealed some positive opportunities for giving information to the public. On the other, it showed how implementation could be hindered if the Directive was interpreted in a less than optimal way, for example, by taking the formal openness of licensing as adequate for compliance.

The accident at Sandoz happened when the deficiencies in the public information requirement of the Seveso Directive were becoming clearer. The Directive as it stood was shown to be inadequate with respect to some of the compounds that make a plant notifiable. The accident spurred the revision of the Directive, permitting other information issues that had surfaced in the interim to be incorporated as well.[20] Instead of a vague requirement to inform the public "in an adequate way," the requirement now became that people should be actively informed. As a result, information provided in the framework of licensing was no longer seen as adequate from the point of view of the Seveso Directive.

A second round of systematic consideration began with an EC conference, attended by officials, industrialists, and researchers, in Varese, Italy, in 1989, and a new study of the implementation process by Brian Wynne.[21] The Varese meeting disclosed the variations that were developing in national practices and stood out as a watershed. Wynne's study was intended to form the basis for a code of good practice, which in turn was supposed to provide additional impetus for improving the information process.

Conducted in four countries (UK, France, the Netherlands, and Denmark), the study was to compare the information activities around a chosen site in each country. It became clear from this comparison that member states of the EC had legitimately different cultural and institutional contexts within which the legal obligations of the Seveso Directive were defined and implemented. These in turn affected the responsibilities of different actors in the process and the collaboration among them. On the basis of observations like these, it seems futile to impose uniform codes of conduct across countries and to prescribe precisely how to inform the public. Differences among national cultures, for example, affect the way information is provided and who takes responsibility for it. In the Netherlands the mayor of a town is the responsible authority in case of an emergency. The mayor is expected to sign any letter related to emergency preparedness; to enhance the effectiveness of such a letter, the site manager, a company employee, should preferably also sign. In no case is it sufficient for the manager to sign alone. This latter, however, is a common practice in the United Kingdom, although not the preferred one. In both countries the presumption is that a message about risk and emergency should not look like a commercial message. In France, on the other hand, glossy information leaflets have been distributed by authorities and companies without signatures.

Information Provision and the Public

In the evolution of EC information practices and their implementation, the public's role seems to be most conspicuous by its absence. In a sense this is a genuine void. Public action is seldom directly aimed at influencing policy at the EC level. Instead, the public tends to focus on national legislation, such as the information requirements in Dutch licensing procedures or the right to be heard in the German ones. When legislation in a certain area has been enacted in a member state, officials from that country may try to get the EC onto a similar legislative track. This may be done for instance during the half-year period during which each country holds the EC chair. More general action to place an issue on the EC agenda can be taken by European parliamentarians. Public interest groups may refer to EC legislation in order to expose noncompliance by their own government. For instance, the Dutch government was accused by an environmental group of not generating enough information on risk in the licensing process, and the government was indeed judged liable by the European Court.[22]

But the framing of the Seveso Directive involved little public participation. In France members of the public were involved in the design of the information campaigns. In other countries they were not involved in any organized way. In the Netherlands representatives of public interest groups were consulted about the information that they considered necessary. Some members of the public were also asked to evaluate a preliminary version of the information to be provided. But public interest groups were not seriously considered by local government and industry as partners in setting up information campaigns. It is not clear whether other European countries considered a more active public role. It is seductive to think, especially from the standpoint of U.S. norms of participation, that the partnership of the public in information campaigns is something to be aimed at. Such close collaboration, however, may entail too much commitment to the message that is being sent. It is not clear that such a sharing of responsibility is in all cases advantageous to the public.

European legislation, in contrast to that in the United States (see Hadden, this volume, Chapter 5), interprets the public's relationship to information as a *need* to know rather than a *right* to know. The former implies a right of access only to that information which is needed for a specific purpose, such as self-protection. The latter suggests an open-ended right of access to all available information. The right-to-know principle has generally been interpreted as more far-reaching than the need to know. The history of the implementation of the Seveso Directive, however, shows that this may not necessarily be true.

In Europe, different countries have widely varying rules with respect to the information that people are entitled to get. As already noted, in the Netherlands and Germany industry needs to acquire an environmental license before starting operations. Risk data are part of the information that is openly available to all who wish to argue against the granting of such a license. In the Netherlands a meeting has to be held before the license is granted so that everyone who has objections can present them. Legal action can also be taken against proposed licenses. The availability of this type of information is based on the right-to-know concept. Citizens have a right to know what potential dangers are inflicted upon them; if they think these are untoward, they can act against them. Other countries, however, like the United Kingdom, lay much less emphasis on the right to know. The Health and Safety Executive, for instance, advises about granting licenses without informing the public. The right-to-know principle also seems to be a much less general starting point for policy in Europe than in the United States. In the Netherlands, for instance, the legislative framework for disaster prevention is geared toward providing the information that people need in case of a major accident.

Indeed, during the second revision of the EC Directive, the point was made that information resulting from a right-to-know approach could well be insufficient for purposes of public safety. The insufficiency might result not only from the fact that too little information was given, although that could and did happen in many cases, but also from the fact that too much information might be given in the wrong way. Unfiltered risk information is often too technical, not sufficiently geared toward the needs and capabilities of lay people, and too cumbersome and difficult to acquire. This is why the Dutch licensing authorities are obliged to provide a popular version of the licensing conditions in addition to the technical version. More importantly, the EC has explicitly stated that providing information on a right-to-know basis is insufficient, because people do not receive the information that they need to act upon. The Seveso Directive provides not only that people must receive all necessary emergency response information but also that they must be informed in such a way that they can understand the risks they run. If people only get highly technical information, the latter objective is not fulfilled. In the Netherlands the need-to-know principle has been translated into an obligation to provide information with various amounts of detail to varying groups of people. In risk-communication campaigns, simple information is provided door to door. The opportunities for acquiring additional information are indicated, and meetings are organized for those who wish to be further informed. For the really committed, the original licensing materials and risk analyses are always available.

These attitudes and practices stand in sharp contrast with the presumptions underlying SARA Title III. As Hadden's chapter indicates, U.S. law provides only for the disclosure of information, not for its transmission in usable form to the public at risk. In the U.S. framework, the task of interpreting information and mobilizing citizen action accordingly falls to organized public interest activists, such as state and national environmental groups. In the EC countries, where the state plays a more actively protective role toward its citizens, not merely the provision of information but also its screening and repackaging are seen as appropriately the obligation of the state.

Incremental Learning

In this chapter I have reviewed a number of accidents that shook Europe in the last few decades and impelled disaster management to the point where it now stands. The implication of this history is that new accidents are needed to push disaster management forward. We see disaster management highest on various political agendas shortly after a disaster has occurred. At that moment public attention is drawn to the issue. Questions are asked in newspapers about the responsibility for the occurrences, the way in which the disaster happened, and why it was not prevented. Suddenly the possibility of a disaster, which is usually downplayed, becomes a dramatic reality. Everyone realizes that a small probability of disaster does not mean that it is absolutely impossible. At such a moment, room opens up for new measures, either in legislation or in implementation practices.

The picture that emerges is one in which risk management slowly grows in importance, but in ways that are strongly influenced by earlier disasters. Disaster policy is adapted stepwise in a direction that is determined by the starting point: the country where the situation occurred, the policy framework that is seen as relevant for the situation, the precise way that accidents happened, and the lessons that are drawn from them. The media and the public strongly influence the policy agenda.[23] Politicians react. These activities shape political attention at the time of the disaster, but do not determine the long-term influence on disaster-management practices. When described in this way, risk management appears to be an incremental process in which disasters are the most important directing factors. Although this may to some extent be a realistic picture, it needs to be balanced with a more sociopolitical account. As important as the disasters themselves is the way in which they are interpreted by various actors and the availability of operationalized management approaches for mitigating them.

Accidents, then, are necessary to generate attention for risk management, but they do not necessarily provide sufficient impetus to create a permanent solution. Comprehensive solutions take time to develop, during which time attention can drag. When an issue is complicated, it takes a lot of commitment to find a solution, and if it is not periodically reconsidered on the political agenda a drop in attention will certainly occur. Disasters provide one of the strongest arguments for reconsidering existing policy.

Should we then conclude that only disasters are capable of keeping risk management on the agenda? Lloyd Etheredge drew such a conclusion for the learning potential of governments, when he suggested that only in crisis situations are normal procedures overcome so as to adapt behavior in a constructive way.[24] A more optimistic view, however, is warranted once an issue is taken up as part of the routine policy process. The process may then go forward without accidents to push it further. Accidents then may even be welcomed as a chance to showcase progress in policy development. An example relating to public information provision in the Netherlands illustrates this ironic possibility. When Dutch officials were just starting to implement the public-information article of the Seveso Directive, they organized a press conference to announce their activities. Some relatively minor accidents with dangerous materials occurred at just that time. These were covered as dramatically as possible in the news media. Accidents of this scale would never have gained so much attention if there had been no need for public legitimation. They were picked up by the media to make the other activities surrounding disaster preparedness seem more newsworthy. One saw here a reversal of the usual pattern: the accident was not the cause for media and policy attention; rather, media attention was instigated by policy, and accidents were used as exemplars.

Large disasters such as Bhopal may well be a shock to everyone involved and—except where they completely overwhelm a society's learning capacity—may open up completely new ways of thinking about disaster management. But smaller accidents tend to be taken up strategically as illustrative examples to adapt behavior. When a conceptual framework already exists, new occurrences serve mainly as a checkpoint against which to gauge the direction and the urgency of the chosen risk-management policy. In this respect, relatively minor accidents serve to keep the learning process from stagnating.

Finally, the history that I have sketched documents dramatic changes in the world that Europeans see as relevant to their disaster-management regulations. Before the Seveso Directive, safety regulation was handled primarily as a national activity. The Seveso regulation marked the beginning of supranational thinking on accidents in Europe. The trans-boundary characteristics of Seveso and later accidents undoubtedly played a part in this change of perspective. But possibly more important is the fact that the world the Europeans are prepared to see as their responsibility has also grown. The nation state is no longer seen as the only part of the world that a European citizen belongs to and takes responsibility for; instead, "Europe" has become the world in which he or she lives. In coming years this feeling may become an even more important vehicle for changes in safety and environmental regulation. The disappearance of the Berlin wall has brought Europe into a strong state of flux, and the area that is seen as "our world" by most Western Europeans is now expanding rapidly. European countries have begun to think in terms of trade-offs between investing in safety and the environment in their own nation states and in parts of Eastern Europe. The increasing feeling of all human beings that they belong to one world may well become an important "push factor" in helping the newly reconstituted Europe to learn from disaster.

Notes

1. Brian Wynne, "Implementation of Article 8 of the Directive 82/501/EEC; A Study of Public Information, 1987," conducted for the Commission of the European Communities, contract no. 86-B-6641-11-006-11-N, p. 49.
2. From May 30 to June 1, 1989 an EC conference was held in Varese, Italy, on Communicating with the Public About Major Accident Hazards. Many of the speakers referred to earlier accidents as important in shaping risk communication, but only two of them, Jim Makris from EPA and Michael Baram, both speakers from the United States, mentioned only Bhopal by name. See Jim Makris, "Community Right-to-Know," pp. 65–78, and M. S. Baram, "Risk Communication Law and Its Implications," pp. 110–124, in H. B. F. Gow and H. Otway, eds., *Communicating with the Public About Major Accident Hazards* (New York: Elsevier, 1990).
3. *The Flixborough Disaster* (London: HMSO, 1975)
4. Wynne, "Implementation of Article 8," p. 122.
5. Ibid., p. 50.
6. Ibid., p. 35. Some countries had such experiences in an earlier period. A speaker from the Federal Republic of Germany stated at the Varese conference (see note 2): "This is probably due to the fact that we experienced serious incidents in the course of industrialization of our country which led to an enhanced sensitivity towards risks caused by industry." Also see H. Pettelkau, "Effects of the Second Amendment to Directive 82/501/EEC on Emergency Planning in the Federal Republic of Germany," in Gow and Otway, eds. *Communicating with the Public*, pp. 53–57.
7. Tom Margerison and Marjorie Wallace, *The Superpoison* (London: Macmillan 1979).
8. Brian Wynne, *Risk Management and Hazardous Waste* (Berlin: Springer, 1987).
9. Commission of the European Communities, *Chemical Risk Control in the European Community* (Brussels: Commission of the European Communities 1987).
10. "Council Directive of June 24, 1982 on the Major Accident Hazards of Certain Industrial Activities," 82/501/EEC, *Official Journal of the European Communities*, L230, August 5, 1982.
11. Commission of the European Communities, *Chemical Risk Control*.
12. The public information article (Article 8) specifically provides that:

1. Member States shall ensure that persons liable to be affected by a major accident originating in a notified industrial activity within the meaning of Article 5 are informed in an appropriate manner of the safety measures and of the correct behavior to adopt in the event of an accident. 2. The member States concerned shall at the same time make available to the other Member States concerned, as a basis for all necessary consultation within the framework of their bilateral relations, the same information as that which is disseminated to their own nationals. Plants that produce only

chemicals that are not listed in the Seveso Directive will not be regulated by it; also the Directive does not regulate the transport of hazardous materials.

13. H. Otway and A. Amendola, "Major Hazard Information Policy in the European Community: Implications for Risk Analysis," *Risk Analysis* 9,4(1991): 505–512. At another place Otway ventures that it may be simply an expression of a general trend to translate everything into information terms. See H. Otway, "Communication with the Public About Major Hazards: Challenges for European Research, in Gow and Otway, eds., *Communicating with the Public*, pp. 26–36 (note 2).

14. Brian Wynne and Josée Van Eijndhoven, "Risk Communication in Europe: Ways of Implementing Article 8 of the Post-Seveso Directive," in R. E. Kasperson and P. J. M. Stallen, eds., *Communicating Health and Safety Risks to the Public: International Dimensions* (Dordrecht: Reidel, 1991).

15. Pettelkau, "Effects of the Second Amendment."

16. Josée van Eijndhoven and Cor Worrell, eds., *Communicatie over risico's van industriële activiteiten* (Den Haag: NOTA March 1991).

17. Radiation doses, for example, were measured in picocuries in Germany and in becquerels in the Netherlands.

18. Wynne, "Implementation of Article 8."

19. See Wynne; Otway and Amendola, "Major Hazard Information Policy"; and EEC 1988. Council Directive of 24 November 1988, amending Directive 82/501/EEC on the Major-Accidents Hazards of Certain Industrial Activities, 88/610/EEC. Official Journal of the European Communities. No. L336/14–18.

20. Brian Wynne, "Empirical Evaluation of Public Information on Major Industrial Accident Hazards," Report on Study, contract no. 3646-89-03-ED ISP GB. For the Commission of the European Communities.

21. Ibid.

22. In practice such information was almost always asked in a licensing procedure, but some local authorities did not and could not be legally forced to supply it. Therefore additional legislation was issued. See Josée van Eijndhoven and Cor Worrell, "Active and Passive Provision of Risk Information in the Netherlands," in Kasperson and Stallen, *Communicating Health and Safety Risks*, pp. 15–35.

23. E.g., Ortwinn Renn, "Risk Communication and the Social Amplification of Risk," in Kasperson and Stallen, *Communicating Health and Safety Risks*, pp. 287–324.

24. Lloyd S. Etheredge, *Can Governments Learn? American Foreign Policy and Central American Revolutions* (Elmsford, NY: Pergamon Press, 1985).

Chapter 7
The Transnational Traffic in Legal Remedies

Marc Galanter

The December 1984 disaster in Bhopal, in which upwards of 3,500 persons were killed and as many as 150,000 seriously injured, invites our reflection on many matters. I shall examine the strikingly different role played by tort law in the risk-management complexes of India and the United States, the two sites of the ensuing legal battle. Flows of capital, goods, people, and information mean that injurious events may be transnational in significant ways. What do the national differences displayed in the aftermath of Bhopal imply for the transnational traffic in legal services and legal remedies?

To place tort law in some perspective, I begin by imagining the introduction of a new productive technology—for example, the production of pesticides—into a new setting—for example, India. This new technology brings with it new risks. At the same time, it effects a reduction of the risks of starvation, malnutrition, and harms associated with older agricultural technologies. Let us assume that the overall quantum of risk in the recipient society is now less than it was before the advent of the new technology. But now there are new risks that impinge on the workers in the pesticide plants, on those who live near the plants, on those who transport the product, use it in the fields, ingest it, and so forth. At least some of these new risks are more focused, more visible, and more controllable than the old risks that they have replaced. And they are apprehended in a very different way, for they are palpably the result of identifiable human interventions, associated with particular human agencies.

The Various Layers of Control

What kinds of controls are there to protect against these new risks? There are several overlapping layers[1]:

- A first layer consists of controls intrinsic to the technology itself: preventive design, safety procedures, worker training, and other devices to minimize risk that are built into the technological package itself. Just how these devices will work will vary in different cultures—for example, with workers' literacy, comprehension, obedience, risk adverseness, and so on.
- A second layer consists of administrative control by government authorities: determining acceptable risks, requiring preventive practices, and monitoring compliance. Such administrative regulation is typically not included as part of the transfer of technology. To include it would be difficult, since insistence by the transferor would offend the honor of the sovereign recipient and might thwart its policies. Typically there is some administrative counterpart in the recipient country that is assigned some regulatory tasks. These may be more or less appropriate and more or less effective, but again this is ordinarily considered a matter of domestic concern.

These first two layers attempt to address risks before injuries occur; the next two come into play only when injuries have occurred. Because they influence the activity in the first two layers, we can think of them as additional sources of control of the risks from the new technology.

- The third layer consists of institutions for absorbing and spreading losses when the new technology does result in injuries: relief and health institutions that help to reduce losses; welfare institutions like social security and insurance that compensate victims.
- Finally, there is a fourth layer of control made up of private law, which generates and broadcasts standards in the course of vindicating the claims of injured persons. That is, private persons can move courts (or other bodies, like workers' compensation boards) for awards to compensate for damage suffered when the new technology produces actual injuries and damage. This compensation may or may not be conditioned on a finding of fault or wrongdoing. Compensation may be designed to be variable or it may be measured by a fixed schedule.

In the following I contrast the heavy reliance on the most typical manifestation of the fourth layer—tort litigation—in the American setting and the neglect of tort remedies in India. A brief overview of the working of tort controls and their characteristic strengths and weaknesses is followed by an examination of the collision between the

United States' high accountability-high remedy system and India's low accountability-low remedy system in the Bhopal litigation. Finally, I take up the implication of such imbalances for the transnational traffic in legal remedies.

Characteristics of the Tort System

The United States relies heavily on the fourth layer of private law controls, more so than do other industrialized countries. One comparative survey estimated that "Comparing costs relative to each country's gross domestic output, the U.S. tort system—at 2.5 percent of GNP—ranges between three and eight times the relative cost of tort systems in major European countries as well as in Australia and Japan" (Sturgis 1989:12).[2]

Our expansive system of private remedy is as much a sign of what we do not have as of what we do have. We do not have a Bismarckian administrative state with intensive and efficient governmental regulation, nor do we have a comprehensive welfare state. The same comparative study noted that "America's social welfare system is considerably smaller than that of any other country studied" (Sturgis 1989:14). Because we have weak administrative controls and a ragged safety-net welfare state, tort looms large as part of our system of compensating injuries.[3] In terms of our layers, our heavy reliance on the fourth layer is associated with our comparative under-reliance on the second and third layers. Numerically, the system of private law controls is dominated by routinized administrative remedies like workers' compensation that provide low recoveries without much contest, and which attract little investment of legal talent and little public attention. A minority of injuries are handled by the tort system, which is manned by a dynamic entrepreneurial bar, and which produces higher, uneven, expensive, and sometimes more visible recoveries.[4]

Tort is a curious straddle that combines public standards with passive, reactive public institutions, leaving the initiative to private sector actors (victims and lawyers). The use of private law marks a shift from prospective and preventive control to retrospective and remedial control. Preventive effects depend on potential injurers extracting appropriate signals from what the courts do and modifying their behavior. The enforcement initiative is shifted away from the productive enterprise (cf. layer 1) and the government (cf. layer 2) as surrogates for potential victims—surrogates who have many other responsibilities and commitments—to the actual victims and their agents. These victims obviously have strong interests in controlling these risks, but this interest may be so diffuse that they have little incentive to invest in prevention (Komesar 1990). Their low capability to control these risks directly means that prevention initiatives depend on surrogates, such as lawyers and potential injurers. This diffusion of enforcement initiative is matched by the decentralization of pronouncement of standards. Tort standards are formulated largely by courts responding incrementally to specific cases that are brought before them. Tort standards are "context sensitive,"[5] incorporating changing popular values and understandings. In the United States this incorporation of popular views is accelerated by the use of civil juries.[6]

The tort system marries the compensation function with the prevention function. Information about instances in which injurers (and their insurers) are forced to compensate victims cumulate into a kind of knowledge that generates prevention. This process of knowledge generation and preventive action can be analyzed into several distinct steps. First, the compensation may be effectuated either by running the entire course of legal contest or by "voluntary" settlement at an earlier stage in the light of the anticipated outcome of that contest. In fact most injury claims, even serious ones, are settled without trial; many are granted without formally invoking the system by filing suit. Second, information about such instances of enforced compensation has to be disseminated, so they become known to potential injurers. The fulfillment of this condition entails such institutional arrangements as public courts, public records, and reporting by the trade publications and general media. It is noteworthy that much of this information is lost or suppressed by confidential settlements and by the difficulty of retrieving relevant information. Third, this information has to be gathered into a kind of usable knowledge that is predictive. This is done by published legal doctrine, by specialized publications such as jury-reporting services in the United States and *Current Law* in the United Kingdom, and in the lore of lawyers, insurers, and risk managers. Fourth, potential injurers have to pay attention to it and alter their behavior in light of it.[7]

The linkage of this knowledge to prevention, often condensed into talk about deterrence, is complex and multiple.[8] Imposition of tort liability may generate both "special effects" and "general effects." Special effects are the effects produced by the impact of litigation (full-blown, attenuated, or threatened) on the parties immediately involved. General effects are effects of the communication to others of information about litigation, including effects of the response to that information.[9]

Special effects are changes in the behavior of the specific actors involved in a particular lawsuit. We can, in theory at least, isolate various kinds of effects on the subsequent activity of such actors. An actor may be deprived of resources for future violations. This is *incapacitation*. Or the result of litigation may be increased *surveillance* that renders future offending behavior less likely. Or the offending actor may be deterred by fear of being caught again. This is *special deterrence*. Or the experience of being exposed to the law may change the actor's view that the behavior in question is right. This is *reformation*.[10]

In addition to these special effects on the parties before the court, there may be effects on wider audiences that we may call general effects. Litigation against one actor may lead others to reassess the risks and advantages of similar activity. This is *general deterrence*. It neither presumes nor requires any change in the moral evaluation of the acts in question, nor does it involve any change in opportunities to commit them. It stipulates that behavior will be affected when actors acquire more information about the costs and benefits that are likely to attach to the act—information about the certainty, celerity, and severity of "punishment," for example. Thus the actor can hold to what H. L. A. Hart called the "external point of view" (Hart 1961:86), treating law as a fact to be taken into account rather than a normative framework that he or she is committed to uphold or be guided by. The information that induces the changed estimate of costs and benefits need not be accurate. What a court has done may be inaccurately perceived; indeed, the court may have inaccurately depicted what it has done.

On the other hand, communication of the existence of a law or its application by a court may change the moral evaluation by others of a specific item of conduct. To the extent that this involves not the calculation or the probability of being visited by certain costs and benefits, but a change in moral estimation, we may call this general effect *enculturation*. There is suggestive evidence to indicate that at least some segments of the population are subject to such effects (Berkowitz and Walker 1967; Colombatos 1969).[11] Less dramatically, perceiving the application of law may maintain or intensify existing evaluations of conduct, an effect that Jack Gibbs calls *normative validation*.

In addition to these effects on the underlying behavior, litigation may produce effects on the level of disputing behavior. It may encourage or discourage the parties to a case from making (or resisting) other claims. It may encourage claimants and lawyers to pursue claims of a given type. It may provide symbols for rallying a group, broadcasting awareness of grievance, and dramatizing challenge to the status quo. On the other hand, grievances may lose legitimacy, claims may be discouraged, and organizational capacity dissipated. The ef-

TABLE 7.1. Comparative Total Cost of Delivering $1.00
          of Benefits to a Recipient

Delivery mechanism	Cost
Tort (Michigan) [c. 1960] (*a*)	$2.26
Product liability torts (U.S.) [c. 1978] (*b*)	$2.25
Tort (England) [c. 1978] (*b*)	$1.85
Automobile torts (U.S.) [c. 1971] (*b*)	$1.77
Workers compensation (U.S.) [c. 1960] (*a*)	$1.44
Private loss insurance (U.S.) [c. 1960] (*a*)	$1.22
No-fault compensation (New Zealand) [c. 1980] (*b*)	$1.095
Workers compensation (Ontario) [c. 1980] (*b*)	$1.09
Social Security (U.S.) [c. 1960] (*a*)	$1.02

Sources: (*a*) Conard et al. 1964: 48, 54, 59; (*b*) Fleming 1984: 1207.

fects may be labeled *mobilization* and *demobilization*. One of the most evident effects of recent litigation has been its profound mobilizational effect on various groups like doctors and insurers who are involved in political initiatives to curtail liability. For similar effects on victim groups following industrial disasters, see Reich, this volume, Chapter 9.

While supposition about the effects of litigation is abundant, serious studies that measure these effects are relatively rare. Some recent studies trace out the complex effects of single tort cases.[12] Other researchers have examined the way that an array of judicial decisions impinges on decisionmaking by private actors. Thus a study of large manufacturers found that

except for firms subject to the maximally intrusive regulation of such agencies as the Food and Drug and the Federal Aviation administrations, product liability is the most significant influence on product safety efforts. Product liability, however, conveys an indistinct signal. The long lags between the design decision and the final judgment on product liability claims (frequently five or more years), the inconsistent behavior of juries, and the rapid change in judicial doctrine in the area, all tended to muffle the signal. . . .
Of all the various external social pressures, product liability has the greatest influence on product design decisions. The other influences largely work through the product liability mechanism. (Eads and Reuter 1983: vii–viii)

But the production of these preventive effects by the tort system does not come cheap. Tort carries very high transaction costs compared to other systems of compensating victims. Because each instance of compensation involves individualized determinations of liability and damages, it is an expensive way to move money around. Table 1 compares the administrative or overhead cost of delivering one dollar of benefits to a recipient in various compensation systems.

A very large portion of the money extracted from injurers by the tort process is consumed by the tort process itself. Analyzing data from a number of studies, Rand researchers estimated that the costs of tort litigation consumed roughly half of the $29 to $36 billion of private expenditure on that litigation in 1985 (Hensler et al. 1987: 26).[13] As Table 7.1 suggests, the overhead differs from one field of tort liability to another. Institute for Civil Justice researchers concluded that, in 1985, costs amounted to 48 percent of total expenditures on auto tort litigation, 57 percent of expenditures on tort litigation that did not involve autos, and 63 percent of expenditures on asbestos claims (Hensler et al. 1987:27–28).[14] This relatively expensive system requires justification to offset its inefficiency as a system for compensating specific classes of injuries. One such justification, as noted above, is the generation of preventive effects. Another is its flexibility and adaptiveness: the tort system and its personnel are in place and need not be reformulated and reinstitutionalized for every new task of risk control. Its open texture permits rapid adaptation to new technologies and new encounters. (On the "accumulation of unregulated technologies," see Shrivastava, this volume, Chapter 12, p. 259.)

Tort is more than a technical device for providing compensation and prevention. It has become a major symbolic presence, dramatizing our sense of the high value of human life, a kind of rough and uneven egalitarianism of high expectations, and our sense of the efficacy of money-driven arrangements.[15] At the same time, as manifested in the current campaign for "tort reform," it has come to symbolize extravagant and erratic compensation, a loss of individual self-reliance, and a source of social misallocation.

Mass Injuries in the Good Old Days

The tort system grew up as a way of providing individualized remedies to individual victims. In recent decades tort recovery for individuals has become more ample, and tort has become established as a component of our response to those injuries on a vastly greater scale. How does this system work as a way of handling mass injuries—either single-event disasters like Bhopal or epidemics such as the thousands of Dalkon Shield injuries?

We should begin by recalling that a tort system imposing high standards of accountability and awarding sizable remedies is a fairly recent phenomenon in the United States. Lawrence Friedman describes the tort system of the late nineteenth century as a "system of noncompensation" in which few claims were brought and plaintiffs faced an array of doctrinal, practical, and cultural barriers to recovery (Friedman 1987:355). In the first decade of this century, fewer than one in twelve of those filing tort claims for personal injury "successfully pursued their claims through filing, trial and on to final judgment" (Friedman and Russell 1990:310). Some cases ended in settlement, but the harsh "working system" of "roadblocks and obstacles, with a pot of gold for a few very lucky, very gallant and persistent survivors . . . denied recovery to victims, and allowed industries to avoid internalizing the full costs of their operation by shielding them from what many considered excessive exposure to lawsuits" (Friedman and Russell 1990:310). This system of non-compensation co-existed with a visible body of tort doctrine that appeared to mandate relief to victims (Friedman and Russell 1990:310).

Compensation was uncertain and meager; seeking it was arduous and could provoke retaliation (Gersuny 1981). Of 212 married employees killed in work accidents in Pittsburgh in 1906–1907, over half received $100 or less from their employers, and only 8 percent received more than $1,000 (Eastman 1910:121).[16] A 1908 study of work-related fatalities in Manhattan and in Erie County, New York found that 41 percent received no compensation; those settled without suit averaged $703; those who settled after filing suit averaged $1,477; the 3 percent whose cases were tried recovered over $5,000 (Bale 1987:40).[17]

If anything, victims of mass disasters received smaller recoveries on average than workers injured individually.[18] Three years after the 1911 fire in the Triangle Shirtwaist Company, in which 145 young women were killed due to a locked fire escape, the twenty-three civil cases against the building owner were settled for the sum of $75 each (*New York Times* 1914).[19] The early 1930s Hawk's Nest disaster, in which over seven hundred tunnel workers died of silicosis and which has been labeled America's worst industrial disaster, led to the bringing of a total of 538 suits, thirty-four of them for wrongful death. The total amount of settlements was $200,000, "only two thirds of which actually accrued to [the victims]" (Cherniack 1986:73).[20] If every claimant shared in the recovery, the average recovery would have been about $390, reduced by the lawyers' one-third or one-half. When those who did not recover are eliminated, the shares are correspondingly higher. And it should be noted that those who filed were only a minority of those who contracted silicosis or other maladies.[21]

Victims of "consumer" disasters—theater fires, capsized excursion steamers, and so forth—fared no better. When the "Absolutely Fireproof" Iroquois Theater burned in Chicago in 1903, killing 602 patrons, "a few dozen of the civil suits were settled for payment of $750 per death" before the company was discharged in bankruptcy (Speiser 1980:134). There was no recovery for the 1,031 fatalities of the excursion steamer *General Slocum*, which burned in the East River on June 14, 1904 (Werstein 1965:148). Even the $15 to $18 million in claims generated by the 1912 sinking of the *Titanic*, in which 1,500 lost their lives, led in 1916 to settlements with the American claimants for $664,000. The largest settlement for death was $50,000, with the recovery for the death of immigrants set at $1,000 (*New York Times* 1916). In the 1942 Coconut Grove nightclub fire in Boston, in which 492 were killed, each claimant eventually received about $160 (after legal expenses) from the bankrupt defendant (Keyes 1984:160). The legal treatment of mass disasters before World War II is a story of hapless victims encountering ineffectual and sometimes predatory lawyers, unflinching antagonists, unresponsive law, callous lawmakers, and a largely indifferent public.

The Transition to a High Accountability-High Remedy System

Half a century later there is a new legal world with a legal doctrine more favorable to claimants, a more skilled and sophisticated (and less exploitative) plaintiffs' bar, and judges and juries that award more ample recoveries. These legal institutions are set in a far richer and more educated society, with higher expectations of institutional performance. Lawyers, scholars, and journalists generate much richer information about that performance. National media connect regions, classes, and races; the softening of social divisions has extended the bounds of empathy.

This new legal world reflects changes in the incidence of risk and expectations of remedy. Lawrence Friedman reminds us that in nineteenth-century America "a person could not expect to pass through life without sudden catastrophe" (Friedman 1985:50). "In life there was no general expectation of justice or fairness; no general expectation that somebody or some agency would provide compensation for material loss. In the legal system, too, the situation was basically the same: no general expectation of justice, no norms that promised justice in every circumstance, no rules that generally promised compensation" (Friedman 1985:51). But technology has "made the world over," bringing "dramatic . . . far reaching reductions in the uncertainties of life" (Friedman 1985:51, 52) and raising public expectations of life and of law.

Legal institutions in the United States have been reshaped to support a high accountability-high remedy system that corresponds with these values and expectations.[22] Changing expectations have been accompanied by increasing investment in each of our four layers: there is more safety technology, more government control, more welfare and insurance, and more control by the tort system. (This does not imply a claim that the present mix is optimum.)

Cases involving what we might call "consumer" disasters—crashes of commercial airliners or hotel fires—routinely lead to substantial compensation. A study of recovery for 2,113 victims of air crashes on major U.S. airlines from 1970 to 1984 found that the average compensation was $363,608—but even this was only about half of the full economic loss of the survivors (King and Smith 1988: viii). In the 1977 Beverly Hills Supper Club fire in Southgate, Kentucky, some 260 claimants (including survivors of the 165 fatalities) settled for a total of $34 million. In the 1980 MGM Grand Hotel fire in Las Vegas, in which 84 persons were killed, a $155 million settlement fund was established for the 1,357 plaintiffs (Lewin 1984). The total settlement of thirty-nine claims arising from the 1980 fire at Stouffer's Inn in Harrison, New York, in which there were twenty-five deaths, was $48.6 million. All but one of the claimants settled for seven-figure amounts (Flaharty 1984). One hundred claims (involving 85 deaths) arising from the 1981 fire at the Las Vegas Hilton Hotel were settled for $22.8 million. (Tarr 1985).

With industrial disasters the record is more mixed, but the movement is in the same direction. Consider the 1972 Buffalo Creek disaster in West Virginia, less than a hundred miles southwest of the Hawk's Nest tunnel. Over 125 persons were killed, communities were demolished, and thousands had their lives disrupted when a Pittston Corporation mine dam collapsed, flooding the valley below (Erikson 1976). A suit on behalf of 600 victims was brought as an intense, and ultimately profitable, pro bono effort by a major Washington law firm.[23] It involved a massive deployment of legal resources, intensive investigation, the development of innovative theories of recovery, strenuous and effective legal maneuvers—and ultimately a settlement of $13.5 million (Stern 1977).[24] The result was an unusual instance of a major legal campaign for a group of victims operating under unified direction. In spite of the high levels of skill and coordination, this campaign focused exclusively on compensation; it did not address the victims' problems of reestablishing community, nor did it address what Robert Rabin calls one of the "central features of the case, the total absence of an administrative enforcement system that could have prevented the tragedy" (Rabin 1978: 286). Early on, plaintiffs' counsel announced his intention to press for a remedy that would control future corporate conduct, but no trace of this appeared in the settlement agreement (Stern 1977:86–87).[25] Other claimants settled on their own, apparently for a total of more than $14 million. Another large group of cases on behalf of affected children, managed by another major Washington firm, was settled for $4.88 million in early 1978 (*Wall Street Journal* 1978).

Buffalo Creek is not a typical industrial disaster story. On February 3, 1971, a year before the dam burst at Buffalo Creek, an explosion at the Thiokol Corporation plant in Camden County, Georgia killed twenty-nine workers and injured more than fifty while they were making incendiary flares for the U.S. government. Some sixty-five lawsuits were filed. The victims, like those in Buffalo Creek, were settled workers with ties in the locality. But again we have a pattern of relatively marginal claimants—here, rural black women—matched against organizations that are powerful, resourceful, and centrally located (Scardino 1986:9). Both Thiokol and the government were held liable in a 1977 ruling,[26] but tort recovery from Thiokol was preempted by Georgia's workers compensation law. Protracted resistance by the government led to an extended series of appeals, including a rehearing before a bench of twenty-four judges of the United States Court of Appeals[27] and a reference to the Georgia Supreme Court.[28] By 1986, some forty-four suits had been settled. The victims had sued for $717 million in compensation, but it was estimated that the settlements would total less than $20 million.[29] The litigation was still winding down in late 1989. Its sixteen-year span would not be out of place in India. Still, this is not Hawk's Nest; we have rigorous accountability and substantial damages.

In recent decades the processing of mass disaster recovery through the tort system has become more efficient. In the single-event "disaster," courts have fashioned devices for aggregating multiple claims and processing them more expeditiously. The 1986 arson fire that killed ninety-seven and seriously injured over one hundred more at the San Juan Dupont Plaza Hotel gave rise to 275 suits filed by some 2,337 plaintiffs against more than 250 defendants. By mid-1991 settlements of $220.9 million had disposed of the victims' claims; the amount and division of plaintiffs' lawyers' fees had been litigated; and the court was turning to the resolution of insurance coverage issues (Blum 1991). A complex mediation by federal and state court judges resolved all claims arising from the 1987 collapse of the L'Ambiance Plaza in Bridgeport, Connecticut in eighteen months (Verhovek 1988). The $41 million settlement involved "92 lawyers representing 16 injured workers, the estates and families of 28 . . . killed [workers] and 40 contractors, subcontractors and other defendants" (Ravo

1988). On the other hand, as Tom Durkin and William Felstiner show in the next chapter, the courts and lawyers have struggled in vain to find a mode of expeditious resolution of the vast epidemic of asbestos cases.[30]

As asbestos—or Thiokol—reminds us, even in a strong, high accountability system, compensation of victims through lawsuits involves tremendous transaction costs—uncertainty, delay, lawyers' fees. Typically claimants have to grant tremendous discounts from announced entitlements to overcome them. And the relief comes late—not when it would do most good in terms of rebuilding shattered lives.

We know that as a compensation device, tort is extremely costly and uneven in performance. Barriers of information and initiative mean that many or most potential cases are never brought (Abel 1987). How good is tort in controlling risk? Frankly we do not know. Indeed, current attacks on the tort system vacillate between accusing it of overdeterring and of being ineffectual. The complex undertaking of assessing these claims remains to be done. In the meantime we can surmise that had the United States pursued the more traveled path of industrial nations by developing comprehensive administrative and welfare measures to deal with the injurious effects of industry, there would have been little for it to offer *ex post* in the Bhopal case. But by fostering a market in potent retrospective private remedies (which in turn become powerful symbols), American society created a resource that could be put to unanticipated transnational uses.

The Collision with India

Having taken this detour through the tort system, let us return to our example of a new productive technology arriving in India accompanied by its complement of new risks. Safety technologies are attenuated by a less educated and skilled workforce. Administrative controls are weak, for example, factory inspectors in Madhya Pradesh are few and lack resources to monitor sophisticated production facilities. India's welfare state provisions were sparse. Not only were all these layers weak, but the private law layer was weak as well. India has a low accountability-low remedy tort system. At the risk of distortion by condensation, let me briefly set out some of the principal components of that system at the time of the Bhopal accident.[31]

• India had an undeveloped tort law. Few tort cases were brought. There had been little doctrinal development. Tort is little used and has remained largely outside the consciousness of Indian lawyers and public.

- Delays of Bleak House proportions are routine. In a survey I conducted of reported tort cases in the ten years 1975–1984, these cases took an average of twelve years and nine months from filing to decision. They did not involve matters of great complexity, either logistical or technological: in the twenty-two negligence cases, the most common fact situation was a railroad crossing accident (7); next was a downed electrical line (3). There was not a single product liability case among the fifty-six cases located in my survey, nor any case involving any industrial process or chemical mishap. Nor did these cases involve massive amounts of evidence, large numbers of experts, or large numbers of parties.
- The sources of the amazing longevity are several. First, there are relatively few courts—about one-tenth as many on a per capita basis as in the United States (Galanter 1985b:attachment C). Staggering backlogs have been building for a generation. Lawyers' and judges' work habits of dealing with cases piecemeal and lavish provision for multiple interlocutory appeals (originally designed for colonial supervision of unreliable locals) equip the determined adversary with abundant opportunity to prolong litigation almost indefinitely.
- Upon invoking the courts, claimants must pay substantial fees, proportional to the size of their claim, which are charged whether they are successful or not. These fees divert disputes (and legal experience) away from money damages tort cases into other channels (e.g., criminal law, injunctive relief).
- Where tort cases are brought, recovery is far from assured. Of the 56 cases, 48 had been resolved. Some twenty-three of these failed to recover anything. The average recovery of the plaintiffs who won was only Rs 15,159. The median recovery was Rs 7,895.[32]
- High *ad valorem* court fees, protracted delay, and meager recoveries discourage claimants. Neither contingency fees nor legal aid are present to overcome financial barriers to access. Rules shifting costs to losing parties raise the risks of pioneering litigation.
- India has a numerous and well-established legal profession. Lawyers in India are courtroom advocates; their role does not include investigation and fact-development; specialization is rudimentary; barring some recent exceptions, there are no firms or other forms of enduring professional collaboration that would allow a division of labor and pooling of resources to support the development of expertise in tort law. One may visualize Indian lawyers as stuck in a hyper-individualized bazaar economy in which virtually all lawyers offer the same narrow range of services.
- The setting in which Indian lawyers work is devoid of institutional

support for specialized knowledge: there are no specialist organizations, no specialized technical publishing, no continuing legal education; nor is there a vigorous scholarly community.

- Indian civil procedure does not include provisions for wide-ranging discovery that would permit factual investigation in complex problems of technology or corporate management. There are no special procedures for handling complex litigation involving massive amounts of evidence or large numbers of parties. Bar and bench, though they contain many brilliant and talented individuals, have a very limited fund of experience, skills, and organizational capacity to address massive cases involving complex questions of fact.

The cumulative effect of these factors, together with cultural and political predispositions, is that there has been little connection between tort law and disasters in India. Such a negative is hard to document. I can only say that I have never heard of an instance of an industrial explosion, mine cave-in, building collapse, food adulteration, or other mass injury leading to tort claims. Surveys of all the tort cases reported by India's leading series of law reports since 1975 did not reveal a single case that arose from such an incident.[33] What typically happens in disasters is that the government announces that it is making *ex gratia* payments of specified amount to the victims. For example, when four people were trampled to death in a March 1989 stampede at the New Delhi railway station, the railway announced an *ex gratia* payment of Rs 5,000 [approximately $320 at then current exchange rates] to the kin of the deceased and of Rs 1,000 to the injured. A departmental inquiry was ordered and a criminal case was registered on the basis of the negligent announcement that was thought to have triggered the stampede (*Hindu* 1989). Attributions of responsibility, if pursued at all, would be done by a governmental investigation or perhaps a criminal prosecution or a commission of inquiry. In each case, the inquiry into responsibility is dissociated from the administration of compensation.

We need not take the present level of controls as representing a calculated choice and conclude that Indians have consented to that level of protection. As in most societies, including our own, there is a pretense that government affords more protection than it does in fact. Lackadaisical administration, failures of implementation, and the expense of remedies attenuate even the most ample substantive standards. What was so striking in the Bhopal case was that the Government of India took the unusual step of dropping the ordinary pretense and conceding—at least momentarily—that its private law controls were inadequate, a move that earned it the severe reproach of the Indian legal establishment.

In Bhopal, India's low accountability-low remedy system collided with the high accountability-high remedy system of the United States. Because the Bhopal event was transnational, it was not contained within either the Indian or the U.S. system. Had Bhopal been a purely Indian event, there would most likely have been a modest *ex gratia* payment by the company and/or the government and that would have been the end of the matter. If it had been an American event, it is likely that there would have been very substantial payments to the victims, possibly on a scale that would have significantly diminished the company, and the proceedings would have generated strong preventive effects on safety practices (storage, warnings, etc.). Indeed, as documented by numerous other contributors to this volume, the specter of Bhopal did generate a whole range of preventive activity in the United States—as far as one can tell—with far more reduction of risk than in India.

The contrast between the two systems drove a series of attempts at arbitrage. The great ambulance chase by American lawyers in Bhopal can be read as testimony to the gap. So can the Government of India's insertion of itself as representative of the victims to pursue their claims in the United States. But these attempts to connect the victims with the most promising forum should be placed in the context of increasing transnational flows of legal services. The arrival of the plaintiffs' lawyers in Bhopal was only the most visible spurt of a sustained flow of American lawyers servicing transnational transactions. Union Carbide's international operations, including its Indian ones, were already served by transnational lawyers. What is unusual is that the Bhopal victims managed to get connected as well. Jet planes, instantaneous transmission of news, and an open society allowing unimpeded flow of news and people made it possible for the gap to be bridged. The possibility of U.S. jurisdiction and massive recoveries induced entrepreneurial personal injury lawyers and the Indian government to use these resources to bridge the gap.

These efforts were abrogated by Judge John Keenan's decision to grant Union Carbide's motion to dismiss the case from the United States courts.[34] Having overestimated the capacity of the Indian system, Judge Keenan hedged by attempting to devise his own linkage, lending some of the strength of the U.S. system to the victims while relieving his own court from the onerous burden of this mega-case. In granting Union Carbide's motion to dismiss on grounds of *forum non conveniens*,[35] Judge Keenan was persuaded that the Indian courts and lawyers were capable of improvising procedures adequate to dealing with this case of a kind and scale unknown to them. In the event, no such innovative response was forthcoming.[36] Indeed, the two notable innovations, both from the public interest sector and each intended to help the plaintiffs' cause, both arguably redounded to the detriment of the claimants. The first of these was a ruling by the Supreme Court of India in a case involving a gas leak that occurred in New Delhi just weeks before the hearing scheduled in Judge Keenan's court on the forum issue (see also Rosencranz et al., this volume, Chapter 3). The Supreme Court of India's aggressive response, later crystalized into a doctrine of expanded liability for dangerous industrial processes, was urged by Carbide as a warrant of the innovative capacity of the Indian courts and apparently contributed to Judge Keenan's decision. (That this centerpiece of Indian judicial activism ended up being used by Union Carbide, but not by the plaintiffs, suggests that even favorable substantive doctrine does not make a decisive difference in a setting in which procedural and institutional tools are lacking.) A second innovation by a dedicated intervenor who persuaded the District Judge hearing the case to award interim relief provided the occasion for appeal to the Supreme Court of India, which imposed a settlement in February 1989.[37] The settlement for $470 million, by far the largest recovery in any Indian litigation, was far short of the $3.1 billion that the Government had sought.

To earlier misgivings about the inadequacy and callousness of the relief efforts was added new disquiet with the amount of the settlement and the termination of the case without either a definitive finding of fault or establishment of norms of corporate conduct. In the end, both the Government of India and the Supreme Court declared themselves defeated by intractable gridlock and delay. The Government justified the settlement on the ground that "Eminent lawyers have argued that this case, which has already been four years in various courts in the pretrial stage, would in the most optimistic circumstances need anywhere from 15 to 25 more years for an ultimate decision" (*Hindustan Times* 1989). This was not a claim that the settlement represented the victims' true entitlements; rather it was an assertion that whatever the magnitude of those entitlements, the character of India's legal system made it inevitable that they could not be obtained before passage of so long a period that the discounted present value of the claims was less than the amount to be delivered under the settlement. The features of the system that prevented a timely and adequate adjudication were treated, by the Government itself, as given and unalterable.[38]

While the merits of the settlement continued to be hotly debated, the money, which was paid over immediately, was not distributed to the victims because the government had not assembled machinery for distribution nor devised a policy for distributing it.[39] Unable to devise a system for identifying the actual victims, the government made uniform (and miniscule) interim payments to residents of some thirty-six wards in the city of Bhopal. The first determinations of individual compensation took place in mid-1992, eight and a half years after the event and over three years after the settlement. By June 1993 only 5 percent of the claims had been adjudicated; of these, all death cases, 70 percent were rejected (N.K. Singh 1993). Typical awards in death cases were about Rs. 100,000 (equivalent to $3,200 at the 1993 exchange rate) (N.K. Singh 1993; S. Hazarika 1993).

To some observers, including myself, the course of events reinforced earlier apprehensions that Indian courts and lawyers were unlikely to bring the matter to a satisfactory conclusion and confirmed the conviction that the matter would have had a more satisfactory outcome had it remained in the courts of the United States. In the end, the heroic interventions of a few "public interest" actors were too isolated to overcome the endemic inertia and mismanagement.

Transnational Remedies in a World of Unequal Remedial Capacities

We have seen that tort is a very expensive and unwieldy system of controlling the risks of new technologies. The compensation it delivers is often inadequate—especially for the most seriously injured[40]— and too late. The transaction costs are very high. And in mass disasters there are severe administrative problems. But these defects must be looked at in the context of comparison with other institutional alternatives.[41] Tort does offer some advantages that are particularly telling where the other layers of controls are weak, as in most developing countries. Tort can be "self-enforcing" through mobilizing a class of bounty-hunting lawyers. And it can operate without the extensive *ex ante* investment that it takes to put into place safety regulations or administrative controls or welfare state provisions.

Disputes involving complex technology typically involve large organizations. As societies industrialize, an increasing portion of serious disputes are between entities of different sizes—typically between individuals and large organizations—rather than between comparable entities. Legal systems will differ in their ability to handle disputes arising from complex technology and large organizations and to offset the advantages of organizations in legal combat with individuals.

It is likely that in the foreseeable future, legal systems will differ greatly in their capacities, their goals, and their priorities. Like engineering, banking, insurance, and other specialized information services, legal services will not be evenly dispersed, but will be concentrated at central locations. Expectably, agents and brokers will appear to make available elsewhere the services produced at these central nodes. So far most of these transnational innovations are extensions of the "corporate hemisphere" of the legal profession that services large organizations.[42] We can see only the glimmerings of transnational activity among lawyers who occupy the hemisphere of the legal profession that services individuals.[43] One can imagine devices for linkage that are more sophisticated and more enduring than the ad hoc exertions of the American plaintiffs' lawyers and the Government of India. Such devices might include multinational law firms, networks of lawyers like corresponding banks, international placement and matchmaking services, or trade union insistence on favorable choice of forum provisions in technology-transfer agreements.

The growing transnational traffic in legal services is predominantly, though not exclusively, a matter of the spread of American lawyers and their highly rationalized, client-oriented lawyering style.[44] J. Gillers Wetter suggests that we are living in the midst of a "singular movement," comparable to the reception of Roman law in Europe, "the adoption and absorption throughout the world of a less clearly defined legal heritage in which many characteristic elements can be traced back to the common law, with an American flavor" (Wetter 1980:217; Wiegand 1991). The appeal of U.S. lawyers is connected to the strength of the U.S. remedy system.[45] The strength of U.S. legal technologies suggests the possibility of a second wave of transnationalization of law, in which the capacity for local legal systems to investigate and remedy harms to individuals from technological risks is upgraded or linked to stronger forums.[46]

Notes

1. I have omitted here those arrangements in the recipient country (like the placement of housing or the adequacy of roads) which, though not designed with an eye to exposure to the risks in question, may increase or decrease such exposure.

2. Cf. Atiyah 1987 on contrast with England.

3. Pfennigstorf and Gifford (1991:129) attribute the less frequent resort to tort remedies in other industrialized democracies to the presence of public entitlement systems or to public and private insurance; these "alternative compensation sources do much of the work that is accomplished under the tort system in the United States." On the scantier coverage and lesser coordination of American social security schemes, see Grana 1983; Kaim-Caudle 1973.

4. On the shape and costs of the tort system, see Hensler et al. 1987.

5. Cf. Schuck 1991:27.

6. Juries are a significant component of the civil remedy system in the United States and to a lesser extent in parts of Australia and Canada. See Galanter 1990b.

7. For a discussion of the problems of extracting and applying this knowledge, see Galanter 1990b.

8. In a review of the sizable literature on deterrence, Gibbs 1986 observes that, since deterrence research has proceeded without controls for other general effects, "all previous reported tests of the deterrence doctrine . . . were really tests of an implicit theory of general preventive effects; and that will remain the case as long as nondeterrent mechanisms are left uncontrolled." The literature on the effects of tort law displays the same conflation of deterrence with other preventive effects that Gibbs finds in the criminal law literature.

9. This notion of "general effects" takes off from the very helpful discussion of general preventive effects of punishment by Gibbs (1975:ch. 3), as usefully elaborated by Feeley (1976:517ff). It is simply a generalization from the illuminating and now familiar (if not entirely serviceable, as Gibbs points out) distinction between special deterrence and general deterrence introduced by Andeneas 1966.

10. Some of the labels used here for the various effects are inspired by those carefully discussed by Gibbs 1975. A fuller taxonomy of the effects of litigation can be found in Galanter (1983:124ff).

11. Other studies provide suggestive but contrasting hypotheses about the conditions under which such enculturation takes place and its relation to the coercive aspects of law. Cf. Muir 1967 with Dolbeare and Hammond 1971.

12. See, for example, the studies by Wiley 1981 and Givelber, Bowers, and Blitch 1984.

13. This estimate was for all cases resolved after filing in courts of general jurisdiction, but did not include claims resolved without filing. Nor did it include the cost of the governmental institutions, which another team of Rand researchers estimates as $320 million for 1982 (Kakalik and Robyn 1982:62).

14. None of these studies compare costs at different points in time, but there is some reason to think that there is variation from time to time as fields become more routine or more problematic.

15. Thinking that other people are entitled to compensation (by the wrongdoer or some impersonal organ of society) when they suffer is an attenuated expression of human solidarity. It is not a willingness to sacrifice for others, to succor them, to share their burdens—but it is not indifference or dismissal either. It stands in contrast to societies in which the suffering of others may be seen, if it is seen at all, as in the nature of things.

16. In addition, in thirteen instances suit was still pending and in ten others there was recovery of an unknown amount.

17. In Michigan in 1910, the average recovery for death on the job was $388 for industrial workers and $1,158 for miners (Bale 1987:44).

18. A striking exception was the 1909 Cherry Mine fire, in which some 270 miners were killed. Although the St. Paul Mining Company originally proposed to pay $100 for each death, outside intervention led to average payments of over $1,400, remarked at the time as extremely generous. The heirs of unmarried victims received $800; widows were given $1,800 (State of Illinois 1910).

19. The owner of the Triangle Shirtwaist Company, a known insurance claim "repeater," collected $64,925 in insurance—some $445 for each dead worker (Stein 1962:176).

20. This report of the amount withheld by the lawyers is at variance with the other accounts that reported contingency fees of 50 percent (Cherniack 1986:66; U.S. House of Representatives 1936:4, 69).

21. The House Subcommittee Resolution referred to 476 dead and an additional 1,500 "now suffering from silicosis" (U.S. House of Representatives 1936:1). Cherniack reports that about 2,500 worked in the tunnel, including about 1,200 who were heavily exposed (Cherniack 1986:29, 98).

22. Although it is evident that something has changed, it is less clear just how to characterize this shift. Friedman views it as a shift in popular culture, but compare Sanders, who suggests that it is not a general change in views but an increase in variance, so that there are now sizable (but not necessarily majority) portions of the population that hold views more favorable to high accountability and high recovery (Sanders 1987:610). In any case, it is necessary to explain why the impulse to general protection in America has taken the form of strong tort law rather than the kind of comprehensive welfare state that is found in other industrial societies.

23. Although Arnold & Porter's involvement was "pro bono" in the sense that the firm would probably not have taken the case absent the "doing good" aspects, the financial arrangement was actually a standard contingency fee set at the modest level of 25 percent.

24. Some observers were troubled by the chanciness of the whole proceeding. Robert Rabin points out that the outcome was very much affected by a series of contingencies—the identity of the judge, untested theories, bargaining in "an Alice-in-Wonderland atmosphere in which the lawyers traded monetary claims made out of whole cloth" in "negotiations [that] took no account of precedent or of individual claims—normal guidelines were suspended" (Rabin 1978:294, 295).

25. The settlement abandoned the demand for public attribution of blame. The expertise of Arnold & Porter was dismantled and no further representation of flood victims was undertaken, although plaintiffs' counsel insisted on placing the entire results of his investigation in the record, so the loss of knowledge was limited. The Arnold & Porter representation covered only a minority of the survivors—650 out of more than 2,000.

26. *Artez v. United States*, 503 F. Supp. 260 (S.D. Ga., 1977), damages awarded 456 F. Supp. 397 (S.D. Ga., 1978), aff'd 604 F.2d 417 (5th Cir. 1979).

27. *Artez v. United States*, 635 F.2d 485 (1981).

28. *United States v. Aretz*, 248 Ga. 19, 280 S.E.2d 345 (1981).

29. This account is from Scardino 1986.

30. Courts inundated by asbestos cases adopted innovative case-management plans, such as the Ohio Asbestos Litigation Plan (Orlando 1988). Other courts devised novel procedures for handling massive insurance indemnification litigation. In 1985 thirty-four asbestos producers and sixteen insurers established the "Wellington Facility" to use "alternative dispute resolution techniques" to resolve claims. The Facility collapsed in 1988 (Mitchell and Barrett 1988), leading to a reported surge of asbestos trials (Carter 1988). In the Manville proceedings, a solution was eventually negotiated among contending groups—management, stockholders, various classes of creditors, insurers, injury victims, future claimants, and so forth—placing more than half

of the company's stock in a trust for the asbestos injury claimants. The Manville Personal Injury Settlement Trust, an entirely new kind of creature, was established to pay some $2.5 billion to claimants over a twenty-six-year period (Alternatives to the High Cost of Litigation 1988). The Manville Trust subsequently developed its own financial difficulties (Schachner 1993).

31. This summary is borrowed from Galanter 1990a. A fuller discussion of these features may be found in Galanter 1985 a, b.

32. The exchange value of the rupee was approximately twelve to the U.S. dollar in late 1984, seventeen to the U.S. dollar in 1989, and twenty-five to the dollar in mid-1991. On damages and their determination in India, see Galanter 1985a: 276. A more recent survey by Mary Versailles (1991) of cases reported in the *All-India Reporter* analyzed recoveries for death of an adult male in a motor vehicle accident case. The average recovery in cases decided in 1985 was Rs 74,084 and the median was Rs 56,640. Taking inflation into account, the size of recoveries remained constant from 1976 to 1986.

33. I rely here on surveys of cases reported in the *All-India Reporter* conducted by my students, Gary Wilson, J.D. (1986) University of Wisconsin, and Mary Versailles, J.D., University of Wisconsin (1991).

34. *In re* Union Carbide Corporation Gas Plant Disaster at Bhopal, India in December 1984, 634 F. Supp. 842 (S.D. N.Y., 1986).

35. That is, on the ground that the American court was not the most convenient forum and that an adequate alternative forum existed in which the case could be heard.

36. Earlier talk about special courts, limitation of interlocutory appeals, and so forth was never implemented.

37. On the settlement and its aftermath, see Barr 1989. The Supreme Court's definitive response to questions engendered by the settlement is found in *Union Carbide Corporation v. Union of India* (A.I.R. 1991 S.C. 248).

38. In the decision of the Supreme Court of India dismissing objections to the settlement, this same unalterability argument was endorsed by the Chief Justice of India:

> If the litigation was to go on merits in the Bhopal Court it would have perhaps taken at least 8 to 10 years; an appeal to the High Court and a further appeal to this Court would have taken in all around another spell of 10 years with steps for expedition taken. We can, therefore, fairly assume that litigation in India would have taken around 20 years to reach finality. (*Union Carbide v. Union of India*, A.I.R. 1992 S.C. 248).

39. In the meanwhile, the Government of India has reduced by more than half its commitment to funding a seven-year rehabilitation program (*India Today* 1989).

40. Where many pursue legal remedies together, the most seriously injured may be less well served than the larger number of less seriously injured. Cf. the observation that: "Other things being equal, plaintiffs are likely to receive a higher recovery in an individual action than in a class action" (Coffee 1987). A study of civil actions in Cook County, Illinois found that each additional co-plaintiff added to civil actions reduced the original plaintiff's compensation by 27 percent (Chin and Peterson 1985).

41. Cf. Komasar 1990.

42. In their analysis of the structure of the Chicago bar, Heinz and Lau-

mann (1982:48) described the fundamental structural division in the practice of law between those lawyers (typically organized into larger offices) who represent corporations and other organizations and those lawyers (typically in smaller practices) who represent individuals.

43. For a fascinating account of the transfer of expertise from German to Japanese thalidomide claimants, see Ino et al. 1975.

44. The unplanned export of U.S. legal institutions that is "quietly emerging through the international market for U.S. legal services" (Garth 1985:6.) is an ironic variation on the vision of legal influence that animated the law and development movement of the 1960s, which sought to replicate legal institutions, rules, and training to produce local approximations of advanced legal institutions (which, as critics pointed out, turned out to be remarkably similar to our own). See Trubek and Galanter 1974; Gardner 1980.

45. "When breakdowns in the system do occur, the international actors prefer to fight with the best available technology, and for a variety of reasons that tends to mean "metalitigation" in the United States. In no other country do the parties have such power—stemming especially from liberal discovery—to escalate a dispute into a tremendously costly lawsuit. . . . Despite recent discussion of the efficiency of settlements, it can be suggested that the deterrent impact of large-scale litigation helps to bolster the peaceful regime of international legality and access to the U.S. arsenal of weapons helps to maintain that stability" (Garth 1985:10).

46. India is a society with a lot of lawyers, a vast pool of scientific and technical expertise, and well-established judicial institutions; it contains the resources needed to develop a stronger system of remedies. Such a development would entail a massive rearrangement of existing components of the legal system. But there are many countries that probably do not have the potential to have legal systems that contain procedures and expertise to handle gigantic, complex lawsuits. Consider that half of the sovereign nations in the world have populations of less than five million; there are sixty countries with less than two million.

References

Abel, Richard. 1987. "The Real Tort Crisis—Too *Few* Claims." *Ohio State Law Journal* 48: 443–467.

Andeneas, Johannes. 1966. "The General Preventive Effects of Punishments." *University of Pennsylvania Law Review* 114: 949–983.

Atiyah, Patrick. 1987. "Tort Law and the Alternatives: Some Anglo-American Comparisons." *Duke Law Journal* 1987:1002–1044.

Bale, A. 1987. "America's First Compensation Crisis: Conflict Over the Value and Meaning of Workplace Injuries Under the Employers' Liability System." In David Rosner and Gerald Markowitz, eds., *Dying for Work: Workers' Safety and Health in Twentieth-Century America* (Bloomington: Indiana University Press).

Barr, Cameron. 1989. "Carbide's Escape." *American Lawyer* (May, 1989): 99–105.

Berkowitz, Leonard and Nigel Walker. 1967. "Laws and Moral Judgments." *Sociometry* 30: 410–422.

Blum, Andrew. 1991 "Dupont Plaza Steering Committee Gets Paid." *National Law Journal* (August 19): 5.

Cherniack, Martin. 1986. *The Hawk's Nest Incident: America's Worst Industrial Disaster*. New Haven, CT: Yale University Press.

Colombatos, John. 1969. "Physicians and Medicare: A Before-After Study of the Effects of Legislation on Attitudes." *American Sociological Review* 34: 318.

Conard, Alfred F., James N. Morgan, Robert W. Pratt, Jr., Charles E. Voltz, and Robert L. Bombaugh. 1964. *Automobile Accident Costs and Payments*. Ann Arbor: University of Michigan Press.

Dolbeare, Kenneth and Phillip Hammond. 1971. *The School Prayer Decisions: From Court Policy to Local Practice*. Chicago: University of Chicago Press.

Eads, George, and Peter Reuter. 1983. *Designing Safer Products: Corporate Responses to Product Liability Law and Regulation*. Santa Monica, CA: Institute for Civil Justice.

Eastman, Crystal. 1910. *Work Accidents and the Law*. A volume of the Pittsburgh Survey. New York: Charities Publication Committee. Reprinted 1969.

Erikson, Kai. 1976. *Everything in Its Path: Destruction of Community in the Buffalo Creek Flood*. New York: Simon and Schuster.

Feeley, Malcolm. 1976. "The Concept of Laws in Social Science: A Critique and Notes on an Expanded View." *Law and Society Review* 10: 497–523.

Flaharty, F. 1984. "Stouffer Fire Suit Settles for $48.5 M." *National Law Journal* (June 4): 4.

Fleming, John. 1984. "Is There a Future for Tort?" *Louisiana Law Review* 44: 1193–1212.

Friedman, Lawrence. 1985. *Total Justice*. New York: Russell Sage Foundation.

———. 1987. "Civil Wrongs: Personal Injury Law in the Late 19th Century." *American Bar Foundation Research Journal* 1987: 351–78.

Friedman, Lawrence M., and Thomas D. Russell. 1990. "More Civil Wrongs: Personal Injury Litigation, 1901–1910." *American Journal of Legal History* 34: 295–314.

Galanter, Marc. 1983. "The Radiating Effects of Courts." In K. Boyum and S. Mather, eds., *Empirical Theories About Courts* New York: Longman.

———. 1985a. "Legal Torpor: Why So Little Has Happened in India After the Bhopal Tragedy." *Texas International Law Review* 20: 273–295.

———. 1985b. Affidavit, *In re* Union Carbide Corporation Gas Plant Disaster at Bhopal India in December 1984. MDL No. 626, United States District Court, S.D. N.Y. (December 5).

———. 1990a. "Bhopals, Past and Present: The Changing Legal Response to Mass Disaster." *Windsor Yearbook of Access to Justice* 10: 3–22.

———. 1990b. "The Civil Jury as Regulator of the Litigation Process." *University of Chicago Legal Forum* 1990: 201–271.

———. 1991. "Case Congregations and Their Careers." *Law and Society Review* 24: 271–395.

Gardner, James A. 1980. *Legal Imperialism: American Lawyers and Foreign Aid in Latin America*. Madison: University of Wisconsin Press.

Garth, Bryant. 1985. "Transnational Legal Practice and Professional Ideology." *Michigan Yearbook of International Studies* 7: 3–21.

Genn, Hazel. 1987. *Hard Bargaining: Out of Court Settlement in Personal Injury Actions*. Oxford: Oxford University Press.

Gersuny, Carl. 1981. *Work Hazards and Industrial Conflict*. Hanover, NH: University Press of New England.

Gibbs, Jack P. 1975. *Crime, Punishment and Deterrence.* New York: Elsevier.
————. 1986. "Punishment and Deterrence: Theory, Research, and Penal Policy." In L. Lipson and S. Wheeler, eds., *Law and the Social Sciences.* New York: Russell Sage Foundation.
Givelber, Daniel J., William J. Bowers, and Carolyn L. Blitch. 1984. "*Tarasoff,* Myth and Reality: An Empirical Study of Private Law in Action." *Wisconsin Law Review* 1984: 443–497.
Grana, John M. 1983. "Disability Allowances for Long-Term Care in Western Europe and the United States." *International Social Security Review* 36: 207–221.
Hart, H.L.A. 1961. *The Concept of Law,* Oxford: Clarendon Press.
Hensler, Deborah R., Mary E. Vaiana, James S. Kakalik and Mark A. Peterson. 1987. *Trends in Tort Litigation.* Santa Monica, CA: Institute for Civil Justice.
The Hindu. 1989. "Toll Rises to Four in Railway Station Stampede." March 21, p. 9.
Hindustan Times. 1989. "Bhopal Gas Settlement: Govt Justifies Amount." March 8.
India Today. 1989. "Cruel Cut." August 31, p. 74.
Ino, Masaru, et al. 1975. "Diary of a Plaintiffs' Attorneys' Team in the Thalidomide Litigation." *Law in Japan* 8: 136–187.
Kaim-Caudle, P. R. 1973. *Comparative Social Policy and Social Security.* New York: Dunellen, 1973.
Kakalik, James S., and Abby Eisenshtat Robyn. 1982. *Costs of the Civil Justice System: Court Expenditure for Processing Tort Cases.* Santa Monica, CA: Institute for Civil Justice.
Keyes, Edward. 1984. *Coconut Grove.* New York: Atheneum.
King, Elizabeth M., and James P. Smith. 1988. *Economic Loss and Compensation in Aviation Accidents.* Santa Monica, CA: Institute for Civil Justice.
Komesar, Neil K. 1990. "Injuries and Institutions: Tort Reform, Tort Theory and Beyond." *New York University Law Review* 65: 23–77.
Lewis, Tamar. 1984. "Faster Settling of Mass Claims." *New York Times,* Aug. 7, p. 32.
Litan, Robert E. 1991. "The Liability Explosion and American Trade Performance: Myths and Realities." In Peter H. Schuck, ed., *Tort Law and the Public Interest* (New York: W. W. Norton).
McInturff, Patrick S., Jr. 1981. "Products Liability: The Impact on California Manufacturers." *American Business Law Journal* 19: 343.
Mitchell, Cynthia F. and Paul M. Barrett. 1988. "Novel Effort to Settle Asbestos Claims Fails as Lawsuits Multiply." *Wall Street Journal,* June 7, p. 1.
Muir, William. 1967. *Prayer in the Public Schools.* Chicago: University of Chicago Press.
New York Times. 1914. "Settle Triangle Fire Suits." March 12, p. 1.
Orlando, Jacqueline. 1988. "Asbestos Litigation and the Ohio Asbestos Litigation Plan: Insulating he Courts from the Heat." *Ohio Journal of Dispute Resolution* 3: 399–414.
————. 1916. "Pays Titanic Awards." January 28, p. 9, col. 2.
Pfenningstorf, Werner, and Daniel G. Gifford. 1991. *A Comparative Study of Liability Law and Compensation Schemes in Ten Countries and the United States.* Oak Brook, IL: Insurance Research Council.

Rabin, Robert. 1978. "Dealing with Disasters: Some Thoughts on the Adequacy of the Legal System." *Stanford Law Review* 30: 281–298, at 294, 295.

Ravo, Nick. 1988. "Courts Complete Collapse Accord." *New York Times*, December 2.

Sanders, Joseph. 1987. "The Meaning of the Law Explosion: On Friedman's *Total Justice*." *American Bar Foundation Research Journal* 1987:; 601–615.

Scardino, Albert. 1986. "A Tragedy in South Georgia." *New York Times*, July 20, sec. 3, p. 1.

Schuck, Peter H. 1991. "Introduction: The Context of the Controversy." In Peter H. Schuck, ed., *Tort Law and the Public Interest* (New York: W. W. Norton).

Speiser, Stuart M. 1980. *Lawsuit*. New York: Horizon Press.

State of Illinois, Bureau of Labor Statistics. 1910. *Report on the Cherry Mine Disaster*. Springfield: The Bureau).

Stein, Leon. 1962. *The Triangle Fire*. Philadelphia: J. B. Lippincott.

Stern, Gerald. 1977. *The Buffalo Creek Disaster*. New York: Vintage Books.

Sturgis, Robert W. 1989. *Tort Costs Trends: An International Perspective*. Darien, CT. Tillinghast.

Tarr, A. 1985. "Megatrial Averted in Hilton Blaze: Settlement of 115 Claims Approved." *National Law Journal* (October 28): 3.

Trubek, David and Marc Galanter. 1974. "Scholars in Self-Estrangement: Some Reflections on the Crisis in Law and Development Studies in the United States." *Wisconsin Law Review* 1974: 1062–1102.

U.S. House of Representatives. 1936. 74th Cong., 2d Sess., Hearings Before a Subcommittee of the Committee on Labor: An Investigation Relating to Health Conditions of Workers Employed in the Construction and Maintenance of Public Utilities.

Verhovek, Sam Howe. 1988. "$41 Million Settlement Reached by Mediation in Fall of Connecticut Building." *New York Times*, Nov. 16, p. 14.

Viscusi, W. Kip, and Michael J. Moore. 1991. "Rationalizing the Relationship Between Product Liability and Innovation." In Peter H. Schuck, ed., *Tort Law and the Public Interest* (New York: W. W. Norton).

Wall Street Journal. 1978. "Pittston Settles Claims from '72 Dam Collapse Totaling $4,880,000. January 25, p. 17, col. 1.

Werstein, Irving. 1965. *The General Slocum Incident: Story of an Ill-Fated Ship*. New York: John Day.

Wetter, J. Gillers. 1980. "The Case for International Law Schools and an International Legal Profession." *International and Comparative Law Quarterly* 29: 206–218.

Wiley, Jerry. 1981. "The Impact of Judicial Decisions on Professional Conduct: An Empirical Study." *Southern California Law Review* 55: 345–396.

Chapter 8
Bad Arithmetic: Disaster Litigation as Less Than the Sum of Its Parts

Tom Durkin and William L. F. Felstiner

In attempts to compensate methyl isocyanate (MIC) victims at Bhopal and asbestos victims in the United States, vast differences in process led to a final similarity. At Bhopal, the Indian legal system did not deliver timely, equitable compensation to injured parties. Similarly, with asbestos-related diseases (ARDs), the U.S. legal system failed to deliver timely, equitable compensation to most affected workers. Both legal systems thus reached similar results, but by radically different paths. Both industrial disasters[1] have spawned efforts to explore how legal systems and actors learn. This chapter asks the general question of how legal failures come about in mass disasters[2] by evaluating what happened in the aftermath of Bhopal in the light of compensation efforts for ARDs in the United States.

For a number of reasons, U.S. ARD litigation is a particularly appropriate case for examining the upper limits of systemic legal responses. Almost no expenses were spared by plaintiff and defense lawyers seeking new ways to process ARD claims. This makes the ARD case an especially stark contrast with Bhopal, where an unprepared legal system arguably provided the lower limits of systemic responses. In India, a pathetically narrow range of legal options were available to victims. However, in the end the U.S. system, with its extraordinary advantages of resources and experience, reached equally unsatisfactory results.

In contrast to the legal systems of most developing countries, the U.S. tort system is experienced, complex, and well financed; it expeditiously processes many hundreds of thousands of cases annually. Litigation in the asbestos cases is "mature" (McGovern 1988:1); that is, it continues to receive intense judicial and public attention (see

In re Asbestos Products Liability Litigation, No. VI, 1991), it has already consumed somewhere between $5 and $8 billion dollars in damage awards and defense costs (Forbes 1991:19), it affects large numbers of people distributed across wide geographic areas (Peto and Schneiderman 1981), and it can be compared cross-nationally (Felstiner and Dingwall 1988). There is extensive research on ARD litigation in the United States (Durkin 1991). Finally, there is a long history of liability litigation involving the same participants. Many legal innovations have been greeted with predictions that *the* solution to the ARD crisis was at hand (*Business Insurance* 1988; *Insight* 1988:41; Willging 1987:xii, 22; but see Hensler 1989:1). If it is possible for legal actors and organizations to "learn from disaster," the experienced and involved students of ARD victim compensation should most likely have done it.

Organizations and legal actors in the United States are generally active, innovative, flexible, and committed leaders. Most are continually willing to change a losing game. Nevertheless, the U.S. legal system, despite extremely high incentives to learn on all sides and more than a decade of concerted effort, has failed to provide nearly enough compensation to nearly enough victims (Gaskins 1989:262–276). Unlike the victims of ARDs, the Bhopal victims were able to frame and name their diseases more quickly (Durkin 1991; Reich, this volume, Chapter 9). The compensation process was greatly expedited not only by the presence of obvious physical evidence, but by the efforts of many organized supporters. However, this benefit was outweighed by other problems: the indeterminate cause of the explosion itself, the accompanying confusion, legal and structural constraints, and the "hyperindividuality" of Indian plaintiffs' lawyers (Galanter 1988 and this volume, Chapter 7) precluded quick resolution. We argue that the cause in both the ARD and Bhopal cases is scale: disasters of this magnitude simply overwhelm the capacity of legal institutions to meet victim compensation needs.

What types of strategic efforts were employed by the U.S. actors, and with what effect? In the U.S. ARD litigation, there are four key groups to consider: defendants, courts, plaintiffs' lawyers, and victims' associations. Their tactics are reviewed below in rough chronological order. This history reflects the reality of consecutive efforts, and this is where we would expect evidence of learning to appear. The failed attempts provide evidence that what occurred in the United States overall was more a series of unrelated attempts to shift financial responsibility than it was cumulative "learning." This series of repeated and frustrated strategies does not resemble the incremental learning posited by Charles Lindblom (1979:519), but rather a set of unrelated attempts to shift financial responsibility. Far from learning, new strategies appeared to gain little from prior families.

Defendants

Asbestos manufacturers and their insurers have been the object of tens of thousands of liability claims and have been exposed to the possibility of paying thousands of millions of dollars in damages and incurring correspondingly large transaction costs, mostly the expenses of legal defense. Originally, their goal was to minimize these costs. Eventually, the manufacturers and some insurers—for example, Raytech, Keene, and Lloyds—realized that their goal had become organizational survival. Defendants sought, usually unsuccessfully but nevertheless repetitively, to escape by pleading standard defenses such as statutes of limitation, assumption of risk, contributory negligence (smoking), and state of the art. Their options, unlimited yet burdened by the complexities of the U.S. legal system, allowed defendants to experiment with a wide range of imaginative tactics not available in India.

Buy silence

A technique used in the early days of ARD litigation was to settle a claim contingent on the plaintiffs' lawyers' agreement not to pursue similar cases (Brodeur 1985; Castleman 1990). This device originated as early as 1933 (Peters and Peters 1980:H6) and continued sporadically into the late 1970s, when its use was limited to mass settlements. It has from time to time proven successful in suppressing liability claims in other industrial disasters (Cherniack 1986:41–42; *Chicago Daily Law Bulletin* 1989:3; Lord 1987:45; Sunday Times of London Investigative Team 1979; Yates 1987:17). It fails when caseloads increase to the extent that defendants lose the benefit of secrecy and plaintiffs' lawyers become reluctant to forgo the income derivable from subsequent cases or other qualified lawyers are available to pursue them.

Worker Compensation

Until the early 1970s most ARD claims were brought by workers employed by asbestos manufacturing concerns. With few exceptions, these early victims could seek damages only through worker compensation programs. In the early 1970s several court cases extended liability to manufacturers for failure to warn of the dangers involved in the use of their products. Victims who used, rather than manufactured, asbestos products had the choice of bringing a workers' compensation claim against their employer (a shipyard or chemical plant, for instance) or bringing a tort suit against the manufacturers of the asbestos products they used in their work. Victims chose not to rely on worker compensation, since compensation claims paid significantly less than tort recoveries and were vulnerable to many of the same defenses (Field and Victor 1988).

The defects in workers' compensation claims were legion, which led to increasing manufacturer responsibility. ARD latency periods (15–50 years) made proof of causality difficult (Viscusi 1988:168–169); statutes of limitation excluded many potential claimants; indirect victims, such as workers' spouses and employees of asbestos-using firms, were excluded; defendants often challenged the connection between the disease and employment hazards; and retirement or lack of lost work time reduced claims because no wage loss was involved (Field and Victor 1988:22–23). Deborah Hensler et al. (1985:118) summarize the drawbacks of workers' compensation:

Many of the problems we have noted about the tort system, including timing of claims, standards for proving causation, and issues arising out of the involvement of multiple defendants have not been solved by state workers' compensation systems either. In addition, workers' compensation systems have usually provided less than full compensation of wage loss, and no compensation for pain and suffering.

At Bhopal, worker compensation was not a major issue, since the injuries were sustained mainly by people outside the plant. In addition, the Indian government had no program or organizational structure to serve as a model for handling the claims that actually arose (Chapter 7, this volume). Based on prior experience, India's government, when it did respond to the disaster, could only grant an *ex gratia* pittance to the families of victims.

Federal Legislation

Since 1977, a number of federal ARD compensation acts have been proposed, but all have failed. Representative Millicent Fenwick (R-NJ) filed the first, the Asbestos Health Hazards Compensation Act of 1977. The Act would have barred lawsuits against asbestos manufacturers and required that compensation claims be filed against a federal fund. Senator Gary Hart (D-CO) proposed a comparable law the following year, and similar bills have been filed in most subsequent sessions of Congress (Hensler et al. 1985:29). More recently, an Ad Hoc Committee on Asbestos Litigation (1991) recommended a White Lung compensation program to compensate victims.

Brodeur (1985:195) attributed the failure of the early proposals to their transparently political character. Fenwick and Hart represented districts where the Manville Corp. had its largest factory and its corporate headquarters, respectively. Congressional disinclination to enact an administrative remedy has also been linked to perceived chaos in the Black Lung compensation program (Litan and Winston 1988:14–15; Huber 1988:153).[3] Of course, the major obstacle to socializing the cost of ARD through a federally financed compensation scheme has been the significant burden such a program would impose on the federal budget.

Involving the Federal Government and/or Tobacco Manufacturers as Tort Defendants

Defendants sought to reduce their exposure by involving other "deep pocket" actors—the federal government and the tobacco companies. The federal government had not asserted sovereign immunity in an early class action suit settled in Tyler, Texas in 1977 and paid $5.75 million as its share of the settlement. Since then it has successfully asserted sovereign immunity on every occasion on which defendants have sought to join it to ARD litigation (Brodeur 1985:85). Defendants have tried to overcome this defense by alleging that the government was a sophisticated intermediate user of asbestos products and thereby bore the responsibility for warning end users such as shipyards and heavy chemical plants of the dangers in materials that it supplied to them. Defendants have also alleged that the government is responsible for asbestos products that it has included in procurement specifications. Neither the "sophisticated user" nor contract defenses, as they are called, have proved successful.

A related strategy was to include tobacco producers as co-defendants. This followed epidemiologist Irving Selikoff's (Selikoff, Hammond, and Churg 1968) finding of a synergistic relationship between tobacco and asbestos: among those exposed to asbestos, cigarette smoking greatly increases the probability of contracting an ARD. This effort failed because its proponents miscalculated the power of the target. Although Commercial Union Insurance Company fought to involve tobacco manufacturers, few defendants followed suit. Most realized that attacking this powerful industry, with its demonstrated history of legal and lobbying effectiveness, would increase costs without measurably increasing the potential for reducing exposure (Brodeur 1985:207–208). Many insurers also insured tobacco manufacturers and would, in effect, be suing themselves.

Legal efforts to shift responsibility did not occur in India, although many activists viewed the state as morally culpable. Union Carbide's responsibility could not be diluted unless the Indian Government, 49 percent owners of the Bhopal factory, was willing to accept partial responsibility, which, as others in this book document, it refused to do.

Bankruptcy[4]

Chapter 11 bankruptcy has been used by defendants to insulate their future activities from ARD claims and by plaintiffs' lawyers to force the liquidation of asbestos defendants before their assets were consumed by defense expenses. Some firms followed the model set by A. H. Robins Company in disposing of tens of thousands of Dalkon Shield claims.

This model has a trust fund financed by insurer contributions and by contributions from the reserves of the company and from future profits of the company's non-asbestos-related operations. Latecomers arrived considerably weaker, and used bankruptcy to liquidate the company. In some cases, the trust fund can become the dominant stockholder in the post-bankruptcy company. After the reorganization ARD claims must be presented to the trust for settlement negotiations before a lawsuit can be brought against it. Of course, the utility of this device to the claimants depends on the size and available resources of the trust fund. The utility to the company depends on the extent to which post-bankruptcy earnings can meet its responsibilities to the trust and the stockholders.

UNR led the way into voluntary bankruptcy in 1982, followed closely by fellow early-comers Manville and Amatex. All three companies were able to use the trust fund strategy to insulate post-Chapter 11 operations from ARD claims. Victims received only a fraction of the value of their claims from UNR and Amatex (*Wall Street Journal* 1990:B2), while the Manville trust has not been able to pay most of the current claim against it and its ability to meet claims over the long term is very much in doubt.

The fate of those companies who became enmeshed in Chapter 11 voluntarily or involuntarily in the late 1980s or early 1990s is less clear. So, of course, is that of those who have filed ARD claims against them. Nicolet, a late filer, was liquidated in bankruptcy (*ALR*, Oct. 6,

1989), and ARD claims against them were paid only a small fraction of their value. Eagle Pitcher initiated "voluntary" bankruptcy after resisting efforts by ARD victims to force it into Chapter 11 and after unsuccessful efforts to settle all claims against it in class action proceedings (*New York Times* 1991:C1). Most of these companies, including National Gypsum, Celotex, and Hillsborough, chose Chapter 11 voluntarily and today are enmeshed in the difficult task of juggling the interests of stockholders, trade creditors, insurers, ARD claimants, and the sometimes separate interests of their lawyers.

The Asbestos Claims Facility

The Asbestos Claims Facility (ACF) was a coordinated effort by most defendants and insurers to impose order on, and reduce the costs of, ARD litigation. At the time of its formation, which antedated most manufacturer bankruptcies, defendants faced a universe of litigation in which contradictory defenses were being asserted, damage awards varied widely, important rules varied from court to court, transaction costs were high and spiraling higher, and the triple-trigger rule (insurers held liable whether their policies covered the period of exposure, while asbestos fibers were "in residence" in victims, or when ARDs became manifest) had been announced.

The ACF strategy was to persuade plaintiffs' lawyers to file claims with the facility rather than the courts. The payoff would be the enhanced prospects of recovering similar amounts of damages more rapidly than possible in court. Claimants dissatisfied with ACF results could return to court. Liability was unchanged from tort standards. Defendants anticipated transaction cost savings from economies of scale, a streamlined claims procedure, minimized duplication of efforts, and automatic allocation of damages among defendants and insurers (see Hensler et al. 1985:31).

The ACF failed because it made several faulty assumptions: that future rates of claiming would parallel those of the past; that consensus could be reached about the pace at which claims were to be processed; and that a fixed procedure for allocating responsibility for paying claims among defendants and insurers was workable. The initial estimate of 500 new claims per month was exceeded by factors of four to six. Some defendants insisted that resources that could be used to pay compensation were being wasted in unnecessary investigation, but more protested that claims were not being adequately investigated. Since claims in fact were processed more quickly than anticipated, some defendants withdrew from the ACF because the pace of payments strained their liquid resources (*ABA Litigation News* 1988). Finally, the ACF's procedures for assigning liability shares proved to be insufficiently flexible. Initial shares could be adjusted by a maximum of 15 percent every three years. But unanticipated increases in types of claims (including from talc and tire factories and from brake mechanics) imposed liability on defendants with no connections to those industries. Firms continued to withdraw in protest until the ACF was disbanded in 1988 (*ALR*, Feb. 12, 1988, March 25, 1988, April 22, 1988, May 13, 1988; *Business Insurance*, 1988a).

In Bhopal, an ACF-like organization might profitably have been introduced to reduce transaction costs and to compensate for the bureaucratic failures that beset the Indian government's remedial efforts. There was, however, no precedent for such an innovation, and the negotiations between Union Carbide and the Indian government proceeded without institutional reforms and apparently with little concern for effective claim settlement.

Center for Claims Resolution

The Center for Claims Resolution (CCR) was formed from the remnants of the ACF. Several of the defendants and insurers who had supported ACF's activities formed a much more modest settlement facility called the Center for Claims Resolution. It exists today, employs former ACF personnel, and uses many ACF procedures. Although there were a number of early coordination and fee payment problems between CCR and its lawyers (*ALR*, Nov. 11, 1988, Nov. 25, 1988, June 23, 1989), it continues to settle claims. Its efforts, however, have been swamped by the tens of thousands of new claims that have been filed in court since its organization.

The Payoff Matrix

The ACF failure led Raymark, a major defendant, to develop a new strategy that was later joined only by Celotex. In a complex corporate reorganization, Raytech emerged with Raymark's assets while all ARD liabilities remained with Raymark (*ALR*, May 27, 1988). Raymark embarked on a litigation strategy that specified that claims would only be settled according to (very low) payments dictated by a payoff matrix that reflected type of disease, length of exposure, proportion of exposure attributable to Raymark products, and no other case characteristics. If a claimant would not accept the matrix amount, Raymark went to trial. At one time, matrix settlement offers ranged from $42 to $452 for diseases that were securing damages in seven figures at trial.

The matrix strategy yielded two types of success. As in Bhopal, defendants exploited the weaknesses of victim representation. Despite the preposterously low amounts involved, the matrix made it possible to settle some cases for matrix values after plaintiffs had settled claims against other defendants for substantial amounts and did not want to incur the burdens of trial against Raymark and Celotex alone. In these cases Raymark not only escaped with minimal payments but incurred only minimal defense costs. The secondary benefit of the matrix strategy was its effect on court calendars and settlement schedules. By insisting on trying a larger proportion of cases, Raymark reduced the pace of settlements and lengthened the trial queue for all defendants (*National Law Journal,* 1989:15–16; *ABA Litigation News* 1989).

Although the matrix approach worked for a time, it eventually collapsed. It upset judges, juries, and other plaintiffs' lawyers (*National Law Journal* 1989:3); trial verdicts against Raymark and Celotex were numerous and substantial (*ALR*, Nov. 11, 1988). Plaintiffs' suspicions that the defendants used the matrix to postpone inevitable bankruptcy petitions were apparently borne out when Raytech (formerly Raymark) (March 1989) and Celotex (October 1990) filed for Chapter 11.

Wall Street Tactics

Strategies recently pioneered by Wall Street investment banking firms were appropriated by ADR defendants. By use of "poison pills, scorched earth, golden parachutes, and Leveraged Buy Outs" (Hirsch 1986:830–831), defendants sought survival strategies as well as protection from outsider threats. Sharplin (1986, 1989) describes how Manville fashioned a parody of "golden parachutes" by selling off assets to departing management. Both Raytech and Kohlberg, Kravis and Roberts, the buy-out specialists (in its manipulation of Celotex, Hillsborough, and Jim Walters Corporation [*ALR*, Oct. 19, 1990; *National Law Journal* 1991]), engaged in elaborate asset-shielding, liability divestiture, and name-changing efforts. All concerned except Kohlberg, Kravis and Roberts ended up in bankruptcy.

Fiberboard was the most innovative defendant in mobilizing takeover defense strategies to slow the cash demands of ARD settlements. Fiberboard's financial prospects were clouded by two threats—pending ARD claims and hostile takeovers.[5] To meet both threats simultaneously Fiberboard used ARD claims as a "poison pill." Fiberboard created "Fiberbucks," a settlement program that paid off claims in installments. With a change of ownership, however, the balance owed victims would be due immediately. This program allowed Fiberboard to pay off ARD claims gradually while the company both generated profits to pay off the claims and avoided takeover bids (*New York Times* 1986). Despite some ridicule from plaintiffs' lawyers, a number accepted the Fiberboard offer. Shortly afterward, H. K. Porter Company adopted this survival tactic by creating "Porterbucks" (*ALR*, Nov. 25, 1988). In the end, innovation was not enough and both Fiberboard and H. K. Porter ended up in bankruptcy.

Settlement Trusts[6]

We have described the theory of Chapter 11 settlement trusts. The only trust to make substantial payments to a significant number of claimants is the Manville Personal Injury Settlement Trust, the controversial result of protracted bargaining in the bankruptcy court that began in 1982 but did not produce payments until 1988. Sometimes heralded as the solution to mass toxic torts, the Manville and A. H. Robins Dalkon Shield trusts were to provide compensation, superior claims-handling efficiency, equity between similar claims, and decreased transaction costs.

The Manville trust, however, had problems from the beginning. Despite initial liquid assets of $1.7 billion, it quickly ran out of cash and was forced to suspend all payments to claimants. The operational problems were the excess of claims over projections (164,900 claims were filed in 1990; *ALR*, March 1, 1991), settlements that ran 50 percent higher than projections, and a pace of settlements that outstripped projections. Structural problems included trust terms that mandated the settlement of claims on a first-in, first-out basis, which meant that priority was given to place in queue rather than seriousness of injury; a failure to regulate the high legal fees paid to plaintiffs' lawyers; and a trust-financing plan in which needs became manifest long before resources were to be provided or generated. The Manville trust is currently being reorganized.

A Bhopal trust was considered at one stage but failed because of its questionable legality. The courts, which instigated the trust fund idea, had few institutional models at their disposal and tried to impose their wishes on Carbide through unprecedented and contradictory decrees. An order that a fund be established foundered under the improbable condition that Carbide essentially admit guilt by making interim payments to victims.

Producer-Insurer Cross-Claims

A liability-shifting effort has been underway for many years between asbestos producers and their insurers and between insurance companies (*ALR*, Feb. 6, 1988). The issues in scores of lawsuits have ranged from the definition of injury (*ALR*, Oct. 19, 1990), to coverage (*ALR*, Aug. 25, 1989), to successor liability (*ALR*, June 9, 1989), to payment of defense costs (*ALR*, April 22, 1988). Many were considered in a large consolidated case in San Francisco involving seventy-five manufacturers and insurers. This case was filed in March 1983; the trial ran from March 1985 until May 1989. Judgment was entered in January 1990 and is currently under appeal. This strategy produces huge transaction costs. It will eventually assign liability to specific defendants and insurers, but only after the expenditure of huge litigation costs by parties that are hard pressed to pay off legitimate ARD claims.

In Bhopal, the two major antagonists were Union Carbide and the Indian state. Union Carbide and their insurers maintained a united front in the battle with India. When Union Carbide signed the final settlement, it included the agreement that all claims against Carbide were closed. Although factions in the Indian government successfully reopened the case against Carbide, the financial terms of the settlement were left undisturbed.

Early Exit

Some defendants whose asbestos products were infrequently used at a large number of sites had limited comparative responsibility for ARDs, but were nevertheless made defendants in large numbers of lawsuits. They could, of course, defend each suit, escape liability altogether in many of them, pay major damages in a few, and incur significant defense costs in all. But many of these marginal defendants chose instead to pay small amounts of money in virtually all suits against them early in the case process, thus eliminating discovery costs. Hensler et al. (1985:95) called this strategy "an administrative procedure closer in spirit to workers' compensation than to tort litigation." They noted that "the plaintiff lawyer must simply allege exposure during a time when the defendant's products were used at a site where the plaintiff worked, and some minimal injury. The defendant then paid the amount fixed in advance with that lawyer." This arrangement reduced the sum of liability and transaction costs paid by these marginal defendants and was favored by plaintiffs' lawyers, for such easy and early recoveries and enabled them to pay all or some of the out-of-pocket expenses involved in the more protected claims against the major defendants.

Other Unusual Settlement Practices

Hensler et al. (1985:95) have reported two other mass settlement techniques. The first is block settlement, where a lawyer accepts a block sum for all of her or his cases. That lawyer would then determine the value of each case, either alone or with expert assistance. The second is batch settlement, where

a plaintiff lawyer and a defendant settle large batches of claims one at a time, but within a short period. In these sessions, scores of cases may be settled in a day, hundreds in a week. With such numbers, the individual attention devoted to each case is perfunctory, and categorization schemes or rules of thumb must be used to allow this process to work.

What happened in India was, in Indian terms, an extraordinary type of block settlement, but it was slow to benefit the victims. Union Carbide paid India, the Bhopal victims' sole representative, a lump sum of $470 million intended to compensate victims and close claims. As shown elsewhere in this book, the buck literally did stop there. The lack of victim influence in the legal system was demonstrated by the fact that the monies intended for them were distributed instead to a range of existing government agencies, with little or no continuing accountability to the courts or to the victims themselves.

Courts

Court efforts to expedite ARD litigation have taken two different forms. One generally successful effort is to streamline the pretrial process through specialization of judicial personnel and active judicial involvement in case management and standardization of pleadings, motions, and discovery. (See Hensler et al. 1985:68–77 for the details of these efforts.) The other effort has been to effect substantial issue preclusion and case consolidation.

Both efforts have often been tried at the trial court level, but generally rebuffed by appellate courts. The rationale for issue preclusion is that it is inefficient to try the same issues over and over again against the same or similar defendants (e.g., the dangerousness of particular products or the connection between asbestos exposure and lung cancer) and that, after some time, such matters ought to be considered closed. Various labels have been put on these efforts—collateral estoppel, judicial notice, or res judicata—but none have stood up to the due process challenge that the prior cases would be binding on parties who were not present in the earlier litigation or, if present, did not have an incentive to litigate the issue actively (Hensler et al. 1985:61–62).

Case consolidation takes three forms—class actions, multidistrict- ing, and consolidation for trial. Class actions have traditionally been considered inappropriate for tort cases because the individual issues, such as damages and exposure (to asbestos in ARD cases), are thought to outweigh the common issues, such as product defect and the state of medical and scientific knowledge. Many class actions have been de- nied in asbestos and other mass torts, but a few ARD class actions have survived, especially in plaintiff-oriented east Texas. After incurring large losses in east Texas, defendants generally were successful in op- posing new class actions.

The federal courts in east Texas have also been the site of experi- ments in consolidating cases for trial. In this procedure, also used in Ohio and New York (Ad Hoc Committee on Asbestos Litigation 1991:17–18), a large number of cases are aggregated for trial, but the actual proceedings concern only a sample of the group. The jury verdicts in the sample are then used by the lawyers and judge to pro- duce settlements of the remaining cases in the group. This procedure sometimes produces very large settlements and defense interests are wary of it (see Ad Hoc Committee on Asbestos Litigation 1991). A variant of this procedure is followed in the northern district of Ohio, where settlement values endorsed by the court are derived from a satistical analysis of prior settlements.

Multidistricting, a procedure that centralizes cases in many federal courts in a single forum for pretrial, was denied to various kinds of asbestos cases in 1977, 1980, 1985, 1986, and 1987, but finally granted in July 1991. The 1991 order consolidated 26,639 actions pending in eighty-seven federal districts (*In re* Asbestos Products Li- ability Litigation, No. VI, 1991). This action had been recommended by a 1990 letter signed by nine federal judges responsible for thou- sands of ARD cases in their districts and by the Judicial Conference Ad Hoc Committee on Asbestos Litigation, appointed earlier in 1991 by the Chief Justice. The transferee judge faces a difficult set of man- agement issues: whether the centralized pre-trial proceedings will lead to one form or other of a single class action trial, whether defer- ral programs will be established for plaintiffs who are not critically ill, whether limits on contingent fees can be established, whether nation- wide product data bases and corporate histories ought to be initiated, whether punitive damages ought to be restricted, whether case dis-

position ought to be accelerated to provide relief to victims or slowed
down to permit defendants to generate the money needed to pay victims, and whether alternative dispute resolution measures ought to
be employed (Judicial Panel on Multidistrict Litigation 1991:9–10).
Whatever the success of multidistricting in the federal courts, there
are approximately twice as many (unconsolidated) cases pending in
the state courts.

The report of the Judicial Conference Ad Hoc Committee on Asbestos Litigation (1991) is the first acknowledgment by a formally constituted representative of the judiciary that compensation for ARDs
may be beyond the powers of the U.S. court system to organize and
the defendants to subsidize (see also Weinstein 1991:61–63). In con-
firming what had already been recognized by academic experts (see,
e.g., Hensler and Shubert 1991), the Ad Hoc Committee concluded
that "exhaustion of assets threatens and distorts the process; and future claimants may lose altogether" (1991:3). In the end, it concluded
that Congress ought to fashion a legislative solution that would remove ARD claims from the legal (tort) system.

In this as in other cases, a resolution of sorts was accomplished outside the law's standard operating procedures. Bhopal was settled in
1989 by the same sort of legal innovation that allowed Judge Weinstein to quasi-resolve the Agent Orange case in the U.S. (Shuck 1987).
In each case, strict precedent was replaced by the overwhelming prag-
matic need to "do something" about mass suffering. As these decisions signal, it has become more common for participants in the
legal system to acknowledge that traditional tort law cannot solve the
problems created by large disasters. Rosencranz et al.'s review (this
volume, Chapter 3) of the Indian Supreme Court's handling of Bhopal shows the Court's striking disregard for legal convention in its
effort to bring an end to the case.

Plaintiffs' Lawyers

Plaintiffs' lawyers developed two major innovations during the course
of ARD litigation—a formal cooperative organization, the Asbestos
Litigation Group (ALG), and techniques of mass case mobilization.[7]
In the ALG, the relatively small number of plaintiffs' law firms involved in most of the ARD cases (fewer than one hundred) shared
information about defendants, insurers, medical research, expert
witnesses, and legal developments and took, or debated the prospects for, common positions on bankruptcy proceedings, trust funds,
claims facilities, sociolegal research, and proposed legislation. Al-

though there has frequently been controversy among leading figures in the ALG (see Singer 1990), the group played a major role in coordinating the sustained discovery that underlies the liability case against most defendants. The ALG also effectively organized the liability, exposure, and medical dimensions of ARD litigation to the point that the typical claim is nearly risk-free, and has become a model for coordination efforts in other mass tort litigation in the United States (Galanter 1990).

In 1986, before the Asbestos Claims Facility lowered the threshold on claims costs, about 50,000 ARD suits had been filed in U.S. courts. Five years later the number was near to, or exceeded, 200,000. Although no research has been done on the point, it is unlikely that this number of claimants found their way one by one to the lawyers that represent them. This mass mobilization of claims was apparently accomplished by experienced asbestos lawyers capitalizing on ties to unions, doctors, victims' organizations, other lawyers, and, of course, their own considerable, often national, reputations. Among the more unusual solicitation techniques is one characterized by defendants as a variant on ambulance-chasing. Radiologists in lawyer-subsidized x-ray vans screen workers at factory gates, providing both a fast radiographic diagnosis and an obvious offer of legal representation (*Wall Street Journal*, 1990a: B8).

The Bhopal litigation began with U.S. plaintiffs' lawyers swarming over India, signing up thousands of victim clients (in some cases, victims signed with several lawyers). But these U.S. lawyers, with their strong victim advocacy perspective, were soon excluded from Bhopal, when India ruled that the state would be the victims' sole representative. Victims then faced the prospect that their only possible legal advocates would be relatively inexperienced, hyper-individualistic lawyers and a clearly uninterested state. As Marc Galanter (this volume, Chapter 7) shows, Indian lawyers were not specialists nor were they willing to coordinate their work with others. The absence of lawyer networks and specialization put victims at a serious legal disadvantage if they wished to pursue their claims individually; collectively, they were dependent on a fragmented and politically compromised state.

Victims' Organizations

ARD victims' groups have been organized on a national basis, with chapters in cities where asbestos diseases occur in large numbers, and occasionally on a local basis as well. The largest organizations are the Asbestos Victims of America with 15–20,000 members and the White

Lung Association with 11–15,000 members. There is no umbrella organization. These organizations act primarily as information clearing-houses. Information is sought from, and provided to, individual victims, lawyers, and networks of lawyers, doctors, researchers, congressional and regulatory panels, other victims' groups, and the general public. Victims' organizations also identify victims and assist them through the legal, medical, financial, social, and emotional difficulties posed by ARDs.

These groups have attracted media support (Ravanesi 1990), medical and legal assistance (Peters and Peters 1988), and consulting services (Sharplin 1986, 1989) from a wide range of professionals. They publish newsletters, co-sponsor x-ray screening vans, and organize public information fairs. National group leaders are often sought out by the media for information and reaction to bankruptcies, court rulings, and regulatory changes.

Victims' groups, however, face formidable difficulties. External institutional support and funding are scarce (see Reich 1991). The groups tend to be internally fragmented and short-lived. Since mortality among members is high, leadership succession is particularly difficult. There is controversy about goals and focus—case assistance versus education, local versus national or global emphasis. More than the other actors in the ARD world, these groups are constrained by bargains made with stronger allies and opponents: some have aligned themselves with public interest groups and other actors, which provides access to shared resources, but dilutes their public message (see Pfeffer and Salancik 1978).

Paradoxically, the underdevelopment of the Indian legal system may have contributed to efforts to organize victims. Armin Rosencranz, Shyam Divan, and Antony Scott (Chapter 3, this volume) report that almost two dozen victims' groups became interested in the Bhopal victims. Frustrated by an unresponsive legal system, victims sought out, and were sought out by, various groups of actors. The invasion of U.S. plaintiffs' lawyers focused attention on Bhopal as a public, political issue. Social activists' networks then began to champion the victims' interests. New social organizations came to their aid. The victims' struggles became attached to other social and political causes. A wide range of political, public interest, and community groups became involved, helping to increase the visibility of victims. Although these alliances were unable to speed the compensation process in the courts, they did focus Indian and world attention on the situation of Bhopal victims, and thereby created incentives for the final settlement.

Conclusion

Let us now reexamine the failures of legal compensation in Bhopal in the light of what we have learned about the general futility of the highly resourceful American efforts to respond to large numbers of ARD cases. Coping with the consequences of industrial disasters can be difficult for the participants either because they strain the legal system or because they overwhelm its capacity altogether. Industrial disasters often involve quite ordinary remedial or compensatory challenges, but in such number and distribution that the cumulative effect is, at least temporarily, disabling. These "normal" disasters may inspire novel legal and medical theories of causation and the number of claims may exceed the processing capacity of local courts in which they are filed. Because they are out of the routine, they may impose high transaction costs, they may be difficult to settle or try on an individual basis, and it may be awkward, under existing rules of tort law, to aggregate them for disposition. Where they involve multiple defendants and insurers they may trigger high levels of ancillary litigation. Because of their devastating impact on a few private enterprises, they may lead to serious, but generally doomed, efforts to socialize the costs of compensation. Because of the way in which the cases may be concentrated in a few courts, local systems may break down even though the absolute number of cases is relatively low.

But some industrial disasters constitute something more than simply a large number of individually difficult claims. They are instead to industrial production what war is to politics, in that transformation caseloads become military casualty lists. The numbers of injured and dead become so large that there can be no real possibility that they can be compensated according to the rules that apply to ordinary victims: the legal, private, and public resources that can realistically be made available are inadequate to meet such demands. We have never thought that we could afford to pay for wartime injuries and deaths by measures worked out on an individual basis, as if they were highway casualties. Instead we have provided small, lump-sum death benefits and limited pensions and medical care for the survivors. Wars produce administrative solutions of partial compensation and horizontal equity.

Our analysis of ARD cases in this chapter shows that despite the creative, energetic, and sustained response of most participants, acting to protect their own interests as they are intended to do in ordinary litigation, the U.S. tort regime could not cope with the scope of the demands made upon it. One of the most sophisticated legal systems in the world, capable of processing millions of ordinary claims, broke down in the face of the ARD disaster. In dealing with these cases, it would have been better to treat worker victims like dead and wounded soldiers, not because they deserved less than workers injured in ordinary accidents but because there were so many of them that all efforts to provide ordinary relief necessarily led to gross inequities. The alternative to taking up these challenges in a systematic way was the chaos and social indifference of the U.S. asbestos debacle.

This is not to say that all of the efforts to cope with ARD cases in the United States were reasonable, well designed, well executed, and concerned with social consequences. The efforts of the litigators did not in the aggregate demonstrate learning. Quite to the contrary, many of the efforts that we document in this chapter reflected an excess of individuality and a set of remedies that incorporated more ingenuity on the part of individual actors than good sense across the entire remedial system. But the flexibility of the tort system and the advantages that the players took of the opportunities that it offered were not *the* exclusive problems. The more intransigent problem was the number of victims. In parallel fashion, the efforts of the Bhopal parties to avoid the American regress to self-interested experimentation—through Union Carbide's escape from the U.S. courts and the Indian government's assumption of *parens patriae* status—did not resolve the problem of numbers and the related need to deal with mass disasters through means other than litigation.

We began this chapter by asking if differences between highly sophisticated legal systems and underdeveloped legal systems lead to different capacities to compensate disaster victims. We found in Bhopal and in the U.S. ARD cases a surprising convergence of negative results. The U.S. legal system, because of its very complexity and openness to multiple and sophisticated legal strategies, was choked by the number of asbestos claims. The Indian legal system, because of its lack of capacity, long delays, and insularity, never provided an adequate forum for processing all the victim claims.

The lesson of ARD litigation for India and for other developing countries, then, seems to be that "high remedy-high accountability" tort systems of the U.S. type (see Chapter 7, this volume) should be approached with caution. Although such tort regimes can effectively process thousands of ordinary claims, even the most developed, experienced, and innovative tort arrangements can be overwhelmed by too large a number of claimants. For disasters involving so many victims, compensation at the ordinary levels cannot be organized and provided. Bhopal's litigation history looks in retrospect curiously similar to the asbestos cases in the United States. Although the number of deaths was much lower in Bhopal, the number of claims was comparable, and the impact from Bhopal was more difficult to absorb because the claims originated at a single stroke in a forum that had no experience in coping with industrial catastrophes on such a scale. We conclude that India, like the United States, should strive to make its tort regime more fair and efficient and should seek to benefit from the U.S. historical experience in that effort. But India ought to recognize, as more industrialized countries ought to recognize, that when faced with disasters of mass proportions, the tort system must be shunted aside in favor of an administered response that is, in part at least, socially financed. Relief so organized and financed cannot be delivered at the level provided to the victims of ordinary accidents. The objective of compensation should be as efficient distribution as possible.

Notes

1. See Erikson 1976 p. 255 for justification of treating long-term traumas as disasters.
2. Disasters involving human agency are common in modern life. Legal efforts to cope with many disasters have been chronicled by social scientists and lawyers. Examples in addition to Bhopal (Kurzman 1987) include coal mining (Braithwaite 1985; Erikson 1976; Stern 1976), pharmaceuticals (Sunday Times of London Investigative Team 1979; Hills 1987), chemicals (Clarke 1989; Perrow 1984; Schuck 1987), hydroelectric plants (Cherniak 1986), oil production (Carson 1982), and asbestos use (Artibane and Baumer 1986; Brodeur 1985; Castleman 1990; Hensler et al. 1985; Peters and Peters 1980, 1988).
3. Viscusi (1988:182–183) argued that the cost explosion found in the Black Lung program would almost certainly occur in an asbestos program. A judicial consultant indicated that Congress would not consider an administrative plan because of the widespread perception that the Black Lung program was chaotic. But these views should be contrasted with Barth's (1987) careful investigation of the Black Lung program. He argues that costs escalated chiefly because its administrators responded to the heavy political pressures of Congress and mine owners. While the Black Lung program obviously experienced large cost increases (Viscusi 1988:192), they were not the result of a bureaucracy running amok. Although the Ad Hoc Committee on Asbestos Litigation (1991) concluded by noting the need for such an administrative program, they began by intending to find a purely judicial solution. A clear call for a Black Lung type of program is found only in the dissenting opinion.
4. Companies filing for Chapter 11 because of asbestos claims include Amatex, Carey-Canada, Celotex, Eagle Pitcher, Forty Eight Insulation, Hillsborough, Johns-Manville, National Gypsum, Raymark, Standard Insulation, UNARCO, UNR, and Jim Walters (Ad Hoc Committee, 1991:51).
5. Management believed their stock was seriously undervalued due to the uncertainty surrounding asbestos litigation.
6. There is a Manville Property Damage Claims Trust, but it suspended

operations for thirty-two years to prevent further depletion of resources (*ALR*, Dec. 7, 1990).

7. The only defense analogs to the ALG are liaison counsel sometimes appointed to coordinate pre-trial activity in specific cases or for specific time periods and cooperation in securing, organizing, analyzing, and distributing medical information about specific plaintiffs (see Hensler et al. 1985:75–76).

References

ABA Litigation News. 1988. "Novel Settlement Experience Fails" December, p. 2.

Ad Hoc Committee on Asbestos Litigation Report. 1991. March. Washington DC: The Committee.

ALR [*Asbestos Litigation Reporter*]. 1988–1989. Various issues.

Artibane, Joseph and Catherine Baumer. 1986. *Defusing the Asbestos Litigation Crisis: The Responsibility of the U.S. Government*. Washington, DC: Washington Legal Foundation.

Barth, Peter. 1987. *The Tragedy of Black Lung*. Kalamazoo, MI: Upjohn.

Braithwaite, John. 1985. *To Punish or Persuade: The Enforcement of Coal Mine Safety*. Albany: State University of New York Press.

Brodeur, Paul. 1974. *Expendable Americans*. New York: Viking Press.

———. 1985. *Outrageous Misconduct: The Asbestos Industry on Trial*. New York: Pantheon.

Business Insurance. 1988. "Save the Facility." March 21, p. 4.

Carson, W. G. 1982. *The Other Price of Britain's Oil: Safety and Control in the North Sea*. New Brunswick, NJ: Rutgers University Press.

Castleman, Barry. 1990. *Asbestos: Medical and Legal Aspects*. 3rd ed. New York: Prentice-Hall.

Cherniack, Martin. 1986. *The Hawk's Nest Incident: America's Worst Industrial Disaster*. New Haven, CT: Yale University Press.

Chicago Daily Law Bulletin. 1989. "Offer to Buy Out Toxic Shock Lawyer Reported." October 26, p. 3.

Clarke, Lee. 1989. *Acceptable Risk? Making Decisions in a Toxic Environment*. Berkeley: University of California Press.

Dingwall, Robert, Tom Durkin, and William L. F. Felstiner. 1990. "Delay in Tort Cases: Critical Reflections on the Civil Justice Review." *Civil Justice Quarterly* 9:353–363.

Durkin, Tom. 1991. "Bibliography on Asbestos Related Legal Issues." Unpublished manuscript.

Erikson, Kai. 1976. *Everything in Its Path: Destruction of Community in the Buffalo Creek Flood*. New York: Simon and Schuster.

Felstiner, William L. F. and Robert Dingwall. 1988. *Asbestos Litigation in the United Kingdom*. Oxford: Centre for Socio-Legal Studies.

Field, Robert, and Richard Victor. 1988. *Asbestos Claims: The Decision to Use Workers' Compensation and Tort*. Boston: Workers Compensation Research Institute.

Forbes. 1991. "Who Will the (Asbestos) Monster Devour Next?" February 18, pp. 75–79.

Galanter, Marc. 1990. "Case Congregations and Their Careers." *Law and Society Review* 24:371–390.

Gaskins, Richard. 1989. *Environmental Accidents: Personal Injury and Public Responsibility*. Philadelphia: Temple University Press.

Hensler, Deborah. 1989. "Resolving Mass Toxic Torts: Myths and Realities." *University of Illinois Law Review* 1989:1–16.

Hensler, Deborah and Gustave Schubert. 1991. "Second Nightmare for Asbestos Victims." *Los Angeles Times*, March 29, p. B5.

Hensler, Deborah, William L. F. Felstiner, Molly Selvin, and Patricia Ebner. 1985. *Asbestos in the Courts: The Challenge of Mass Toxic Torts*. Santa Barbara, CA: Rand.

Hills, Ben. 1987. *Blue Murder*. Sydney, Austr.: McMillan.

Hirsch, Paul. 1986. "From Ambushes to Golden Parachutes: Corporate Takeovers as an Instance of Cultural Framing and Institutional Integration." *American Journal of Sociology* 91:800–837.

Huber, Peter. 1988. *Liability: The Legal Revolution and Its Consequences*. New York: Basic Books.

Judicial Panel on Multidistrict Litigation. 1991. *In re* Asbestos Product Liability Litigation, No. VI, July 29.

Insight. 1988. "Reorganization Gives Manville New Life Amid Asbestos Suits." August 1, pp. 40–43.

Kurzman, Dan. 1987. *A Killing Wind*. New York: McGraw-Hill.

Lindblom, Charles. 1979. "Still Muddling, Not Yet Through." *Public Administration Review* 39 (November/December): 517–526.

Litan, Robert and Clifford Winston. 1988. *Liability: Perspectives and Policy*. Washington, DC: Brookings Institution.

Lord, Miles. 1987. "A Plea for Corporate Conscience." In Stuart Hills, ed., *Corporate Violence* Totowa, NJ: Rowman and Littlefield.

McGovern, Francis. 1988. "Resolving Mature Mass Torts Litigation." Yale Law School Working Paper no. 78.

National Law Journal. 1988. "It's Over: Robins Plan Gets the Nod." August 1, p. 10.

———. 1989. "Asbestos Lawsuits Grind to Halt." January 30, pp. 3–17.

———. 1991. "Asbestos Cases Turn on LBO." September 2, p. 3.

New York Times. 1986. "Asbestos Bomb Takeover Defense." December 16, p. C6.

———. 1991. "Bankruptcy Sought by Eagle-Pitcher." January 8, p. C5.

Perrow, Charles. 1984. *Normal Accidents: Living with High Risk Technologies*. New York: Basic Books.

Peters, George and Barbara Peters. 1980. *Sourcebook on Asbestos Diseases*, vol. 1. New York: Garland.

———. 1988. *Sourcebook on Asbestos Diseases*, vol. 3. New York: Garland.

Peto, Richard and Marvin Schneiderman. 1981. *Banbury Report: Quantification of Industrial Cancer*. New York: Cold Spring Harbor Laboratory.

Pfeffer, Jeffrey and Gerald R. Salancik. 1978. *The External Control of Organizations: A Resource Dependence Perspective*. New York: Harper and Row.

Ravanasi, Bill. 1990. "Breath Taken: A History and Landscape of Asbestos." Boston: Center for Arts in the Public Interest.

Reich, Michael. 1991. *Toxic Politics*. Philadelphia: Temple University Press.

Schuck, Peter. 1987. *Agent Orange on Trial: Mass Toxic Disasters in the Courts*. Cambridge, MA: Harvard University Press.

Selikoff, Irving, E. C. Hammond, and J. Churg. 1968. "Asbestos Exposure, Smoking, and Neoplasm." *JAMA* 204:106–112.

Sharplin, Art. 1986. "Liquidation Versus "The Plan": A Report Prepared for the Asbestos Victims of America." Mimeo.

———. 1989. Open letter to Judge Lifland. November 15.

Singer, Amy. 1990. "Leon Silverman: $4.5 Million; His Clients ???" *American Lawyer*. (October): 58–67.

Stern, Gerald. 1976. *The Buffalo Creek Disaster: The Story of the Survivors' Unprecedented Lawsuit*. New York: Random House.

Sunday Times of London Investigative Team. 1979. *Suffer the Children*. London: Sunday Times.

Viscusi, W. Kip. 1988. "Liability for Occupational Accidents and Illnesses." in Robert Litan and Clifford Winston, eds., *Liability: Perspectives and Policy*. Washington, DC: Brookings Institution.

Wall Street Journal. 1990a. "Judge Chides Lawyers Facing Suit for Thousands of Asbestos Claims." June 7, p. B8.

———. 1990b. "Amatex Survives Sometimes Scary Stay in Chapter 11." October 1, p. B6.

Weinstein, Judge Jack. 1991. Report on Manville Trust. May 19.

Willging, Thomas. 1987. *Trends in Asbestos Litigation*. Santa Monica, CA: Rand.

Yates, R. 1987. "Burn Victims—Big Settlements." *American Bar Association Journal* (June 1) 1987:17–18.

Chapter 9
Toxic Politics and Pollution Victims in the Third World

Michael R. Reich

Among the various groups involved in chemical disasters, the problems of "institutional learning" are most severe for one group in particular: the victims of toxic contamination. The victims must confront two main obstacles to institutional learning. First, the victims rarely constitute an existing institution; in some cases, they do not even belong to the same community. The victims therefore begin their struggle at a decided disadvantage, with few resources, little information, and no organization—in short, as relatively powerless. When the victims of a chemical disaster suffer also from poverty and marginality, these barriers assume even larger proportions, especially in comparison to the advantages of existing public and private institutions. Second, while established organizations may be slow at learning how best to assist the victims, they usually are relatively fast at learning how to protect their own institutional interests. And the institutional interests of governments and companies involved in industrial disasters rarely correspond to the collective or individual interests of the victims.

What, then, can the victims of a chemical disaster do to protect their interests and to seek redress for harms suffered? How can the victims learn as well as the institutions? In a separate study, I compared the politics of redress in three chemical disasters: polychlorinated biphenyl contamination of cooking oil in western Japan, polybrominated biphenyl contamination in cattle in Michigan, U.S.A., and dioxin contamination from a factory in Seveso, Italy.[1] The study concluded that victims of toxic contamination seek redress through politics in three phases, first by making the problem public, next by organizing group actions, and finally by mobilizing political allies. The political process of empowerment, however, creates its own conflicts and costs, its own process of victimization. For the victims, paradoxically, the politics of contamination can become as toxic as the chemicals themselves.

In this chapter I use the model of toxic politics developed in that comparative study to examine the process of empowerment for victims of chemical disasters in poor countries. The first half of the chapter presents the three political phases that toxic victims struggle through in seeking redress, and applies the model to the chemical disaster in Bhopal. This inquiry suggests that victims of chemical disasters in poor countries confront political dilemmas that are fundamentally similar to those faced by victims of chemical disasters in rich countries.

In the second half of the chapter I examine the distinctive political context faced by Third World pollution victims. These victims often confront a state with different characteristics from rich countries—with a priority on economic development, a lower saliency of environmental concerns, limitations on political liberty, and dependencies on richer countries. In addition, when affected by multinational corporations, these victims suffer further disadvantages from the weakness of international regulation. The recent emergence of an international environmental movement, however, promises to provide an important source of support for Third World pollution victims. Evolving networks of environmental groups represent a new form of international cooperation among nongovernmental organizations, with important implications for the ecological hazards produced (or tolerated) by both states and markets.

The Bhopal case illustrates how the structural problems of toxic politics and the broader international context of Third World politics affect the search for redress by Third World pollution victims. Their search for redress encounters predictable and recurring obstacles, stemming in part from national and international political economies. To overcome these obstacles, victims must engage in the three phases of political learning (non-issue, public issue, and political issue) at both national and international levels, through the engagement of international organizations (which have their limits) and, above all, through the emerging international environmental movement.

Toxic Politics and Bhopal[2]

People struck by a chemical disaster become suddenly involved in another world of problems, conflicts, identities, and institutions. As victims of toxic contamination, they want redress—to be made whole again, to return to their previous existence. This impulse seems to be universal, regardless of national identity or cultural context. But the notion of "wholeness" is ambiguous. Victims need to articulate their vague desires as specific demands. The victims' demands for redress commonly form around three basic problems of toxic contamination: care, compensation, and clean-up. These problems commonly evolve into foci of political conflict in chemical disasters.

Obtaining what the victims consider appropriate and adequate redress is not automatic; it depends on political and social processes. Both public and private institutions are often unwilling to provide immediate or full redress. Much of the burden of obtaining redress therefore depends on the initiative of victims themselves—on their identification of their problems as an issue, on their collective mobilization in group action, and on their alliances with other groups in the political arena. Victims use these political and social processes to define and resolve the problems of redress. How they use these processes both reflects and can change the balance of power between victims and social institutions.

The political process by which victims seek redress in a chemical disaster goes through three phases. The first phase focuses on the individual's discovery of a private trouble and the institutional processes that maintain social problems as a *non-issue*. Following the distinction made by C. Wright Mills, I consider a private trouble as a problem perceived as concerning an individual or family, and a public issue as a problem perceived as involving a larger group of people and institutions in society.[3] The phase of non-issue lasts until the toxic agent is publicly identified, often through the efforts of the victims and through the mass media. In the second phase, the problem appears on the agenda of society as a *public issue*. While private companies and public administrations generally seek to contain the issue, victims seek to expand the issue, struggling to assert their grievances through organization and through protest. In the third phase, the issue expands to include groups of non-victims, in alliances with victims' groups. These alliances use social conflict around the problem as a *political issue*, to pressure private and public institutions to provide redress through a redistribution of resources.

In contrast to some others, my approach to the study of chemical disasters investigates the processes of issue formation more from the bottom-up perspective of victims than from the top-down perspective of officials. Other analysts who have examined power and powerlessness in studying social problems and political mobilization[4] have identified similar phases, suggesting that the three phases I propose for the politics of redress for toxic victims represent three broader processes in the political evolution of issues in society.

E. E. Schattschneider, in *The Semisovereign People*, his classic work on the social processes of conflict in democracy, stressed that the scope of a conflict, especially the number of people involved, determines the outcome:

Every change in the scope of conflict has a bias; it is partisan in nature. That is, it must be assumed that every change in the number of participants is about something, that the newcomers have sympathies or antipathies that make it possible to involve them. By definition, the intervening bystanders are not neutral. Thus, in political conflict, every change in scope changes the equation.[5]

Moreover, as more people become involved and the equation changes, the conflict changes its nature, and "the original participants are apt to lose control of the conflict altogether."

As the scope of the issue expands, the victims gain power but also must pay some costs. These trade-offs constitute the dilemmas of empowerment, which change form through the three phases. When a chemical disaster first appears as a non-issue, victims confront the dilemma of going public. When the contamination becomes a public issue, victims face the dilemma of group action. And when the problem develops into a political issue, victims encounter the dilemma of political alliance.

Non-Issue

In the first phase, victims confront the problem as a non-issue, from a position of individual powerlessness. In the case of chemical disasters, the significant non-issue phase generally occurs before the precipitating event, when institutional and cultural factors inhibit the recognition of signals that could have helped avert a tragic outcome. The phase of non-issue in Bhopal actually extended back quite some time before the night of December 2–3, 1984. Both private companies and public agencies in Bhopal used their resources to maintain as a non-issue the potential for a chemical disaster. Various events occurred during this period.[6] A worker at the factory died of an accident on December 24, 1981, resulting in an investigative report submitted in March 1984 that blamed the worker as well as poor coordination between the plant's production and maintenance staffs. Raajkumar Keswani, a Bhopal journalist for the Hindi weekly *Rapat*, had warned about the potential for disaster at the factory. And the Madhya Pradesh legislative assembly debated the factory's safety on December 21, 1982. Yet none of these events transformed the problems at Union Carbide's factory into a significant public issue or resulted in significant official action to reduce the risks of the factory's production.

In Bhopal as in other areas of toxic politics four basic difficulties of information and power delayed the transition from non-issue to public issue: inadequate detection systems, inadequate understanding of the problem, inadequate internal communication systems, and inadequate external coordination systems.[7] As described in other chapters, these problems existed at the local, national, and international levels within Union Carbide,[8] and also in the public agencies involved with the Carbide factory in Bhopal.[9] Even when private and public institutions detected significant problems, they did not fully understand the implications,[10] and rarely did effective communication occur within or between the involved organizations. These problems of information and power persisted as the Bhopal disaster evolved.

In Bhopal, victims fell ill in the middle of the night on December 2–3, 1984 without knowing that the cause was toxic contamination. Toxic victims commonly begin from this position of injury and ignorance. The Bhopal disaster most resembled the Seveso case of a factory explosion. As in Seveso, the toxic agent in Bhopal was visible, as a white cloud, which allowed many victims to identify the source of the problem as the chemical factory owned by Union Carbide India Limited. The visibility greatly collapsed the length of the phase of non-issue compared to other chemical disasters that have involved invisible and slow toxic contamination. A difference from Seveso was the toxicity to human beings; the gas at Bhopal turned out to be highly lethal.

Even at Bhopal, however, many people assumed at first that their problems were personal. The nonspecificity of the first toxic symptoms—burning eyes and sore throat—suggested briefly that individuals suffered from some personal illness. That perception changed as the severity of the illness increased and as other victims were discovered. The nature of the toxic contamination and the geographical proximity of victims facilitated discovery of the problem as something other than a private trouble. One account of the "night in hell" at Bhopal reported:

In all the cases the pattern of discovery seems to have been the same. At first everybody imagined it was a problem with their own eyes, then on learning that other people's eyes were similarly affected, they thought something was the matter with their homes. When they got out and began to run they would soon discover that the route they had taken was useless.[11]

Without a correct diagnosis of their illness as chemical poisoning, Bhopal victims (as elsewhere) confronted multiple obstacles in getting effective medical care and other assistance. During Bhopal's "night in hell," doctors sought to help the victims, but had little clear idea what to do. "Confronted with an unprecedented flow of patients and an unknown combination of symptoms whose root cause was not immediately traceable, doctors in Bhopal were in a quandary, resorting merely to treating the symptoms."[12] All sorts of remedies were tried, some that helped, some that made things worse. Even after the first night, however, Bhopal victims continued to struggle at an individual level with the search for effective medical care, with an ambiguously defined set of toxic symptoms, and with psychological stress due to uncertainty, fear, and stigma associated with victimization.

On the night of the disaster, the phase of non-issue was prolonged by the company's delay in officially notifying local authorities and residents. The lack of external coordination is symbolized by the silence of the company's public siren that night. The lack of public warning about the toxic gas release and the lack of company information to nearby residents on what to do in case of an emergency reflected a broader attitude of corporate indifference.[13] Subsequently, state officials and local physicians emphatically faulted Union Carbide for not informing them about the nature of the poison gas in the early hours of the disaster and for not directly communicating with them about the physical condition of victims.[14]

Public identification of the cause as a specific chemical contaminant—methyl isocyanate—represented a major turning point at Bhopal, transforming the problem from a private trouble to a public issue. That shift in perception, which began the night of the disaster, marked the transition from a non-issue to a public issue. Victims became tragically aware of other fellow sufferers; they knew that the problem was social and not individual, that the disaster was not a private fate or an act of god.

Public Issue

In the second phase, as the issue becomes public, the victims begin to organize themselves, achieve public recognition, and influence public and private institutions, whose most common initial response is to look for measures to contain the issue. In the early hours of the Bhopal disaster, until 9 A.M. on December 3, company officials insisted on the low toxicity of the gas, that "MIC is an acute irritant, but certainly not lethal."[15] Subsequently, both the medical officials of the state government and the physicians of Union Carbide played down the toxicity of the poison gas by denying the possibility of cyanide exposure. Similarly, the health secretary of Madhya Pradesh, as late as December 27, 1984, about three weeks after the disaster, was reported as still declaring that the gas only affected the eyes and lungs of its victims and that all other systems were normal.[16] The invasion of Bhopal by competing teams of U.S. lawyers, soon after the disaster, raised the stakes for all parties involved, but especially for the company and the government.[17] (Also see Rosencranz et al. this volume, Chapter 3.)

Controversy over the definition of the poison—whether it involved cyanide—persisted. Different medical institutions within the city of Bhopal (and even different medical specialties within the same hospital) took opposing sides on the controversy. A German clinical toxicologist, Dr. Max Daunderer, was invited by the Government of India to visit Bhopal. He arrived with 50,000 doses of thiosulfate to treat cyanide poisoning, but was prohibited from administering the drug when one advanced poisoning patient died.[18] The controversy over thiosulfate continued and acquired broader symbolic and political implications. As in other chemical disasters, the definition of the disease and its treatment became a symbolic battlefield, with sometimes violent outbursts, in the conflict over redress for Bhopal gas victims.

Carbide sought to establish its definition of the problem through limited administrative action and through legitimation. The limited action included Carbide's decision on December 3 to fly in their physician, along with medicines, oxygen, respirators, and 120,000 rupees ($10,000), while providing treatment for 6,000 victims at the company dispensary.[19] The legitimation of company policy appeared as a scientific report, prepared by a Carbide "investigation team" and released to the public in March 1985, on the "Bhopal methyl isocyanate incident."[20] Even the name of the report symbolically downplayed the significance, the damage, and the human suffering that had occurred. The company also hired "leading medical authorities here in the United States, not otherwise associated with Union Carbide," to evaluate the health condition of victims. By early January, the company's Chairman of the Board, Warren M. Anderson, was proclaiming that "those injured by methyl isocyanate are rapidly recovering and display little lasting effects."[21] Reports on the scene in Bhopal indicated otherwise.[22]

The state of Madhya Pradesh, meanwhile, engaged in its own administrative action and legitimation efforts. The arrest of Carbide's Chairman of the Board, the day after he arrived in Bhopal soon after the disaster, served symbolically to support the public impression that the state government's Chief Minister was doing all he could, even though the Carbide official was released after a six- or seven-hour stay in a guesthouse. The State Minister declared, "The letter and the spirit of the law have been observed."[23] On December 16, in a transaction presumably intended to remove any residual threat from MIC remaining in Carbide's tank, the state ordered a mass evacuation of Bhopal residents and agreed to a company conversion of MIC into pesticide, all under the title of "Operation Faith." The administrative confusion that pervaded this event translated into additional trauma for Bhopal victims, compelling them to leave their homes again and removing them from adequate medical treatment and from adequate food and shelter.[24]

The victims of toxic disasters respond to the phase of public issue by creating formal organizations and by conducting protests to counter the power of social institutions. Through these activities, victims seek to expand rather than contain the issue's scope. Both responses represent efforts at empowerment. Through organization, victims seek to create their own self-help mechanism to negotiate with social institutions and bring the public issue under the victims' control. Through protest, victims seek to use the creative disruption of normal society as a means to change the perception of the public issue and compel concessions for redress from social institutions. As a public issue, the problems of care, compensation, and clean-up become fields of public struggle.

In Bhopal, formal groups of gas victims appeared soon after the disaster became public knowledge. On December 16, 1984, the day of the government's "Operation Faith," a group was formed by some victims and by concerned organizations (such as Kishore Bharati and Ekalavya), with the name "Organization to Protest Deaths by Gas Poisoning," to patrol areas evacuated by victims and prevent looting.[25] The first demonstration, or *morcha*, occurred soon thereafter on January 3, 1985, organized at the initiative of social activists and including 10,000 victims and supporters. The group marched from the Union Carbide factory to the residence of the state's Chief Minister, chanting protests against the company, the state government, the federal government, and the United States.[26] A second demonstration occurred on March 13.

The transition from the victims' struggle as a public issue to society's conflict as a political issue occurs through another expansion of the issue's scope. A dramatic event of some sort, often a protest by victims, serves to shake up the symbolic boundaries of the problem and to expand the groups involved in the issue. Some victims search for outside political allies, while issue-entrepreneurs seek out the problem and the victims.[27] Issue-entrepreneurs rarely take up all aspects of a contamination problem. But they can catalyze the transition of the problem into a political issue and assist the victims in their search for redress.

Political Issue

In the third phase, when the problem emerges as a political issue, victims become involved in organizations that seek to help the victims but also to use them. Governments, companies, media, and political groups adopt and adapt the issue into their repertoire of interests. Tension develops between victims' groups that seek to solve their immediate and specific problems and outside organizations that pursue other long-range and more general goals. This phase highlights the victims' dilemma of political alliance: their need to ally with other forces, and the loss of control produced by alliance. The victims gain power through their alliances with other organizations but in return they also become incorporated into other social conflicts and organizational plans.

In Bhopal, a great number of Indian and non-Indian voluntary groups became active in seeking to assist the victims.[28] Within India, new groups included the Bhopal Poison Gas Struggle Front (Zahreeli Gas Kand Sangharsh Morcha), the Citizens Committee on Relief and Rehabilitation (Nagrik Raahat aur Punarvas Samiti), the Delhi Committee on the Bhopal Gas Disaster, the Bhopal Group for Information and Action, and the Trade Union Relief Front. Existing organizations included the Medico Friends Circle, the Delhi Science Forum, the Voluntary Health Association of India, the Centre for Science and Environment, and the Lawyers Collective. Foreign organizations included the No More Bhopal Network (formed by the International Organization of Consumers' Unions, Malaysia), the Japan Bhopal Monitoring Group, the Citizens Commission on Bhopal (New York), and People Concerned About MIC (Institute, West Virginia).

The support groups at Bhopal developed their own conflicts and divisions. According to S. Ravi Rajan, four major categories of voluntary-action groups became involved in assisting Bhopal victims: groups that participated in the government's relief and rehabilitation effort (such as the Self Employed Women's Association); groups that functioned as conscience keepers through systematic research reports (such as the Delhi Science Forum); groups that sought to connect the victims' struggle with the workers' struggle through an alternative production plan for the factory (such as the Trade Union Relief Fund for Gas Victims of Bhopal); and groups that rejected the "establishment idea of voluntarism" and sought to mobilize and empower the gas victims (such as the Bhopal Poison Gas Struggle Front).[29] This conflict among the support groups reflects the structure of political competition in society, as in other chemical disasters.[30]

Victims also became involved in political conflict over the criteria for "official" victims, which affected both care and compensation. In chemical disasters, public organizations often engage in a process of line-drawing, seeking to decide who should receive benefits and who should not. This process structures the conflict among victims and also the conflict between support groups and officials. In Bhopal, a major conflict arose over the extent of the symptoms and who was affected. While the government (and the company) sought to contain the definition of a gas-poisoning victim, the activist groups sought to expand it. When a state health official's announcement that the gas affected only the eyes and lungs of victims, the leader of the Bhopal Poison Gas Struggle Front responded, "To us activists in the field, working with the injured, the statement was shocking. Our survey teams had established that almost every organ of the body was showing one or another affliction."[31] Five years after the disaster, medical authorities admitted that it was virtually impossible to distinguish between individuals with symptoms due to poison gas exposure and those with similar symptoms due to something else. Yet the processes of documenting injuries and assigning them to one of four categories continued, despite ambiguities, uncertainties, and controversy.[32] These processes had distinct consequences for redress. If an individual did not meet the government's criteria as an authentic victim, the claims were not recognized as genuine.

Victims inevitably became involved in conflicts over the state's definition of the disease and its treatment. While members of the Bhopal Poison Gas Struggle Front insisted that the victims were poisoned by cyanide and that sodium thiosulfate was an effective treatment, the state refused to accept either, claiming that any positive effects came from psychosomatic responses.[33] In mid-June 1985, the state resorted to official violence to enforce its position, ordering the police to break into volunteer clinics, confiscate the thiosulfate, and arrest volunteer physicians dispensing the treatment to Bhopal gas victims. The government then imposed an emergency regulation to restrict public assembly and contain the conflict.[34] The Struggle Front continued to expand conflict over thiosulfate, filing a case against the government at the Indian Supreme Court, which resulted in an independent Supreme Court committee to design an alternative medical relief plan.[35] In this way, political alliances to expand conflict over the nature of the disease and its treatment helped to expand redress for the gas victims, although tensions between supporters and victims remained.

The victims' agendas also become entangled in Carbide's agendas. The company responded to the politicization at Bhopal through dissociation, confrontation, and diversion—patterns found in other chemical disasters as well.[36] Its efforts at dissociation emphasized that the Bhopal factory and the Indian company were separate entities, over which the U.S. corporate headquarters had little influence or control.[37] Carbide's strategy of confrontation began with hints that someone may have deliberately added water to the MIC tank (in the company's investigation report of March 1985) and ended up by mid-1987 as a public and insistent claim of sabotage as the cause of the poison cloud in Bhopal.[38] This strategy of symbolic reversal—seeking to transform the company from victimizer to victim—corresponds to similar responses by firms in other chemical disasters, for legal as well as political objectives.[39]

Nature of the State

While the above analysis suggests that pollution victims must struggle through a series of fundamentally similar political obstacles, pollution victims in the Third World often confront a different political context from that found in rich countries. A first important difference is the nature of the state, which impinges in different ways on the victims' search for redress. Political processes within national boundaries critically affect the policies for dealing with the social victims and costs of chemical disasters. More broadly, political processes influence the policies for the choice and control of industrial technology. The nature of the state shapes government priority to industrial production over risk reduction, the limited protection of political liberty, and the impacts of rich countries on the transnational transfer of industrial risks—all of particular importance to Third World pollution victims.

Priority to Production

Many poor countries seek to alleviate poverty through an emphasis on economic growth, with intentional disregard to the accompanying environmental costs. The case of Japan during the 1950s and 1960s exemplifies a government strategy of single-minded devotion to economic growth combined with a stubborn official neglect of the environmental and human health consequences.[40] China now seems to be following a similar path, with its push for the four modernizations, and a resulting increase in environmental pollution and industrial hazards.[41]

Yet, in recent decades, a sea change has occurred in Third World attitudes about the need to control the negative environmental consequences of industrial development. At the time of the Stockholm

Conference in 1972, the dominant attitude of poor countries considered environmental quality to be a luxury item for the rich countries. At that conference, Indira Gandhi asked, "How can we speak to those who live in the villages and in the slums about keeping the oceans, the rivers, and the air clean, when their own lives are contaminated? Are not poverty and need the greatest polluters?"[42] Yet Mrs. Gandhi did attend the meeting, marking the start of India's environmental efforts.[43]

Third World perspectives on the environment have shifted 180 degrees since the Stockholm meeting. Demands have risen sharply for better controls within countries and between countries. Many poor countries have established governmental agencies for environmental controls: up from 11 in 1972 to 102 in 1980, according to a survey by the Center for International Environmental Information.[44] While these agencies represent an institutional commitment to environmental protection, practical problems remain. The agencies tend to be small in size and weak in power, and they confront all sorts of obstacles in implementation (a common problem for policy in the Third World). In India, the weakness of environmental controls and the government's emphasis on employment, production, and agricultural chemicals contributed to creating the risk of industrial disaster at Bhopal.[45]

In many Third World nations, concern about the environment must compete with crisis in the economy. Many countries are mired in economic decline and environmental degradation. The World Commission on Environment and Development urged that environmental controls be integrated into development plans.[46] But the reality for governments in the world's poorer countries is that the environment continues to take a back seat to the economy.

Political Liberty

Although not true for the victims of Bhopal, Third World pollution victims often confront a political climate that restricts freedom of expression and freedom of organization. Many developing countries and many socialist countries have not tolerated political dissent. The state has not allowed public opposition to the production-first strategy or to other government policies. The lack of protection for political liberties raises the personal risks of environmental protest and constrains environmental organizations from public actions. Pollution victims are discouraged from organizing in their own groups (to make the problem a public issue) and from seeking allies in other sectors of society (to make the problem a political issue).

Examples abound of state repression of environmental activists in non-liberal polities. In Malaysia, in October 1987, the government, under the pretext of preventing an explosion of racial and religious tensions, made at least 63 arrests of persons considered as "security risks," including two public health activists who had publicly criticized government policy.[47] In the Philippines, in 1989, two priests who criticized the logging industry and its environmental costs were killed, while death threats were issued against a reporter for the *Far Eastern Economic Review* and a $1.2 million libel suit was filed against the magazine and its reporters for a story on Philippine logging. In Brazil, the rubber tapper and labor-environmental activist Chico Mendes was assassinated.[48] These examples show the dangers of speaking up against powerful economic interests in countries where violence against social protesters is tolerated (and sometimes encouraged) by the state.

The severe environmental degradation in the former Soviet Union and throughout Eastern Europe graphically illustrates the consequences of restricting political liberties and prohibiting environmental protests while pushing ahead with industrialization. Opposition to state policies or actions was thoroughly and effectively squashed, as part of the Stalinist heritage. According to Nicholas Robinson, a specialist on Soviet environmental policies, Stalin opposed forest conservation and exterminated "an entire generation of ecologists."[49] Throughout Eastern Europe, the concept of pollution in a socialist state was taboo, enforced by the full weight of state power.[50] The degree of environmental destruction that resulted is staggering.

But in the 1980s, environmental activism increased throughout the Soviet Union and Eastern Europe, with important political consequences.[51] Many people came to identify the political system with environmental disaster. While rising environmental activism reflected the weakening of state controls, it also contributed to expanding the boundaries of accepted political activities under state controls. Environmental groups became a leading edge of the pro-democracy movement in Eastern Europe and a major force in bringing down the Iron Curtain. In the former Soviet Union, environmental groups contributed to resurgent nationalism and to centrifugal pressures that resulted in fragmentation.

India, as a relatively open Third World state, did not impose systematic restrictions on the political organizations and activities of Bhopal victims. But political tensions did reach the point where the state of Madhya Pradesh took direct action against some groups, exemplified by the police raid on medical clinics in June 1985 and the subsequent government imposition of an emergency regulation to restrict public assembly. Overall, Bhopal victims could articulate their problems with relatively few obstacles, but they still could not achieve solutions due to structural constraints. In the early 1990s, police harassment of environmental activists in India, especially in the anti-Narmada dam movement, raised concerns about a broader effort by the state to contain environmental protest through restrictions on civil liberties.[52]

Policy Choices in Rich Countries

The environmental and economic policy choices in rich countries shape the risks of industrial processes in poor countries, and thereby affect the probabilities of chemical disasters. Policies on hazardous exports illustrate how protective decisions in rich countries affect the toxic hazards confronted by people in poor countries. The chemical disaster at Bhopal tragically illustrates how rich countries allow the export of risk-production technology without requiring the export of risk-limitation technology and culture. Other transnational industrial hazards that involve policy choices by rich countries include the export of hazardous wastes, of pharmaceutical products not approved by the exporting country, and of potentially hazardous production facilities.

What kind of state might reduce the shift of industrial risks from rich to poor countries, in a politically feasible and ethically acceptable way? Whose standards of risk should take precedence? Perhaps the most desirable solution would be an internationally accepted standard and institution to control the trade of industrial risks. This form of international governance, however, seems unlikely to occur in the near future, leaving several alternatives. One possibility would be a state that respects the sovereignty of other countries and refuses to impose its own standards on other nations. This libertarian approach to international trade in industrial risks would require each state to set its own standards, and would place no particular obligations on rich countries (or poor countries) to regulate the export of products or technologies. The problems with this free-market approach are well known.

Another approach would require rich states to set standards for other nations, either directly or indirectly, as in the case of U.S. drug export policy.[53] This paternalistic approach might reduce the flow of industrial risks from rich to poor countries, but could also be interpreted as denying the sovereign rights of poor countries to exercise their own choices over products and risks. In addition, in the competitive international market, it would be difficult to persuade one rich country's private sector to restrict its trade in certain products and thereby forgo potential profits, unless other countries could be persuaded to follow suit.

A third possibility would be a state that relies on a principle of "informed consent" in international relations of industrial hazards,[54] requiring the exporting party fully to inform the importing party of the potential risks involved in specific products or processes, and to allow the importing party to decide whether to accept the risks. This approach avoids problems of libertarianism and paternalism, but poses difficult questions of implementation.[55] (Also see Laird, this volume, Chapter 10). Because of these difficulties, the principle of informed consent among states can yield a practice of continued ignorance among users.

International Regulation

In recent decades the world has experienced an extraordinary diffusion of ideas, products, and technologies, but without effective international mechanisms to monitor or manage the unintended negative environmental consequences. The establishment of the United Nations Environment Programme marked an important step in promoting international governance of this area, along with international treaties and agreements on specific problems. International action can help overcome some of the domestic barriers that Third World victims confront (such as the nature of the state, and economic and political chaos made in other "worlds") through international codes that govern corporate behavior and through the development of national regulatory capacity.

International Codes

The ratification of international codes in several fields has demonstrated that it is possible to change the terms of discourse worldwide about industrial hazards in poor countries. International agencies and other bodies have turned to codes of conduct as a mechanism to affect the behavior of private corporations and thereby to prevent or reduce the transnational transfer of industrial risks. These codes, as a form of world governance, seek to establish international minimum standards of conduct in many fields, including health, environment, economic matters, and consumer protection.[56] The codes have served to introduce new principles for the selection and regulation of technology at the national level.

Two examples in the health field, both involving actions by the World Health Organization, are the WHO International Code of Marketing of Breast Milk Substitutes (passed in 1981),[57] and the WHO ethical guidelines for marketing practices of pharmaceutical products, setting international standards in 1988 for advertising, labeling, and packaging of commercial drugs.[58] Both the infant formula and pharmaceutical codes seek changes in private marketing and distribution systems, with the goal of preventing specific hazards and thereby improving health conditions. In both cases, it was possible to formulate the codes, despite opposition from the industries involved. In both cases, an international movement in support of the codes effectively outmarketed the industries involved,[59] an important point discussed below.

Yet international agencies are limited in overcoming domestic barriers confronted by Third World pollution victims through codes of conduct. Important differences exist between international passage of codes of conduct and national enactment of laws. Even when countries translate the international codes into national legislation, problems arise in implementation. The actual health impacts of the codes are difficult to document through empirical study, in part because of the multifactorial nature of the problems. In addition, changes in leadership in international agencies, such as has occurred in the World Health Organization, can produce dramatic shifts in activities in these areas, reducing the policy's prominence within the organization, lowering the issue on the international agenda, and diminishing the incentives and pressures for national implementation.

International codes of compensation also hold the potential for assisting Third World pollution victims achieve redress. The Stockholm Declaration on the Human Environment of 1972 declared in Principle 21 that nations shall have a "responsibility to ensure that activities within their jurisdiction and control do not cause damage" outside of their jurisdiction. According to legal theory, responsibility carries with it a corresponding legal obligation to provide compensation in cases where harm occurred. Because of concerns about state sovereignty, the Stockholm Declaration's concept of responsibility for transnational environmental harm has remained ambiguous, rendering the corresponding legal obligation for compensation "a hollow concept."[60]

The Stockholm Declaration implicitly recognized some of these difficulties, in its explicit call in Principle 22 for greater efforts to develop international law "regarding liability and compensation for the victims of pollution and other environmental damage" with a transnational character. Various international organizations have promoted international agreements and international legal principles designed to achieve the objectives set out by Principles 21 and 22 of the Stockholm Declaration to prevent and to compensate for transnational environmental harm These efforts, however, remain impaired by "the unwillingness of governments to yield State sovereignty over national resources in order to secure a clear definition of State responsibility."[61]

The Bhopal case illustrates the difficulties in applying international legal principles on compensation for transnational environmental damage. Y. K. Tyagi and Armin Rosencraz identified numerous international instruments that establish standards of environmental protection and accountability and examined how those legal obligations might apply to transnational corporations (such as Union Carbide Corporation) as well as to states.[62] At Bhopal, they concluded, the problem was the lack of incentives to comply with the principles: "International law is rich in articulation but poor in implementation. Sovereign states are jealous in guarding their sovereignty."

The difficulties in implementing the international legal codes for compensation, even in the case of Bhopal, suggest that we have a long way to go before pollution victims in Third World countries can rely on international legal mechanisms to assist them in obtaining redress. The principles and codes continue to evolve, becoming more highly articulated and accepted in the international community. Some observers have argued that international law might gain more practical relevance for transnational environmental damage, if nongovernmental organizations received (or seized) standing.[63] Until that time, the potential role of international law, even in Bhopal-like disasters, will remain unfulfilled for the compensation of Third World victims. Consequently, national institutions will continue as the primary venue for pursuing redress.

Development of National Capacity

International agencies can also reduce the risks of transnational transfers of industrial technology by promoting the development of national capacity in Third World countries. The World Bank, for example, in the 1980s introduced major changes in its policies and procedures for industrial risks and environmental hazards associated with Third World development projects. One example of efforts to promote national capacity is the Bank's publication on techniques for assessing industrial hazards.[64] Despite these efforts, however, problems of implementation and effectiveness remain. A tendency still exists in the Bank to focus on environmental problems, without adequate attention to the health consequences of industrial development, such as occupational health.

By building national capacity for institutions in Third World countries, international agencies can change the relative bargaining power between poor countries and multinational corporations. Assistance in the analysis and assessment of hazardous technologies, for example, could make a difference in negotiations between a Third World country and a multinational corporation. But international efforts to strengthen national capacity can also be interpreted as an infringement on national sovereignty. Conflicts have arisen between international agencies and private industry federations, constraining the actions of the international agencies. Some rich countries, such as the United States, have vigorously protested the "supranational regulatory activities" of supposedly technical assistance agencies, such as the World Health Organization (as occurred in the debate over the infant formula marketing code). And a growing number of Third World countries have their own multinational enterprises, which are responsible for the transnational transfer of industrial hazards and oppose interventions by international agencies. The development of institutional capacity within Third World countries to improve the assessment and control of industrial hazards thus confronts various political obstacles within both the international agencies and the national context.

International Environmental Movement

The emergence of an international environmental movement, based on networks of nongovernmental organizations, may offer the greatest hope of assistance to Third World pollution victims. These evolving international networks do not represent a movement in the conventional sense of mass collective action to protest a specific problem within a community in times of transition;[65] but they do represent, I would argue, a new organizational response to the increasingly international nature of environmental problems. The similar values, constituencies, strategies, and organizational forms of these networks— and the linkages that connect the various networks—give them the character of an international movement. From the perspective of Third World pollution victims, the most important locus of "institutional learning" is within the nongovernmental organizations (in both rich and poor countries) that are joining international networks for environmental protection, especially given the limits of learning that exist within international organizations, as discussed in the preceding section.

The 1980s witnessed the development of an increasingly sophisticated environmental movement in many Third World countries, placing new pressures on government and business to reduce the hazards associated with industrial development. These groups operate at numerous disadvantages, with limited resources in information, scientific and legal expertise, personnel, and financial support. But in some countries, such as India, Malaysia, Brazil, and Indonesia, the groups have become an effective political voice that requires government and business to listen and implement environmental policies.

During the same decade, an increasing number of internationally oriented environmental groups appeared in the United States, Europe, and Japan and initiated programs to support environmental and consumer protection in the Third World. These rich country groups have influenced policies in international organizations and bilateral aid agencies and have provided information and financial support for Third World groups.

These two patterns of organizational development—the strengthening of domestic movements in poor countries and the internationalization of existing groups in rich countries—have contributed to the formation of international networks. Examples include the Pesticide Action Network (PAN), Health Action International (HAI), the International Baby Food Action Network (IBFAN), the Action Groups Against Advertising and Sponsoring by the Tobacco Industry (AGHAST), the International Network of Victims of Corporate and Government Abuse, and the International Coalition for Justice in Bhopal. In the 1980s, the International Organization of Consumer Unions adopted a strategy of promoting such networks on specific issues as an effective method for mobilizing public opinion and resources in the international arena.

The emergence of these networks represents a fundamental change in the international politics of the environment in the late twentieth century. The new networks are changing the agenda-setting process in the field of international development and the environment, for rich and poor countries and for international agencies. The power of these new networks derives from multiple sources, including the following: the organizational flexibility of a network to undertake innovative approaches, the high level of commitment by members to address a specific issue, the capacity to link previously isolated groups and exchange information in multiple directions, the heightened legitimacy created by connecting First and Third World organizations, and the enhanced flow of material resources to weaker groups in the network.

These networks hold the potential for affecting the politics of Third World pollution victims and lowering the political and economic costs of obtaining redress. For example, the international environmental movement can articulate a set of values that emphasizes environmental protection, management, and redress, rather than economic growth at all costs, and can provide domestic groups with an external source of legitimacy and power for seeking to change national policy. The international movement can also connect the protection of human rights with the protection of environmental integrity, and can "adopt" environmental activists whose personal liberties are threatened or denied, much in the way that Amnesty International has done in the field of human rights.[67]

The international environmental movement has innumerable opportunities in rich countries to change policies that influence the transnational transfer of risk to poor countries, and can become a countervailing force to assure compliance by multinational enterprises with both national and international regulations, thus overcoming one of the most vexing obstacles to effective controls over the transnational transfer of environmental risk.[68] On international codes, the potential exists for nongovernmental organizations to transform international law from an academic exercise into a practical instrument of defence of Third World environments and thereby become "guardians of the international environment."[69] Finally, nongovernmental groups have shown a capacity to change the environmental policies of international development agencies and thereby affect national policies in Third World countries.

Conclusion

I have suggested in this chapter that the process through which the victims of Bhopal gained redress followed a pattern of political empowerment that paralleled the experience of victim groups in other countries and situations. In Bhopal as elsewhere, the difficulties faced by the sufferers arose in part as a consequence of their initial powerlessness. It appears that victims of chemical pollution, regardless of their place of origin, must learn to overcome similar obstacles on their path to compensation. They must cope with daunting psychological, institutional, and political barriers, as well as resource limitations, to elevate their problem from a non-issue to a public issue and then a political issue. Only when the last stage is achieved and maintained can they begin to count on redress.

Third World victims confront two additional kinds of obstacles to those faced by victims elsewhere. The nature of the state presents an important, and sometimes overwhelming, barrier to recovery, especially when the state puts priority on economic production, imposes limits on political freedom, or does both. The transnational transfer of risk from rich to poor countries represents a further obstacle. If Third World victims learn to harness the potential power of international regulation and international environmental networks, they can then counteract (to a degree) the state's inattention to industrial safety and effect some control over the transnational flow of risks. But the capacity of Third World victims to learn at the international level occurs perhaps more slowly and unpredictably than at the national. The problems of managing the politics of Third World states and international relations significantly complicate the victims' processes of learning about how to obtain redress in chemical disasters.

Notes

1. Michael R. Reich, *Toxic Politics: Responding to Chemical Disasters* (Ithaca, NY: Cornell University Press, 1991).
2. This section draws on *Toxic Politics*, especially pp. 7–11.
3. C. Wright Mills, *The Sociological Imagination* (New York: Oxford University Press, 1959).
4. John Gaventa, *Power and Powerlessness: Quiescence and Rebellion in an Appalachian Valley* (Urbana: University of Illinois Press, 1980), pp. 257–258; Stuart A. Scheingold, *The Politics of Rights: Lawyers, Public Policy, and Political Change* (New Haven, CT: Yale University Press, 1974), p. 131.
5. E. E. Schattschneider, *The Semisovereign People: A Realist's View of Democracy in America* (New York: Holt, Rinehart and Winston, 1960), pp. 4–5.
6. Robert Reinhold, "Disaster in Bhopal: Where Does Blame Lie?" *New York Times*, January 31, 1985.
7. *Toxic Politics*, pp. 147–168.
8. Praful Bidwai, "Plant Design Badly Flawed," *Times of India*, December 27, 1984, in Lawrence Surendra, comp., *Bhopal: Industrial Genocide? A Compilation* (Hong Kong: Arena, 1985), pp. 63–69.
9. Reinhold, "Disaster in Bhopal."
10. Radhika Ramaseshan, "Government Responsibility for Bhopal Gas Tragedy," *Economic and Political Weekly* 19, 50 (December 15, 1984): 2109–2110.
11. Dhiren Bhagat, "A Night in Hell," *Sunday Observer*, in Surendra, *Bhopal: Industrial Genocide?* p. 24.
12. Radhika Ramaseshan, "Profit Against Safety," *Economic and Political Weekly* 19, 51 (December 22/29, 1984): 2147–2150.
13. Bharat Bhushan and Arun Subramaniam, "The Catastrophe at Bhopal," *Business India* (December 30, 1984): 109.
14. Wil Lepkowski, "Bhopal: Indian City Begins to Heal but Conflicts Remain," *Chemical & Engineering News* (December 2, 1985): 25.

15. Bhushan and Subramaniam, "Catastrophe at Bhopal," p. 67.

16. Lepkowski, "Bhopal," p. 26.

17. "Compensation for Bhopal," editorial, *Washington Post*, reprinted in *International Herald Tribune*, December 14, 1984.

18. Bhushan and Subramaniam, "Catastrophe at Bhopal," p. 115.

19. Lepkowski, "Bhopal," p. 25.

20. Union Carbide Corporation, *Bhopal Methylisocyanate Incident Investigation Team Report* (Danbury, CT: Union Carbide Corporation, 1985).

21. Letter from Warren A. Anderson, Chairman of the Board, Union Carbide Corporation, to People's Research Institute on Energy and the Environment, Tokyo, January 3, 1985.

22. Padma Prakash, "Bhopal Gas Disaster: Continuing Nightmare," *Economic and Political Weekly* 20 (April 6, 1985): 579.

23. Sreekant Khandekar and Suman Dubey, "Bhopal: City of Death," *India Today*, December 31, 1984, p. 10.

24. Radhika Ramaseshan, "Bhopal Gas Tragedy: Callousness Abounding," *Economic and Political Weekly* 20 (January 12, 1985): 56–57.

25. Ibid.

26. Paul Shrivastava, *Bhopal: Anatomy of a Crisis* (Cambridge, MA: Ballinger, 1987), pp. 105–108.

27. John W. Kingdon, *Agendas, Alternatives, and Public Policies* (Boston: Little, Brown, 1984), pp. 129–130.

28. For a somewhat tongue-in-cheek analysis of ten different strata of voluntary groups that became involved in Bhopal, see Shiv Visvanathan and Harsh Sethi, "Bhopal: A Report from the Future," *Lokayan Bulletin* 7, 3 (1989): 47–67. See also Shrivastava, *Bhopal*, pp. 150–151, n. 2, and p. 161, n. 27.

29. S. Ravi Rajan, "Rehabilitation and Voluntarism in Bhopal," *Lokayan Bulletin* 6, 1–2 (1988): 3–31.

30. Reich, *Toxic Politics*, pp. 231–235.

31. Lepkowski, "Bhopal," p. 26.

32. Siddharth Dube, "Five Years After: Compensation? The Government Hasn't Even Identified the Victims of the Bhopal Gas Disaster Yet," *Sunday*, December 17–23, 1989, pp. 66–69.

33. Lepkowski, "Bhopal," p. 29.

34. Shrivastava, *Bhopal*, pp. 108–109.

35. Rajan, "Rehabilitation and Voluntarism," p. 27.

36. Reich, *Toxic Politics*, pp. 235–251.

37. Arun Subramaniam, Javed Gaya, and Rusi Engineer, "Why the Guilty Must Be Punished," *Business India*, December 2–15, 1985, p. 44.

38. Steven R. Weisman with Sanjoy Hazarika, "Theory of Bhopal Sabotage Is Offered," *New York Times*, June 23, 1987.

39. Reich, *Toxic Politics*, pp. 240–243.

40. Norie Huddle and Michael Reich, *Island of Dreams: Environmental Crisis in Japan* (1975; reprint Rochester, VT: Schenkman Books, 1987).

41. Peter J. Poole, "China Threatened by Japan's Old Pollution Strategies," *Far East Economic Review*, June 23, 1988, pp. 78–79.

42. Cited in H. Jeffrey Leonard and David Morell, "The Emergence of Environmental Concern in Developing Countries: A Political Perspective," *Stanford Journal of International Law* 17 (1981): 281–313.

43. Sheila Jasanoff, "Managing India's Environment," *Environment* 28, 8

(1986): 12–16, 31–38. A similar turnabout has been noted in other countries such as Algeria, as reported in Peter Haas, *Saving the Mediterranean: The Politics of International Environmental Cooperation* (New York: Columbia University Press, 1990).

44. Leonard and Morrell, "Emergence of Environmental Concern," p. 283.

45. Shrivastava, *Bhopal*, pp. 41, 61.

46. World Commission on Environment and Development, *Our Common Future* (Oxford: Oxford University Press, 1987).

47. Stephen Duthie, "Malaysian Premier Faces Criticism After Crackdown," *Wall Street Journal*, October 29, 1987.

48. Alexander Cockburn, "Amazon Symbiosis: Social Justice and Environmental Protection," *Wall Street Journal*, December 29, 1988.

49. Larry Tye, "The Scars of Pollution," *Boston Globe*, December 17, 1989.

50. Andras Biro, "East Europe: 'Greens' Force Change," *Panoscope* 17 (March 1990): 16–17.

51. Janos Vargha, "Green Revolutions in East Europe," *Panoscope* 18 (May 1990): 7.

52. "Environmental Movements: Changing Status," *Economic and Political Weekly* 26, 19 (May 11, 1991): 1189–90.

53. Rebecca J. Cook, "The U.S. Export of 'Pipeline' Therapeutic Drugs," *Columbia Journal of Environmental Law* 12 (1987): 39–70.

54. Rashid Shaikh and Michael R. Reich, "Haphazard Policy on Hazardous Exports," *The Lancet* 8249, 2 (1981): 740–742.

55. Michael R. Reich, "International Trade and Trade-Offs for Third World Consumers," in E. Scott Maynes and ACCI Research Committee, eds., *The Frontier of Research in the Consumer Interest* (Columbia, MO: American Council on Consumer Interests, 1988), pp. 375–396.

56. Cook, "U.S. Export," pp. 61–63.

57. Reich, "International Trade," pp. 375–396.

58. World Health Organization, *Ethical Criteria for Medicinal Drug Promotion* (Geneva: WHO, 1988).

59. Michael R. Reich, "Essential Drugs: Economics and Politics in International Health," *Health Policy* 8 (1987): 39–57.

60. Sanford E. Gaines, "International Principles for Transnational Environmental Liability: Can Developments in Municipal Law Help Break the Impasse?" *Harvard Environmental Law Journal* 30 (1989): 311–349.

61. Ibid., p. 313.

62. Y. K. Tyagi and Armin Rosencranz, "Some International Law Aspects of the Bhopal Disaster," *Social Science and Medicine* 27 (1988): 1105–1112.

63. Philippe J. Sands, "The Environment, Community, and International Law," *Harvard International Law Journal* 30 (1989): 393–417.

64. Technica, Ltd., *Techniques for Assessing Industrial Hazards: A Manual*, World Bank Technical Paper No. 55 (Washington, DC: World Bank, 1988).

65. Sidney Tarrow, *Struggle, Politics, and Reform: Collective Action, Social Movements, and Cycles of Protest* (Ithaca, NY: Cornell University Center for International Studies, 1989), pp. 17–20.

66. Patricio Merciai, "Consumer Protection and the United Nations," *Journal of World Trade Law* 20 (1986): 206–231.

67. Sands, "Environment, Community, and International Law," pp. 416–417.

68. Gunther Handl and Robert E. Lutz, "An International Policy Perspective on the Trade of Hazardous Materials and Technologies," *Harvard International Law Journal* 30 (1989): 351–374.

69. Sands, "Environment, Community, and International Law," p. 417.

Chapter 10
Information and Disaster Prevention
Frank N. Laird

Why, in a world awash in information, did no one in Bhopal have the information needed to prevent or mitigate the disaster? Accounts of the accident demonstrated widespread ignorance at all levels, both public and private: many plant personnel were unaware of the risks of MIC, local authorities did not know what chemicals were in fact in use at the plant, and local physicians had no idea about how to treat victims of MIC exposure (Bhushan and Subramaniam 1985:109; Bowonder, Kasperson, and Kasperson 1985:31; Reinhold 1985; Subramaniam 1984; Varma 1986). Policy makers understandably have drawn the conclusion that better information at any of these points might have lessened the devastating consequences of the disaster. As discussed in this volume and elsewhere (Jasanoff 1988), governments have moved to correct the perceived deficiencies through right-to-know legislation.

In this chapter I critique some familiar types of programs that seek to provide information as a means of managing risk, particularly in relation to technology transfer across national boundaries. Technical information in the context of actual or potential disasters is not simply data that one can use easily and at will. It is both a complex technical good and a strategic good within the policy process. Programs for using information must take these properties into account or else technical information will contribute little to risk management. I do not mean to imply that information per se has no value. Rather, information is valuable only in the context of a program that recognizes its properties as a complex technical resource requiring certain social constructs for its use and as a strategic political resource that can and will be used for myriad purposes.

The focus in this chapter is on transnational information programs. In what sense have institutions that manage such programs learned to do better since Bhopal? Conventional notions of information, critiqued below, would suggest the need to get more information to more people, a service that international agencies may be uniquely situated to deliver. In contrast, my analysis suggests that institutional learning must entail a different approach to information transfer, one that confronts explicitly the sociological and political-strategic properties of information.

From the outset, I make a distinction between information, which I take to mean useful knowledge, and data, which are simply facts about some phenomenon. Raw data, the stuff that comes out of experiments and other primary scientific sources, are usually of very little use to most people involved in risk management, especially at the local level. Information, as used here, denotes data that have been processed, interpreted, and otherwise made into a form that is immediately useful.

Information as a Technical Resource

There is an extensive literature on the social nature of the creation and interpretation of scientific and technical knowledge and artifacts (e.g., Barnes and Edge 1982). What concerns us in this chapter is how the social and political components affect the use of knowledge in preventing and coping with disasters. At heart, the issue is the control of technology and management of risk, and the role information can play in that process. Such analysis requires that we understand two important features of technology. Technologies are not separate, discrete entities, such as pieces of hardware. They are instead relatively unbounded, both functionally and socially (Sclove 1982:45–46; Wynne 1989a:121; Chapter 1, this volume). For example, the UCIL plant in Bhopal had multiple functions, not all of which were explicit or consciously known to all its users. The plant was a part of India's attempt to be self-sufficient in Green Revolution technology. It was a source of employment for the town. It was a focus for squatter settlements. It was a repository of an immense quantity of lethal chemicals, and therefore a potential and real hazard. All these were in addition to its nominal purpose of producing Sevin.

The social unboundedness of technology means that its functioning depends heavily on the social practices and institutions in which it is embedded (Wynne 1989b), and the safe functioning of diverse technologies depends on just those social factors. Information programs in turn can only be successful in controlling technology if they are designed to cope with social and political problems. Any attempt to use information to prevent or mitigate disasters must take into account the widely varying needs and abilities of different groups such as lay people and experts (Slovic 1987). Even the informational needs of experts are not as simple as one might think. Different experts have a great diversity of informational needs, and none of them are likely to have the broad range of local knowledge needed to apply their information. For example, details about the volatility and toxicology of MIC would have been useful to officials trying to make siting and regulatory decisions about the UCIL plant but would not have helped physicians treating Bhopal victims or workers or residents running from the poison cloud. In short, technically skilled people must work within organizational and institutional structures that give them access to relevant information and enable them to apply that information to the local situation.

Information as a Strategic Resource

The notion of information which underlies the right to know policies enacted after Bhopal is that it is instrumental, that is, merely a means to an end. Moreover, this view sees both means and ends as nonproblematic. In this sense, information is seen as a simple tool, even if the actual use of the tool may require some technical skill. This tool analogy could be applied to the needs for information in the Bhopal case. The ends lay clearly in preventing the catastrophic release of MIC or, failing that, mitigating its effect on workers and the public. The informational means to the ends also seemed obvious: knowledge of the hazards of exposure to MIC, the manufacturing processes using it, and ways to treat people exposed to it. Of course, many of these categories of information had uncertainties, even very large ones. Nonetheless, such uncertainties were only part of the problem, and did not reflect the full range of complexities involved in using information. The conventional conception of information as a neutral tool, however, makes the problem look simpler than it really is. In fact, information is a complex good that is strategic as well as instrumental (Stone 1989: chs. 7 and 13). In addition to applying information to its nominal purpose, this conception recognizes that information serves a variety of other purposes as well. The strategic exploitation of information may consist of withholding it, releasing it selectively, or releasing it to selected persons.

Consider the instance of toxicology data on MIC. The nominal purpose of such data is to understand better the hazards of working with

MIC and the measures needed to protect workers and the public from harm. As such an instrumental entity, the data clearly seem to constitute a public good, and the only issues relate to sponsoring research where the data are uncertain and seeing to it that the right people receive the results. However, a strategic analysis of information suggests an additional set of uses for the data and better explains what actually happened in Bhopal. The toxicology data on MIC in the open literature were not very reliable or complete. Union Carbide Corporation (UCC) possessed better data since they had the opportunity and incentives to study MIC in more detail. Nonetheless, up to the time of the accident, UCC regarded the data they had generated as proprietary information, as trade secrets. After the accident, UCC shared its knowledge with the National Toxicology Program and the Environmental Protection Agency, but still did not allow it to be published in the open literature (Dagani 1985:39). Clearly, Union Carbide did not regard this information as simply instrumental to protecting public health and safety. The company may have seen it as instrumental to different ends, or seen it more strategically. For example, technical information may give the holder a market advantage if it can be kept secret. A company that thinks it can make a product better or cheaper because of proprietary ownership of data would be reluctant to release it. It seems unlikely that toxicology data on MIC had to be kept secret in order to protect profits and market share. Nonetheless, large corporations, like any large organizations, operate as bureaucracies in the sense that they adopt standard procedures for a broad range of complex operations. Since it is easier for bureaucrats to declare all data related to a production process to be confidential than for them to protect data selectively, toxicological data could easily end up as proprietary.

As second strategic use has to do with community relations. A company may not want its plant to be thought of as a serious hazard by the host community. One way to manage those relations is simply to withhold information about hazards associated with the plant, as was the case in Bhopal (Jasanoff 1988). After the accident, representatives from the chemical industry declared their intention to improve communications with the communities in which they operate (Worthy 1986:10). Yet improved communication is also a strategic use of information. The purpose is not simply to inform the public, but to generate more trusting relations between the public and the source of information, an objective that may, in turn, influence the timing, content, and form of the information disclosed.

Third, information can be used strategically as a bureaucratic resource. In both public and private bureaucracies, information is a means of controlling an issue area. If exclusive possession of information enables a bureaucracy to control an issue, its members may be very reluctant to share that information freely with others. Thus, information relevant to occupational safety or disaster management may exist somewhere within a government, but not be available to other agencies when they need it.

The fact that information is a strategic good must be incorporated into plans to provide it more effectively to prevent or mitigate future Bhopals. There is no point in exhorting people not to use information strategically. Policy-makers must recognize that other public and private sector actors may have different goals from their own and will use information to seek those diverse goals. Information programs must allow for negotiating and, if possible, integrating those different purposes.

Prerequisites of Using Information

There are three major institutional requirements for a system to use information effectively: experts, infrastructure, and adaptive feedback. First and most obvious, any organization that needs to use complex information needs people who can select and interpret it. These people are commonly thought of as experts. Just as information is not a simple tool, so experts are not simple tool-users. Their very presence in a community, government agency, or firm can affect their procedures as well as their internal and external relationships. The specific ways in which experts can be incorporated into institutions may vary enormously (see Jasanoff 1986 for some comparative examples). However, two features seem essential to their success as interpreters of information. First, they must be connected to information sources and be able to use them. Second, they must be close to and sensitive to the needs of people within institutions who make decisions and otherwise need to use the information. Otherwise, they will be cut off from a crucial source of information on local environmental and social practices, without which their technical data may be hard to use effectively. As straightforward as these conditions appear at first glance, there is no single way to achieve them in practice and, unfortunately, there are many ways to fail to achieve them.

Infrastructural issues seem obvious, but they are worth noting explicitly. It is not enough simply to supply communication and information technologies, such as computers and telephone lines, though such items are clearly part of the infrastructure. In addition to hardware, experts within institutions need to be connected to both formal and informal networks of information in order to stay current in their field. Therefore, such things as journals, conferences, informal networks, and workshops all count as part of the infrastructure.

An important lesson from Bhopal is that the institutions in which experts are situated, in both the public and private sectors, must have adequate capacity to make use of the information and to control important decisions about the management of technology. These expert and political capacities were sadly lacking in Bhopal. By all the accounts of the accident, the state had neither the expertise nor the political authority required to understand the plant, to control it, or to cope with the accident when it did happen.

For a government agency to help protect a population from industrial technological hazards, it must have the capacity to regulate the actions of private and public firms. The precise way in which a government tries to exert such control varies from country to country (Jasanoff 1986) and in no country can a government perform all regulatory tasks alone, least of all in poor countries. Nonetheless, in any country the state needs certain capacities in order to execute some regulatory functions. It must have the expert capacity to understand both the threat that a facility poses and how to minimize that threat. Also, it must have the political capacity to influence the way in which the facility is run in order to minimize the threat. This political capacity in part depends on the state's ability to balance a large variety of conflicting interests, not the least of which are attracting foreign capital on the one hand and imposing regulations on firms that choose to locate there on the other. Finally, it must have the political and social capacity to mobilize and use the appropriate resources in the event that an accident does occur.

The development of political capacity to regulate industries is, if anything, harder to acquire than technical capacity. Such capacity is not the same thing as popular or elite hostility toward a single company, such as Union Carbide. Involved are more profound questions and deeply entrenched political arrangements concerning the role of the state in the private sector. These questions and arrangements are complicated all the more by the presence in the private sector of large foreign multinationals. Altering these patterns is a substantial political task. Moreover, the form regulation ought to take is a difficult question, given the variety of models in various industrialized countries, none of which may be compatible with a host country's political culture.

Finally, an effective use of information requires adaptive feedback. Woodhouse (1888) has argued that scientific and technical information is, because of uncertainties, always difficult to use. A system of feedback that conveys both positive and negative results from applying information enables an institution to get better at such use, that is, creates more usable knowledge by better matching technical data with local knowledge and context. Yet again, there are a number of political and bureaucratic obstacles to feedback, complicating the situation. For example, bureaucratic careers may suffer if programs do not receive glowing reviews, instead of more candid ones that would enable people to learn from example. Political leaders, too, may have time horizons that are very short, further inhibiting learning from negative feedback.

Nonetheless, some feedback is essential for improved performance, or a system may be overwhelmed by catastrophic error. Perrow's (1984) arguments about coupling in technological systems demonstrate this difficulty. Tightly coupled systems can propagate and amplify errors more quickly than remedial actions can respond to them. Bureaucrats or politicians confronted with such systems will have few incentives for an open display of feedback, particularly when there is the chance that negative feedback could expose potentially serious consequences.

These organizational requirements for using information are made all the more difficult to satisfy by the strategic and proprietary nature of information. One cannot assume that the various actors involved in trying to establish information programs will share the program's nominal goal or work under the same incentives as the program's designers. Transnational programs, where the actors come from widely disparate countries and cultures, only exacerbate the problem of divergent goals. Without addressing and perhaps altering the deep structural arrangements within countries—an ethnically and politically troublesome task—it may be useless simply to transfer information across national boundaries.

Institutions for Information Transfer Before Bhopal

Organizations concerned with the Third World's need for technical information have built up institutional structures to try to meet the requirements I have outlined. One U.N. publication (United Nations 1988) lists nine separate programs designed to provide member countries with technical information related to environmental or industrial health and safety. These programs vary in format and focus, but all share characteristics that indicate a failure to take into account the full complexities of using information discussed above. They can be divided into two groups: passive databases and export notification schemes.

There are a wide variety of databases, some of which refer users to other databases. The United Nations Environment Programme (UNEP) runs two programs particularly aimed at making information more accessible. The first is the International Environmental Information System (INFOTERRA). Its purpose is to direct users to other institutional sources of more specialized information. Its directory lists over 6,000 such sources, is indexed, and is machine readable. To make this information even more accessible, INFOTERRA has established 134 National Focal Points all over the world, including India, which usually employ nationals of the recipient countries, often employees of the environmental ministry, and which have a copy of the directory and can assist people in that country more easily than could an office in Geneva or New York (United Nations 1988). This program is an index of other information sources. To use this service, state and local officials need to contact the national ministry, locate the information source that they need, then find and use that source, all tasks requiring time and substantial expertise. A strength of the program is that it contributes, through the National Focal Points, to building technical capacity to deal with environmental issues within Third World governments.

The second UNEP Program is the International Registry of Potentially Toxic Chemicals (IRPTC), part of the broader Earthwatch program established by UNEP to identify and gather data on important environmental issues (Goldberg 1985:1041). The IRPTC, which was started in 1976, maintains a database that currently covers about six hundred chemicals. The IRPTC will make that database available free of charge to Third World countries and will respond to specific inquiries. Like INFOTERRA, the IRPTC maintains a network of local contacts, called National Correspondents, in countries around the world, including India (United Nations 1988). This system is, in a sense, more immediately useful, since it can answer technical questions directly if they concern a chemical in the database. If the National Correspondent office is qualified to interpret the data with regard to the requester's specific needs, then it could partially ameliorate some of the local technical deficiencies.

Like the other programs, however, the IRPTC is reactive. Such structures make powerful, and unrealistic, assumptions about the user community, for example, that people recognize that they have a problem with toxic chemicals. They further assume that people know of the existence and content of these programs, can find what they want in these sources, and know how to use the data they do find. These programs also illustrate the need for in-house expertise. All of them require substantial technical training to be used effectively.

Export notification schemes are somewhat different in orientation; they are older and better-developed transnational data programs related to international trade in hazardous chemicals, particularly pesticides. Beginning long before the Bhopal disaster and continuing to the present day, they are a patchwork of assorted unilateral, bilateral, and multilateral programs intended to improve the regulation of hazardous chemicals in developing countries by better informing decision making. Despite their diversity in detail, these programs reveal some common structural features and assumptions about the utility of information in risk management that illustrate well the difficulties of using information for preventive purposes.

In 1972 the U.S. Federal Insecticide, Fungicide, and Rodenticide Act (FIFRA) addressed the problem of exporting pesticides to developing countries by requiring that information about products banned or restricted in the United States be provided to importing nations (Goldberg 1985). Specifically, Section 17 of the Act required the Environmental Protection Agency (EPA) to notify foreign governments of the exports of banned or restricted pesticides and of EPA regulations of "international significance" (Halter 1987:9). Such notices go from the EPA to the State Department and thence to the American embassies in the relevant importing country (Halter 1987:9). By 1978, however, critics were arguing that such information schemes were not providing effective international regulation of toxic chemicals (Alston 1978). In that same year, the Government Operations Committee of the U.S. House of Representatives investigated the FIFRA notification system; the Committee found that EPA often did not implement the procedures adequately and that, when EPA did send out notification, "the information rarely went further than the United States embassy overseas" (Goldberg 1985:1034). Congress responded by toughening up the notification procedures. In January 1981, just before leaving office, President Jimmy Carter instituted even stricter notification requirements. These, however, were rescinded by President Ronald Reagan shortly after he took office (Goldberg 1985:1035).

Notification procedures were the linchpin of pre-Bhopal multilateral information programs as well. In 1984, the Organization for Economic Cooperation and Development (OECD) and UNEP adopted notification plans, with varying degrees of volunteerism, that ask exporting countries to provide both regulatory and export notices regarding hazardous chemicals either directly to governments of importing countries or through the IRPTC. The Food and Agriculture Organization, another U.N. agency, promulgated similar guidelines in 1985 for pesticides (Halter 1987:16–17). These notification programs only cover part of the problem of control of hazardous chemicals in the Third World, namely, international trade in certain classes of hazardous products and waste. However, hazardous chemicals produced in the Third World, or hazardous processes in use there, are unaffected. Of still more importance for our own purposes is that all these programs are intended to function from the top down. The information is supposed to come from national governments and flow either to international organizations or to the national level of the government of the importing country and from there to the final users. This structure makes strong and largely unsupported assumptions about the channels of information flow, the expert capacity within those channels, the regulatory capacity at the end of the channel, and the absence of strategic uses of information all along the way. Each of these assumptions bears a closer look.

To begin with, the environmental agency in the importing country may not be willing or able to get the information to the people who most need it. The appropriate national agency must have a close working relationship with relevant local government officials, local health authorities, and, ideally, the workers who will handle the dangerous material (Goldberg 1985:1035). The chance of this happening is contingent on the details of the governmental structure within the host country and the organizational and individual behavioral norms of all the various agencies involved. Effective community information programs, discussed in van Eijndhoven's and Hadden's chapters in this volume make the channels more effective, while political barriers in the Third World discussed in Chapter 9 make them less so.

The second major problem is the possible lack of expertise within the developing country. National-level agencies must have expertise that enables them to interpret the incoming data, decide how important they are, decide what actions they suggest, figure out to whom they should be further transmitted, and put them into a form that is intelligible to its numerous eventual recipients. These tasks add up to a tall order, and require substantial expertise at numerous points in the information channel. Consequently, developing countries, even if flooded with technical data, may not be able to use it (Goldberg 1985:1045).

Third, data flows, and even useful information, do not determine domestic policies. If the importing country lacks the regulatory capacity, supplying the country with more information, particularly at the top level, is, at best, only a very partial solution to the problem. Notification can satisfy the sender's legal requirements without helping the recipient. Information is usually not the critical element that determines whether an environmental agency has or exercises the political capacity to regulate manufacturing firms or farming enterprises. The fundamental problem of regulatory capacity is deeper than the possession or deprivation of information (Halter 1987:31, 34–35).

Finally, the strategic properties of information will affect its availability and use at every level in the notification process. To begin, companies in developed countries may refuse to release data that they claim are proprietary even to their own national governments. These governments may then refuse (or simply neglect) to send the information to importing countries or the relevant international organization, such as the IRPTC. Further down the channel, the receiving national government may not send the information to local governments, in order to preserve some bureaucratic advantage or, again, from neglect. The local government may not understand the data, or, if they do, may not share the useful information with health officials for fear of provoking a scare and arousing opposition to a development project. All along the way, actors have numerous incentives to use the information strategically and thereby defeat the intended purpose of the notification system.

Information Systems After Bhopal

Since Bhopal, there have been numerous attempts by a variety of organizations to strengthen the transnational flow of information related to environmental health and safety. These programs can be grouped into three conceptual categories: top-down, strong Prior Informed Consent (PIC), and bottom-up. These activities do not constitute an exhaustive list, but they do include important programs by most of the major international actors.

Top-Down Programs

At the Third OECD High Level Meeting on Chemicals in March 1987, environmental ministers from all twenty-four member states agreed that OECD should initiate new programs and take a leading role in reducing the risks from chemical accidents. Plans for information dissemination were seen as an important part of such actions (BNA 1987b:145–146). At a higher level conference in February 1988, OECD representatives further agreed on the importance of the issue, and promoted a work program within OECD that would address several of the problems related to accident prevention and preparedness. Improving information dissemination was depicted as the "crucial" part of this effort (BNA 1988a:158–159). The conference established an Accidents Program, which was made part of the OECD Environment Program. The Accidents Program has two major tasks. One is the development of information exchange mechanisms. The second is the "development of common principles, procedures and policy guidance and accident prevention, preparedness and response" (Schulberg and Visser 1990:2). The core of the OECD information programs is top-down because the guidelines mainly address information exchange among states at the national level, or between states and new international institutions. Thus the OECD Council passed a binding decision requiring information exchange between states when an accident (or accident potential) poses trans-frontier risks (Schulberg and Visser 1990:3). The issue of trans-frontier risks remains prominent for OECD. On July 8, 1988, the OECD Council passed a Decision of Council—that is, a binding decision—requiring member states to exchange information to reduce such risks. The resolution, which contains eight separate titles, spells out in detail the states' responsibilities toward their neighbors, including neighbors that are not members of OECD (OECD 1990:176–179). These top-down programs have the same difficulties as did the pre-Bhopal ones discussed above.

Several other international groups have promoted top-down information systems. In June 1989, the Commission of the European Communities proposed a European Environment Agency and a European Environmental Monitoring and Information Network. These organizations would provide information needed for environmental regulation by the Commission and by the member states (DiMeana 1990:161). The United Nations Center on Transnational Corporations has published a list of banned or restricted products and is in the process of putting out an anthology about various international policies for industrial safety (BNA 1987b:431). The publications are available to anyone who wants to buy them, but are obviously of most use to those who can make use of the information. The Economic and Social Council of the United Nations has developed a "Draft United Nations Code on Transnational Corporations." The Code asks transnational corporations to provide the host country governments with information about the possible environmental effects of the corporations' operations in that country (Burns 1990:66–67). Again, the information appears to go to national-level agencies. It is hard to be completely dismissive of top-down information systems. At the very least, providing national authorities with access to information is undoubtedly better than not doing so, unless it permits a minimal level of compliance to absolve exporters of legal or political responsibility for accidents. Nonetheless, the point I argue here is that the value of information as an instrument of risk management is very limited in a top-down strategy.

Prior Informed Consent (PIC)

The second general category of information programs includes those which try to strengthen PIC, the requirements that an importing country be fully informed if it imports a chemical that is banned or severely restricted in the exporting country. Since Bhopal, a number of organizations have endorsed the PIC, including the Commission of the European Communities (DiMeana 1990:163). The European Economic Community has been drafting binding regulations requiring PIC (Halter 1987:17–18). In the United States, less than one year after Bhopal, a coalition of industry, environmental, and labor groups proposed amendments to FIFRA, strengthening its PIC provisions by requiring an exporter of a banned pesticide to notify both the importer and the appropriate regulatory official in an importing country thirty days prior to the export (Goldberg 1985:1036–1037). These amendments failed to become law. FIFRA was not amended until 1988, principally due to domestic issues (Greene 1989). Several years later the United States did not sign the Basel Convention on the Control of Trans-boundary Movements of Hazardous Wastes and Their Disposal which requires PIC in the import and export of hazardous wastes. However, the U.S. government claimed that it lacked the statutory authority to implement the Convention domestically and said that it would seek such authority ("Environmental Protection Agency 1989 Activities" 1990:184). In addition, in 1989 the United States encouraged the adoption of PIC by U.N. agencies, such as UNEP (ibid.: 185).

UNEP has been a strong supporter of PIC. In 1989 the UNEP Governing Council adopted the London Guidelines, which, in part, mandate the use of PIC procedures. Shipments of restricted chemicals would not proceed if they were opposed by the "designated national authority in the importing country" ("UNEP 1989 Activities" 1990: 156). Under these guidelines, importing countries (whose participation is optional) would send a formal notice to the IRPTC that they wish to receive banned or restricted chemicals. The exporting countries, in turn, must notify the IRPTC of regulatory restrictions. That information is to be passed along to potential importers, along with other data on the chemical. If an export does occur, the exporter should "ensure that . . . the designated national authority of the state of import [is provided] with relevant information" ("UNEP 1989 Activities" 1990:156).

Depending on the specifics of the procedure, PIC can address some of the issues raised earlier concerning the strategic uses of information, particularly withholding it. The UNEP Guidelines try to get around the problems of withholding in two ways. First, they add another link in the chain, the IRPTC. By having both importers and exporters funnel information through the IRPTC, they set up an arbiter with fewer axes to grind and whose raison d'être is to release, not hold back, information. Moreover, if the exporting country provides the IRPTC with regulatory notices as a routine matter, then there will not be the same pressure for withholding as there would be if the information had to be exchanged at just the time one was trying to close a deal. Second, requirements such as those in the Basel Convention for written prior consent help to ensure that the procedures are actually being followed in a transaction. It would be important for an independent organization like the IRPTC to oversee the paper trail as a guarantee of impartiality.

Bottom-Up Programs

I have argued above that information coming from national or transnational sources may not reach local users or, if it does, may not be what they need or in the form that is most useful to them. These problems, all of which were tragically evident in Bhopal, may be alleviated, at least in part, by information programs that can be called bottom-up. Bottom-up programs have two advantages. First, they can allow people at the local level to determine what information they actually need, thereby overcoming problems of fit between general and local knowledge. Second, they can provide a mechanism whereby those local demands for information can be channeled to national and transnational sources. In this sense, bottom-up programs are active and "information-forcing," in contrast to top-down programs, which are largely reactive. Two 1990 OECD monographs, part of the activities of the Accidents Program, have pointed to the informational needs at the local level (OECD 1990a, b). They particularly emphasize the importance of industry's providing information to local authorities and to the public.

These ideas are more developed in the APELL program (Awareness and Preparedness for Emergencies at Local Level) recently put out by UNEP. APELL grew out of an initiative by the UNEP director in 1986 in response to a number of disasters (UNEP 1988:9) and a meeting in June 1987, when UNEP announced a work program aimed at better preparation for emergency response. At the meeting were representatives from a number of industry associations, including the U.S. Chemical Manufacturers Association (CMA). The CMA had developed a program to help local communities in the United States prepare for emergencies, the Community Awareness and Emergency Response program, and was willing to share its experiences with UNEP (BNA 1987c:371–372). By April 1988, UNEP, working with the CMA and the European Council of Chemical Manufacturers Federations, had produced a draft of the APELL handbook (BNA 1988b:289).

The core idea behind APELL is not only that local responders must have adequate knowledge and planning to respond to an emergency but that the local groups themselves must help decide what information they need. APELL recognizes the importance of the national government, but considers its role to be that of assisting the local user. Emergency response depends first and foremost on preparation at the local level (BNA 1988b:148–149). Thus, the information strategy in APELL is bottom-up. An information system rooted in the self-defined needs of local groups is socially constructed in a very different way from top-down systems, and will have a very different structure and operation. Central to the APELL process is the formation of a local Coordinating Group. The Group is intended to be inclusive. It brings together the three major "partners" in emergency planning and response: local authorities, industry representatives, and community-group leaders. Having this diverse group draw up the response plans serves two purposes. First, local responders can provide input into the process about what their real needs are in an emergency. Second, the process is intended to develop positive working relationships among all these groups as they get to know and trust each other. In short, the process builds capacity within the community to cope with emergencies.

APELL would have information flowing in several directions: from responders and community groups to industry officials, from industry to the community about the hazards and needed remedies associated with the plants, and from national and international sources, such as the IRPTC, to the local Coordinating Groups (BNA 1988b:152–158, 166). The handbook emphasizes industry's responsibility to provide data (BNA 1988b:156, 165–166). The incentive for industry to do so is the maintenance of a close working relationship with other members of the Coordinating Group, coupled with the desire to avoid harm if an accident does occur.

APELL addresses four of the most important problems in information use outlined earlier in the chapter: getting information to those who really need it, developing local expert capacity, developing regulatory capacity, and preventing or mitigating the strategic misuse of information. In these respects, APELL represents a successful instance of social learning. Consider each problem in turn. Precisely because APELL begins planning at the local level, responders have the opportunity to learn and articulate their informational needs. There is an implicit recognition in this program that useful information is context-specific, tailored to local conditions, though there is, of course, no guarantee that local officials will in fact get what they need. Nonetheless, when planning is based in broad participation, information systems are shaped by local needs and social relations and should be more responsive to them. APELL develops local expert capacity by making industrial expertise more readily available to the government, expertise crucial to interpreting complex data. The Coordinating Group is a forum in which agreements can be worked out to share that expertise. Nonetheless, the strategic problems of information are still present. Experts loaned occasionally from industry are not the same as governmental in-house expertise. Furthermore, experts are not without their biases, and the availability of loaned experts may not meet local needs. APELL, despite improvements, does not address any of the fundamental issues that erode regulatory capacity. The relationships and knowledge that government officials gain from their membership in the Coordinating Group can aid them in doing their job. Nonetheless, APELL per se makes no formal changes in government structure or authority, does not solve resource problems, and does not resolve conflicting policy goals.

Finally, APELL helps to alleviate some of the problems caused by the strategic use of information. By putting local plant managers directly into contact with local officials, and by providing a strong mandate that the plant managers share their information, it reduces the strategic manipulation by national, transnational, or corporate actors. As local officials become more sophisticated about the nature of the problems they face, they will be better able to ask the right questions of their industrial counterparts. Nonetheless, APELL is only a partial solution to these strategic problems. Plant managers can still use information strategically, and they are subject to a complex mix of incentives. While the APELL process may provide one set of incentives to cooperate with local authorities and their representatives, their responsibilities to their company and higher management may provide a different set. If secrecy is a deep part of their corporate culture, the APELL process will not change that.

Conclusions: Information Flow as Risk Management

Information, useful knowledge, is not a neutral, simple tool. It is a complex good, difficult to use technically, and politically strategic because it is embedded in the social and political circumstances of its creation, distribution, and use. Users will exploit it for multiple ends, not simply that for which it is designated. Early international information programs did not acknowledge this problem of social and political embeddedness. Databases and clearinghouses are static and reactive, not sensitive to local needs in preventing disasters, and not designed to avoid the problems that come with information's strategic value. PIC is only a very modest improvement on databases.

In attempting to innovate after Bhopal, international organizations concerned with information reacted in two ways. First, they tried to improve on old systems, such as strengthening various PIC programs. Second, and more important, they developed a new program based on a different approach to the problem, exemplified by APELL. By developing a bottom-up instead of top-down system, UNEP and its allies displayed real learning, rethinking the approach to this problem. What constitutes innovative learning and why does it come about? What can be done to promote such innovation by international organizations? Though answers are necessarily tentative and incomplete, the record of information systems suggests a way to look at the problem.

Ernst Haas has argued for a typology of learning by international organizations that draws a distinction between adaptation and learning. Both are organizational responses to outcomes perceived as failures. Adaptation, however, is the simpler response. It consists in trying out a new method for achieving the same goal and is characterized by an incremental, trial-and-error approach to problem-solving (Haas 1990: chs. 1–2). Neither the goals of the organization nor its (often implicit) theories about the natural and social world are reexamined in the light of new knowledge.

Learning is a more profound change in the way an international organization operates, and a rarer one. It requires accepting new knowledge (consensual, as Haas calls it) that changes prevailing ideas about the purpose of the organization, its definition of the problem, the theories that guide its actions, or all of these. The role of knowledge is key in reevaluating both means and ends. An organization that learns undergoes more substantial changes than one that merely adapts incrementally. Entirely new approaches are evidence of learning. To say that an international organization learns means that key groups of bureaucrats in the secretariat, and selected representatives of member states that constitute a governing body, learn. Learning does not require that everyone in the organization or all states associated with it learn (Haas 1990: ch. 7).

The new knowledge that enables learning usually comes from outside the international organization. The knowledge may not be perfect or complete or even correct, but it is persuasive for some reason to the members of the organization just at a time when they are seeking new ways to solve their problems. Ernst Haas suggests that some external epistemic community is the source of the new knowledge, which may often be the case. However, other actors or organizations that lack the breadth or intellectual coherence of epistemic communities may also be a source. Crises of various sorts often result in organizations' being willing to put established agenda items on the table and rethink what their job is and how to do it, making it possible for them to develop new conceptions of the world and their role in it, often based on knowledge championed by persons outside the organization.

The establishment of bottom-up information systems in the wake of the Bhopal disaster was a form of learning. It was a different approach to the problem, one that was qualitatively different from top-down approaches and it suggested a different theory about the workings of the world, specifically one that took account of the needs and potentials of local officials in trying to prevent and cope with disaster. The urgency to do something new came from the sheer magnitude of a series of disasters, including Bhopal. But urgency by itself is never enough. The relevant officials in UNEP had to see a desirability in changing, presumably to please certain constituencies important to the organization, and the possibility of change lay in UNEP's being able to draw on the experiences of the CMA in developing APELL (UNEP 1988: 14).

How and why UNEP learned in this instance is difficult to show, absent a detailed case study. However, one can argue for some more general lessons. It seems clear that for an international organization to learn it must be in touch with other organizations, such as NGOs, which are likely to be the source of knowledge that will lead to innovations. Operational organizations cannot be expected to be the source of their own new knowledge; they need to be connected to scientific communities or operational organizations in other environments that have had a chance to operate under a different set of theories and values. Ernst Haas has argued that UNEP is in fact poised to learn, partly because of the catalytic role that it plays. It depends upon the actions of other organizations and needs to be able to persuade them to follow its lead, since it has no real enforcement power. This linkage to other organizations can be a valuable resource when it seeks new knowledge (UNEP 1988:161–164).

Finally, the organization must have structural incentives to learn, which may mean reasons to attend to negative feedback. While intense self-examination is going to be rare in any organization, those responsible for its operation and support must not feel so threatened by bad outcomes that they are never open to assimilating new knowledge. In a way, a disaster like that at Bhopal makes learning easier because it is so dramatic that resistance to negative feedback tends to be overwhelmed, and international actors of all sorts scramble to find new ways of doing things. When we better understand these dynamics we will have a chance of learning before disaster rather than from it.

I am grateful to Ms. Kim Jennings of the U.S. EPA and Mr. Rob Visser of the OECD for providing me with information and documents. I am also grateful to Alan Ames, Jack Donnelly, Pamela W. Laird, Lucy Nolan, and the Bhopal group for help and discussions in preparing this chapter.

References

Alston, Philip. 1978. "International Regulation of Toxic Chemicals." *Ecology Law Quarterly* 7:397–456.

Barnes, Barry and David Edge, eds. 1982. *Science in Context: Readings in the Sociology of Science*. Cambridge, MA: MIT Press.

Bhushan, Bharat and Arun Subramaniam. 1985. "Bhopal: What Really Happened?" *Business India* (February 25–March 10): 102–116.

Bowonder, B., Jeanne X. Kasperson, and Roger E. Kasperson. 1985. "Avoiding Future Bhopals." *Environment* 27, 7 (September): 6–13 and 31–37.

Bureau of National Affairs. 1987a. "OECD Nations to Take 'Leading Role' on Accident Prevention, Chemicals Testing." *International Environment Reporter* (April 8): 145–147.

———. 1987b. "Publications." *International Environment Reporter* (December 9): 430–431.

———. 1987c. "UNEP Unveils Program to Reduce Industrial Effects on Environment. *International Environmental Reporter* (August 12): 371–372.

———. 1988a. "OECD High Level Conference Addresses Chemical Accidents, Information Needs. *International Environment Reporter* (March 9): 158–160.

———. 1988b. "UNEP Hosts Meeting to Review Draft Handbook on Industrial Accident Prevention, Response." *International Environment Reporter* (May 11): 289–290.

———. 1990. "United Nations Program on Preparing for Hazardous Accidents Said Growing." *International Environment Reporter* (April): 169.

Burns, William C. 1990. "The Report of the Secretary General on Transnational Corporations and Industrial Process Safety: A Critical Appraisal." *Georgetown International Environmental Law Review* 3:55–84.

Dagani, Ron. 1985. "Data on MIC's Toxicity are Scant, Leave Much to Be Learned." *Chemical & Engineering News* 63, 6 (February 11): 35–40.

DiMeana, Carlo Ripa. 1990. "Commission of the European Communities: 1989 Environmental Activities." *Colorado Journal of International Environmental Law and Policy* 1:159–165.

"Environmental Protection Agency 1989 Environmental Activities." 1990. *Colorado Journal of International Environmental Law and Policy* 1:181–187.

Goldberg, Karen A. 1985. "Efforts to Prevent Misuse of Pesticides Exported to Developing Countries: Progressing Beyond Regulation and Notification." *Ecology Law Quarterly* 12:1025–1051.

Greene, Janice L. 1989. "Regulating Pesticides: FIFRA Amendments of 1988." A BNA Special Report. *Chemical Regulation Reporter* 12 (January 6).

Greenwood, Carolyn D. 1985. "Restrictions on the Exportation of Hazardous Products to the Third World: Regulatory Imperialism or Ethical Responsibility?" *Boston College Third World Law Journal* 5:129–150.

Greenwood, Ted. 1984. *Knowledge and Discretion in Regulation.* New York: Praeger.

Haas, Ernst B. 1990. *When Knowledge Is Power: Three Models of Change in International Organizations.* Berkeley: University of California Press.

Halter, Faith. 1987. "Regulating Information Exchange and International Trade in Pesticides and Other Toxic Substances to Meet the Needs of Developing Countries." *Columbia Journal of Environmental Law* 12:1–37.

Jasanoff, Sheila. 1986. *Risk Management and Political Culture.* New York: Sage Publications.

———. Sheila. 1988. "The Bhopal Disaster and the Right to Know." *Social Science and Medicine* 27, 10:1113–1123.

"OECD 1989 Environmental Activities." 1990. *Colorado Journal of International Environmental Law and Policy* 1:167–187.

OECD. 1990a. *Workshop on the Role of Public Authorities in Preventing Major Accidents and in Major Accident Land-Use Planning.* OECD Environmental Monograph No. 30. Paris: OECD, December.

———. 1990b. *Workshop on Emergency Preparedness and Response and Research in Accident Prevention, Preparedness, and Response.* OECD Environmental Monograph No. 31. Paris: OECD, December.

Perrow, Charles. 1984. *Normal Accidents: Living with High-Risk Technologies.* New York: Basic Books.

Reinhold, Robert. 1985. "Disaster in Bhopal: Where Does Blame Lie?" *New York Times,* January 31, p. 1.

Schulberg, Francine, and Rob Visser. 1990. "Accident Prevention, Preparedness, and Response: The OECD Accidents Program." OECD Doc. ACC/90.298/6.08.1990.

Sclove, Richard E. 1982. "Decision-Making in a Democracy." *Bulletin of the Atomic Scientists* 38 (May): 44–49.

Slovic, Paul. 1987. "Perceptions of Risk." *Science* 236:280–285.

Stone, Deborah A. 1988. *Policy Paradox and Political Reason.* Glenview, IL: Scott, Foresman, and Co.

Subramaniam, Arun. 1984. "The Catastrophe at Bhopal." *Business India* (December 17–30): 67, 69, 73, 75, 76.

United Nations. 1988. *Accis Guide to United Nations Information Sources on the Environment.* New York: United Nations.

United Nations Environment Programme. 1988. *APELL: Awareness and Pre-*

paredness for Emergencies at Local Level. UN Publication No. E.88.III.D.3. New York: United Nations.

United Nations Environment Programme/Industry and Environmental Organization. 1989. "APELL: Awareness and Preparedness for Emergencies at Local Level—A Process for Responding to Technological Accidents." *Toxic Substances Journal* 9 : 145–221.

"UNEP 1989 Environmental Activities." 1990. *Colorado Journal of International Environmental Law and Policy* 1 : 147–156.

Varma, Vijaya Shankar. 1986. "I. Bhopal: The Unfolding of a Tragedy." *Alternatives*, 11, 1 (January): 137–145.

Woodhouse, Edward J. 1988. "Sophisticated Trial and Error in Decision Making About Risk." In Michael E. Kraft and Norman J. Vig, eds., *Technology and Politics*. Durham, NC: Duke University Press.

Worthy, Ward. 1986. "U.S. Chemical Industry Moving to Assure No More Bhopals." *Chemical & Engineering News* 64, 1 (June 6): 9–16.

Wynne, Brian. 1989a. "Building Public Concern into Risk Management." In J. Brown, ed., *Environmental Threats: Perception, Analysis, and Management.* London: Bellhaven Press, Pinter Publishers.

———. 1989b. "Frameworks of Rationality in Risk Management: Towards a Testing of Naive Sociology." In J. Brown, ed., *Environmental Threats: Perception, Analysis and Management.* London: Belhaven Press, Pinter Publishers.

Chapter 11
The Capacity of International Institutions to Manage Bhopal-like Problems

Peter M. Haas

The Bhopal disaster is an example of a broader class of problems that involve managing transboundary risks associated with the production of potentially hazardous substances. International institutions have been coming to grips with such problems only since the 1972 United Nations Conference on the Human Environment (UNCHE). This chapter investigates the extent to which the United Nations system has responded to such new risks and the extent to which international institutions have learned, or are capable of learning, to capture the linkages that produce disasters like Bhopal. This chapter begins with a description of the major transboundary dimensions of industrial risk management, describes institutional responses to them, and evaluates these responses in light of their relationship to the relevant transboundary dimensions and the special needs of developing countries. Thus, the chapter has a normative concern with institutional design: I specify the important features of Bhopal-like problems whose treatment I regard as essential for effective public management. However, this exercise also serves an analytic purpose in identifying the major parameters against which a policy change can be measured, and in assessing whether appropriate lessons can be drawn by the responsible institutions and the parameters within which such institutional learning may occur.

In using the term "institutional learning," I follow Ernst Haas's definition of a "change in the definition of the problem to be solved by a given organization" on the basis of new information.[1] Information is a key factor in institutional change to environmental problems because of the high uncertainty and risk involved with managing highly technical and unfamiliar issues. In this chapter I focus on institutional learning, although references may be made in passing to the relation

TABLE 11.1. Major Accidents Involving Hazardous Substances, 1970–1989.

Year	Number	Year	Number
1970	3	1980	11
1971	3	1981	8
1972	4	1982	6
1973	3	1983	6
1974	10	1984	12
1975	5	1985	15
1976	7	1977	7
1977	7	1987	12
1978	9	1988	10
1979	14	1989	9

Source: OECD, *State of the Environment 1990* (Paris: OECD, 1990), pp. 200–203. Data cover incidents with at least 25 deaths, 125 injuries, 10,000 people evacuated or deprived of water, or $10 million (U.S.) in damages. Data do not include oil spills at sea from ships or mining accidents.

between institutional learning and the broader process of social learning by which states improve their capacity to deal with industrial risks and environmental problems.

Accidental pollution, such as the MIC release at Bhopal, is but one of many forms of low probability-high risk disruptions that unfold within interactive and tightly coupled systems in which consequences of action occur in a non-linear manner.[2] Industrial risk, in short, is but one of many forms of transboundary environmental risk that public authorities seek to manage. Industrial risks include accidents, water and air pollution resulting from operational discharges, hazardous and toxic wastes disposal, and the risks associated with the transport and handling of such substances.

Risky activities occur in most countries with industrialized sectors of the economy. Such activities often have transboundary effects, and are causally related to other activities in multiple subtle ways. The Organization for Economic Cooperation and Development (OECD) has recorded 178 major industrial accidents from 1970 to 1989 (see Table 11.1).[3] Of these, 65 (38%) occurred in developing countries. India alone accounts for 9 percent of the world's major industrial accidents occurring worldwide during this period and 25% of those occurring in developing countries.

The problem for international management is that the often irreversible effects of human decisions are felt in places separated by time and distance from the place where those decisions were initially made. Had Bhopal not been located in the heart of the Indian subcontinent, it could easily have posed direct transboundary threats to environ-mental quality and public health as Chernobyl did. Present choices threaten to circumscribe a future range of action, often in ways that are not fully understood. When there is potential for transboundary effects, no one country is able to guard against insults to its environ-ment through its own actions, unaided by other countries' concurrent actions. Solutions may be imported from abroad—or imposed, as when U.S. lawyers descended on Bhopal. Yet the state of understand-ing about the nature and extent of these interlinkages remains sketchy at best, and the full extent of possible environmental dis-ruptions and resilience are seldom known in advance.

Bhopal, as we saw in earlier chapters, also implicated problems specific to managing industrial risks in developing countries. Third World governments often lack the administrative experience or ca-pacity to assess environmental risks, to design effective institutions, or even to monitor and enforce decisions. With little local participation in formulating decisions, public policies seldom reflect local knowl-edge or preferences. Even more than in the North, governments are obsessed with promoting short-term economic objectives, often at the expense of public health or longer-term environmental quality.

The Bhopal disaster revealed that the private sector, including even experienced multinationals, is incapable of effectively managing such problems alone. Investment decisions relating to the construction and siting of industrial facilities such as the Bhopal plant are commonly taken without regard to distinctive local contexts or conditions, such as poorly trained workforces, shortage of capital, and proximity to highly concentrated population centers. Established operational prac-tices used in industrialized societies may not be easily transferred to developing countries. With only rudimentary regulatory frameworks in many developing countries, transnational corporations, such as Union Carbide at Bhopal, have no incentive to apply the strict rules they follow in developed countries. Moreover, as the United Nations Center on Transnational Corporations notes, "External constraints, like required foreign minority ownership or inadequate local infra-structure, sometimes impede the use of up-to-date technologies in de-veloping countries."[4]

International institutions may be of help in coping with the growing transboundary dimensions of risk associated with industrial activities. I speak here of institutions in the broad sense of "established rules, norms and conventions" mediated by formal international organi-zations that "prescribe behavioral roles, constrain activity, and shape expectations."[5] Through their activities, international institutions may influence or modify patterns of state behavior within a given area of activity, such as the management of transboundary risks associated with industrial projects in developing countries. They can help provide information about the transnational effects of industrial projects, and thus contribute to their better design (see Laird, this volume, Chapter 10). They can provide facilities through which member states may coordinate measures to manage the transboundary externalities from their activities and their responses to actual disasters. They may also help to develop and provide the kind of integrative policy models whose application is necessary to manage the tightly coupled nature of these problems. Through training they may also help to build national administrative and technical capabilities to deal with such problems in the future.

There are reasons to doubt the ability of international organizations to help countries manage such a challenge adequately. Few organizations have the interdisciplinary competence to formulate and disseminate policy relevant to the cross-cutting nature of these problems, and the difficulties of coordination between international organizations are well known. Future generations, who are likely to suffer most heavily from environmental degradation, are represented poorly or not at all in present decisionmaking fora.[6] Is the decentralized United Nations system, in particular, able to respond to the interdisciplinary and nonlinear (and hence nondiscrete) nature of such problems?[7]

Analytic Dimensions of Transboundary Environmental Problems

International environmental problems, in particular hazard exports and transboundary pollution, are widely regarded as a composite of tightly coupled relationships between a variety of social activities. The environmental effects of policy choices are transmitted between countries along three analytic dimensions, reflecting the interdependencies that characterize industrial policy in a global economy.

The first dimension is intersectoral. Choices affecting one sector or area of activity are felt in other sectors as well. Effects are transmitted from one issue to another by the functional linkages between issues. Functional connections may be determined by whether activities or issues are tightly or loosely coupled to other activities or issues, and to which ones.[8]

Transboundary effects are also felt over time, as when the consequences of immediate choices are felt by future generations. The temporal dimension may be short term (such as under six months), medium term (such as six months to 5 years), and long term (over five years). With most ordinary uses of economic discounting techniques, planners generally disregard or heavily discount long-term effects, thereby downplaying the latent consequences of present industrial activity.

Finally, issues are related spatially, both when hazardous products such as pesticides are shipped across boundaries and when pollution travels over long distances, as in the case of radiation from Chernobyl. This dimension may be scaled according to the number of countries producing and consuming a given problem: from global (countries all around the world contribute to and are affected by the problem) to regional (the transboundary effects are limited to a regional scope) to widely distributed (a number of countries are affected by a problem but the problem itself is generated purely within national boundaries).

There are also three modes by which such effects are actually transmitted or mediated. First-order effects are the physical effects of action or inaction. Second-order effects are the social effects that occur as a consequence of physical degradation of the environment. Third-order effects are the consequence of actions taken to protect the environment or defer deterioration, including the opportunity costs of varying policies and mobility of investment and resources as environmental quality changes.[9] Not all of these can be covered in this brief chapter.

Functional Linkages

At Bhopal the siting of a potentially hazardous facility was tightly coupled with a number of other activities. Decisions regarding the production and management of MIC at Bhopal were closely affected by such conditions as population growth, urbanization, agricultural production, transportation and energy use, and economic policy. The industrial siting decision in turn had effects on public health, environmental quality, and agricultural production. While regularized use of MIC-based pesticides was intended to increase agricultural production, excessive use and ecosystemic build-up of such materials were destined to lead to longer-term declines.

In Bhopal, a potentially hazardous substance was produced in a densely populated area with weak technological and administrative controls. Accordingly, the accident had widespread and unanticipated consequences. Yet the proximate factors associated with the magnitude of the disaster cannot be separated from the broader social factors that laid the groundwork for such an event. Locating industrial sources nearest to the major inputs, such as incidental labor supply, reflects deeper political choices that developing countries can seldom evade: in particular, a potentially tragic choice of economic efficiency over serious public health or environmental considerations.

Events like Bhopal must be seen as part of a broader web of tightly coupled decisions that cut across many areas of public policy. In a country like India, high rates of urban growth and urbanization and limited availability of transportation and infrastructural support relate in turn to patterns of resource and energy consumption. The Union Carbide factory would not have been producing insecticides if it were not for India's broader need for agricultural chemicals to expand food production to satisfy a growing population and to obtain foreign exchange through exports. Throughout the world, but particularly in developing countries, planning and managing urban systems and improving the environment of human settlements pose a daunting challenge, particularly when urban populations are often growing at 6–8 percent per year from natural increase and rural migration.

Thus one can argue that the siting decision was preceded by (possibly unavoidable) social choices regarding centralized and large-scale industrial production, which entailed the location of factories near the major industrial inputs—labor, energy, and intermediate products—with an attendant rise in the potential for disaster. This industrial development strategy is endemic throughout the world, and surely continues in India, where concentrated growth zones are planned for the future.[10] For the present, at least, the inadequacy of infrastructure rules out less centralized industrial development that would keep centers from being located in such vulnerable areas.

Spatial Linkages

Many environmental problems emerge as a result of flows of polluting facilities and pollutants transmitted spatially between countries. That is, policy effects are felt across international borders, either physically, through more or less complex biogeochemical cycles, or by markets that transmit the price effects of local disruptions. Had Union Carbide built its factory closer to a border we could well have been discussing a physical transboundary case similar to Chernobyl or the pollution of the Rhine from the accident at Sandoz (see Chapter 6, this volume). With greater reliance on international trade for enhancing national welfare, market channels, too, are becoming increasingly important for the transnational dispersal of environmental risks.

Except for its legal ramifications, the most salient spatial dimension of the Bhopal disaster was ultimately national. The accident involved purely private goods which appeared within the boundaries of one territorial state and whose effects remained within those boundaries. Nonetheless, Bhopal called attention to the transnational dimension inherent in technology transfer. Decisions developed within one region's economic or cultural context were transplanted elsewhere, such as the engineering design features of the Bhopal plant, including infrastructure, management practices, and labor skills, which were originally created for market conditions in the United States. Thus, technological decisions that appear at first to be purely national can in reality produce widely distributed effects in countries throughout the world.

Temporal Linkages

Temporally, the effects of an environmental mishap may be felt in the future both by victims of that episode and in areas that suffer longer-term impacts through multiple feedback loops. The effects of toxic substances are often not fully understood when they are originally developed (as, for example, in the case of methyl isocyanate), and when populations are exposed, the full effects may not be felt for as much as twenty to fifty years. Environmental detriments, too, may be irreversible, at least in the short to medium run. Adverse effects in functionally related areas may take even longer to make themselves felt. An accident of significant proportions may cause significant changes in food and agricultural production, energy use, and population level, but such effects are unlikely to occur for at least five to ten years. Formulating better policies to address such temporal linkages is difficult because of the poor information generally available about these issues.

Institutional Design

While no existing international organizations have competency to deal with all three dimensions by which Bhopal-like problems acquire transnational status, we may investigate how such institutions have responded to environmental problems within their traditionally de-limited domains. Which institutions have developed new activities to take account of all three dimensions of policy linkages? The most effective institution for responding to new environmental challenges would be one that is sufficiently resilient to avoid making irreversible decisions and expert enough to respond to unfolding understanding about environmental conditions, while possibly even contributing to a better understanding of environmental threats and dynamics. Its institutional design is best seen as that of a switchboard operation, rather than a centralized or strictly hierarchically designed body. Such a design is most likely to improve the ability of governments and societies to deal with industrial and environmental risks because the institution is able to encourage social learning by ensuring that policy-relevant knowledge claims and new ideas about environmental management are provided to the organization and its members and are widely disseminated.

At a minimum, institutional learning requires an institutional design that provides for the provision of non-partisan scientific information about the physical environment, the regularized feedback of information regarding activities by governments and firms, the support of developing countries' capacity to conduct the environmental monitoring and research and apply it indigenously to their policy process, and the widespread dissemination of such information in a readily usable manner, so that private groups can keep track of each other's activities and hold governments accountable for enforcing their environmental commitments. By soliciting input from a variety of different actors with different experiences and concerns, including the scientific community, multinational corporations (MNCs), governments, and grassroots nongovernmental organizations (NGOs), such an institution is able to help the international system respond more effectively to environmental issues.

Tightly coupled issues that give rise to events such as Bhopal can best be treated by institutions with a broad range of competencies for studying and coordinating policies and for initiating and coordinating research and monitoring activities by other agencies. The wider the functional interlinkages underlying environmental problems, the broader the range of functional skills that are required for policy making, and a coordinative and, at times, catalytic agency is needed to avert disjointed policies. While analysts may regard international standard-setting and rulemaking as necessary to assure adequate management of transboundary environmental problems, such functions are more commonly performed through coordination among nations than through supranational administration.

Most importantly, institutions with the capacity to develop useful policy guidance must offer integrated management procedures that simultaneously address the multiple interlinkages that characterize transboundary problems. The United Nations Environment Programme (UNEP) notes that "what must be borne in mind, however, is that to be effective the activities that make up the environment programme demand a systems approach to their conceptualization and a multidisciplinary input to their planning and execution."[11]

Memberships must be appropriate to include participants across the likely spatial spread of possible effects. Thus, problems arising out of physical flow of pollutants should be relegated to regional or small bodies with limited membership for most efficient responses. Regional bodies are likely to have more experience and localized knowledge about the context of such flows. Widely distributed national problems, by contrast, may be better treated by multilateral development banks and aid agencies, with global or regional membership, which may provide information about management styles and technology as well as financial assistance.

Unlike environmental problems originating with physical transnational flows, widely distributed problems do not need coordinative institutions for their resolution. Rather, their effective management relies more heavily on providing timely information about the scope of the problem, expert advice on alternative policies, training of national officials, and financial support for projects. Many initiatives have already been undertaken within such institutions as the World Bank and multilateral development agencies, which possess the appropriate membership and institutional resources. Preventing or mitigating such problems in the future will require the involvement of institutions with regional to global membership, as well as technical capabilities to identify problems, gather data, monitor and evaluate environmental quality, estimate risks, assess projects' impacts, disseminate information, provide consultants and expert advice, conduct training, and coordinate national and international programs.[12]

Institutional Responses

International institutions were alerted to issues of environmental management in the late 1960s by a host of widely publicized disasters. Two years of preparations for the 1972 United Nations Conference on the Human Environment made national governments sensitive to a variety of new environmental policy concerns. The conference adopted a declaration with 26 principles and 109 recommendations aimed at getting UN agencies to integrate major environmental issues within their programmatic activities.[13]

Since 1972, numerous existing institutions created new programs to cope with newly revealed policy needs. Some dimensions of these problems corresponded to existing institutional channels for dealing with international issues. Some others, however, because they cut across the narrower functional authority of existing international agencies, required the establishment of new bodies or the creative coordination of ongoing programs by intergovernmental and non-governmental organizations. As different institutions modified their activities to cope with the environmental aspects of their domains of action, their efforts were orchestrated by UNEP, which was created at UNCHE with a "catalytic" mission to spur and coordinate environmental action throughout the United Nations system. Since its inception in 1973, UNEP has expanded its focus to incorporate the activities of non-governmental organizations as well.

Even with the creation of UNEP and the Environment Co-ordination Board in 1972, efforts to coordinate and catalyze environmental activities within the United Nations were fraught with interorganizational jealousies and conflicts. The consolidation in 1978 of coordinating responsibilities within a single senior-level working committee of the heads of the major U.N. agencies with environmental responsibilities, known as the Designated Officials for Environmental Matters (DOEM), was but a modest institutional reform.

In attempting to instill comprehensive environmental policies throughout the U.N. system, UNEP tried to link decisionmaking across a host of functionally interlinked issues, including population growth, agricultural production, industrial siting and general industrial practices, and energy use.[14] UNEP officials hoped to capture the interconnected nature of all environmental policy problems, including industrial wastes and the environmental aspects of development planning, through a master plan by which the Program would coordinate its own projects with those of other U.N. agencies. This approach, UNEP officials hoped, would lead to more coherent planning, as well as imbuing the other U.N. agencies with a more thoroughgoing environmental orientation.[15] In 1988 UNEP adopted the System-Wide Medium-Term Environment Programme for 1990–1995. Overall, however, UNEP's experience has been disappointing, as it lacks the financial resources to induce other agencies or governments to adopt environmental programs and the bureaucratic clout to compel them to do so.[16]

In 1988 the World Bank developed dramatically new environmental assessment procedures for many of its projects, including industrial siting for chemical and fertilizer factories. A manual was published in 1988 specifying techniques to assess industrial hazards in new projects.[17] Environmental assessments are now required for new Bank projects and components that have "diverse and significant components that "may have specific environmental impacts."[18] Cross-sectoral guidelines were issued in 1991 to alert project designers to heed possible cross-sectoral links associated with all industrial projects, as well as possible physical transboundary effects. The new guidelines also called for strengthening the administrative capabilities of local environmental authorities.[19]

The Bank approved programmatic changes as well. Over the last two years the Bank has begun to consider ecological factors in its traditional development-oriented activities. New funds were allocated to support projects that would promote environmental protection or compensate for environmental degradation. About 25 percent of all World Bank projects were assessed for their environmental impact during 1990. While structural adjustment loans are excluded from environmental assessment, four of the 14 structural adjustment loans administered in 1989 had explicit environmental objectives; agriculture and the environment in the Gambia, natural resources management in Ghana, and forestry in Guinea-Buissau and Laos. Five sector adjustment loans specifically addressed environmental objectives. Loans for free-standing environmental projects increased in number from two during the 1989 fiscal year to eleven in fiscal 1990, and 107 of 222 total approved sectoral loans contained environmental components. The Bank announced in 1990 that from 1990 to 1992 it planned to conduct environmental assessments for 376 projects in the pipeline, although only 58 (15%) will receive intensive assessment. Of intended projects, 47 percent will receive environmental assessments: 40 percent of African projects; 59 percent of Asian projects; 53 percent of European, Middle East, and North African projects; and 41 percent of Latin American and Caribbean projects. Most of the work relates to investments in power, energy, and agriculture, followed by transportation and industry, reflecting the Bank's overall portfolio.[20] The $3.5 billion Global Environment Fund was established by the World Bank, UNEP, and the United Nations Development Program (UNDP) in 1990 to finance projects in developing countries with global or regional environmental benefits.

These new operational policies also created an expanded role for NGOs, who are now consulted and involved in Bank operations, particularly in providing advice on consultants and in making available local information on development sites. While these initiatives can be seen as an effort to coopt NGO critics by bringing them inside and investing them with a stake in continued Bank lending, they have also had the effect of establishing NGOs as watchdogs. U.S. and Indian NGOs, for example, now work together in exchanging and publicizing information about World Bank activities. They also provide local information to the Bank that officials do not otherwise receive.

Other dimensions of industrial and environmental risk have been confronted by institutions directly involved with industrial risk problems and with functionally tightly coupled issues. Population problems have fallen under the purview of the World Bank and the United Nations Fund for Population Assistance (UNFPA). By 1987 UNFPA had provided more than $1.5 billion to nearly 150 countries for support of family planning, population information, education, data collection and analysis, establishment of research institutes, and formulation and implementation of population policies.[21] The United States, however, cut off its contributions to UNFPA in 1986 to protest its support for abortion. Public health efforts more generally are supported by the World Health Organization (WHO) and national aid agencies.

Several institutional efforts exist to deal with agricultural production and the second- and third-order effects of agrochemicals such as were produced at Bhopal. The thirteen institutes in the Consultative Group on International Agricultural Research conduct research on various new high-yield agricultural crops. More resistant strains are expected to reduce the need for chemical pesticides. The Food and Agricultural Organization (FAO), the World Food Council (WFC), and the International Fund for Agricultural Development (IFAD) support other efforts aimed at expanding agricultural production.

Information on the management, transport, and use of farm chemicals is collected and disseminated by many institutions. Information about agrochemicals is circulated through FAO's and WHO's Codex Alimentarius Commission, which has also adopted some two hundred international standards for food quality standards and maximum residue levels for pesticides and agrochemicals. Some forty codes of practice, guidelines, and other texts covering food products have also been developed. UNEP works with WHO and FAO to create demonstration projects on correct use of pesticides, now in place in more than thirty countries.

FAO's Code of Conduct on the Distribution and Use of Pesticides recently imposed a voluntary "prior informed consent" provision on international trade in pesticides. FAO administers technical assistance projects and training programs on the correct use and safe handling of pesticides in developing countries. Future plans include efforts to prevent groundwater contamination by pesticides and to promote correct use and safe handling of pesticides. While ambitious in conception and well intentioned in practice, such projects all too frequently lack the resources and host country commitment to affect workplace practices significantly.[22]

Some steps have been taken since 1984 to improve disaster response procedures. UNEP sponsors a program for training local officials to respond to industrial accidents.[23] Since 1986 UNEP has conducted training workshops for officials from developing nations in managing hazardous wastes and controlling disasters. Draft laws and regulations are also provided to developing countries for possible national adoption. The World Bank, too, is currently developing training programs in disaster response.

In 1987 UNEP developed the London guidelines for the exchange of information on chemicals in international trade, and, with the FAO, began developing and distributing lists of chemicals banned and severely restricted by more than ten countries. With the ILO and WHO, UNEP is involved in the International Programme on Chemical Safety (IPCS) intended to conduct and disseminate assessments of the risk to human health from exposure to chemicals, as well as to support future research. Started in 1980, the program by 1992 involved twenty-seven countries and sixty-seven institutions.[24] In 1984 the General Assembly approved the continuing update of a Consolidated List of five hundred potentially dangerous products banned, restricted, or unapproved in sixty countries, covering pharmaceuticals, agricultural chemicals, industrial chemicals, and consumer products.

UNEP is helping to design and promote hazardous waste management strategies, particularly for developing countries. UNEP provides information on the management of toxic substances, and national standards through its International Registry of Potentially Toxic Chemicals (IRPTC), which keeps a file on approximately 450 chemicals with national and international recommendations and legal requirements related to their control (see Laird, this volume, Chapter 10, for an appraisal of IRPTC). UNEP's Paris-based Industry and Environment Office circulates information on hazardous waste management techniques. UNEP developed in 1987 the Cairo Guidelines and Principles for the Environmentally Sound Management of Hazardous Wastes, and is preparing with WHO a technical manual for the safe disposal of hazardous wastes with special emphasis on the problems and needs of developing countries.

To date, developing policies for routine industrial practices largely remains an activity of the industrialized countries. Research, information transfer, and policy advice come from the Organization for Economic Cooperation and Development (OECD), the United Nations Economic Commission for Europe (ECE), and the European Community (EC). The EC responded to industrial disasters by adopting the 1986 Seveso Directive, which requires much more extensive reporting from companies and public notification of industrial siting decisions (see van Eijndhoven, this volume, Chapter 6). EC directives have been issued on toxic wastes, waste handling and disposal, sewage sludge, used oils, PCBs and PCTs, titanium dioxide wastes, and packaging.[25] Few infractions of these directives have been reported.[26]

The International Labor Organization (ILO) has proposed a convention concerning safety in the use of chemicals in the workplace, stressing chemical hazard evaluation and information provision to workers, along with preventive measures and programs.[27] Institutional measures also exist for the transport of hazardous wastes. The OECD adopted the first Decision on the Export of Hazardous Waste from its member countries in 1986, and the EC has a directive on the transboundary transfers of hazardous wastes. No comparable specialized programs exist as yet for managing toxic and industrial wastes in the Newly Industrializing Countries, although with high rates of industrialization and economic growth, these countries will surely soon be encountering such problems at home and in their relations with other Third World countries.

Most recently, some efforts have been taken by international organizations to capture the cross-cutting dimensions of environmental problems. Programs have been developed that are sensitive to the intersectoral nature of environmental threats and that contain elements for monitoring and linking sectors previously considered to be discrete. UNEP and WHO have developed global monitoring networks that are capable of tracing the multiple sources of environmental degradation. These illustrate for decision makers the extensive functional interlinkages among environmental issues by identifying chemical inputs into the environment and relating their introduction to observed health effects in various regions.[28] UNEP's Global Environment Monitoring System (GEMS), run in conjunction with other specialized agencies, coordinates monitoring stations in 142 countries including some 30,000 scientists and technicians. The modeling efforts and systems analysis underway at the International Institute for Applied Systems Analysis (IIASA) in Vienna lends further scientific credibility to the linkages identified between such issues.

Institutional efforts have also shifted somewhat from the physical transmission of hazards to the social factors that promote the spread of environmental hazards. Whereas the physical effects were, in most cases, limited to the regional or widely distributed scale, the globalization of international economic relations has made the second- and third-order consequences of environmental decisions also of a global nature. International financial institutions, such as the World Bank and the International Monetary Fund, have attempted to harmonize the way in which second-order market effects are transmitted by promoting the Polluter Pays Principle and through efforts to reduce state subsidies for activities that contribute to environmental degradation.

The OECD and EC also support the Polluter Pays Principle as a way to promote environmental protection consistently with their formal responsibility for harmonizing economic policies and eliminating market barriers. Economists are trying to revise the United Nations System of National Accounts in order to account for the environmental stocks from which countries generate wealth and which were traditionally not factored into systems of national accounting.[29]

UNEP trains officials in developing countries to apply economic planning techniques that pay closer attention to the multiple connections between economic development and environmental protection. UNEP has been influential in helping draft and administer multilateral treaties regulating transboundary dimensions of environmental risk. The 1989 Basel Convention on Trade in Hazardous Substances and the 1973 Convention on International Trade in Endangered Species constrain the use of markets that promote environmentally damaging activity. The Basel Convention, which closely regulates the export of hazardous wastes and demands extensive reporting from exporting to importing states, may be seen in part as a response to the worldwide outcry that greeted Bhopal.

International Institutions and Environmental Learning

Despite bureaucratic inertia and a generalized reluctance to change fixed patterns of action, the programmatic changes described above indicate a moderate shift in international institutions' approach to managing industrial risks. Three themes are striking in this twenty-year period of institutional responses to shocks such as Bhopal and to the growing mass of new information about the complex nature of environmental risks.

First, interagency coordination to manage environmental programs systematically within the U.N. system failed, due to a lack of bureaucratic leverage by UNEP and by the uniform reluctance among funding countries to support such a massive overhaul of the UN system.

Second, while most institutional efforts do not deal explicitly with the underlying social causes of such problems, many institutions modified their traditional activities in order to integrate environmental considerations that directly affected their operational missions. Virtually all organizations developed projects to deal with industrial risks, and also supplemented their activities to deal with some of the direct environmental linkages to their missions, such as population for UNFPA, public health for WHO, and pesticide use for FAO.

Third, a variety of more important, functional linkages were recognized by UNEP and the World Bank. Each organization developed new programs, and the World Bank modified old programs to take account of the spatial, temporal, and functionally related environmental effects of their activities. Recent IMF and World Bank efforts that have begun to integrate long-term environmental considerations into shorter-term structural adjustments are also consistent with this pattern of more comprehensive programmatic accommodations.[30]

Recent writing in political science about institutional learning helps to explain this variation in institutional responses to environmental challenges. Institutional learning is a political process through which collective behavior is modified in light of new collective understanding.[31] Such learning may take one of two forms: single-loop or double-loop. Single-loop learning refers to modifications in organizational practices that take into account new problems. Double-loop learning refers to the modification of an institutional mission, as members and officials reflect on new understanding about the world to modify their mission in light of what they now understand to be desirable or possible. New institutional objectives and means of control are adopted out of a recognition of the complex pattern of causal relations in the issue that the policy addresses. Ernst Haas regards only this second form as "true" learning; the first is adaptation to changed circumstances, which does not entail the scope that institutional responses require to manage industrial and environmental issues effectively within the context of the new ecological "problematique."

Most of the organizational responses documented above reflect merely single-loop learning. Institutions applied new information about environmental linkages to modify their existing patterns of activity incrementally. While numerous institutions developed new programs for environmental monitoring, circulating guidelines and standards, and coordinating state policies, such responses by the UNFPA, ILO, and FAO were merely adaptive: new means or instruments were appended to preexisting ends. Nor were the results comprehensive enough to be deemed adequate for designated policy purposes.

Most of the single-loop resources neglect the different context of industrial siting in the Third World. The new projects continue to reflect an overarching concern and experience with the environmental problems of the industrialized countries. The training projects sponsored by international institutions tend to retain the technocratic perspective of public planning in the North. Few provisions exist to improve administrative capabilities in developing countries, to include indigenous participation in project planning, or to inject traditional knowledge and local experience into new projects.

The World Bank and UNEP demonstrated double-loop learning by virtue of their systematic efforts to redefine their activities. Questions about the institution's prior programmatic ends led to substantially new, comprehensive programs for dealing with industrial siting and environmental planning. These institutions' programs were also more sensitive to the different conditions in developing countries. The institutional changes of greatest potential value to developing countries are those that stress the provision of environmental information and model policies, as well as training in new technology and techniques. Examples include measures for training LDC officials in planning for emergency responses and managing hazardous wastes. Recent efforts to include NGOs in international planning may also provide a channel for local groups that lack such standing within their own states to express their concerns about industrial planning and to provide an understanding that is often absent from development projects.

Not all international institutions are equally capable of learning. Ernst Haas notes that two necessary conditions for institutional, or double-loop, learning are "a relatively stable coalition of like-minded states . . . and sufficient consensual knowledge . . . to provide the rationale for the novel nesting of problems and solutions."[32] Since the Second Industrial Revolution in the late twentieth century, policy makers have accorded respect to specialists in science and technology because of the growing technical nature of international relations and because national power and wealth have become intimately tied to a country's scientific and technological resources. Where true institutional learning has occurred, it has often been spurred by the inclusion of transnational networks of experts in the operations of international institutions. The policy lessons learned by the institutions reflect the technical understanding and beliefs of these experts. These groups are known as epistemic communities. They are composed of professionals who share common causal beliefs, common values, common truth tests, and a common policy enterprise.[33] Because of their shared command of potentially instrumental technical knowledge, national decision makers often defer to their advice, and they are hired by international institutions as officials and as consultants. Thus, they are responsible for articulating the precise knowledge relevant to the functional responsibilities of international institutions.

During the 1980s, members of a global ecological epistemic community emerged as key actors in international environmental protection. They were trained in the new sciences of systems ecology and informed with holistic beliefs about the nature of social and physical systems. Their preferred policies and programs reflected their causal beliefs regarding the widespread existence of tightly coupled systems, including the choices associated with industrial siting, which required comprehensive environmental planning and participation from local citizens groups in areas where development projects were planned. Many of them were hired by international organizations and helped to draft the new environmental programs intended to cope with industrial accidents and other environmental threats. Epistemic communities imparted new information to national decision makers and to the staffs of international institutions. In turn they helped redirect the programmatic activities of their institutions through a combination of measures. They persuaded their colleagues of the need for new approaches. They helped identify projects and ideas that served as focal points around which other groups could mobilize. Finally, they gained positions of influence in national administrations and international institutions, from which they projected their desired programs. Significant policy change has been limited to those institutions—the World Bank and UNEP for the problem of industrial accidents—in which ecological epistemic community members have greatest bureaucratic influence.

While information about the magnitude of industrial problems and environmental threats has been widespread for at least a decade, only UNEP and the World Bank took significant steps to modify their operations in light of this new perspective. Double-loop learning occurred only in the institutions in which epistemic communities existed and were able to consolidate bureaucratic power within the institution.

In UNEP, for instance, a staff committed to holistic environmental planning helped design a number of programs that integrated environmental considerations into the activities of other institutions, as well as expanding UNEP's role in training developing country officials in more comprehensive planning techniques. The 1988 World Bank reforms were drafted by a like-minded group.[34] Once inscribed in the Bank's policy, these procedural reforms exercised far more leverage than had been anticipated by the Bank's major critics in the United States Treasury Department, Congress, and the Washington NGO community, each of which had initially used environmental arguments expediently to promote its own aims. Such moves even exceeded the wishes of major donors, the Bank's primary clientele, who opposed any massive rethinking that would disrupt the flow of development finance. Still more profound and long-lasting impacts of the programmatic changes at the World Bank may be experienced through the new perspectives on economic development and environmental management that the Bank imparts in its training seminars and publications for developing country officials.

Inhibitions to institutional learning surely exist as well. Governmental opposition can inhibit the effectiveness of new institutional programs. The conceptual policy changes and programmatic reforms conceived in international institutions were not easily converted to changes in practice in developing countries that lacked resources for institutions, equipment, or training programs. As noted earlier, U.S. opposition to abortion after 1985 undercut the UNFPA budget, just as U.S. opposition to projects that would provide concessionary technology transfer to developing countries led to the limiting of U.S. financial support to UNEP after 1977.

Other general inhibitions to institutional learning may be easily identified. Institutions are unlikely to adopt programs that run counter to the interests of the stronger countries on their governing boards who contribute the majority of their budgets and who vote on programmatic matters. The FAO was long regarded as a captive of agricultural producers, and not surprisingly has limited its environmental activities to increasing agricultural yield rather than to limiting the use of farm chemicals. IMO has long been the bailiwick of tanker owners, and its focus on navigation and safety over stringent discharge standards reflects this distribution of power. The most extensive management strategies have addressed problems encountered in the North, for which it is easier to mobilize financial support from multilateral institutions which are funded primarily by the Northern countries. There are few institutional efforts of comparable scope for problems specific to developing countries, and the programs that exist remain underfunded.

Few institutions, moreover, have the organizational capacity for sustained institutional learning. They are typically staffed by people with applied skills, rather than with the interdisciplinary and holistic expertise that leads staff to recognize intersectoral linkages and act on them. Moreover, organizational habits and inertia lead bodies to avoid making dramatic or transformational programmatic shifts. Most responses remained consistent with the organizations' traditional responsibilities.

In the absence of proactive epistemic communities, institutional responses have generally been of the adaptive variety. The functionally most complex issues, for which the least amount of learning has occurred, are the ones that continue to pose the greatest challenges to international organizations responsible for environmental programs.

Conclusion

International institutions responded in a variety of ways to Bhopal and similar environmental challenges. Management of discrete aspects of the transboundary risks associated with industrial accidents was assumed by institutions within the United Nations system whose traditional responsibilities most closely resembled the analytic dimensions of the new problems. Little effective interagency coordination occurred, as most UN agencies developed new projects consistent with their traditional responsibilities. But institutions in which ecological epistemic communities gained control developed more holistic and comprehensive programs. In short, international institutions, and countries participating in them, recognized the importance of a new set of multidimensional and interconnected problems. A new, though still inadequate, pattern of practices appears to be emerging as these actors adjust their behavior to capture some of the most obvious dimensions of environmental interconnectedness.

The spatial and temporal dimensions of many environmental issues were fairly well addressed by existing international bodies. New programs were directed at compensating for administrative weaknesses in developing countries that inhibit them from effectively preventing or managing such problems. However, some of the complex functional interlinkages disclosed by the Bhopal disaster elude satisfactory treatment, because they exceed the limited functional resources of current organizations and because epistemic communities capable of articulating the new scientific information to the institutions were unable to obtain access.

Major gaps therefore remain in the institutional treatment of international environmental problems, and many of the programs developed by these institutions are still only incipient. A new wave of environmental consciousness, such as the one that propelled UNCHE, may be needed in order to push the UN system and other international bodies to expand their search for relevant knowledge into a deeper phase of institutional learning. This responsibility will now lie with the Commission for Sustainable Development, established in the United Nations to coordinate institutional and international activities for sustainable development after the United Nations Conference on Environment and Development. By facilitating access of the scientific community and grassroots organizations to international discussions, and by encouraging the UN agencies to more fully integrate environmental dimensions into their activities the Commission may further promote institutional learning about the management of industrial risks.

I wish to acknowledge the valuable research assistance of Jenifer Conrad in this enterprise. My thanks to Ernst B. Haas, Sheila Jasanoff, Gene Rochlin, Peter Sand, and Oran Young for their comments on previous drafts.

Notes

1. Ernst B. Haas, *When Knowledge Is Power* (Berkeley: University of California Press, 1990), p. 3.

2. Charles Perrow, *Normal Accidents: Living with High Risk Technologies* (New York: Basic Books, 1984). See also Henri Smets, "The Cost of Accidental Pollution," *UNEP Industry and Environment* (October/November/December 1988): 28–33; Jean-Louis Fabiani and Jacques Theys, eds., *La société vulnerable* (Paris: Presses de l'École Normale Supérieure, 1987).

3. OECD, *State of the Environment 1990* (Paris: OECD, 1990), pp. 200–203. Data cover incidents with at least 24 deaths, 125 injuries, 10,000 people evacuated or deprived of water, or $10 million (US) in damages. The data do not include oil spills at sea from ships or mining accidents.

4. "Companies Think Globally on the Environment," *Transnationals* (October 1991): 6.

5. Robert O. Keohane, *International Institutions and State Power* (Boulder, CO: Westview Press, 1989), pp. 1, 3; Peter M. Haas, Robert O. Keohane, and Marc A. Levy, eds., *Institutions for the Earth: Sources of Effective International Environmental Protection* (Cambridge, MA: MIT Press, 1993).

6. Paul Streeten, "What Do We Owe the Future?" *Resources Policy* 12, 1 (1986): Edith Brown Weiss, *In Fairness to Future Generations* (Ardsley-on-Hudson: Transnational Publishers, 1989).

7. Philippe de Seynes, "Prospects for a Future Whole World," *International Organization* 26, 1 (1972): 1–17. John Gerard Ruggie, "On the Problems of 'the Global Problematique': What Roles for International Organizations?" *Alternatives* 5 (1979–1980): 517–550.

8. For a discussion of coupling and the related notion of decomposability see Herbert Simon, "The Architecture of Complexity," in *The Sciences of the Artificial* (Cambridge, MA: MIT Press, 1969); Charles Lindblom, "Incrementalism and Environmentalism" in U.S. Environmental Protection Agency, *Managing the Environment*, EPA-600/5-73-010 (Washington, DC: EPA, November 1973) Lindblom stresses the need to make policy choices regarding such complexly organized issues in the absence of a full understanding of their interactive influence. See also W. C. Clark, and R. F. Munn, eds., *Sustainable Development of the Biosphere* (Cambridge: Cambridge University Press, 1986).

9. A partial cut at these dimensions appears in Horst Siebert, *Economics of the Environment*, 2nd revised and enlarged ed. (Berlin: Springer-Verlag, 1987), pp. 166–67.

10. See Anilla Cherian, "What Happened to the Model Plan?" *Times of India, Bombay*, July 31, 1991, p. 19; Anilla Cherian, "Chembur—a Dead-End for Safety," *Times of India, Bombay* August 1, 1991, p. 15.

11. United Nations Environment Program, *The United Nations System-Wide Medium-Term Environment Programme, 1990–1995* (Nairobi: UNEP, 1988), p. 3.

12. This list of functional needs is drawn from David A. Kay and Harold K. Jacobson, eds., *Environmental Protection: The International Dimension* (To-

towa, NJ: Allanheld, Osmun, 1983); and Eugene Skolnikoff, *The International Imperatives of Technology*, Research Series No. 16 (Berkeley: Institute of International Studies, University of California, 1972).

13. David A. Kay and Eugene B. Skolnikoff, eds., *World-Eco Crisis* (Madison: University of Wisconsin Press, 1972).

14. Lynton Caldwell, *International Environmental Policy* (Durham, NC: Duke University Press, 1990).

15. UNEP, *The United Nations System-Wide Medium-Term Environment Programme, 1990–1995*.

16. Peter S. Thacher, *Global Security and Risk Management* (Geneva: World Federation of United Nations Associations, 1991), pp. 16–20; Martin Holdgate, "UNEP: Some Personal Thoughts," *Mazingira* (March 1984): 17–20; John McCormick, *Reclaiming Paradise: The Global Environmental Movement* (Bloomington: Indiana University Press, 1989), pp. 110–123.

17. Technica, Ltd., *Techniques for Assessing Industrial Hazards: A Manual*, World Bank Technical Paper No. 55 (Washington, DC: World Bank, 1988).

18. Operational Directive 4.00, Annex A3, *World Bank Operational Manual* (Washington DC: World Bank October 1989), p. 1.

19. World Bank, Environment Department, *Environmental Assessment Sourcebook*, vol. 1: *Policies, Procedures, and Cross-Sectoral Issues*, World Bank Technical Paper No. 139 (Washington, DC: World Bank, 1991); World Bank, Environment Department, *Environment Assessment Sourcebook, vol. 3: Guidelines for Environmental Assessment of Energy and Industry Projects*, World Bank Technical Paper no. 154 (Washington, DC: World Bank, 1991).

20. World Bank, *The World Bank and the Environment: First Annual Report, Fiscal Year 1990* (Washington, DC: World Bank, 1990), pp. 5–7, chapter 4; Robert Goodland, "New Environmental Assessment Unit Promotes Operational Directive to Share 'Best Practice' Experience," *Environment Bulletin* 2, 2 (September/October 1990): 7; World Bank, *Annual Report, 1990* (Washington, DC: World Bank, 1990), pp. 65–66.

21. "Population Commission Recommends Continued Monitoring of World Population Trends and Policies," *UN Chronicle* 24, 1 (March 1987): 68.

22. Robert L. Paarlberg, "Managing Pesticide Use in Developing Countries," in Haas, Keohane, and Levy, eds., *Institutions for the Earth*.

23. UNEP, *APELL Awareness and Preparedness for Emergencies at Local Level* UN Publication No. E.88.III.D.3. (New York: UNEP, 1988).

24. Michel Mercier and Morrell Draper, "Chemical Safety: The International Outlook" *World Health* (August/September 1984): 4–6; Jenny Pronczuk de Garbino, "Do We Need All These Chemicals?" *World Health* (January/February 1990): 13–15.

25. Stanley P. Johnson and Guy Corcelle, *The Environmental Policy of the European Communities* (London: Graham and Trotman, 1989).

26. "Alleged Environmental Infractions Among European Community Members," *International Environment Reporter* 13, 3 (March 1990): 133–134.

27. Preparatory Committee for the United Nations Conference on Environment and Development, "Annex I to the Report of the Secretary-General of the Conference," A/CONF. 151/PC/5 (June 28, 1990).

28. Tord Kjellstrom "Health Hazards of the Environment: Measuring the Harm," *World Health* (June 1988): 2–5. For a selection of such findings see United Nations Environment Programme, *Environmental Data Report* (London: Basil Blackwell, 1989); UNEP and WHO, *Assessment of Urban Air Quality*

(London: Monitoring and Assessment Research Centre, 1988); UNEP and WHO, *Assessment of Freshwater Quality* (London: Monitoring and Assessment Research Centre, 1988); UNEP, FAO, and WHO, *Assessment of Chemical Contaminants in Food* (London: Monitoring and Assessment Research Centre, 1988).

29. "The Economy and the Environment: Revising the National Accounts," *IMF Survey* (June 4, 1990): 161–169.

30. For a more thorough review of the types of policy changes with which such conceptual transformations are associated see John Gerard Ruggie, "Social Time and International Policy: Conceptualizing Global Population and Resource Issues," in Margaret P. Karns, ed., *Persistent Patterns and Emergent Structures in a Waning Century* (New York: Praeger, 1986); and John Gerard Ruggie, "International Structure and International Transformation: Space, Time, and Method," in James N. Rosenau and Ernst-Otto Czempiel, eds., *Global Changes and Theoretical Challenges* (Lexington, MA: Lexington, 1989).

31. Chris Argyris and Donald Schon, *Organizational Learning* (Reading, MA: Addison-Wesley, 1978); Joseph S. Nye, Jr., "Nuclear Learning," *International Organization* 41, 3 (Summer 1987): 378–382; Ernst B. Haas, *When Knowledge Is Power* (note 1); Peter M. Haas, *Saving the Mediterranean: The Politics of International Environmental Cooperation* (New York: Columbia University Press, 1990), pp. 58–63; George W. Breslauer and Philip E. Tetlock, eds., *Learning in U.S. and Soviet Foreign Policy* (Boulder, CO: Westview, 1991).

32. Haas, *When Knowledge Is Power*, p. 164.

33. Peter M. Haas, ed. *Knowledge, Power, and International Policy Coordination. International Organization* 46, 1 (Winter 1992).

34. Peter M. Haas, "From Theory to Practice: Ecological Ideas and Development Policy," Harvard University Center for International Affairs Working Paper 92-2 (Cambridge, MA: Center for International Affairs, 1992).

Chapter 12
Societal Contradictions and Industrial Crises

Paul Shrivastava

For me the Bhopal tragedy was a personal and professional watershed. As a past native and resident of Bhopal (for twenty-three years) I found the death and devastation caused by the accident painfully personal. As a professor of management, I was staggered by the enormity of managerial failure that the accident represented. To understand this crisis fully, I have engaged with it for the past six years in multiple roles, as a participant in relief work for Bhopal victims, as a scholar and teacher, as an author, and as a conduit of information to resolve conflicts between Union Carbide and the Government of India. The essential questions driving my efforts have been: Why did Bhopal happen? How can future Bhopals be averted? How can we cope with other disasters like Bhopal?

The social science and management literatures have not been particularly perceptive in answering these questions. Bhopal represents a social and technological phenomenon that was barely investigated before it happened. We lacked the language, concepts, and frameworks to describe and understand it adequately. It was variously referred to as an "incident," an "accident," a "disaster," a "crisis," a "tragedy," a "massacre," and even as "genocide." While each of these words conveys part of the meaning of Bhopal, they also point out the diversity of responses that such events evoke. It is not possible to understand the causes of such a complex phenomenon, much less draw from it suitable policy responses, if we cannot even agree on appropriate moral or analytical concepts to describe it.

I have used the concept of "industrial crisis" to examine Bhopal and other similar events. Industrial crises have three defining characteristics. First, they are processes of major disruption and harm triggered by hazardous events and activities such as industrial accidents, environmental pollution incidents, product injuries, toxic waste disposal, and occupational diseases. Crises should not be equated with the events that trigger them. The triggering event typically harms human health and the natural environment in a circumscribed area. But crises expand beyond the immediate harm to disrupt economic, social, and political processes in organizations and communities.

A second characteristic of industrial crises is that they bring about a restructuring of technological, organizational, and societal systems. Restructuring may involve redesign of products and production technologies, reorganization of corporate financial, ownership, or governance structures, regulatory reshaping of industries, social and political realignment in communities, and reorientation of cultural values. The Bhopal disaster, like the Three Mile Island and Chernobyl nuclear accidents, is an example of such a transforming event.

The third defining characteristic of industrial crises is that they necessitate urgent strategic decisions within organizations and affected communities. These decisions are aimed at coping with immediate emergencies, mitigating harm, long-term recovery, and prevention of future crises. Crises spawn new policies, new regulations, and new corporate strategies.

Many causal factors that trigger crises have been studied by researchers in the past. These include failures in technological systems (Perrow 1984), interorganizational failures (Turner 1976), management decision-making errors (Rogers 1986), and organizational reliability issues (Roberts 1989). These explanations focus for the most part on crisis-triggering events, rather than on the broader social and technological context. They are often limited to analyzing the failures within and between organizations that contributed to the crisis-triggering event. Such analyses are useful for identifying organizational deficiencies and fixing low-level managerial responsibility for accidents. While this is a useful approach, it neither constitutes a complete theoretical explanation of the causes of crises nor supplies a basis for radical remedial action. It does not, for example, take account of failures outside the corporation, failures in the larger economic, political, and cultural systems. Yet these external failures are at least as important as internal organizational failures and deserve further study. Focusing on them can provide insights into deeper structural causes of crises (Quarantelli 1987).

In this chapter I examine deep-rooted social and structural contradictions that make technological and organizational failures inevitable. This focus does not imply that societal variables are more important than the technological or organizational variables that have been examined elsewhere (Cox 1987; Perrow 1984; Shrivastava

1990b), or that these are easily separable. In fact, technological and organizational variables are clearly at the root of most industrial accidents (Perrow 1984; Weick 1988). My focus here is on societal variables because these, as Edward Woodhouse and Joseph Morone (1986) have pointed out, have received less attention in the existing literature.

I begin by providing a framework for explaining the causes of crises, using the concepts of contradictions and vicious circles to explain failures. In the next section, I illustrate these concepts using data from the Bhopal crisis. Economic, political, and cultural contradictions that formed the structural roots of the Bhopal crisis are described. In the final section, I discuss some implications of this analysis for policies to prevent crises and, more generally, for the capacity of societies to learn from events of such proportions.

Explaining the Causes of Crises

Industrial crises originate from technological systems that are embedded within organizations, usually business organizations. Organizations, in turn, are influenced by a host of external environmental conditions. Hence an adequate explanation of crises must provide reasons for failures in technological systems, their organizational contexts, and their societal environment. These factors are highly interpenetrating, have unclear boundaries, and exert mutual influence on each other. Core elements of these factors, however, are analytically distinct, as described below.

Following Charles Perrow (1984), I use "technological system" to refer to an organized scheme of equipment, operators, and work procedures, directed toward some productive activity. Technological systems use raw materials and labor as inputs and produce products and services. Examples of such systems include industrial production and storage facilities, and transportation systems. These systems are complex in that they are composed of many units and subsystems. Constituent parts of the system are tightly coupled and interdependent. Technological systems are often energy-intensive and involve hazards to life and natural environment. They are vulnerable to many types of failures. Failures may occur in individual parts, units, and subsystems. Human operators, designers, and systems managers are another source of failures. They may err in judgment or analysis. Such systems may also fail due to faulty operating procedures or contaminated supplies.

The organizational context in which technological systems are embedded adds to their complexity and susceptibility to failure. Organizational strategies, structures, and financial and human resources determine the level of attention devoted to technological systems. Policies, working conditions, and safety practices determine their integrity. Thus the organizational context determines the level of reliability and safety at which a technology can operate. Organizational variables can exacerbate hazardous conditions. They can amplify the effects of even small technological failures. They also determine the capacity of organizations to cope with crises (Roberts 1989). Organizational failures in the form of high-risk corporate strategies, inadequate safety policies, and managerial and interdepartmental miscommunications create preconditions for crises (Turner 1976; Shrivastava 1987).

Organizations are influenced by the larger economic, social, political, and cultural reality in which they operate. This external environment is also an important source of crises. Preconditions for industrial crises arise in society through the proliferation of hazardous technologies without corresponding development of preventive and emergency management capabilities. Damage from accidents can be amplified by poorly adapted societal conditions and inadequate physical infrastructure supporting technological facilities. Thus, in poor developing countries, which usually have marginal industrial infrastructures, the damage from crises (especially the loss of lives) is much larger than in developed countries.

Economic, social, and political factors affect the pace and character of industrialization and consequent technological risks facing communities. Historically in the West and currently in the Third World, economic development strategies have fostered environmentally insensitive industrialization, coupled with rapid and haphazard urbanization. Technological hazards have expanded much faster than the regulatory systems designed for controlling them. These societal factors have created preconditions for industrial crises whose repercussions are being felt especially in developing countries.

Organizational and societal failures underlying crises have a systemic logic that I describe below in terms of *contradictions* and *vicious circles*. Contradictions are opposing tendencies or forces within a system that place competing and irreconcilable demands on the system's performance. They create tensions or pressures that have dysfunctional effects on the system. Contradictions increase uncertainty within a system because they make the effects of actions less predictable. Actions dealing with one set of pressures may unintentionally exacerbate other opposing pressures.

Organizational reactions to contradictory pressures simultaneously solve some problems and exacerbate others, and perhaps even create new problems. This process can give rise to vicious circles of harm within organizations and in their environments. Vicious circles are sequences of causally related activities that escalate the dysfunctional consequences of organizational activities. The cumulative effect of vicious circles is the creation of structural suboptimalities. Structural limitations lead to underperformance, stagnation, and decay. They create hazardous conditions that contribute to crises (Heydebrand 1977; Kinghorn 1985; Masuch 1985).

The root causes of industrial crises may be traced to contradictions inherent in technological systems, their organizational context, and the organization's societal environment. The main focus of this analysis is on contradictions in the societal environment. However, I begin by listing the technological and organizational contradictions. Inside the technological system, contradictions take many forms. One is the conflicting and competing demands of efficiency and flexibility in the design of technology. There is also a contradictory relationship between the size of technological systems and their control and communications characteristics. A third form is the contradictory effects of automation on the reliability of technological systems. Organizational contradictions include the contradictory demands of organizational stakeholders, contradictions between productivity and safety objectives in organizations, and the competing interests of different organizational departments and divisions.

Vicious circles of behavior created by these internal contradictions may lead to the adoption of inherently unsafe technological designs. They lead to poor communication systems with unreliable warnings. They erode controls, safety, and surveillance. The risk associated with such systems builds up over time and eventually reaches explosive levels, where even minor errors can cause runaway accidents. I have examined these internal (technological and organizational) contradictions and vicious circles in detail elsewhere (Shrivastava 1990b).

But internal contradictions and vicious circles tell only half the story behind crises. They do not explain how preconditions for industrial crises develop in society, and how technological accidents interact with societal factors to create large-scale crises. To understand this aspect of crisis development, we must look at the contradictions and vicious circles in the social conditions within which technological systems exist. Countries pursuing environmentally unsustainable industrial policies, for example, are caught in a vicious circle of economic growth and environmental decline. Developing countries in particular are rapidly accumulating hazardous technologies for which they do not have a safety infrastructure, thus inviting crises in the future (Redclift 1987).

As suggested by the definition of industrial crisis earlier, all technological accidents do not lead to crises. The impacts of accidents within technological facilities is greatly amplified if the societal infrastructure surrounding the facility is incapable of coping with its effects. This infrastructure includes physical facilities and services such as electricity, water supply, transportation, and communication. These services are essential to run industrial facilities safely. In addition, medical systems, waste management services, and civil defense services can help in mitigating industrial hazards. The infrastructure also includes cultural factors such as community awareness of hazards. Other aspects of the infrastructure include community preparedness for emergencies, and safety and environmental-protection regulations. The quality of this societal infrastructure is a function of economic, political, and cultural institutions in a society. In developing societies these institutions are riddled with conflicts and contradictions. Governments are fiscally strapped. They do not have adequate funds to finance infrastructural projects to the extent needed. The people who bear most of the risks from industrial hazards are poor and disenfranchised. They have poor connections with or access to the existing institutions.

Societal Contradictions and the Bhopal Crisis

In examining the contradictions and vicious circles that underlay the Bhopal crisis, I focus particularly on the structural contradictions in Indian society that must be addressed if future crises are to be prevented. This does not in any way reflect my assessment of the culpability of Union Carbide and is not intended to exonerate the company of responsibility for the accident that triggered the crisis. Rather, my approach presumes that complex modern technologies cannot be made risk-free through the "fixes" of machinery or management. Hence, preventing crises must go beyond technological and organizational solutions to addressing larger issues of social structure.

The analysis of the Bhopal disaster presented here is colored by my personal familiarity with social conditions in Bhopal, as well as my experiences in dealing with victims, Union Carbide, and the bureaucracy and political system in Madhya Pradesh and in New Delhi. While this close familiarity is an asset, and perhaps a prerequisite, for unearthing deep-seated contradictions, it also limits my ability to be a totally "disinterested" and "objective" analyst.

The Failures in Bhopal

The immediate dimensions of the Bhopal crisis can be captured with a few simple facts and statistics, many of which have been rehearsed elsewhere in this volume. On the early morning of December 3, 1984, forty tons of methyl isocyanate (MIC) leaked from underground storage tanks at the Union Carbide Corporation's pesticide production plant located at the edge of the city. The gas spread over densely populated neighborhoods around the plant. By the end of the day over 3,500 people were killed and more than 150,000 were injured. Before the incident was over nearly 400,000 residents fled the city in two major waves of panic-stricken evacuations. In addition, 2,000 animals were killed and 7,000 were injured.

But this accident's wider impacts were no less remarkable and took years to play themselves out. The event and its aftermath overwhelmed Union Carbide Corporation, as discussed by Wil Lepkowski earlier in this volume (Chapter 2). Union Carbide stock plummeted, the company was subjected to a hostile takeover attempt, and it emerged from this attack only by selling off one-third of its most profitable assets. For the Government of India, Bhopal opened the door to a series of legal, political, and administrative defeats. The government's lawsuit against Carbide was dismissed by a U.S. court and dragged on inconclusively in India. Its meager resources turned out to be grossly inadequate for providing interim relief to victims. The out-of-court settlement reached in 1989 was challenged both politically and legally on the grounds that the compensation amount was inadequate and that the conditions granting Union Carbide immunity from criminal prosecution were unconstitutional. This challenge further delayed distribution of the $470 million paid by Union Carbide.

The accident itself was largely the result of failures inside the company. These have been extensively investigated in previous studies. An illustrative list of these failures compiled from my own work and other published literature (Bogard 1989; De Grazia 1985; Morehouse and Subramaniam 1988; Shrivastava 1987; Union Carbide Corporation 1985) is provided below:

- Defective plant design that allowed storage of vast quantities of MIC in underground tanks.
- Faulty "pipe washing" procedure that permitted vast quantities of water to enter into the storage tanks.
- Cost-cutting measures that eroded safety by halving the manpower to run the plant from 1980 to 1984.

- Faulty maintenance that caused simultaneous failure of four safety devices—the vent gas scrubber, the water sprays, the flare tower, and the tank refrigeration system.
- Failure to follow up and implement the safety recommendations of the Operational Safety Survey conducted by a team of international experts in 1982.
- The absence of contingency/emergency plans at the plant.
- Lack of management awareness of hazard posed by the plant.

These multiple failures within the Union Carbide organization sufficiently explain what caused the accident to occur. But the accident escalated into a crisis largely because of six social conditions outside the plant.

1. The haphazard urbanization and industrialization policy of the state government of Madhya Pradesh and the government's consequent failure to provide safe and adequate housing for people living around the plant. The state government knew that the plant was hazardous but allowed squatters to live in its vicinity. Indeed, in an election ploy six months before the accident, it legalized squatters' rights by giving them legal title to the small strips of land that they occupied. This created a situation in which thousands of poor people legally lived around the plant; in due course they became the victims of the toxic gas released by the accident.

2. Failure of the state government to provide basic infrastructural services (such as water, electricity, transportation, and communication) necessary for the safe operation of any industry. The inadequate supply of water was responsible for the failure of the water spray safety device. The erratic supply of electricity made the use of computerized data loggers, considered standard safety equipment in U.S. plants, both inconvenient and unreliable. Hence, computerized data loggers were not installed at the Bhopal plant. As a result this plant did not possess the same safety capabilities as other similar plants operated by Union Carbide.

3. Failure of the central and state regulatory agencies to identify the plant as a major hazard during licensing or regular factory inspections and to eliminate it from the community. In fact, the state government perpetuated the hazard. In 1978, local municipal officials raised safety objections to Union Carbide's plans to install the hazardous MIC production unit at a location that was zoned for light industry and commercial activity. The Madhya Pradesh state government came to the company's rescue, vetoing the municipal government's order to relocate the plant on the grounds that it represented a major

investment and provided jobs. Thus, the company was permitted to install an extremely hazardous facility in a densely populated, commercially zoned area.

4. Failure of Bhopal residents to become informed of the hazard posed by the plant and to prepare for an emergency. Several people whom I interviewed said they thought the plant was producing "plant medicine," which approximately translates the Hindi term for pesticides. Hence, they had considered it to be a safe facility. The community repeatedly ignored as "alarmist reporting" two warnings published by a local newspaper about the extremely hazardous substances stored at the plant.

5. Failure of civic or community organizations and government agencies to be prepared for an emergency. The unpreparedness of civic, civil defense, and other public agencies led to haphazard evacuation, which worsened the damage from the accident.

6. Failure of the medical system to cope with the large number of victims streaming into city hospitals. Lacking any specific diagnostic or treatment protocols, medical facilities ended up providing only symptomatic treatment.

Contradictions and Vicious Circles

The failures listed above were not random events. They were caused by deep systemic contradictions in India's economic, political, and cultural systems. These contradictions influenced the Bhopal community's choices with respect to accepting and controlling a major technological hazard. They created the social preconditions in which a technological accident could have devastating impacts. They also constrained the community's ability to respond to the crisis. In the longer run, they impeded effective learning not only in Bhopal but in India and in the industrialized nations of the world.

Economic Contradictions

A basic economic contradiction lies in the industrially based strategy of economic development adopted by India and common to much of the Third World. Industrialization generates contradictory effects. It speedily improves the economic welfare of a segment of people, but simultaneously imposes new and unevaluated risks on their lives.

A prime source of risks is the urbanization pattern that accompanies industrialization. The creation of industries, and consequently jobs, in urban locations attracts large populations from surrounding rural areas. The inflow of people ordinarily outpaces the development of housing and infrastructural services such as water supply, sewage, electricity, communications, and transportation. Industrialization and urbanization reinforce each other to create a vicious circle of increasing public risks. First, the gap between available and needed physical and social infrastructure increases. Second, more industries get established near densely populated areas to draw upon the pool of labor and the sparse infrastructure, in turn imposing still higher risks on neighboring populations (Dogan and Kasarda 1988; Minocha 1981).

Bhopal was a prime example of this pattern of development. For nearly three decades it was the second fastest growing city in India, rife with all the problems of uncontrolled urbanization. By the time of the accident nearly 30 percent of the city's residents lived in slums near industrial plants. The supply of electricity, where available, was erratic and limited to a few hours a day. Water supply and sewage systems were available to fewer than 50 percent of city residents. Water was usually available only for three to four hours a day, and only half an hour a day during summers. Medical services in the city were primitive and inadequate for even normal conditions. The operating rooms of the two major hospitals were often and routinely shut down because of contamination by tetanus virus. In a visit to the largest hospital, which served as the main medical resource for the Bhopal victims, I saw stray dogs, goats, and rats in the "Critical Care Unit." Communications services (only 10,000 telephones) and transportation systems (a congested mixture of autos, bicycles, horse-drawn carriages, pedestrians, and animals) were drastically inadequate to serve a city with a population of 695,000 (Shrivastava 1987).

Bhopal is not unique in these respects. In many Third World cities (Bombay, Calcutta, Caracas, Lagos, Mexico City, Sao Paolo, to name just a few), some 50 to 80 percent of the population live in slums or shantytowns, without running water, sewage and waste disposal, and other modern amenities. More important, many residential neighborhoods are located dangerously close to hazardous industrial facilities. In highly industrialized Western countries, urban residents also confront elevated risks from urban congestion, transportation bottlenecks, environmental pollution and industrial facilities. But more than a century of experience with zoning, urban planning, and emergency management has enabled them to prevent accidents from escalating into crises.

A second economic contradiction lies in the logic underlying the industrial mode of production. Most industrial societies have organized their economies on some variant of the capitalist system, consisting of privately owned or state-owned enterprises operating in quasi-regulated markets. Managers attempt to maximize production and surplus value (profits) from an enterprise, often (as in Bhopal) at the cost of the interests of other stakeholders, such as labor's interest in safe and healthful work conditions and the public's interest in product safety and environmental protection.

The logic of industrialism requires and legitimizes the externalization of dysfunctional effects of production onto the public. It shields firms from having to pay all the costs associated with the control of pollution, hazardous wastes, and other harmful by-products of the production process. Indeed, the industrial mode of production has proved particularly resistant to internalizing such externalities as latent occupational diseases and long-term environmental degradation. The costs of remedying these harms are supposed to be borne by the state. The state, however, is rarely able to cope with these escalating demands, especially in countries like India, since it is perpetually constrained by fiscal deficits.

This contradiction creates a vicious circle in the context of economic competition. The more competitive an industry becomes, the more pressure its firms face to cut costs to maintain rates of profit. This goal is often achieved by reducing manpower and cutting back non-production services, such as worker training, maintenance, safety, and environmental protection. Competition thus creates and externalizes still more hazards.

The history of the Bhopal plant illustrates this dynamic. Increasing competition in the pesticides industry forced Union Carbide to continue cutting costs even for essential services. Even before the plant went into production the company knew it could not be made profitable, since pesticide demand in India had collapsed. During the three years it was in operation, the plant never made a profit and ran at less than 50 percent of capacity. Its poor financial position made it impossible for the plant to compensate internally for the lack of external infrastructure. As a result, the plant operated with marginal levels of safety. This condition was identified in the company's own *1982 Operating Safety Survey*, which listed over two hundred safety problems in the plant and its surroundings. At the same time, tight resource constraints prevented local and state governments from creating safe living conditions around the plant.

Political Contradictions

The most important political contradiction contributing to the Bhopal crisis involved the role of the state. The state has meant very different things in advanced industrial countries, developing Third World countries, and, until recently, the Soviet bloc countries. It varies in character, in historical development, in degree of centralization, in public participation, and in economic orientation from country to country. In most countries, however, the state serves the function of providing techno-administrative coordination to economic and political systems. It mediates the positive and negative consequences of economic and political choices. It is in this role as coordinator that the state is saddled with contradictory responsibilities.

In the Third World, as in more prosperous countries, the state is responsible for preventing crises by regulating hazards and monitoring and controlling their spread. Customarily, however, it lacks the necessary financial resources, technological information, institutional experience and capacity, and political power to fulfill this responsibility. In India, this contradiction of "responsibility without authority" limited the ability of both federal and state agencies to prevent Bhopal from happening.

India's rapid industrialization has created a situation in which the creation of technology far outpaces its regulation and monitoring by the government. Over the past thirty years, the public sector has made planned investments of billions of dollars to establish a modern industrial economy. Competitive market forces have simultaneously pushed the private sector into myriad new and potentially risky technologies, including chemicals, pesticides, biotechnology, weapon systems, and computers. Consequently, between 1947 and 1987 the percentage of India's GNP coming from the industrial sector rose from under 10 percent to over 40 percent. The economic pressure to commercialize technologies has continually expanded, with the consequence of proliferating technological risks.

The vast expansion of industrial and technological capacity has not been accompanied by commensurate regulatory and monitoring capacities. The Indian government has run deficit budgets for nearly two decades and is faced with chronic resource shortages. The government's ability and political will to raise revenues through taxes is limited by its precarious hold on power since the mid-1970s. Available resources were seldom sufficient for creating adequate regulatory and safety infrastructure for new technologies or for maintaining them over time. The Indian government was also reluctant to regulate industries for fear of reducing jobs and tax revenues and alienating foreign investment.

The contradiction in the Indian state's ability both to create and regulate technologies has set up a vicious circle that leads to accumulation of unregulated technologies. The creation and regulation of the pesticide industry offers a good example of the effects of this contradiction. The pesticide industry was created by a huge short-term government demand for pesticides to control the spread of malaria in the mid-1960s, augmented by private farmers' demand for crop protection. The government encouraged companies to enter this industry with subsidies, tax breaks, low-cost loans, and lax safety regulations. Within a few years over 250 manufacturers of pesticides were established, many of them fly-by-night garage operations that simply formulated and packaged pesticides with available ingredients.

The resulting intense competition forced bigger firms like Union Carbide to cut production costs through backward integration. Carbide entered into production of ingredient materials, including MIC, by establishing a multi-million dollar plant in Bhopal. By the mid-1970s malaria had seemingly been eradicated and the governmental demand for pesticides had dropped. Simultaneously poor crops led to a decline in farmers' demand for pesticides. Virtually overnight, the pesticide industry became sick. By the time the Bhopal MIC plant started production in 1981, there was little demand for pesticides, few future prospects, high installed production capacity in the industry, intense competition, and little incentive to regulate the leftover industry. Manufacturers could not make money in it and either exited it if they could or neglected it if they could not. This environment of disinterest and abandonment created fertile conditions for the crisis that occurred.

A second political contradiction lies at the micro-level of state actions in emergency preparedness and planning. Emergency planning for natural disasters, and increasingly also for technological disasters, is now routine in India. But formal plans created by state bureaucracies or by industries tend to be "paper plans" that fail during major crises, because they are rarely supported with preparatory activities, safety equipment, and backup resources to make them work. They give the public an impression of increased safety. The public trusts these plans and loses vigilance over hazards under the impression that the government is taking care of this task. Under reduced public vigilance hazards easily multiply in communities. Thus, there is an escalating harmful circle of hazard generation, superficial emergency planning, decreased public vigilance, and further hazard creation.

In Bhopal, residents were lulled into complacency about the hazard posed by the Union Carbide plant. They were repeatedly told by plant and government officials, who operated in tacit collusion, that there was no imminent danger from it. They were assured that the plant maintained high levels of safety and was capable of dealing with any emergency. In fact, the plant was touted as an example of a well-kept and properly maintained facility. Moreover, the impoverished and uneducated at-risk public in Bhopal had little choice but to trust the government and the company on matters of safety; it possessed neither resources nor information to judge the issues on its own (Morehouse and Subramaniam, 1988).

Cultural Contradictions

The cultural contradictions at the root of the Bhopal crisis are the most difficult to identify. Since cultural values are implicit and taken for granted, cultural contradictions are often intangible. They do not take the concrete forms that economic and political contradictions often manifest.

An important cultural contradiction is apparent in the ambivalent Indian attitudes toward nature. There is a deep conflict between the respect for nature inherent in Hinduism, the dominant religion of India, and the nature-destroying and anthropocentric values inherent in modern secular India's aspirations of industrialization. Traditional religious values of *ahimsa* (non-violence among humans and nature), high respect for natural elements (trees, land, water, air), deification of animals, and the naturalism advocated by such mid-century leaders as Mohandas Gandhi and Rabindranath Tagore were formally rejected by the Indian Constitution, which made India a "secular" state. In contrast to these traditional values, anthropocentrism and its attendant consumerist orientation serve as the base for Indian economic plans for rapid industrialization in the Western mold.

Anthropocentrism is a cultural value deeply rooted in the Judeo-Christian religious traditions of the West and has been an essential part of the ideological base for Western industrialism. Anthropocentrism relegates nature to an inferior status as compared to humans. It is consistent with the humanist vision of Christianity, in which nature is viewed as being available for domination and control in order to improve human welfare (McKibben 1989; Berry 1988; White 1967).

In India's modernization as well, the pro-nature values of indigenous religions have lost out to a secular anthropocentrism that is more consistent with industrialization. The attractiveness of anthropocentric development is obvious in a country with a huge, impoverished population. From the time India gained independence, the government's economic development policy was aimed at converting a largely agricultural society into a "modern" industrial nation in the image of the industrialized West. This required reducing the relative size of the agricultural sector, at the same time boosting agricultural productivity to meet total food requirements. The government encouraged the use of chemical pesticides, fertilizers, and hybrid seeds to improve agricultural productivity. The pesticide plant at Bhopal was an extension of this high-input Green Revolution, which exemplified the technological domination of nature for human needs.

This pattern of industrial development was also responsible for progressive urbanization of Bhopal and the under-development of agricultural hinterlands. With the loss of jobs in the agricultural sector, rural populations migrated to regional cities like Bhopal in search of work. Bhopal was not equipped to handle this influx of people. Its population grew from about 90,000 in 1950 to nearly 700,000 in 1980. This included a large pool of low-skilled, unemployed people living in slums and shantytowns, such as those that crowded around the periphery of the Union Carbide plant. The Bhopal crisis thus was the product of an industrial policy that disrupted the stable relationships between human communities and their natural environments and perpetuated a vicious circle of environmentally destructive development.

Conclusion: Limits on Learning

Industrial crises are becoming more frequent and affecting every aspect of modern life. To prevent them from multiplying, we must understand their causes and design appropriate policies for eliminating them. In this closing chapter, I have examined some social roots of industrial crises and argued that the logic of failures stems from inherent systemic contradictions and the vicious circles of harm that they generate. Indeed the structural contradictions that are at the root of industrial crises are so deep and pervasive that it is difficult to be optimistic about the potential for learning from these events. Simply identifying these contradictions should serve as a cautionary warning for industrial policy makers.

Two important limitations of this analysis need to be acknowledged before we turn to its implications for social learning and public policy. First, the framework presented here focused on crises triggered by industrial accidents in hazardous facilities. There are, however, many other types of industrial crises, such as those caused by product injuries (Dalkon Shield), environmental pollution incidents (Love Canal), and occupational hazards (lung cancer among asbestos workers). While my analysis did not directly address these, some of the explanations I have suggested in this chapter may apply more broadly to other kinds of crises as well. Second, although the framework I present here extends earlier explanations, it identifies only a tentative set of relevant contradictions. The categories of economic, political, and cultural contradictions provide a useful way of understanding the causes of crisis. It was not my intention here to provide a comprehensive list of all possible contradictions in each category; those I described form only an illustrative set.

As elaborated in the foregoing chapters, learning from the Bhopal disaster and other similar events has taken many forms: legal and regulatory changes, organizational improvements, technological innovations, safety enhancements, and technological design changes. These changes have been both incremental and wide-ranging, as for instance in the passage of community "right-to-know" laws (see Chapters 5, 6, and 10, this volume) and in the mobilization of victim groups to create a new politics of compensation (see Chapter 9, this volume). But while these changes are impressive in the aggregate, it is questionable whether they have reduced the overall level of technological risk the world faces today. Largely reactive and remedial in nature, most of the "learning" has failed to address the internal systemic contradictions that are the fundamental structural causes of industrial crises.

A more fundamental limitation of these changes lies in the fact that they attempt to modify existing institutions, but do not question their underlying assumptions. These changes are in some sense on the surface. They do not address the deeper structural contradictions indentified here as the sources of crises. The improvement of existing institutions does not affect people who are beyond the reach of these traditional institutions, as victims of industrial crises often are. Hence, learning from disasters must seek to create new institutions, in addition to modifying existing ones.

Clearly, if industrial crises are to be averted or coped with effectively, we need concerted action on several fronts. Technological fixes and minor organizational improvements alone cannot accomplish the task; they must be supplemented by basic structural changes that address deep-seated contradictions in technological, organizational, and societal systems. Given the international character of crises, such restructuring will need to be transnational as opposed to the largely domestic forms of learning that disasters have triggered in the past. In each possible domain of structural change—the economic, the political, and the cultural—there are debates over the best pathways to follow (Douglas and Wildavsky 1982; Perrow 1984; Woodhouse and Morone 1986). My purpose in this brief presentation is to suggest directions of analysis and not to provide a precise blueprint for change.

The changes envisaged in this discussion are far-reaching and fundamental. For these changes to occur, the public or people who face technological risks from industrial activities must accept responsibility for being the agents of change. Such changes are frame-breaking and cannot occur within the existing institutional frameworks. In part they aim to revise existing institutional arrangements. It is only through grass-roots learning and action that fundamental change can be accomplished. The economic, political, and cultural rethinking that is necessary if we are to deal with structural contradictions must question our most cherished assumptions in these domains. In some areas such new thinking is beginning to emerge, as exemplified by the theories and practice of radical environmentalism, grass-roots development movements, and indigenous peoples' movements. These movements are based on a radical critique of industrialism. They seek to create communities with different values of community harmony, environmental preservation, small-scale and appropriate technology, peace, and women's rights.

The economic debate will involve reassessing the desirability of market-driven industrial development, as against more controlled, environmentally sustainable economic development strategies that balance economic growth with environmental preservation. Sustainable development implies shielding human and natural environments from the technological risks inherent in industrialization. It implies arresting the environmental destruction and resource extinction that are caused by rapid industrialization. Current industrial growth should be paced in such a way that it does not compromise the ability of future generations to meet their needs. The "sustainability" principle recognizes the physical limits to growth on a planet with finite resources (World Commission on Environment and Development 1987).

Political restructuring will require reexamining the means of controlling the proliferation of technology and technological risks. Currently, social choices about which technological risks society should face are made by private corporations, and to a lesser extent by state agencies. Private companies who own hazardous technologies largely determine the selection of products and processes and the location of plants, and hence who will be exposed to risks. The extent or quantity of risk exposure is also a function of investments in safety infrastructure that enhance the ability of communities to cope with crises. These infrastructural decisions, as we have seen, are largely the domain of the state. Yet decision making by the state fails to involve the citizens whose preferences should have guided decisions about technological investments and risks.

Missing from this arrangement are processes that would allow more democratic social choice of technology. Since Bhopal some Western countries have adopted procedures that permit the public to get relevant information on risks and to participate in decision making. In the United States, some communities have gone beyond government-sanctioned procedures to protest risk proliferation in their neighborhoods. The "not-in-my-backyard" (NIMBY) sentiment has gained momentum in thousands of communities across the country. More ambitious social processes and institutions for facilitating participation across international boundaries still need to be developed, requiring at a minimum much broader dissemination of information about technological risks and hazards to the public (Woodhouse and Morone 1986; Schwartz and Thompson 1990).

Cultural change aimed at remedying the contradictions identified here will require a complete *revisioning of our current cosmologies or worldviews*. Our anthropocentric biases serve as grounding for widespread social values of individualism and consumerism that show little respect for nature and community. Natural resources and other species have no recognized rights in this scheme of things. The notion of sustainability requires an alternative worldview that restores due significance to the natural world, one in which natural resources are not there simply for humans to exploit to meet the needs of the present. Instead, humans must learn to see themselves as part of the natural world, indeed as its most knowledgeable and informed custodians. In this alternative worldview, humans and nature will have to coexist in a symbiotic, dynamic, and harmonious relationship. Cultural values flowing out of such a worldview would foster more benign and protective actions toward nature (Berry 1988).

The tragedy of Bhopal suggests, in sum, the need for a radical reorientation in worldwide thinking about the causes and prevention of industrial crises. Such radical transformation is beginning to occur in small ways. The Kayapo in the Amazon rain forest have established ways of preserving their land, natural resources, and culture while developing economically; rural peasants in the Narmada Valley in India have organized to protest and stop the multibillion-dollar Narmada Dam project. In doing so, they have rejected the traditional views of economic development, in favor of a more bioregionally sustainable approach. In the United States, over 7,000 communities are currently engaged in grass-roots protests against industrial development projects that bring hazardous technologies into their communities. In Madagascar, economic development is being integrated with rain forest protection programs to create an alternative development that is in harmony with both the natural and social-cultural environment. These small beginnings need to be expanded. Our challenge as scholars, policy makers, and citizens is to draw from industrial crises some genuinely new lessons about the future: to articulate actionable principles, to develop new economic and social policies, and to re-envision the relationship between humans and nature in ways that can prevent more Bhopals on our only too fragile planet.

References

Agarwal, Anil. 1986. *The State of India's Environment.* Centre for Science and Environment Development. New Delhi: CSE.

Berry, Thomas 1988. *The Dream of the Earth.* San Francisco: Sierra Club Books.

Bogard, William P. 1989. *The Bhopal Tragedy: Language, Logic, and Politics in the Production of a Hazard.* Boulder, CO: Westview.

Cox, Robert W. 1987. *Production, Power, and World Order: Social Factors in the Making of History.* New York: Columbia University Press.

Cummings-Saxton, J., S. J. Ratick, F. W. Talcott, C. P. Dougherty, A. Vander Vliet, A. J. Barad, and A. E. Crook. 1988. "Accidental Chemical Releases and Local Emergency Response: Analysis Using the Acute Hazardous Events Database." *Industrial Crisis Quarterly* 2, 2:139–170.

De Grazia, Alfred, 1985. *A Cloud over Bhopal.* Bombay: Kalos Foundation.

Dogan, Mattie and John D. Kasarda. 1988. *The Metropolis Era*, vol. 2. Beverly Hills, CA: Sage Publications.

Douglas, Mary and Aaron Wildavsky. 1982. *Risk and Culture.* Berkeley: University of California Press.

Exxon Corporation. 1988. *Annual Report.* New York: Exxon.

Heydebrand, Wolf. 1977. "Organizational Contradictions in Public Bureaucracies: Toward a Marxian Theory of Organizations." *Sociological Quarterly* 18 (Winter): 83–107.

Jasanoff, Sheila. 1988. "Judicial Gatekeeping in the Management of Hazardous Technologies." *Journal of Management Studies* 25, 4:353–372.

Kemeny, John, et al. 1979. *The Need for Change: The Legacy of TMI.* Report of the President's Commission on the Accident at Three Mile Island. Washington, DC: U.S. Government Printing Office.

Kinghorn, Sandra. 1985. "Corporate Harm: An Analysis of Structure and Process." Paper presented at the Conference on Critical Perspectives in Organizational Analysis, Baruch College, CUNY, New York, September 5–7.

Landy, Marc K., Marc J. Roberts, and Stephen R. Thomas. 1990. *The Environmental Protection Agency: Asking the Wrong Questions.* New York: Oxford University Press.

Levine, Adeline. 1982. *Love Canal: Science, Politics, and People.* Lexington, MA: Lexington Books.

Masuch, Michael. 1985. "Vicious Circles in Organizations." *Administrative Science Quarterly* 30, 1:14–33.

McKibben, Bill. 1989. *The End of Nature.* New York: Random House.

Minocha, A. C. 1981. "Changing Industrial Structure of Madhya Pradesh." *Margin* 4, 1:46–61.

Morehouse, Ward, and Arun Subramaniam. 1988. *The Bhopal Tragedy.* New York: Council on International and Public Affairs.

Nelkin, Dorothy, and Laurence Tancredi. 1989. *Dangerous Diagnostics: The Social Power of Biological Information.* New York: Basic Books.

Osborn, Richard N. and D. H. Jackson. 1988. "Leaders, Riverboat Gamblers or Purposeful Unintended Consequences in the Management of Complex, Dangerous Technologies." *Academy of Management Journal* 31, 4:924–947.

Pauchant, Thierry, and Ian I. Mitroff. 1988. "Crisis Prone versus Crisis Avoiding Organizations." *Industrial Crisis Quarterly.* 2, 1:53–64.

Perrow, Charles. 1984. *Normal Accidents: Living with High Risk Technologies.* New York: Basic Books.

Quarantelli, Enrique L. 1987. "What Should We Study? Questions and Suggestions for Research About the Concept of Disasters." *International Journal of Mass Emergencies and Disasters* 5, 1:7–32.

Redclift, Michael. 1987. *Sustainable Development.* London: Methuen.

Roberts, Karlene H. 1989. "New Challenges in Organizational Research: High Reliability Organizations." *Industrial Crisis Quarterly* 3, 2:111–126.

Rogers, William P. 1986. *Report of the Presidential Commission on the Space Shuttle Challenger Accident.* Washington, DC: U.S. Government Printing Office.

Schwarz, Michiel, and Michael Thompson. 1990. *Divided We Stand: Redefining Politics, Technology and Social Choice.* Philadelphia: University of Pennsylvania Press.

Shrivastava, Paul. 1987. *Bhopal: Anatomy of a Crisis.* Cambridge, MA: Ballinger.

Shrivastava, Paul. 1990a. "Hamburger Packages Outlasting the Pyramids." *Los Angeles Times*, May 19.

———. 1990b. "Organizational Sources of Industrial Crises." Paper presented at the Academy of Management Annual Meeting, August. *Technological Forecasting Journal*, forthcoming.

Stevens, William. 1989. "Exxon Valdez Oil Spill." Keynote presentation to the 2nd International Conference on Industrial and Organizational Crisis Management, New York University, New York, November 5.

Tamuz, Michal. 1987. "The Impact of Computer Surveillance on Air Safety Reporting." *Columbia Journal of World Business* 22, 1, 69–78.

Turner, Barry A. 1976. "The Organizational and Interorganizational Development of Disaster." *Administrative Science Quarterly* 21:378–397.

Union Carbide Corporation. 1985. *Bhopal Methylisocyanate Incident Investigation Team Report.* Danbury, CT: Union Carbide Corporation.

Weick, Karl E. 1988. "Enacted Sensemaking in Crisis Situations." *Journal of Management Studies* 25, 4:305–318.

White, Lynn, Jr. 1967. "The Historical Roots of Our Ecological Crisis." *Science* 155 (March 10): 1203–1207.

Woodhouse, Edward J., and Joseph G. Morone. 1986. *Averting Catastrophe: Strategies for Regulating Risky Technologies.* Berkeley: University of California Press.

World Commission on Environment and Development. 1987. *Our Common Future.* New York: Oxford University Press.

Zimmerman, Rae. 1990. *Government Management of Environmental Risks.* Chicago: Lewis Publishers.

Bibliography

Abel, Richard. 1987. "The Real Tort Crisis: Too Few Claims." *Ohio State Law Journal* 48:443–467.

Abraham, C. M. and Sushila Abraham. 1991. "The Bhopal Case and the Development of Environmental Law in India." *International Comparative Law Quarterly* 40, 2:334–365.

Ad Hoc Committee on Asbestos Litigation Report. 1991. Washington, DC.

Agarwal, Anil, Darryl D'Monte, and Ujwala Samarth. 1987. *The Fight for Survival: People's Action for Environment.* New Delhi: Centre for Science and Environment.

Alston, Philip. 1978. "International Regulation of Toxic Chemicals." *Ecology Law Quarterly* 7:397–456.

Andeneas, Johannes. 1966. "The General Preventive Effects of Punishments." *University of Pennsylvania Law Review* 114:949–983.

Argyris, Chris and Donald Schon. 1978. *Organizational Learning.* Reading, MA: Addison-Wesley.

Artibane, Joseph and Catherine Baumer. 1986. *Defusing the Asbestos Litigation Crisis: The Responsibility of the U.S. Government.* Washington, DC: Washington Legal Foundation.

Ascher, William and Robert Healy. 1990. *Natural Resource Policymaking in Developing Countries.* Durham, NC: Duke University Press.

Atiyah, Patrick. 1987. "Tort Law and the Alternatives: Some Anglo-American Comparisons." *Duke Law Journal* 1987:1002–1044.

Bale, Anthony. 1987. "America's First Compensation Crisis: Conflict over the Value and Meaning of Workplace Injuries Under the Employers' Liability System." In Rosner and Markowitz, eds.

Bandyopadhyay, J., N. D. Jayal, U. Schoettli, and C. Singh, eds. 1985. *India's Environment.* Dehra Dun: Natraj Publishers.

Baram, Michael S. 1990. "Risk Communication Law and Its Implications." In Gow and Otway, eds., 110–124.

Barnes, Barry and David Edge, eds. 1982. *Science in Context: Readings in the Sociology of Science.* Cambridge, MA: MIT Press.

Barth, Peter. 1987. *The Tragedy of Black Lung.* Kalamazoo, MI: Upjohn.

Baxi, Upendra and Amita Dhanda, eds. 1990. *Valiant Victims and Lethal Litigation: The Bhopal Case.* New Delhi: Indian Law Institute.

Berkowitz, Leonard and Nigel Walker. 1967. "Laws and Moral Judgments." *Sociometry* 30:410–422.

Berry, Thomas. 1988. *The Dream of the Earth.* San Francisco: Sierra Club Books.

Bhopal Gas Disaster Research Center. 1991. *Annual Report, 1990*. Bhopal: Gandhi Medical College.

Bijker, Wiebe, Thomas P. Hughes, and Trevor Pinch, eds. 1987. *The Social Construction of Technological Systems*. Cambridge, MA: MIT Press.

Biro, Andras. 1990. "East Europe: 'Greens' Force Change." *Panoscope* (March): 16–17.

Blum, Andrew. 1991. "Dupont Plaza Steering Committee Gets Paid." *National Law Journal* 1991 (August 19): 5.

Bogard, William P. 1989. *The Bhopal Tragedy: Language, Logic, and Politics in the Production of a Hazard*. Boulder, CO: Westview Press.

Bowonder, B. 1988. *Implementing Environmental Policy in India*. New Delhi: Friedrich Ebert Stiftung.

Bowonder, B. et al. 1989. *Corporate Responses to Environmental Policies*. Hyderabad: Centre for Energy, Environment and Technology, College of India.

Bowonder, B. and S. S. Arvind, 1989. "Environmental Regulations and Litigation, India." *Project Appraisal* 4: 182–196.

Bowonder, B., Jeanne X. Kasperson, and Roger E. Kasperson. 1985. "Avoiding Future Bhopals." *Environment* 27, 7: 6–13, 31–37.

Bowonder, B. and T. Miyake. 1988. "Managing Hazardous Facilities: Lessons from the Bhopal Accident." *Journal of Hazardous Materials* 19: 237–269.

Boyum, K. and S. Mather, eds. 1983. *Empirical Theories About Courts*. New York: Longman.

Braithwaite, John. 1985. *To Punish or Persuade: The Enforcement of Coal Mine Safety*. Albany: State University of New York Press.

Breslauer, George W. and Phillip E. Tetlock, eds. 1991. *Learning in U.S. and Soviet Foreign Policy*. Boulder, CO: Westview Press.

Brewer, Garry D. 1989. "Perfect Places: NASA as an Idealized Institution." In Byerly, ed.

Brodeur, Paul. 1974. *Expendable Americans*. New York: Viking.

———. 1985. *Outrageous Misconduct: The Asbestos Industry on Trial*. New York: Pantheon.

Brown, J., ed. 1989. *Environmental Threats: Perception, Analysis, and Management*. London: Belhaven Press, Pinter Publishers.

Burns, William C. 1990. "The Report of the Secretary General on Transnational Corporations and Industrial Process Safety: A Critical Appraisal." *Georgetown International Environmental Law Review* 3: 55–84.

Byerly, Radford, Jr., ed. 1989. *Space Policy Reconsidered*. Boulder, CO: Westview Press.

Caldwell, Lynton. 1990. *International Environmental Policy*. Durham, NC: Duke University Press.

Carson, Rachel. 1962. *Silent Spring*. New York: Houghton Mifflin.

Carson, W. G. 1982. *The Other Price of Britain's Oil: Safety and Control in the North Sea*. New Brunswick, NJ: Rutgers University Press.

Carter, Terry. 1988. "Let 1,000 Asbestos Suits Bloom." *National Law Journal* 1988 (December 26): 2.

Castleman, Barry. 1990. *Asbestos: Medical and Legal Aspects*. 3rd ed. New York: Prentice-Hall.

Centre for Science and Environment (CSE). 1983. *The State of India's Environment, 1982*. New Delhi: CSE.

———. 1985. *The State of India's Environment, 1984–85*. New Delhi: CSE.

———. 1991. *The State of India's Environment, 1990*. New Delhi: CSE.

Central Pollution Control Board. 1991. *Annual Report 1989–90*. New Delhi: The Board.

Chemical Manufacturers Association. 1990. *Advisory Panels: Options for Community Outreach*. Washington, DC: Chemical Manufacturers Association.

Cherniack, Martin. 1986. *The Hawk's Nest Incident: America's Worst Industrial Disaster*. New Haven, CT: Yale University Press.

Chin, Audrey and Mark A. Peterson. 1985. *Deep Pockets, Empty Pockets: Who Wins in Cook County Jury Trials*. Santa Monica, CA: Institute for Civil Justice.

Chitnis, V. S. 1987. "Environment Protection Act, 1986: A Critique," In Diwan, ed.

Clark, William C. and R. E. Munn, eds. 1986. *Sustainable Development of the Biosphere*. Cambridge: Cambridge University Press.

Clarke, Lee. 1989. *Acceptable Risk? Making Decisions in a Toxic Environment*. Berkeley: University of California Press.

Coffee, John C. 1987. "The Regulation of Entrepreneurial Litigation: Balancing Fairness and Efficiency in the Large Class Action." *University of Chicago Law Review* 54:877–937.

Colombatos, John. 1969. "Physicians and Medicare: A Before-After Study of the Effects of Legislation on Attitudes." *American Sociological Review* 34: 318–334.

Commission of the European Communities (CEC). 1987. *Chemical Risk Control in the European Community*. Brussels: CEC.

Conn, W. David, William L. Owens, and Richard C. Rich. 1960. *Communicating with the Public About Hazardous Materials: An Examination of Local Practice*. Washington, DC: Environmental Protection Agency.

Conard, Alfred F., James N. Morgan, Robert W. Pratt, Jr., Charles E. Voltz, and Robert L. Bombaugh. 1964. *Automobile Accident Costs and Payments*. Ann Arbor: University of Michigan Press.

Cook, Rebecca J. 1987. "The U.S. Export of 'Pipeline' Therapeutic Drugs." *Columbia Journal of Environmental Law* 12:39–70.

Cox, Robert W. 1987. *Production, Power, and World Order: Social Factors in the Making of History*. New York: Columbia University Press.

Cummings-Saxton, J., S. J. Ratick, F. W. Talcott, C. P. Dougherty, A. Vander Vliet, A. J. Barad, and A. E. Crook. 1988. "Accidental Chemical Releases and Local Emergency Response: Analysis Using the Acute Hazardous Events Database." *Industrial Crisis Quarterly* 2, 2:139–170.

de Garbino, Jenny Pronczuk. 1990. "Do We Need All These Chemicals?" *World Health* (January/February): 13–15.

De Grazia, Alfred. 1985. *A Cloud over Bhopal*. Bombay: Kalos Foundation.

D'Monte, Darryl. 1985. *Temples and Tombs*. New Delhi: Centre for Science and Environment.

De Seynes, Philippe. 1972. "Prospects for a Future Whole World." *International Organization* 26, 1: 1–17.

Dingwall, Robert, Tom Durkin, and William L. F. Felstiner. 1990. "Delay in Tort Cases: Critical Reflections on the Civil Justice Review." *Civil Justice Quarterly* 9:353–363.

DiMeana, Carlo Ripa. 1990 "Commission of the European Communities—1989." *Colorado Journal of International Environmental Law and Policy* 1:159–165.

Diwan, Paras, ed. 1987. *Environment Protection: Problems, Policy, Administration, Law*. New Delhi: Deep & Deep Publications.

Dogan, Mattie and John D. Kasarda. 1988. *The Metropolis Era: Vol. 2.* Beverly Hills, CA: Sage Publications.

Dolbeare, Kenneth and Phillip Hammond. 1971. *The School Prayer Decisions: From Court Policy to Local Practice.* Chicago: University of Chicago Press.

Douglas, Mary and Aaron Wildavsky. 1982. *Risk and Culture.* Berkeley: University of California Press.

Durkin, Tom. 1991. *Bibliography on Asbestos Related Legal Issues.* Unpublished manuscript.

Dwivedi, O. P. 1985. "Environmental Regulations in India." *Environmental Professional* 7:121–127.

Dwivedi, O. P. and Kishore, B. 1982. "Protecting the Environment: India's Legal and Institutional Mechanisms." *Asian Survey* 22, 9:894–911.

Eads, George and Peter Reuter. 1983. *Designing Safer Products: Corporate Responses to Product Liability Law and Regulation.* Santa Monica, CA: Institute for Civil Justice.

Eastman, Crystal. 1910. (reprinted 1969). *Work Accidents and the Law* (a volume of the Pittsburgh Survey). New York: Charities Publications Committee.

Ellul, Jacques. 1964. *The Technological Society.* New York: Alfred Knopf.

"Environmental Protection Agency: 1989 Environmental Activities." 1990. *Colorado Journal of International Environmental Law and Policy* 1:181–187.

Environmental Protection Agency (U.S.). 1986. "Environmental Auditing Policy Statement." *Federal Register* 51:25004–25009.

Erikson, Kai. 1976. *Everything in Its Path: Destruction of Community in the Buffalo Creek Flood.* New York: Simon and Schuster.

Etheredge, Lloyd. 1985. *Can Governments Learn? American Foreign Policy and Central American Revolutions.* Elmsford, NY: Pergamon Press.

Exxon Corporation. 1988. *Annual Report.*

Fabiani, Jean-Luis and Jacques Theys, eds. 1987. *La société vulnerable.* Paris: Presses de l'École Normale Supérieure.

Freeley, Malcolm. 1976. "The Concept of Laws in Social Science: A Critique and Notes on an Expanded View." *Law & Society* 10:497–523.

Felstiner, William L. F. and Robert Dingwall. 1988. *Asbestos Litigation in the United Kingdom.* Oxford: Centre for Socio-Legal Studies.

Ferguson, Jeffrey S. and Yves Alarie. 1991. "Long Term Pulmonary Impairment Following Single Exposure to MIC." *Toxicology and Applied Pharmacology,* 107, 2: 253.

Field, Robert and Richard Victor. 1988. *Asbestos Claims: The Decision to Use Workers Compensation and Tort.* Boston: Workers Compensation Research Institute.

Flaharty, F. 1984. "Stouffer Fire Suit Settles for $48.5 M." *National Law Journal* 1984 (June 4): 4.

Fleming, John. "Is There a Future for Tort?" *Louisiana Law Review* 44:1193–1212.

Friedman, Lawrence. 1985. *Total Justice.* New York: Russell Sage Foundation.

———. 1987. "Civil Wrongs: Personal Injury Law in the Late 19th Century," *American Bar Foundation Research Journal* 1987:351–378.

Friedman, Lawrence and Thomas D. Russell. 1990. "More Civil Wrongs: Personal Injury Litigation, 1901–1910." *American Journal of Legal History* 34:295–314.

Gaines, Sanford E. 1989. "International Principles for Transnational Environmental Liability: Can Developments in Municipal Law Help Break the Impasse?" *Harvard International Law Journal* 30:311–349.

Galanter, Marc. 1983. "The Radiating Effects of Courts." In Boyum and Mather, eds.

———. 1985. "Legal Torpor: Why So Little Has Happened in India After the Bhopal Tragedy." *Texas International Law Review* 20:273–295.

———. 1990a. "Bhopals Past and Present: The Changing Legal Response to Mass Disaster." *Windsor Yearbook of Justice* 10:3–22.

———. 1990b. "The Civil Jury as Regulator of the Litigation Process." *University of Chicago Legal Forum* 1990:201–271.

———. 1991. "Case Congregations and Their Careers." *Law and Society Review* 24:371–395.

Gardner, James A. 1980. *Legal Imperialism: American Lawyers and Foreign Aid in Latin America.* Madison: University of Wisconsin Press.

Garth, Bryant. 1985. "Transnational Legal Practice and Professional Ideology." *Michigan Yearbook of International Studies* 7:3–21.

Gaskins, Richard. 1989. *Environmental Accidents: Personal Injury and Public Responsibility.* Philadelphia: Temple University Press.

Gaventa, John. 1980. *Power and Powerlessness: Quiescence and Rebellion in an Appalachian Valley.* Urbana: University of Illinois Press.

Genn, Hazel. 1987. *Hard Bargaining: Out of Court Settlement in Personal Injury Actions.* Oxford: Oxford University Press.

Gersuny, Carl. 1981. *Work Hazards and Industrial Conflict.* Hanover, NH: University Press of New England.

Gibbs, Jack P. 1975. *Crime, Punishment and Deterrence.* New York: Elsevier.

———. 1986. "Punishment and Deterrence: Theory, Research, and Penal Policy." In Lipson and Wheeler, eds.

Ginsburg, Robert. 1990. "Present Danger, Hidden Liabilities—Environmental Profile of the Union Carbide Corporation in the United States." Prepared for the National Toxics Campaign Fund.

Givelber, Daniel J., William J. Bowers, and Carolyn L. Blitch. 1984. "Tarasoff, Myth and Reality: An Empirical Study of Private Law in Action." *Wisconsin Law Review*: 443–497.

Glasser, Bernhard, ed. 1987. *The Green Revolution Revisited.* London: Allen and Unwin.

Goldberg, Karen A. 1985. "Efforts to Prevent Misuse of Pesticides Exported to Developing Countries: Progressing Beyond Regulation and Notification." *Ecology Law Quarterly* 12:1025–1051.

Goswami, Dilip. 1988. *A Handbook on Pollution Control by Industries and Government Bodies with Supreme Court Decisions.* New Delhi: Emcon Business Review.

Government of Karnataka. 1987. *Report of Task Force on Safety in Karnataka.* Bangalore: Government of Karnataka.

Gow, H. B. F. and H. Otway, eds. 1990. *Communicating with the Public About Major Accident Hazards.* New York: Elsevier.

Grana, John M. 1983. "Disability Allowance for Long-Term Care in Western Europe and the United States." *International Social Security Review* 36: 207–221.

Greene, Janice L. 1989. "Regulating Pesticides: FIFRA Amendments of 1988." A BNA Special Report. *Chemical Regulation Reporter*, January 6.

Greenwood, Carolyn D. 1985. "Restrictions on the Exportation of Hazardous

Products to the Third World: Regulatory Imperialism or Ethical Responsibility?" *Boston College Third World Law Journal* 5:129–150.

Greenwood, Ted. 1984. *Knowledge and Discretion in Regulation.* New York: Praeger.

Haas, Ernst B. 1990. *When Knowledge is Power: Three Models of Change in International Organizations.* Berkeley: University of California Press.

Haas, Peter M. 1990. *Saving the Mediterranean: The Politics of Environmental Cooperation.* New York: Columbia University Press.

———. 1992. "From Theory to Practice: Ecological Ideas and Development Policy." Harvard University Center for International Affairs Working Paper 92-2.

———, ed. 1992. *Knowledge, Power, and International Policy Coordination. International Organization* 46, 1.

Haas, Peter M., Robert O. Keohane, and Marc A. Levy., eds. 1993. *Institutions for the Earth: Sources of Effective International Environmental Protection.* Cambridge, MA: MIT Press.

Habermas, Jürgen. 1970. *Toward a Rational Society.* Boston: Beacon Press.

Hadden, Susan. 1987. "Statutes and Standards for Pollution Control in India." *Economic and Political Weekly* 22, 16:709–720.

———. 1989. *A Citizen's Right to Know: Risk Communication and Public Policy.* Boulder, CO: Westview Press.

Halter, Faith. 1987. "Regulating Information Exchange and International Trade in Pesticides and Other Toxic Substances to Meet the Needs of Developing Countries." *Columbia Journal of Environmental Law* 12:1–37.

Handl, Gunther and Robert E. Lutz. 1989. "An International Policy Perspective on the Trade of Hazardous Materials and Technologies." *Harvard International Law Journal* 30:351–374.

Hart, H. L. A. 1961. *The Concept of Law.* Oxford: Clarendon Press.

Hazarika, Sanjoy. 1993. "Settlement Slow in India Gas Disaster Claims." *New York Times*, March 25, p. A1.

Heinz, John P. and Edward O. Laumann. 1982. *Chicago Lawyers: The Social Structure of the Bar.* New York: Russell Sage Foundation.

Hensler, Deborah, William L. F. Felstiner, Molly Selvin, and Patricia Ebner. 1985. *Asbestos in the Courts: The Challenge of Mass Toxic Torts.* Santa Barbara, CA: Rand.

———. 1989. "Resolving Mass Toxic Torts: Myths and Realities." *University of Illinois Law Review*: 1–16.

Hensler, Deborah et al. 1987. *Trends in Tort Litigation.* Santa Monica, CA: Institute for Civil Justice.

Heydebrand, Wolf. 1977. "Organizational Contradictions in Public Bureaucracies: Toward a Marxian Theory of Organizations." *Sociological Quarterly* 18. (Winter): 83–107.

Hills, Ben. 1987. *Blue Murder.* Sydney: McMillan.

Hills, Stuart, ed. 1987. *Corporate Violence.* Totowa, NJ: Rowan and Littlefield.

The Hindu. 1991. *The Hindu Survey of the Environment, 1991.* Madras: The Hindu.

Hirsch, Paul. 1986. "From Ambushes to Golden Parachutes: Corporate Takeovers as an Instance of Cultural Framing and Institutional Integration." *American Journal of Sociology* 91:800–837.

Holdgate, Martin. 1984. "UNEP: Some Personal Thoughts." *Mazingira* (March): 17–20.

Huber, Peter. 1988. *Liability: The Legal Revolution and Its Consequences*. New York: Basic Books.

———. 1991. *Galileo's Revenge: Junk Science in the Courtroom*. New York: Basic Books.

Huddle, Norie and Michael Reich. 1987. *Island of Dreams: Environmental Crisis in Japan*. Rochester, NY: Schenkman Books.

Hughes, Thomas P. 1983. *Networks of Power: Electrification in Western Society, 1880–1930*. Baltimore: Johns Hopkins University Press.

International Monetary Fund. 1990. "The Economy and the Environment: Revising the National Accounts." *IMF Survey* (June 4): 161–169.

India Today. 1989. "Cruel Cut." August 31, p. 74.

Ino, Masaru et al. 1975. "Diary of a Plaintiffs' Attorneys' Team in the Thalidomide Litigation." *Law and Japan* 8: 136–187.

Jasanoff, Sheila. 1986a. "Managing India's Environment." *Environment* 28, 8: 12–16, 31–38.

———. 1986b. *Risk Management and Political Culture*. New York: Russell Sage Foundation.

———. 1988a. "Judicial Gatekeeping in the Management of Hazardous Technologies." *Journal of Management Studies* 25, 4: 353–372.

———. 1988b. "The Bhopal Disaster and the Right to Know." *Social Science and Medicine* 27, 10: 1113–1123.

Jasanoff, Sheila, Gerald E. Markle, James Petersen, and Trevor Pinch, eds. (forthcoming). *Handbook of Science and Technology Studies*. Newbury Park, CA: Sage Publications.

Jelinek, Mariann. 1979. *Institutionalizing Innovation: A Study of Organizational Learning Systems*. New York: Praeger.

Johnson, Stanley P. and Guy Corcelle. 1989. *The Environmental Policy of the European Communities*. London: Graham & Trotman.

Jones, Tara. 1988. *Corporate Killing: Bhopals Will Happen*. London: Free Association Books.

Joshi, V. T. 1991. "Madhya Pradesh: Not Learning from Experience." In *The Hindu Survey of the Environment*, 1991, pp. 59, 61.

Judicial Conference Ad Hoc Committee on Asbestos Litigation. 1991.

Kaim-Caudle, P. R. 1973. *Comparative Social Policy and Social Security*. New York: Dunellen.

Kakalik, James S. and Abby Eisenshtat Robyn. 1982. *Costs of the Civil Justice System: Court Expenditures for Processing Tort Cases*. Santa Monica, CA: Institute for Civil Justice.

Karan, P. P., Wilford A. Bladen, and James R. Wilson. 1986. "Technological Hazards in the Third World." *Geographical Review* 76: 195–208.

Karns, Margaret P., ed. 1986. *Persistent Patterns and Emergent Structures in a Waning Century*. New York: Praeger.

Kasperson, Roger E. and P. J. M. Stallen, eds. 1991. *Communicating Health and Safety Risks to the Public: International Dimensions*. Dordrecht: Reidel.

Kay, David A. and Harold K. Jacobson, eds. 1983. *Environmental Protection: The International Dimension*. Totowa, NJ: Allanheld, Osmun.

Kay, David A. and Eugene B. Skolnikoff, eds. 1972. *World Eco-Crisis*. Madison: University of Wisconsin Press.

Kemeny, John et al. 1979. *The Need for Change: The Legacy of Three Mile Island*. Report of the President's Commission on the Accident at Three Mile Island. Washington, DC: U.S. Government Printing Office.

Keohane, Robert O. 1989. *International Institutions and State Power.* Boulder, CO: Westview Press.

Keyes, Edward. 1984. *Coconut Grove.* New York: Atheneum.

Khanna, P. 1989. "Conceptual Framework and Role of EIA in Decision Making." Indo-Dutch Seminar on EIA, New Delhi.

Khator, Renu. 1988. "Organizational Response to the Environmental Crisis in India." *Indian Journal of Political Science* 49, 1:14–39.

King, Elizabeth M. and James P. Smith. 1988. *Economic Loss and Compensation in Aviation Accidents.* Santa Monica, CA: Institute for Civil Justice.

Kingdon, John W. 1984. *Agendas, Alternatives, and Public Policies.* Boston: Little, Brown.

Kletz, Trevor A. 1978. "What You Don't Have Can't Leak." *Chemistry and Industry* (May 6): 287–292.

———. 1985. *What Went Wrong? Case Histories of Process Plant Disasters.* Houston, TX: Gulf Publishing Company.

———. 1988. *Learning from Accidents in Industry.* London: Butterworths.

———. 1993. *Lessons from Disasters: How Organizations Have No Memory and Accidents Recur.* Rugby, England: Institution of Chemical Engineers.

Komesar, Neil K. 1990. "Injuries and Institutions: Tort Reform, Tort Theory and Beyond." *New York University Law Review* 65:23–77.

Kraft, Michael E. and Norman J. Vig, eds. 1988. *Technology and Politics.* Durham, NC: Duke University Press.

Kurzman, Dan. 1987. *A Killing Wind.* New York: McGraw-Hill.

Lalvani, G. H. 1985. "Law and Pollution Control." In Bandyopadhyay et al., eds., 284–290.

Landy, Marc, Marc Roberts, and Stephen R. Thomas. 1990. *The Environmental Protection Agency: Asking the Wrong Questions.* New York: Oxford University Press.

Latour, Bruno. 1988. *The Pasteurization of France.* Cambridge, MA: Harvard University Press.

Leelakrishnan, P., ed. 1984. *Law and Environment.* Cochin, India: University of Cochin, Department of Law.

Leonard, H. Jeffrey and David Morell. 1981. "The Emergence of Environmental Concern in Developing Countries: A Political Perspective." *Stanford Journal of International Law* 17:281–313.

Lepkowski, Wil. 1984. "Bhopal: Indian City Begins to Heal But Conflicts Remain." *Chemical & Engineering News* 63, 48:18–32.

———. 1989. "Bhopal Settlement: Carbide to Pay India $470 Million." *Chemical & Engineering News* 67, 8:4–5.

Levine, Adeline. 1982. *Love Canal: Science, Politics, and People.* Lexington, MA: Lexington Books.

Lindblom, Charles. 1959. "The Science of 'Muddling Through.'" *Public Administration Review* 19:79–88.

———. 1979. "Still Muddling, Not Yet Through." *Public Administration Review* 39:517–526.

———. 1990. *Inquiry and Change.* New Haven, CT: Yale University Press.

———, ed. 1973. *The Science of the Artificial.* Cambridge, MA: MIT Press.

Lipson, L. and S. Wheeler, eds. 1986. *Law and the Social Sciences.* New York: Russell Sage Foundation.

Litan, Robert E. 1991. "The Liability Explosion and American Trade Performance: Myths and Realities." In Schuck, ed., 127–150.

Litan, Robert E. and Clifford Winston, eds. 1988. *Liability: Perspectives and Policy*. Washington, DC: Brookings Institution.

Lord, Miles. 1987. "A Plea for Corporate Conscience." In Stuart Hills, ed.

Makris, J. 1990. "Community Right-to-Know." In Gow and Otway, eds., 65–78.

Mann, Dean E. 1991. "Environmental Learning in a Decentralized World." *Journal of International Affairs* 44:301–337.

"The Manville Asbestos Trust." 1988. *Alternatives to the High Cost of Litigation* 6:1.

Marcuse, Herbert. 1964. *One-Dimensional Man*. Boston: Beacon Press.

Margerison, Tom and Marjorie Wallace. 1979. *The Superpoison*. London: Macmillan.

Masuch, Michael. 1985. "Vicious Circles in Organizations." *Administrative Science Quarterly* 30, 1:14–33.

Maynes, E. Scott and ACCI Research Committee, eds. 1988. *The Frontier of Research in the Consumer Interest*. Columbia, MO: American Council on Consumer Interests.

McCormick, John. 1989. *Reclaiming Paradise: The Global Environmental Movement*. Bloomington: Indiana University Press.

McGovern, Francis. 1988. "Resolving Mature Mass Torts Litigation." Working Paper 78, Yale University Law School.

McInturff, Patrick S., Jr. 1981. "Products Liability: The Impact on California Manufacturers." *American Business Law Journal* 19:343.

McKibben, Bill. 1989. *The End of Nature*. New York: Random House.

Merciai, Patricio. 1986. "Consumer Protection and the United Nations." *Journal of World Trade Law* 20:206–231.

Mercier, Michel and Morrell Draper. 1984. "Chemical Safety: The International Outlook." *World Health* (August/September): 4–6.

Meyers, P. W. 1990. "Nonlinear Learning in Large Technological Firms." *Research Policy* 19:97–115.

Mills, C. Wright. 1959. *The Sociological Imagination*. New York: Oxford University Press.

Ministry of Environment and Forests. 1991. *Annual Report 1990–91*. New Delhi: Ministry of Environment and Forests.

Minocha, A. C. 1981. "Changing Industrial Structure in Madhya Pradesh." *Margin* 4, 1:46–61.

Mishra, A. B. 1987. "Mining a Hill and Undermining a Society—The Case of Gandhamardan." In Agarwal, D'Monte, and Samarth, eds., 125–144.

Mitchell, Cynthia F. and Paul M. Barrett. 1988. "Novel Effort to Settle Asbestos Claims Fails as Lawsuits Multiply." *Wall Street Journal*, June 7, p. 1.

Morehouse, Ward and Arun Subramaniam. 1986. *The Bhopal Tragedy*. New York: Council on International and Public Affairs.

Morehouse, Ward, David Dembo, and Lucinda Wykle. 1990. *Abuse of Power—The Case of Union Carbide*. New York: New Horizons Press.

Muir, William. 1967. *Prayer in the Public Schools*. Chicago: University of Chicago Press.

Mumford, Lewis. 1964. "Authoritarian and Democratic Technics." *Technology and Culture* 5:1–8.

———. 1967, 1970. *The Myth of the Machine*. New York: Harcourt, Brace, Jovanovich.

Nathawat, G. S., S. Shastri, and J. P. Vyas. 1988. *Nature and Environmental Law.* Jaipur: RBSA Publishers.

Nelkin, Dorothy and Laurence Tancredi. 1989. *Dangerous Diagnostics: The Social Power of Biological Information.* New York: Basic Books.

Noble, David. 1977. *America by Design.* New York: Oxford University Press.

Nye, Joseph S., Jr., 1987. "Nuclear Learning." *International Organization* 41, 3:378–382.

"OECD 1989 Environmental Activities." 1990. *Colorado Journal of International Environmental Law and Policy* 16:167–187.

OECD. 1990a. *State of the Environment 1990.* Paris: OECD.

———. 1990b. *Workshop on Emergency Preparedness and Response and Research in Accident Prevention, Preparedness, and Response.* OECD Environmental Monograph No. 31. Paris: OECD.

———. 1990c. *Workshop on the Role of Public Authorities in Preventing Major Accidents and in Major Accident Land-Use Planning.* OECD Environmental Monograph No. 30. Paris: OECD.

Orlando, Jacqueline. 1988. "Asbestos Litigation and the Ohio Asbestos Litigation Plan: Insulating the Courts from the Heat. *Ohio Journal of Dispute Resolution* 3:399–414.

Osborn, Richard N. and D. H. Jackson. 1988. "Leaders, Riverboat Gamblers or Purposeful Unintended Consequences in the Management of Complex, Dangerous Technologies." *Academy of Management Journal* 31, 4:924–947.

Otway, H. and A. Amendola. 1991. "Major Hazard Information Policy in the European Community: Implications for Risk Analysis." *Risk Analysis* 9, 4:505–512.

Otway, H. and H. B. F. Gow, eds. 1990. *Communication with the Public About Major Hazards: Challenges for European Research.* New York: Elsevier.

Paarlberg, Robert L. 1993. "Managing Pesticide Use in Developing Countries." In Haas et al., eds., 309–350.

Pauchant, Thierry and Ian I. Mitroff. 1988. "Crisis Prone Versus Crisis Avoiding Organizations." *Industrial Crisis Quarterly* 2, 1:53–64.

Perrow, Charles. 1984. *Normal Accidents: Living with High Risk Technologies.* New York: Basic Books.

Peters, George and Barbara Peters. 1980. *Sourcebook on Asbestos Diseases*, vol. 1. New York: Garland.

———. 1988. *Sourcebook on Asbestos Diseases*, vol. 3. New York: Garland.

Peto, Richard and Marvin Schneiderman. 1981. *Banbury Report: Quantification of Industrial Cancer.* New York: Cold Spring Harbor Laboratory.

Pettelkau, H. 1990. "Effects of the Second Amendment to Directive 82/501/EEC on Emergency Planning in the Federal Republic of Germany." In Gow and Otway, eds., 53–57.

Pfeffer, Jeffrey and Gerald R. Salancik. 1978. *The External Control of Organizations: A Resource Dependence Perspective.* New York: Harper and Row.

Pfennigstorff, Werner and Daniel G. Gifford. 1991. *A Comparative Study of Liability Law and Compensation Schemes in Ten Countries and the United States.* Oak Brook, IL: Insurance Research Council.

Pinch, Trevor J. and Wiebe E. Bijker. 1987. "The Social Construction of Facts and Artifacts: Or How the Sociology of Science and the Sociology of Technology Might Benefit Each Other." In Bijker et al., eds., 17–46.

Pitt, Joseph C. and Elena Lugo, eds. 1991. *The Technology of Discovery and the Discovery of Technology.* Proceedings of the 6th International Conference of the Society for Philosophy and Technology. Blacksburg, VA: Society for Philosophy and Technology, Virginia Polytechnic Institute.

Presidential Commission on the Space Shuttle Challenger Accident. See Rogers 1986.

Project 88. 1988. *Project 88: Harnessing Market Forces to Protect the Environment.* Washington, DC: U.S. Government Printing Office.

Quarantelli, Enrique L. 1987. "What Should We Study? Questions and Suggestions for Research About the Concept of Disasters." *International Journal of Mass Emergencies and Disasters* 5, 1:7–32.

Rabin, Robert. 1978. "Dealing with Disasters: Some Thoughts on the Adequacy of the Legal System." *Stanford Law Review* 30:281–298.

Rajan, S. Ravi. 1988. "Rehabilitation and Volunteerism in Bhopal." *Lokayan Bulletin* 6, 1/2:3–31.

Ramakrishna, K. 1985. "The Emergence of Environmental Law in Developing Countries: A Case Study of India." *Ecology Law Quarterly* 12:907–935.

Ravanasi, Bill. 1990. *Breath Taken: A History and Landscape of Asbestos.* Boston: Center for Arts in the Public Interest.

Redclift, Michael. 1987. *Sustainable Development: Exploring the Contradictions.* London: Methuen.

Reich, Michael R. 1987. "Essential Drugs: Economics and Politics in International Health." *Health Policy* 8:39–57.

———. 1988. "The International Trade and Trade-Offs for Third World Consumers." In Maynes et al., eds., 375–396.

———. 1991. *Toxic Politics: Responding to Chemical Disasters.* Ithaca, NY: Cornell University Press.

Renn, Ortwin. 1989. "Risk Communication and the Social Amplification of Risk." *Risk Analysis* 9, 4:505–512.

Roberts, Karlene H. 1989. "New Challenges in Organizational Research: High Reliability Organizations." *Industrial Crisis Quarterly* 3, 2:111–126.

Rogers, William P. 1986. *Report of the Presidential Commission on the Space Shuttle Challenger Accident.* Washington, DC: U.S. Government Printing Office.

Rosenau, James N. and Ernst-Otto Czempeil, eds. 1989. *Global Changes and Theoretical Challenges.* Lexington, MA: Lexington Books.

Rosencranz, Armin. 1988. "Bhopal, Transnational Corporations, and Hazardous Technologies." *Ambio* 17, 5:336–341.

Rosner, David and Markowitz, Gerald, eds. 1987. *Dying for Work: Workers' Safety and Health in Twentieth-Century America.* Bloomington: Indiana University Press.

Ruggie, John Gerald. 1979–1980. "On the Problems of 'The Global Problematic': What Roles for International Organizations?" *Alternatives* 5:517–550.

———. 1986. "Social Time and International Policy: Conceptualizing Global Population and Resource Issues." In Karns, ed.

———. 1989. "International Structure and International Transformation: Space, Time, and Method." In Rosenau and Czempeil, eds.

Sadgopal, Anil and Sujit K. Das. 1988. "Report on Medical Relief and Rehabilitation of Bhopal Gas Victims." Report prepared for Indian Supreme Court.

Sanders, Joseph. 1987. "The Meaning of the Law Explosion: On Friedman's *Total Justice.*" *American Bar Foundation Research Journal*: 601–615.

Sands, Philippe J. 1989. "The Environment, Community, and International Law." *Harvard International Law Journal* 30:393–417.

Schachner, Michael. 1993. "Court Reverses Own Ruling." *Business Insurance* (May 17): 2.

Schattschneider, E. E. 1960. *The Semi-Sovereign People: A Realist's View of Democracy in America*. New York: Holt, Rinehart and Winston.

Scheingold, Stuart A. 1974. *The Politics of Rights: Lawyers, Public Policy, and Political Change*. New Haven, CT: Yale University Press.

Schuck, Peter H. 1987. *Agent Orange on Trial: Mass Toxic Disasters in the Courts*. Cambridge, MA: Harvard University Press.

———. 1991. "Introduction: The Context of the Controversy." In Schuck, ed.

———, ed. 1991. *Tort Law and the Public Interest*. New York: W. W. Norton.

Schulberg, Francine and Rob Visser. 1990. "Accident Prevention, Preparedness, and Response: The OECD Accidents Program." OECD Doc. ACC/90.298/6.08.1990.

Schumacher, E. F. 1973. *Small Is Beautiful*. London: Blond and Briggs.

Schwartz, Michiel and Michael Thompson. 1990. *Divided We Stand: Redefining Politics, Technology, and Social Choice*. Philadelphia: University of Pennsylvania Press.

Sclove, Richard E. 1982. "Decision-Making in a Democracy." *Bulletin of the Atomic Scientists* 38:44–49.

Selikoff, Irving, E. C. Hammond, and J. Churg. 1968. "Asbestos Exposure, Smoking, and Neoplasm." *Journal of the American Medical Association* 204: 106–112.

Sen, Falguni and William G. Egelhoff. 1991. "Six Years and Counting: Learning from Crisis Management in Bhopal." *Public Relations Review* 17, 1: 69–83.

Shaikh, Rashid and Michael R. Reich. 1981. "Haphazard Policy on Hazardous Exports." *The Lancet* 8249, 2.

Shastri, S. 1988. "Public Interest Litigation and Environmental Pollution." In Nathawat et al.

Shrivastava, Paul. 1987a. *Bhopal: Anatomy of a Crisis*. Cambridge, MA: Ballinger.

———. 1987b. "A Cultural Analysis of Conflicts in Industrial Disaster." *International Journal of Mass Emergencies and Disasters* 5, 3:243–264.

———. 1987c. "Preventing Industrial Crises: The Challenges of Bhopal." *International Journal of Mass Emergencies and Disasters* 5, 3:243–264.

———. 1992. *Bhopal: Anatomy of a Crisis*. 2nd ed. London: Chapman.

Siebert, Horst. 1987. *Economics of the Environment*. 2d ed. Berlin: Springer-Verlag.

Simon, Herbert. 1969. "The Architecture of Complexity." in Lindblom, ed.

Simonis, Udo E. 1987. *Ecological Modernization: New Perspectives for Industrial Societies*. New Delhi: Friedrich Ebert Stiftung.

Singh, C. 1984. "Legal Policy for the Control of Environmental Pollution." In Leelakrishnan, ed., 1–27.

Singh, N. K. 1993. "No Succour in Sight." *India Today*, June 30, p. 36.

Skolnikoff, Eugene. 1972. *The International Imperatives of Technology Research Series, No. 16*. Berkeley, CA: Institute of International Studies.

Slovic, Paul. 1987. "Perceptions of Risk." *Science* 236:280–285.

Smets, Henri. 1988. "The Cost of Accidental Pollution." *UNEP Industry and Environment* (October/November/December): 28–33.

Smith, Cornelius C. 1990. "Bhopal Aftermath: Union Carbide Rethinks Safety." *Business and Society Review* 75:50–53.

Speiser, Stuart M. 1980. *Lawsuit*. New York: Horizon.

State of Illinois. 1910. *Report on the Cherry Mine Disaster*. Springfield, IL: The Bureau.

Stavins, Robert H. 1989. "Harnessing Market Forces to Protect the Environment." *Environment* 31, 1:5–7, 28–35.

Stein, Leon. 1962. *The Triangle Fire*. Philadelphia: Lippincott.

Stern, Gerald. 1976. *The Buffalo Creek Disaster: The Story of the Survivors' Unprecedented Lawsuit*. New York: Random House.

———. 1977. *The Buffalo Creek Disaster: How the Survivors of One of the Worst Disasters in Coal-Mining History Brought Suit Against the Coal Company—and Won*. New York: Vintage.

Stone, Deborah A. 1989. *Policy Paradox and Political Reason*. Glenview, IL: Scott, Foresman and Co.

Stover, W. 1985. *A Field Day for the Legislators in the Chemical Industry After Bhopal* (Symposium proceedings). London: Oyez IBC.

Streeten, Paul. 1986. "What Do We Owe the Future?" *Resources Policy* 12, 1:4–16.

Sturgis, Robert W. 1989. *Tort Costs Trends: An International Perspective*. Darien, CT: Tillinghast.

Sunday Times of London Investigative Team. 1979. *Suffer the Children*. London: Sunday Times.

Sutton, Vickie V. 1989. *Perceptions of Local Emergency Planning Committee Members' Responsibility for Risk Communication and a Proposed Model Risk Communication Program for Local Emergency Planning Committees Under SARA Title III*. Ph.D. dissertation, University of Texas at Dallas.

Tamuz, Michal. 1987. "The Impact of Computer Surveillance on Air Safety Reporting." *Columbia Journal of World Business* 22, 1:69–78.

Tarr, A. 1985. "Megatrial Averted in Hilton Blaze: Settlement of 115 Claims Approved." *National Law Journal* (October 28): 3.

Tarrow, Sidney G. 1989. *Struggle, Politics, and Reform: Collective Action, Social Movements, and Cycles of Protest*. Ithaca, NY: Cornell University Press.

Technica, Ltd. 1988. *Techniques for Assessing Industrial Hazards: A Manual*. World Bank Technical Paper No. 55. Washington, DC: World Bank.

Thacher, Peter. 1991. *Global Security and Risk Management*. Geneva: World Federation of United Nations Associations.

Trubek, David and Marc Galanter. 1974. "Scholars in Self-Estrangement: Some Reflections on the Crisis in Law and Development Studies in the United States." *Wisconsin Law Review* 1974:1062–1102.

Turner, Barry A. 1976. "The Organizational and Interorganizational Development of Disaster." *Administrative Science Quarterly* 21:378–397.

———. 1978. *Man-Made Disasters*. London: Wykeham.

Tyagi, Y. K. and Armin Rosencranz. 1988. "Some International Law Aspects of the Bhopal Disaster." *Social Science and Medicine* 27:1105–1112.

"UNEP 1989 Environmental Activities." 1990. *Colorado Journal of International Environmental Law and Policy* 1:147–156.

Union Carbide Corporation. 1985. *Bhopal Methylisocyante Incident Investigation Team Report*. Danbury, CT: Union Carbide Corporation.

United Nations. 1988. *Accis Guide to United Nations Information Sources on the Environment*. New York: United Nations.

United Nations Environment Programme (UNEP). 1988. *APELL: Awareness and Preparedness for Emergencies at Local Level*. UN Publication No. E.88.III.D.3. New York: UNEP.

―――. 1988. *The United Nations System-Wide Medium-Term Environment Programme for the Period 1990–1995*. Nairobi: UNEP.

―――. 1989. *Environmental Data Report*. London: Basil Blackwell.

United Nations Environment Programme/Industry and Environment Organization (UNEP/IEO). 1989. "APELL: Awareness and Preparedness for Emergencies at the Local Level—A Process for Responding to Technological Accidents." *Toxic Substances Journal* 9:145–221.

―――. 1990. *Environmental Auditing: Report of a United Nations Environment Programme/Industry and Environment (UNEP/IEO) Workshop*. Paris: UNEP/IEO.

United Nations Environment Programme and World Health Organization (UNEP and WHO). 1988. *Assessment of Urban Air Quality*. London: Monitoring and Assessment Research Center.

―――. 1988. *Assessment of Freshwater Quality*. London: Monitoring and Assessment Research Center.

United Nations Environment Programme, World Health Organization, and Food and Agriculture Organization (UNEP, WHO, and FAO). 1988. *Assessment of Chemical Contaminants in Food*. London: Monitoring and Assessment Research Center.

U.S. House of Representatives, 74th Congress, 2nd session. 1936. *Hearings Before a Subcommittee of the Committee on Labor: An Investigation Relating to Health Conditions of Workers Employed in the Construction and Maintenance of Public Utilities*. Washington, DC: U.S. Government Printing Office.

van Eijndhoven, Josée and Cor Worrell, eds. 1991. *Communicatie over risico's van industriele activiteiten*. Den Haag: NOTA.

Vargha, Janos. 1990. "Green Revolutions in East Europe." *Panoscope* (May): 7.

Varma, Vijaya Shankar. 1986. "I. Bhopal: The Unfolding of a Tragedy." *Alternatives* 11, 1:137–145.

Viscusi, W. Kip. 1988. "Liability for Occupational Accidents and Illnesses." In Litan and Winston, eds.

Viscusi, W. Kip and Michael J. Moore. 1991. "Rationalizing the Relationship Between Product Liability and Innovation." In Schuck, ed., 105–126.

Weick, Karl E. 1988. "Enacted Sensemaking in Crisis Situations." *Journal of Management Studies* 25, 4:305–318.

Weiss, Edith Brown. 1989. *In Fairness to Future Generations*. Ardsley-on-Hudson, NY: Transnational Publishers.

Werstein, Irving. 1965. *The General Slocum Incident: Story of an Ill-Fated Ship*. New York: John Day.

Wetter, J. Gillers. 1980. "The Case for International Law Schools and an International Legal Profession." *International and Comparative Law Quarterly* 29:206–218.

White, Lynn. 1967. "The Historical Roots of Our Ecological Crisis." *Science* 155 (March 10): 1203–1207.

Wiegand, Wolfgang. 1991. "The Reception of American Law in Europe." *American Journal of Comparative Law* 39:229–248.

Wildavsky, Aaron. 1988. *Searching for Safety*. New Brunswick, NJ: Transaction Press.

Wiley, Jerry. 1981. "The Impact of Judicial Decisions on Professional Conduct: An Empirical Study." *Southern California Law Review* 55:345–396.

Willging, Thomas. 1987. *Trends in Asbestos Litigation*. Santa Monica, CA: Rand.

Winner, Langdon. 1986. *The Whale and the Reactor*. Chicago: University of Chicago Press.

———. 1991. "Upon Opening the Black Box and Finding It Empty: Social Constructivism and the Philosophy of Technology." In Pitt and Lugo, eds., 503–519.

Woodhouse, Edward J. 1988. "Sophisticated Trial and Error in Decision Making About Risk." In Kraft and Vig, eds., 208–223.

Woodhouse, Edward J. and Joseph C. Morone. 1986. *Averting Catastrophe: Strategies for Regulating Risky Technologies*. Berkeley: University of California Press.

Woodhouse, Edward J. and Susan Cozzens. (forthcoming). "Science and Politics." in Jasanoff et al., eds.

World Bank. 1990. *The World Bank and the Environment: First Annual Report Fiscal Year 1990*. Washington, DC: World Bank.

World Bank Environmental Department. 1991a. *Environmental Assessment Sourcebook Volume I: Policies, Procedures, and Cross-Sectoral Issues*. World Bank Technical Paper No. 139. Washington, DC: World Bank.

———. 1991b. *Environmental Assessment Sourcebook Volume III: Guidelines for Environmental Assessment of Energy and Industry Projects*. World Bank Technical Paper No. 154. Washington, DC: World Bank.

World Commission on Environment and Development. 1987. *Our Common Future*. Oxford: Oxford University Press.

World Health Organization (WHO). 1988. *Ethical Criteria for Medicinal Drug Promotion*. Geneva: WHO.

World Resources Institute. 1990. *World Resources, 1990–91: A Guide to the Global Environment*. New York: Oxford University Press.

Wynne, Brian. 1987a. *Implementation of Article 8 of the Directive 82/501/EEC, A Study of Public Information*. Brussels: Commission of the European Communities.

———. 1987b. *Risk Management and Hazardous Waste: Comparative Institutional Perspectives*. Berlin: Springer.

———. 1988. "Unruly Technology." *Social Studies of Science* 18:147–167.

———. 1989a. "Building Public Concern Into Risk Management." in Brown, ed., 118–132.

———. 1989b. "Frameworks of Rationality in Risk Management: Towards a Testing of Naive Sociology." In Brown, ed., 33–47.

———. 1990. "Representing Policy Constructions and Interests in SSK." *Social Studies of Science* 20:195–207.

Wynne, Brian and Josée van Eijndhoven. 1991. "Risk Communication in Europe: Ways of Implementing Article 8 of the post-Seveso Directive." In Kasperson and Stallen, eds.

Yates, R. 1987. "Burn Victims—Big Settlements." *American Bar Association Journal* (June 1): 17–18.

Zimmerman, Rae. 1990. *Government Management of Environmental Risks*. Chicago: Lewis Publishers.

Contributors

B. Bowonder is Dean of Research at the Administrative Staff College, Hyderabad, India. He has written widely on environmental and technology regulation in India.

Shyam Divan received his legal education in Bombay, India, and at the University of California, Berkeley. He practices as an advocate before the Bombay High Court and has published numerous works on environmental regulation, including *Environmental Law and Policy in India* (1991), of which he is a co-author.

Tom Durkin is Assistant Professor at the Center for Studies in Criminology and Law, University of Florida. He is a former participant in the Asbestos Litigation Project at the American Bar Foundation. His current research focuses on institutional and organizational influences on law.

Josée van Eijndhoven is Senior Lecturer in the Department of Science and Society, University of Utrecht, The Netherlands. Her research focuses on the regulation of hazardous technologies in the European Community, with particular emphasis on public participation and public access to technical information.

William L. F. Felstiner is Visiting Professor of Sociology at the University of California, Santa Barbara and Distinguished Research Fellow at the American Bar Foundation. His research reflects broad interests in the sociology of law, including lawyer-client relations, asbestos litigation, alternative dispute resolution, and procedural justice.

Marc Galanter is Evjue-Bascom Professor of Law and South Asian Studies at the University of Wisconsin-Madison and Director of Wisconsin's Institute for Legal Studies. He is a leading authority on Indian law, as well as on litigation and disputing in the United States. He was retained by the Government of India as an expert in the litigation arising from the Bhopal disaster.

Peter M. Haas is Associate Professor in the Department of Political Science at the University of Massachusetts, Amherst. His research centers on international environmental policymaking, with a particular focus on the role of international organizations and the scientific community in environmental management. He is the author of *Saving the Mediterranean: The Politics of International Environmental Cooperation* (1990) and co-editor and contributor to *Institutions for the Earth: Sources of Effective International Environmental Protection* (1993).

Susan G. Hadden is Professor in the LBJ School of Public Affairs and the Department of Government at the University of Texas, Austin. She has written two books on the use of technical information to manage risk and has also published widely on U.S. and Indian environmental policy, risk communication, computers in government, and telecommunications policy.

Sheila Jasanoff is Professor of Science Policy and Law and Chair in the Department of Science and Technology Studies at Cornell University. Author of *Risk Management and Political Culture* (1986), she has also written numerous books and articles on U.S. and comparative environmental policy, as well as many works on science and the law, risk management, biotechnology policy, and the theoretical implications of science studies for science policy.

Jeanne X. Kasperson is Research Librarian and Director of Publications at the George Perkins Marsh Institute at Clark University and Senior Research Associate at the Alan Shawn Feinstein World Hunger Program at Brown University. Her research includes work on the social amplification of risk, risk communication, corporate culture, and global environmental change.

Roger E. Kasperson is Professor of Government and Geography and senior researcher at the George Perkins Marsh Institute, Clark University. He has written widely on issues connected with technological hazards, risk communication, radioactive wastes, and global environmental change. He is contributing co-editor of *Communicating Risks to the Public* (1991).

Frank N. Laird is Assistant Professor of Technology and Public Policy in the Graduate School of International Studies at the University of Denver. His research focuses on the role of public participation and risk communication, with particular emphasis on how participation can satisfy democratic norms and how values are institutionalized during periods of technological change.

Wil Lepkowski is senior correspondent for *Chemical and Engineering News* in Washington, DC. Since 1977, he has covered all major areas of science and technology, with special focus on their interplay with government, the economy, and ordinary lives. He has authored a series of articles on Bhopal, from the immediate aftermath of the disaster to the present.

Michael R. Reich is Professor of International Health Policy and Director of the Takemi Program in International Health at the Harvard School of Public Health. His research interests are in comparative public policy and political economy, and he is the author, most recently, of *Toxic Politics: Responding to Chemical Disasters* (1991).

Armin Rosencranz is President of the Pacific Environment and Resources Center, Sausalito, CA. As a lawyer and political scientist, Rosencranz specializes in international and comparative environmental policy. His recent research and writing interests have focused on deforestation in Siberia, the Bhopal disaster, and global environmental issues. He is a co-author of *Environmental Law and Policy in India* (1991). He also teaches U.S. and international environmental law at the University of California at Berkeley.

Antony Scott is currently enrolled in the graduate program in Energy Analysis and Policy at the Institute for Energy Studies at the University of Wisconsin. He was Research Director at the Pacific Environment and Resources Center from 1990 to 1992.

Paul Shrivastava is Howard I. Scott Professor of Management at Bucknell University and Editor of *Industrial and Environmental Crisis Quarterly*. He is the author of *Bhopal: Anatomy of a Crisis* and many other books and articles on strategic management of organizations, environmental and crisis management, and management problems in a global economy.

Index

University of Pennsylvania Press
Law in Social Context Series

Roy B. Fleming, Peter F. Nardulli, and James Eisenstein. *The Craft of Justice: Politics and Work in Criminal Court Communities*. 1992

Joel F. Handler. *Law and the Search for Community*. 1990

Robert M. Hayden. *Social Courts in Theory and Practice: Yugoslav Workers' Courts in Comparative Perspective*. 1991

Sheila Jasanoff, editor. *Learning from Disaster: Risk Management After Bhopal*. 1994

Richard Lempert and Joseph Sanders. *An Invitation to Law and Social Science*. 1989

Candace McCoy. *The Politics of Plea Bargaining: California's Proposition 8 and Its Impact*. 1992

Joseph Rees. *Reforming the Workplace: A Study of Self-Regulation in Occupational Safety*. 1988

Jeffrey A. Roth, John T. Scholz, and Ann Dryden Witte, editors. *Taxpayer Compliance Volume I: An Agenda for Research*. 1989

Jeffrey A. Roth, John T. Scholz, and Ann Dryden Witte, editors. *Taxpayer Compliance Volume II: Social Science Perspectives*. 1989

Joachim J. Savelsberg with Peter Brühl. *Constructing White-Collar Crime: Rationalities, Communication, Power*. 1994